Shakespeare and Spenser

The Manchester Spenser

The **Manchester Spenser** is a monograph and text series devoted to historical and textual approaches to Edmund Spenser – to his life, times, places, works and contemporaries.

A growing body of work in Spenser and Renaissance studies, fresh with confidence and curiosity and based on solid historical research, is being written in response to a general sense that our ability to interpret texts is becoming limited without the excavation of further knowledge. So the importance of research in nearby disciplines is quickly being recognised, and interest renewed: history, archaeology, religious or theological history, book history, translation, lexicography, commentary and glossary – these require treatment for and by students of Spenser.

The **Manchester Spenser**, to feed, foster and build on these refreshed attitudes, aims to publish reference tools, critical, historical, biographical and archaeological monographs on or related to Spenser, from several disciplines, and to publish editions of primary sources and classroom texts of a more wide-ranging scope.

The **Manchester Spenser** consists of work with stamina, high standards of scholarship and research, adroit handling of evidence, rigour of argument, exposition and documentation.

The series will encourage and assist research into, and develop the readership of, one of the richest and most complex writers of the early modern period.

General Editor J.B. Lethbridge

Editorial Board Helen Cooper, Thomas Herron, James C. Nohrnberg & Brian Vickers

Shakespeare and Spenser

Attractive opposites

EDITED BY
J. B. LETHBRIDGE

Manchester University Press
Manchester and New York
distributed in the United States exclusively by Palgrave Macmillan

Copyright © J. B. Lethbridge 2008

The right of J. B. Lethbridge to be identified as the author of this work has been asserted by him/her in accordance with the Copyright, Designs and Patents Act 1988.

Published by Manchester University Press
Oxford Road, Manchester M13 9NR, UK
and Room 400, 175 Fifth Avenue, New York, NY 10010, USA
www.manchesteruniversitypress.co.uk

Distributed in the United States exclusively by
Palgrave Macmillan, 175 Fifth Avenue,
New York, NY 10010, USA

Distributed in Canada exclusively by
UBC Press, University of British Columbia, 2029 West Mall,
Vancouver, BC, Canada V6T 1Z2

British Library Cataloguing-in-Publication Data is available

Library of Congress Cataloging-in-Publication Data is available

ISBN 978 0 7190 8642 7 paperback

First published by Manchester University Press in hardback 2008

This paperback edition first published 2011

The publisher has no responsibility for the persistence or accuracy of URLs for any external or third-party internet websites referred to in this book, and does not guarantee that any content on such websites is, or will remain, accurate or appropriate.

Printed by Lightning Source

Contents

General Editor's Preface	vii
Acknowledgments	viii
Introduction: Spenser, Marlowe, Shakespeare: Methodological Investigations J.B. LETHBRIDGE	1
Beyond Binarism: Eros/Death and Venus/Mars in Shakespeare's *Antony and Cleopatra* and Spenser's *Faerie Queene* JUDITH H. ANDERSON	54
Spenser and Shakespeare: Polarized Approaches to Psychology, Poetics, and Patronage ROBERT LANIER REID	79
Perdita, Pastorella, and the Romance of Literary Form: Shakespeare's Counter-Spenserian Authorship PATRICK CHENEY	121
Pastoral Forms and Religious Reform in Spenser and Shakespeare KAREN NELSON	143
The Equinoctial Boar: Venus and Adonis in Spenser's Garden, Shakespeare's Epyllion, and *Richard III*'s England ANNE LAKE PRESCOTT	168
Hamlet's Debt to Spenser's *Mother Hubberds Tale*: A Satire on Robert Cecil? RACHEL E. HILE	187
Fusion: Spenserian Metaphor and Sidnean Example in Shakespeare's *King Lear* SUSAN OLDRIEVE	201
What Means a Knight? Red Cross Knight and Edgar MICHAEL L. HAYS	226
The Seven Deadly Sins and Shakespeare's Jacobean Tragedies RONALD HORTON	242

Works Cited 259

Spenser-Shakespeare Bibliography 291

Index 299

General Editor's Preface

The Manchester Spenser is a monograph and text series devoted to historical and textual approaches to Spenser, his life, times, places, works and contemporaries.

In response to a perceptible approach to the limits of our ability to interpret texts in the absence of new knowledge about them, a growing body of work in Spenser and Renaissance studies based on solid historical research is being produced and lacunae in the historical fields lamented and explored, including much-needed texts for teaching and research. The importance of research in nearby disciplines such as history, archaeology, religious or theological history and book history, is being recognised and renewed, and requires treatment by or for students of Spenser.

The Manchester Spenser, to foster and build on this refreshed attention to historical study, aims to publish historically-based criticism, reference tools, historical, biographical and archaeological monographs on or related to Spenser's life, times, people and works, and from several disciplines; to publish editions of primary texts relating to Spenser, and also classroom texts of a more wide-ranging nature.

The Manchester Spenser seeks work with stamina, of the highest standards of historical scholarship, research, handling of evidence, rigour of argument, exposition and documentation.

One aim is to promote the reading of Spenser; the overriding aim is simply to understand—the man and his works; to understand again perhaps; more fully it may be hoped; and undoubtedly as the generations slip by, again and probably again.

Acknowledgments

First thanks (and for so very much else) must go to Tom Herron who, together with Hannibal Hamlin, to whom also our gratitude, organised the Spenser and Shakespeare Seminar at the 2006 Shakespeare Association of America Conference which was the origin of the papers collected in this volume, and whose urging, emailing, persuading and curial diplomacy landed the book in the laps of editor and authors.

Next, to the contributors whose willingness, faithfulness, patience, fortitude, expertise and friendship have been so generously offered.

I must thank my students at Tübingen University in the Marlowe, Spenser, Shakespeare Seminar which I taught with Tom Herron in the Summer Semester of 2007, and which helped a great deal with the editing of this volume; the enthusiasm, the detailed often learnedly sceptical responses to a rich variety of sometimes rather wild speculations, the solid, patient, scholarly research, the inventiveness—and the sheer fun of it all—all these have been laid under contribution. In particular my thanks to those directly involved: Carmen Adams and Cornelia Düwel.

Thanks are due, too, to the Rivers Foundation at East Carolina University, to the Office of International Affairs which administers the endowment, and to its English Department (first under Bruce Southard, now under Mike Palmer) for giving me a haven for a year, during the first part of which I not only recovered my health but managed to get the bulk of the editing and writing done under ideal conditions and among good scholars and friends—Tom Herron again, Charles Fantazzi, Jerry Leath Mills, David Wilson-Okamura, ... to mention only those names (among very many, very kindly others I was sad to leave), which will be familiar to the readers of these Acknowledgments. My thanks also of course to my own University, Tübingen, for granting me leave of absence; and, with a different sense in 'of course', to its Rector, Professor Bernd Engler, for so many and such good years my shepherd and friend.

For the first time I have had a Research Assistant, a mythical beast like the unicorn that only scientists and American scholars seem to see. Nick Frankenhauser is another gracious gift of ECU, but he has his own identity, and I should like to thank him very heartily. RAs have to earn their keep of course, but to be thrown into the deep end of a collection, and together with a new professor in the midst of many urgent and no doubt puzzling things, must have been a shock to the system; but Nick coped with humour and civility and did sterling work on those tedious things that have to be done towards the end of a book: bibliographical work, proof-reading, managing puzzling indexing software, also some fetching and carrying I'm afraid, poor chap, from ECU's splendid library resources: but all with good cheer and accuracy, and, as I understand, an all-night session or two at home.

My wife, Stefanie Lethbridge, put in some sterling work at libraries around the world checking references and the bibliography, and some of the trickier quotations; Lord knows that if there are mistakes, they are not because of any slackness on her part. *Mea culpa*.

I acknowledge, too, and with the deepest gratitude, personal and professional, the Editorial Board who have seen The Manchester Spenser through its first beginnings and into the wide world, to seek adventures where they may be found; and, for incitement, encouragement, and example, Brian Vickers and Victor Skretkowicz. And of course, nothing would have happened at all without the vision, belief and patience (I fear it has been needed) of Matthew Frost and David Rodgers at Manchester University Press.

Acknowledgments are never done of course, but one word more, for this is not the first, nor will it be the last time that I make heavy and steady and fruitful use of software developed by others, most of whom have day jobs, and freely distributed to the great benefit of the modern academic life. I have used GNU/Linux for many years now; this book has been type-set, indexed and bibliographied using the LaTeX programmes and macros, and I should like to acknowledge with gratitude all those around the world who write the software and who so generously and kindly offer help for idiots via the web and email. Linus Torvalds—it seems impertinent, but I should like to submit thanks to him for the Linux operating system; and to the GNU people whose sorting, concordancing, indexing and editing programmes are simply a basic element in GNU/Linux and sometimes taken for granted. My primary tool is Keith Bostic's nvi editor, a clone of the classic Unix vi, still compiling after all these years and changes in the underlying system software—an incitement to thorough work. The task (thanks to a new computer) was finished on a Kubuntu system. The book is set in Aldine 401.

Introduction: Spenser, Marlowe, Shakespeare: Methodological Investigations

J. B. Lethbridge

> You think that a strange thing to say, but it's true. All my life and all my experience, the events that have befallen me, the people I have known, all my memories, dreams, fantasies, everything I have ever read, all of that has been chucked onto the compost heap where over time it has rotted down to a dark, rich, organic mulch. The process of cellular breakdown makes it unrecognisable. Other people call it the imagination. I think of it as a compost heap. Every so often take an idea, plant it in the compost, and wait. It feeds on that black stuff that used to be a life, takes its energy for its own. It germinates. Takes root. Produces shoots. And so on and so forth, until one fine day I have a story, or a novel.
>
> *The Thirteenth Tale*, Diane Setterfield

I began with a desire to speak with the dead—I began with a desire to speak of the dead to the living.[1] What would we say to Shakespeare? Might not the very idea be impertinent? To the dead we ought to listen, not chatter, and to listen with the greatest attention, with the greatest quietude, with the greatest courtesy and the greatest humility.[2] 'Humility' in this case would mean putting ourselves to one side for the sake of attending to what someone else says, and not allowing our own desire to speak to interfere with what the dead have said or with the need to listen. This is the historical attitude. Part of the art of listening, in conversation, lies in the art of posing questions. History involves the asking of questions.[3] So that it is possible, observing these rules of engagement,[4] to pose the odd question; not to chatter, but to attend to the dead. In this way, although we must tread carefully and considerately, posing an intelligent question and awaiting the answer, we can hear things that have been said by the dead which would otherwise go unheard: hints and guesses, whispers and asides, indirections and slant truths. Such a questioning is the comparative study of one author and another, the reading of one author by another, and the use made by one author of another, in our case, Shakespeare's of Spenser. We can best do this by attending carefully to what Shakespeare has said, and listening, quietly,

---

[1] Stephen J. Greenblatt, *Shakespearean Negotiations: The Circulation of Social Energy in Renaissance England* (Oxford: Clarendon Press, 1990), 1.

[2] See Gordon Teskey, '"And therefore as a stranger give it welcome:" Courtesy and Thinking', *Spenser Studies* 18 (2003), 343–59, and J. B. Lethbridge 'Introduction', in *Edmund Spenser: New and Renewed Directions* (Madison: Fairleigh Dickinson University Press, 2006), 50–4.

[3] See R. G. Collingwood, *Autobiography* (Oxford: Oxford University Press, 1939).

[4] See Paul Grice, *Studies in the Way of Words* (Cambridge, MA: Harvard University Press, 1989).

and possessing ourselves in patience, to the quiet echoes of Spenser in Shakespeare. For some of the echoes are very faint. As when in the dawn chorus it is possible, from the whole lovely cacophony to pick out the lark, the woodpecker, the blackbird, thrush, blue-tit, brawling sparrow, and red-winged buzzard; or when in a field of lambs, the ewe hears her own; and although this is a slow, cumulative process in our case— so with Shakespeare: we can pick out the Holinshed, the Golding, the fainter Ovid or Seneca, the occasional note of the Dead Shepheard, the frequent note of the Prince of Poets.

I

Shakespeare read Spenser with some care.[5] Shakespeare was influenced by the Spenser he read; he was also influenced by the Spenser that others had read before him, principally, or so it seems, by Marlowe. Shakespeare the poet-playwright[6] was ten years younger than the poet of pastorals, epic romance and sonnets. Ten years is not a long time, and after four hundred years it may seem that the two poets are contemporaries. But not all decades are equal and the relevant decade is not that between Spenser's birth and Shakespeare's, but that between the publication of *The Shepheards Calendar* and *The Faerie Queene*, between when Spenser published his ground-breaking, first major work, and when Shakespeare first began to write.

There is an indirect or general influence, and a specific or particular influence. When Marlowe writes,

> Like to an almond tree y-mounted high
> Upon the lofty and celestial mount
> Of evergreen Selinus,[7]

we can be certain that he is borrowing from Spenser's *Faerie Queene* I.vii.32. And we should be certain even if it were the only borrowing instead of being, as it is, only one in a whole nexus of fairly clear borrowings.[8] But when in Sonnet 106 Shakespeare writes of 'ladies dead

---

[5] See the Bibliography at the end of the present volume.

[6] Patrick Cheney has put most emphasis on the fact that Shakespeare was considered by his contemporaries as both a poet and a playwright, as he is beginning to be again by we of the twenty-first century. See his paper in the present volume and the notes there.

[7] *Tamburlaine*. See below 26ff., for an analysis of this and other borrowings.

[8] See T. W. Baldwin, 'The Genesis of Some Passages Which Spenser Borrowed from Marlowe', *ELH*, 3 (1942), 157–87, who raises the possiblity that Spenser might be borrowing from Marlowe, and W. B. C. Watkins, 'The Plagiarist: Spenser or Marlowe?', *ELH*, 11 (1944), 249–65, who disposes of the possibility; Baldwin's response to Watkins is *ELH*, 12 (1945), 165. See also Joan Fitzpatrick, 'Shakespeare's *Titus Andronicus* and Bandello's *Novelle* as Sources for the Munera Episode in Spenser's *Faerie Queene*, Book 5, Canto 2', *Notes and Queries*, 52 (2005), 196–198, the only attempt I know which tries,

and lovely knights', can we be certain at all that he is borrowing from Spenser?[9] And when Shakespeare calls Hero's putative lover a 'ruffian' can we be sure that this detail, not in Ariosto or the others, comes from *The Faerie Queene*, II.vii?[10] And even if the odd potential borrowing from Spenser found in *As You Like It*, for instance, is securely agreed, can we be at all sure that Shakespeare was treating temperance in that play, and that he was influenced to do so and in the process of doing so, by *The Faerie Queene*, Book II?[11]

The subject of Spenser's influence on Shakespeare, Shakespeare's *use* of Spenser, is, sadly, a niche subject. Not to say it has been neglected, as the bibliography at the end of this book shows; but there has been a conviction that there is not much to say on the matter.[12] One of the

---

not very convincingly in my view, to argue that Spenser borrowed from Shakespeare. On Spenser and Marlowe, see Patrick Cheney, *Marlowe's Counterfeit Profession: Ovid, Spenser, Counter-Nationhood* (Toronto: University of Toronto Press, 1997), and n35 below.

[9] Patrick Cheney, 'Shakespeare's Sonnet 106, Spenser's National Epic, and Counter-Petrarchism', *English Literary Renaissance*, 31 (2001), 331–64, and below 35–43.

[10] Alwin Thaler, 'Spenser and *Much Ado about Nothing*', *Studies in Philology*, 37 (1940), 225–35. Spenser and Shakespeare employ a 'base "ruffian"': 'groome of base degree' (*FQ* II.iv.24), 'a ruffian' (*Much Ado*, IV.i.92), unlike Ariosto or Bandello, Thaler, 229–33. In Spenser and Shakespeare the motive is not bitter jealousy—this is important in considering *Othello* of course (230—cf Hieatt *SpEncy* 642, 'animated by villany alone, not by a desire for the same woman'); see also Ronald Horton's paper in the present volume, 246.

[11] Maurice Hunt, 'Wrestling for Temperance: *As You Like It* and *The Faerie Queene*, Book II', *Allegorica: A Journal of Medieval and Renaissance Literature*, 16 (1995), 31–46. I realise that this type of question is not unique to the influence of Spenser on Shakespeare but to all questions of borrowing by whoever from whomever.

[12] 'The divergent lines along which the two authors aggressively develop their quite separate inherited traditions of narrative poetry and dramatic enactmentment create a space between them. Temperamental difference makes the lines diverge farther' (Hieatt, *SpEncy* 641). See Robert Reid citing Arthur Kirsch, at 79 below. On the question of the differences between Spenser and Shakespeare's poetry, and attitudes, see not only Hieatt in *SpEncy*, but also these: Abbie Finlay Potts, *Shakespeare and 'The Faerie Queene'* (Ithaca: Cornell University Press, 1958); and a useful, if slightly old-fashioned in tone, paper by Jane Mayhall, 'Shakespeare and Spenser: A Commentary on Differences', *Modern Language Quarterly* 10 (1949), 356–63. There are some adroit analyses of the temper of the sonnets poetry, and some useful lines: 'To some readers and critics, the structure of the *Faerie Queen* [sic] and its "oversmooth" word relations seem monotonous. These people crave the irregularities and the violences of the Shakespearean style' (358). At 360: alternatives 'live and flourish' in the ingenuities of Shakespeare's style; whereas 'Spenser is another story. ... the diction and characters of Spenser are always clear. ... there is no sign of stuttering indecision, of perverse "imagery"'. There is motion in Spenser, as in Shakespeare, but in the former: 'It is a motion so perfect that it appears almost still' (361), whereas it is characteristic of Shakespeares poetry to twist and turn, verse, perverse and reverse. At times, 'the two styles appear almost incompatible' (362). The paper is impressionistic, as perhaps such discussions require to be; but there are many useful observations, some adroit practical criticism, and it is well-worth turning to; even while one may feel that in the sixty-year interim, much of what Mayhall says of Shakespeare we would say of Spenser now. But what ever the differences, the potential incompatibilities, both men were poets and both men would have sought help wherever possible, and for Shakespeare *qua* poet, where would there be a greater thesaurus of diction, image,

purposes of this volume is to change that conviction, in the counter-conviction (as Patrick Cheney might put it), that there is a great deal to say on the matter—and that the time may have arrived to promote the specific field and present it to a wider scholarly group and in a more systematic manner than heretofore.

II

The question of the relations between Shakespeare and Spenser is not limited to linguistic borrowing. And it is noteworthy that probably the majority of books which carry both names in the title or which devote chapters to each poet, do not treat the *influence* of the elder on the younger, nor the *use* of the one by the other; often the poets are simply laid side by side as comparisons or contrasts, as representatives of their period, or as stages in the alteration of a cultural movement.[13] But to treat their *relations* is not just a question of putting them side-by-side in *comparisons*, however useful that might prove to be, or in relations that we *make up* for them in pursuit of our own interpretative purposes. The question is historical—what impact did they have on each other (though so far it appears that it was uni-directional)? It is the presence of the one *in* the other that is the interesting question here, and then the questions arising from that presence. I am not disparaging those works that only place the two poets side-by-side without considering the influence, only trying to find a means of unpacking in different words, Cheney's expression that we have so rarely 'brought them together'. By 'bring them together', I mean treat the influence of Spenser on Shakespeare. But the concept of 'influence' is broader than word-, phrase- and scene-stealing or shaping; if we call that direct influence, we have an indirect influence which is far more general: the pressure of Spenser on English Renaissance poetry quite generally, as, together with Sidney, practically the inventor of it, and the pervasive pressure on a magpie writer such as Shakespeare of having, figuratively at least, at your elbow as you write a work such as *The Faerie Queene* which seems already to have treated most subjects under the sun; a work which possesses undeniable greatness and an almost infinite invention[14]—to say nothing of hymns and sonnet sequences, including the *Ruines* we know Shakespeare to have read carefully and recalled[15]—a pressure which makes itself felt not only in occasional specific details, though these may well

---

prosodic variety, than *Faerie Queene*? On Spenser's style, see n. 20 below. Here, one needs to consult Cheney's opening and footnotes in 'Sonnet 106', esp., 331–7.

[13] I owe these points to discussions with Patrick Cheney.

[14] What Hieatt in a relevant context calls 'the unique poetic embodiment in English', A. Kent Hieatt, 'The Genesis of Shakespeare's *Sonnets*: Spenser's *Ruines of Rome: by Bellay*', *PMLA*, 98 (1983), 800–14, here 812.

[15] See, Hieatt, 'Genesis'.

accompany this more general influence, but in shaping conception and execution, very possibly unawares. Naturally, such a general influence would be much more difficult to be precise over for scholars trying to winkle it out.[16]

We have been reaching a different stage in the study of relations, no longer merely the occasional hunt for linguistic borrowings, but deeper influences, general and shaping influences.[17] Nonetheless, we cannot afford to leave the linguistic borrowings behind, nor to stray very far from them in exposition of other borrowings, however general, if we wish to stay with the specifically historical question. And it is my view that we have not yet exhausted the linguistic borrowings, even while we may have thought for a while that the work is virtually pointless, antiquarian in the negative sense, or fraught with such uncertainties that it were best left alone for sterner stuff. It is over-hasty to belittle source-hunting; without it we should have no definite information that Shakespeare read Spenser at all; whereas taking the results of source-hunting seriously—it is as if we were presented with an ancient copy of *The Faerie Queene* with faded marginalia in Shakespeare's own hand.

One of the weaknesses of the search for linguistic borrowings, which, I argue, lies at the heart of the enterprise of studying the two poets in relation, is that it is—I do not wish to say 'under-theorised'— but that its methodology has not been systematically treated and its tools have not been re-set over the decades. In fact we have no generalisations over the objects nor over the methods of treating the slippery *Forschungsobjekt*.[18] So that in some sense the subject is treated in an amateur fashion—and perhaps this will prove to be for the best; but while the possiblity of professionalising the subject exists, in the potential for systematisation in the form of computerised texts, comparisons

---

[16] Another type of intertextuality argues that because we have read Spenser, or for that matter Homer or Yeats or Eliot, we read Shakespeare differently as a result, irrespective of Shakespeare's real relations to the other writers we invoke. This can undoubtedly be the case and leads to the fascinating 'influence of Eliot on Keats' in David Lodge's *Small Worlds*. But this is capable of such unrestrained generalisation that it can hardly be called historical to the texts—it has nothing to do with Spenser and Shakespeare, but with ourselves as equipped or over-equipped readers—a history of ourselves, not of Spenser or Shakespeare. Michael Pincombe, in 'Classical and Contemporary Sources of the "Gloomy Woods" of *Titus Andronicus*: Ovid, Seneca, Spenser', in *Shakespearean Continuities: Essays in Honor of E. A. J. Honigmann*, ed. John Batchelor, Tom Cain, and Claire Lamont (Basingstoke: Macmillan, 1997), 40–55, remarks, something in Lodge's vein, on the possibility of Shakespeare becoming the source for Ovid: 'the "gloomy woodland setting" [Jonathan Bate] claims to see in the *Metamorphoses* is actually imported into Ovid's poem from Shakespeare's play. In this instance, then, Shakespeare is the source for Ovid (as it were)', 42.

[17] See the closing pages of this Introduction and the following papers for details on this.

[18] 'The understanding that ought to arise from thinking about them together is still confused and rudimentary' (Hieatt, *SpEncy*. 641).

and searches, or refinements of methodology, we should at least put it to the test to see whether its results are at all commensurate with its promises and our hopes.

A new collection of papers, heralding a resurgence of interest in the relations between two of the greatest of Renaissance English poets, is perhaps the ideal place to make an attempt to gather what has been gained, and to offer some thoughts on some of the ways in which we might gain more. So that I shall begin with some caveats on method in general terms; for indeed the ground is boggy and the path inadequately mapped out or even marked by tufts of greener, thicker grass planted by previous adventurers—and any guidance through the morass might be thought welcome. I shall then propose that we renew our attention to some specific methods and only then come to the description and placing of the papers here included in the general field of Spenser-Shakespeare studies; papers which attempt another departure in this, if nothing else, fascinating, but indeed, important sub-discipline.

III

Before we proceed, it will be as well to consider some distinctions between allusion and borrowing. I think there is no case of an allusion in Shakespeare to Spenser, as clear as there is to Marlowe in *As You Like It*: 'Dead Shepherd now I find thy saw of might / "Who ever lov'd that lov'd not at first sight?"' (3.5.81–2, *Hero and Leander*, I.176), but borrowing is not necessarily intentional, though it requires agency, whereas allusion, like representation, is fully and necessarily intentional.[19]

If I simply borrow a phrase from your email to me, I may be quite unaware of having done so; but if I am actually *alluding* to your email to me of last week, then I must do so deliberately and in complete awareness of doing so. Of course, you may take my unconscious borrowing, the undeliberated echo of your phrase, as an allusion—and this may lead to understanding (you know I have read your email), or misunderstanding (that I mean something more by the borrowing than I actually do); both historical understandings, one true one false. But all that has

---

[19] For literary criticism, the question of representation is wholly a question of whose intention, the critic's or the author's (and therefore of attributive verbs). A great deal of confusion arises from failing to recognise that representation is an intentional concept, and if not the original author's, then the critic's. 'Even if two things do look like each other, it does not follow, just because of that, that one represents the other; the chairs we are sitting on are very alike but one does not represent the other. For one thing to represent another it must be intended to do so, and intended to be seen doing so, and this involves some social convention', Michael Podro, 'Depiction and the Golden Calf', in *Philosophy and the Visual Arts: Seeing and Abstracting*, ed. Andrew Harrison (Dordrecht and Boston: Royal Institute of Philosophy Conferences, 1987), vol. 1985, 3–28, here, 5; see also Erwin Panofsky, *Studies in Iconology: Humanistic Themes in the Art of the Renaissance* (London and New York: Harper and Row, 1972), 3–17.

happened here is that it is not my allusion—only my borrowing—but yours: you have taken my accidental, unconscious thievery *as* an allusion, endowing it with your own intention. These things are quite clear as long as I am here to speak authoritatively (and trustworthily) of my mental state, at least to my own satisfaction if not to yours, for you may disbelieve my testimony; but when we are items in a chronicle of wasted email, then the question would be a deal more difficult to assess. And nor is every conscious, even intended, borrowing, an allusion to its source. The intentionality of allusion is not identical with the intentionality of deliberate borrowing. Again, I may borrow a neat phrase from a third party's email in one to you without intending an allusion, perhaps simply in the safety of knowing that you have not read the third email. And yet these distractions are very much the issue in an attempt to assess Spenser's influence on Shakespeare, or Shakespeare's use of Spenser. For while the linguistic borrowings are basic and primary, there are conscious and unconscious borrowings, the types of influence are both passive and active; and between source and borrowing there may be a great deal of static.

And what do we mean by 'influence'? Alas, a great deal. There is deliberate imitation, which of course takes many forms: full *imitatio* or *aemulo*; the deliberate borrowing of a word or phrase, idea, plot scheme, tone, or what indeed not? But there is also unconscious borrowing where the loan poet influences the borrowing poet in ways that the latter (in this case Shakespeare) could not himself fully account for. Broadly, we can talk of conscious and unconscious influence, and the one can pass into the other.

One reason, perhaps the over-riding reason to study Spenser and Shakespeare in close connection, is to throw light on both poets, so that comparing Spenser and Shakespeare may throw light on Spenser as well as on Shakespeare. No doubt it is only fortuitous, but most papers, it would seem, throw light on Shakespeare, most of those in this volume included; Shakespeare commands the attention. But putting them side by side can illuminate Spenser, too. So it is with style. Spenser's style, the way he puts together his poetry, phrases, rhyme, lines and stanzas is, as it seems to me, under-attended to, and the effects on getting the full benefit of Spenser's poetry can be limiting, so that a close association in criticism between Shakespeare and Spenser is useful for the light it can throw on Spenser's style and therefore on how to read him. This is one reason I have written below at some length on the matter.[20]

---

[20] Besides the older books and papers, by Paul Alpers (see n28, below), Roger Sale, *Reading Spenser: An Introduction to 'The Faerie Queene'* (New York: Random House, 1968), and W.B.C. Watkins, *Spenser and Shakespeare* (Princeton: Princeton University Press, 1950), chap. 8, esp., 279–92; see also Judith H. Anderson, *Words That Matter: Linguistic Perception in Renaissance English* (Stanford: Stanford University Press, 1996), chap 5, esp, 151–65; A.D. Nuttall, 'Spenser and Elizabethan Alienation' *Essays in Criticism*, 55 (2005),

Now, the conviction already mentioned that there was little to say on the question of Spenser's influence on Shakespeare, did not grow up either through idleness, caprice or ignorance, and Hieatt has summarized its causes in the article just cited, and one of the claims is that the one style is so very different from the other. This is true, but does not entail that Shakespeare did not or could not borrow and frequently, too, from Spenser. It will be worth while to look into the style question, for doing so will help to highlight both the terrain and illuminate some of the fox-holes and level places, as well as a steep hill or two. In doing so I shall at first speak quite generally and there will be specific exceptions which I shall for the moment ignore.

IV

Elizabethan and Jacobean drama is neither epic, Greek tragedy, nor French classical drama; nor even, with Shakespeare, deliberately reprised Greek tragedy such as *Samson Agonistes*. Epic, and to a certain extent the Greek tragedy, is a scholarly genre.[21] Renaissance drama in English is very largely a popular genre. Epic is slow and deliberately so, intentionally and consciously writing into itself as much of past civilisation as it can—not just for use, as in borrowing, but for its own sake.[22]

209–25; an excellent paper by Paul J. Hecht, 'Spenser Out of His Stanza', *Style*, 39.3 (2005), 316–35; work by David Wilson-Okamura, for example, 'The French Aesthetic of Spenser's Feminine Rhyme', *Modern Language Quarterly* 68 (2007), 345–62; two papers by Catherine Addison: 'Little Boxes: The Effects of Stanza on Poetic Narrative', *Style*, 37 (2003), 124–43, and 'Rhyming Against the Grain: A New Look at the Spenserian Stanza', in *Edmund Spenser: New and Renewed Directions*, ed. J.B. Lethbridge (Madison: Fairleigh Dickinson University Press, 2006), 337–51. See also, William Blisset, 'Stanza, Spenserian' and Susanne Woods, 'Versification', both in *SpEncy*. These works can be seen as an antidote to over-reading. Style is part of genre and genre is part of the originary, that is historical, context of a text. I cite Montrose as an unexpected ally here: 'Writing and reading are always historically and socially situated events, performed in the world and upon the world by ideologically situated individual and collective human agents. In any situation of signification, the theoretical indeterminacy of the signifying process is delimited by the historical specificity of discursive practices'. Louis A. Montrose, 'New Historicisms', in *Redrawing the Boundaries: The Transformation of English and American Literary Studies*, ed. Stephen J. Greenblatt and Giles Gunn (New York: Modern Language Association of America, 1992), 392–418, here 415.

[21] In the present context I call *The Faerie Queene* an epic because it has a great many epic features—its scholarliness being one of the most important of them, its encyclopaedic nature and allusion and open borrowings others. Many of the relevant romance features are shared with Homeric epic, for example, repetitions of various kinds; many of the epic techniques are specifically not part of the Romance tradition.

[22] By 'slow' I do not mean the surface rhythms of the verse. Both Homer, the *Niebelungenlied* say, and Spenser are rhythmically quick, far more so than Virgil or Milton. But even Homer digresses, dilates and punctuates with extended similes and set pieces. To a very large extent the formulae of Homer and Spenser contribute to rhythmic quickness. Thus, and in a manner that Renaissance drama cannot generally afford, Homer, too, is slow.

Ever since Homer, epic has sought encyclopaedic inclusion, *copia*, wearing its borrowings of all kinds on its sleeve as part of its innate texture; not all of epic's borrowings are allusions in detail, but in principle its borrowings collectively are meant to be noticed and are so far at least allusions. It is part of epic technique to borrow, to imitate, to emulate, to allude. This is no less true of *The Faerie Queene* than of Virgil, Tasso, or, preeminently, *Paradise Lost*. Examples in *The Faerie Queene* would be the catalogue of trees, House of Pride, Timias' wielding of Arthur's sword, the song in the Bower and the boat ride to the Bower.[23]

Epic, even such highly dramatic epics as *The Iliad* or *Paradise Lost*, eschews the normal rhythms of the speaking voice, does so deliberately, and uses a highly literary language removed in other senses, too, from the language of common-or-garden speech:

τὸν δ' ἀπαμειβόμενος προσέφη πόδας ὠκὺς Ἀχιλλεύς[24]

Exactly why Spenser does so is not clear, but he, too, writes a literary language, not giving way to the diction, syntax rhythms of the spoken word.

The poetry of drama, on the other hand, is quick. Quick in the sense that one of its primary objectives is to be absorbed as fully as possible while it is being spoken on the stage. To do this the poetry of drama (quite apart from questions of verisimilitude), tends, or tended, to reproduce the syntax and rhythms of the speaking voice, rhythms occurring naturally in the quotidian, as the most effective when the mouth speaks to the ear. And even where it does not mechanically reproduce the rhythms of the speaking voice, dramatic speech gives the impression of doing so. If it did not, it would not succeed as stage drama (or, less generally, 'succeed in the way that it did and has'), its primary raison d'être. However there may be exceptions to this, particularly once we come to the end of the Nineteenth Century, Shakespearean drama is written for the stage, for various stages and various audiences, but still from mouth to ear, and its success, the success of the playwright and his company, and the fruit-sellers and prostitutes and cut-purses, depended upon this success in communicating at speed from mouth to ear without the audience's having or needing chances of recapitulation. Quite apart from that, by Shakespeare's day the characters on stage had to give the appearance of verisimilitude. Naturally, I do not claim that there is no more in Shakespeare's drama than can be caught on hearing

---

[23] Respectively to Ovid, *Met.* to the House of Pride (Tower of Babel, the house built on sand, Matt. 7:26–7); To the legend of Achilles revealed among the women because he could not resist wielding the sword left lying about for the purpose; to Tasso; the Boat trip is the *Odyssey* writ small.

[24] 'Then he answered and said to the swift-footed Achilles': a line, versions of which are often repeated in the *Iliad*.

a single performance—even then, in an age where aural reception and retention were very much more efficient than our own; and of course a great deal of drama previous to Shakespeare, Marlowe and Kyd is very ornate, syntactically artificial in ways that, with hindsight we can see are not in this sense dramatic. Spenser on the other hand printed his works, and, judged by the standards of the time, took some care over the process; *The Faerie Queene* is a printed poem, it communicates from page to eye, with all the chances of recapitulation that offers. Elizabethans recited and read aloud to each other, Spenser is said to have read parts of his poem to Elizabeth herself; but still *The Faerie Queene* is not oral but printed, not dramatic, but epic.

Drama needs to be, or at any rate Shakespeare's is, direct and dense. By 'direct' I mean: first the verse must give the impression of following ordinary spoken rhythms of speech (as opposed to written rhythms of speech, which can be quite different).[25] Not only does this help to ensure some verisimilitude, but the speech being thus familiar, can be as rapidly heard as spoken.

By 'dense' I mean that there should be no wastage—otherwise the play will not hold the attention. We are not talking about a modern action-movie where exciting events and special effects of great realism hold the attention and move it forwards with the expectation of projection, making up for scripts of extreme simplicity; we are speaking primarily of the verse of Shakespeare and secondarily that of Marlowe, where from practical necessity as much as anything, the word was paramount, and, for all the display, staging was highly stylised and special effects very primitive, though it is not clear that realism was particularly aimed at. There is another practical reason for density in dramatic verse: there is a great deal to pack in to the two hours traffic, and little room for slack writing, padding or digression and excursion, which in any case dissipates attention. The audience will only tolerate so much—even in an age where theatre could consume a great part of the daylight hours, with bear-baiting, comic turns, a tragedy, half a comedy—all demanding attention. Naturally, there is a certain amount of derogation from these principles, particularly in the case of Marlowe where spectacle often helps out with padding from the dramatic point of view, something which we undoubtedly find in places in *Tamburlaine* for example and where it was part of the attraction—the same is true of the emulative *Titus* and of the mature *Macbeth* and *Lear* where it is assimilated into the nature of the dramas played out there and of the characters. The greater verbal directness and density of the opening and closing speeches of Faust or of Barabas' great speeches partly accounts

---

[25] Of course it can be very difficult to assess the spoken rhythms of a past age; but the rhythms of prose speech can be taken as a reasonably reliable guide, particularly that prose in drama and in dialogue forms, such as *The View of the Present State of Ireland*, and in reports of conversation and in letters, depositions and such-like.

for their greater dramatic power relative to some of Tamburlaine's. Additionally, in Marlowe to a lesser degree and in Shakespeare to a very high degree, the poetry must not only be dense with regard to action, but also must additionally work to characterisation—that is, it has an additional function to perform, and this, naturally, leads to an increase in density. Where epic is leisurely, drama is very tightly bound to what is endurable or tolerable at a sitting: it has only a couple of hours in which to do all that it has to do. Consequently it must pack a great deal in, and communicate it at speed; in practice this means that the verse must be dense, yet written in a *spoken* language—it must be direct.

If we take a stanza from *The Faerie Queene* we can see that these dramatic qualities of directness and density are weak or ignored:

> Certes (said she) then bene ye sixe to blame,
> To weene your wrong by force to iustifie:
> For knight to leaue his Ladie were great shame,
> *That faithfull is*, and better were to die.
> All losse is lesse, *and lesse the infamie*,
> *Then losse of loue* to him, that loues but one;
> Ne may loue be compeld by maisterie;
> For soone as maisterie comes, sweet loue anone
> Taketh his nimble wings, and soone away is gone.
>   (III.i.25)[26]

Spenser's 'Then losse of loue to him', doesn't mean what it appears to mean in isolation, where it comes over as a generalisation, but means the loss of the particular knight's particular love, as in 'loss of his lover', that is, of a person, not love in general. 'All losse is lesse ... / Then losse of loue', is perfectly adequate spoken syntax, but here it is interrupted by the phrase 'and lesse the infamie', which is very awkward indeed considered as spoken language—and it means, not that the infamy is less, but that 'even' (the impact of 'and') infamy, and infamy of all or

---

[26] In *As You Like It*, Celia and Rosalind take but 10 lines to plan their disguise, but six to find names, and a further 10 to plan the stealing of Touchstone and the taking of their jewels and wealth. Spenser's Glauce and Britomart take ten stanzas, 90 lines, to make their plans, stanzas which include a lengthy account of the current British wars and other female British warriors. It is not impossible that Shakespeare recalled this passage briefly in *As You Like It*, for Rosalind is also 'more than common tall' and so thinks that manly arms, 'a gallant curtal-axe upon my thigh, / A boar-spear in my hand', would suit her: 'Let vs in feigned armes our selues disguise, ... / The dreadfull speare and shield to exercize: / Ne certes daughter that same warlike wize / I weene, would you misseeme; for ye bene tall, / And large of limbe, t'atchieue an hard emprize' (3.3.53). On *AYLI* and *FQ*, see also J. J. M. Tobin, 'Spenserian Parallels', *Essays in Criticism* 29 (1979): 264–9, here 266. Rosalind's 'curtal-axe' is suspiciously Marlovian: 'Lie here, ye weeds that I disdain to wear! / This complete armour and this curtle-axe / Are adjuncts more beseeming Tamburlaine' (*1Tamb*. I.ii); 'the keenest curtle-axe / That e'er made passage through Persian arms' (*1Tamb*. II.iii); 'Thou shalt have shield and lance, / Armour of proof, horse, helm, and curtle-axe' (*1Tamb*. I.iii); 'or with a curtle-axe / To hew thy flesh, and make a gaping wound?' (*1Tamb*. III.ii).

any sort, is less than the loss of a lover. But even more illustrative is the clause 'That faithfull is' which qualifies 'his ladie' from the previous line, thus: 'For [a] knight to leave his lady, *who is faithful*, were great shame'; as Spenser writes it, it is technically (but absurdly, which is why we tolerate it; eventually the meaning becomes clear), the shame that is faithful. Of course a reader, perceiving visually, manages very well to sort it out, it is neither difficult, nor confusing; but it would be far more difficult in aural perception; above all from the dramatic point of view it departs so far from the normal syntax of spoken language that it would both slow the verse down, interfere with verisimilitude, and need very good justification indeed to be put into a character's mouth. While we tolerate this in *The Faerie Queene* and *Paradise Lost*, anyone who actually spoke like this, or, equally, was represented as talking like this, would be marked down as a fool, a pedant, a foreigner, as pretentious, devious or deceptive—or as a comic character who may be comic precisely because he or she is all of these things (think of Osric or Polonius, or Bottom or Don Armado).[27] And all this because the language departs so far from spoken syntax that it has a very marked tendency to *characterise* its speaker—whereas in an epic, it can pass as neutral in that respect. Recall that it is Britmomart *speaking* here. None of these things applies to Britomart, unless we read unwilling to make the suspension of syntactical belief; for this is not *dramatic* speech at all, a point Spenserians have struggled over.[28]

Milton of course, like Homer, individuates the speech of his characters within the limits of epic diction and syntax; but even so, to put *Paradise Lost* on the stage would be a difficult undertaking; dramatic in one sense it is, with the dynamic clash of idea, personality, and as in the *Iliad,* style, and full of speeches, but it remains, in the sense intended here, an epic nevertheless. It is hard work to neutralise such speech in this fashion, and is obviously not an accident, however Jonson and his ilk might pillory Spenser for such things.[29] The syntax of epic is not that of ordinary speech, Greek or Latin, Elizabethan, Jacobean or Caroline English: some constructions in Spenser would be extremely difficult to convey or receive on a stage: they are not direct.

---

[27] See the paper by Rachel E. Hile in the present volume for caveats about Osric's comic role, however.

[28] Paul Alpers, 'How to Read *The Faerie Queene*', *Essays in Criticism*, 18 (1968), 426–43; and 'Narration in The Faerie Queene', *ELH*, 44 (1977), 19–39, and in *The Poetry of 'The Faerie Queene'* (Princeton: Princeton University Press, 1967). Harry Berger, Jr. responds with a newer version of the old claim in 'Narrative as Rhetoric in *The Faerie Queene*', *ELR*, 21 (1991), 3–48.

[29] Robert L. Reid extracts some of the 'lampoons' at the opening of 'The Fairy Queen: Gloriana or Titania?', *The Upstart Crow*, 13 (1993): 16–32, a paper which also explores some of the contrasts between Spenser and Shakespeare.

If we take another stanza, we can see that it has not the requisite density either: II.viii.5 has been amusingly and perceptively characterised in the relevant manner by the critic Sir Walter Raleigh:

> Beside his head there satt a faire young man,
> (This announces the theme, as in music.)
> Of wondrous beauty and of freshest yeares,
> (The fair young man was fair and young.)
> Whose tender bud to blossom new began,
> (The fair young man was young.)
> And florish faire above his equal peers.
> (The fair young man was fair, fairer even than his equals, who were also his peers.)[30]

Similarly, ringing the changes for the sake of ringing the changes, as in Spenser's tree catalogue, or the many processions and pageants, can have no place in the new Elizabethan drama of Marlowe and Shakespeare, not at any rate verbally.[31]

Finally, consider the following comparison:

> Then was there heard a most celestiall sound,
> Of dainty musicke, which did next ensew
> Before the spouse: that was Arion crownd;
> Who playing on his harpe, vnto him drew
> The eares and hearts of all that goodly crew,
> That euen yet the Dolphin, which him bore
> Through the Aegaean seas from Pirates vew,
> Stood still by him astonisht at his lore,
> And all the raging seas for ioy forgot to rore.
>
> So went he playing on the watery plaine.
>   (IV.xi.24–5)

> Thou rememb'rest
> Since once I sat upon a promontory,
> And heard a mermaid on a dolphin's back
> Uttering such dulcet and harmonious breath
> That the rude sea grew civil at her song,
> And certain stars shot madly from their spheres,
> To hear the sea-maid's music?
>   (MND 2.1.148)

---

[30] Sir Walter Raleigh, *Milton* (London: Edward Arnold, 1922), 200.

[31] Exceptions abound of course: In *Love's Labours Lost* for example, or *Much Ado*, where it is more highly individuated, the simple play of verbal wit is part of the dramatic appeal, and might count, I suppose, as a sort of 'ringing the changes'. But ringing the changes in the manner of *Much Ado* is a very highly developed dramatic technique, at that time available only to a dramatist who had deliberately set himself to school over many years. But when Mercutio spends too long at Queen Mab, Romeo interrupts him, dramatically speaking not a moment too soon, with: 'Peace, peace, Mercutio, peace! / Thou talkst of nothing' (I.iv.95–6).

In the Spenser, there are further undramatic qualities of importance throughout *The Faerie Queene*. For example, his 'Then was there heard' is in the passive voice, whereas Oberon says 'I ... heard', active voice; Spenser's 'vnto him drew / The eares and hearts of all that goodly crew' saps movement by turning a potentially physical activity (drawing people to or after him) into a dead metaphor of it—what is drawn is not bodies in space, but hearts and minds, and even the action of playing is not dramatised: it is the figurative, abstract (that is, unreal), drawing which is emphasised, and the playing is emphatically put to one side in a reduced relative clause: 'Who[,] playing on his harp'; and further, the dolphin, who does act at least, 'stands still' rather than, for instance, 'leaps high' or something; and the sea, too, does nothing positive, only forgetting to roar, a negative action, a privation of activity, like the dolphin's standing still. In Shakespeare's case, besides the far greater compression (omitting the epic *copia* of the dolphin's history for instance), the whole throbs with activity: the mermaid is actually 'uttering', and Oberon is actually listening (active 'heard') and the sea does something, the same something as it happens as Spenser's sea, but it *does* it, 'sea *grew* civil', active voice, and above all the activity in the unforgettable 'And certain stars shot madly from their spheres'.[32] So that Spenser can be seen not to be writing dramatic verse. This need not be a general point: Spenser is not writing either Marlovian or Shakespearean dramatic verse—and in this formulation we see that the crucial difference between Spenser and the two dramatists lies in their much greater density and directness. Curiously, Spenser, while not dense in the manner of Marlowe or Shakespeare is nevertheless quick in his movement through his digressions, divagations and dilations,[33] but he is quick precisely through lack of density, and through formulaic constructions and predictability, as the stanzas quoted above illustrate.

Because Spenser is writing epic, he is freed from the iron need for density and quickness and certain types of directness. No doubt he could have written with the density of Virgil (which is not that of drama) as Milton was to do; for some reason, possibly the pressure of the Romance tradition, features of the style of which are reproduced in *The Faerie Queene*—repetition, hyperbole, paratactic sentence-structure, and to a certain extent paratactic narrative structures—Spenser elected a loose-limbed, formulaic and repetitive style which in these senses is

---

[32] Against Shakespeare's 'rude ... civil', Spenser has 'raging ... rore', which opposition is not quite so tightly focussed as Shakespeare's; once again we find Spenser opening out and Shakespeare closing out.

[33] See Matthew Arnold, *On Translating Homer* (London: Longman, Green, Longman, and Roberts, 1861), 67–8. And it would be perfectly possible to describe Shakespeare's verse, from a different point of view, and meaning something slightly different by the term, as 'slow', exactly becasue it is so dense in the piling up of image on image, connotation on connotation and so on.

Homeric rather than Virgilian. Spenser's poetry is end-stopped, makes use of formulaic repetition, and deserts the syntax of spoken language in favour of a literary style, no doubt also pressured here by his stanza form and the consequent necessity to proliferate rhymes. Spenser also makes use, and as far as one can judge he does so deliberately, of local dilation, another epic feature of his poem—as for instance in the extended simile and in set pieces such as the catalogue of trees or the allegory of Alma's castle, the processions of Pride, Cupid, the Months and Seasons.

These are some of the reasons for thinking that Shakespeare might not have found Spenser, and *The Faerie Queene* in particular, congenial or appealing as a source for his dramatic poetry at least; and Spenser's abstraction—though this is more perceived by ourselves than real and does not apply to every facet or level of Spenser's poetry—might also be thought a deterring factor.[34] In applying the discussion to specific cases and factors, we shall find others.

It is not surprising, looked at historically, that Marlowe's borrowings from Spenser are so much more apparent, those we have noticed at any rate, than Shakespeare's.[35] For Marlowe's dramatic poetry, particularly in *Tamburlaine*, where most of the more obvious and lengthy borrowings occur, is in many respects, epic and stanzaic—to some extent it is dilatory rather than dense (or quick). Marlowe's line is mighty precisely because he has not yet fully attained, or perhaps did not want to attain, absolute freedom from the end-stopped line, some steps towards which he had obviously been taking. And in this respect, it is not surprising that his borrowings from Spenser occur mostly in *Tamberlaine*.[36] This is not

---

[34] Robert L. Reid in the closing pages of 'The Fairy Queen' has managed this question very adroitly.

[35] Gareth Roberts, 'Three Notes on Uses of Circe by Spenser, Marlowe, and Milton', *Notes and Queries*, 25 (1978), 433–35; A. B. Taylor, 'Britomart and the Mermaids: A Note on Marlowe and Spenser', *Notes and Queries*, 18 (1971), 224–5; John D. Jump, 'Spenser and Marlowe', *Notes and Queries*, 11 (1964), 261–262; T. W. Baldwin, 'The Genesis of Some Passages Which Spenser Borrowed from Marlowe', *ELH*, 9 (1942), 157–87; W. B. C. Watkins, 'The Plagiarist: Spenser or Marlowe?', *ELH*, 11 (1944), 249–65; T. W. Baldwin, 'The Genesis of Some Passages Which Spenser Borrowed from Marlowe', *ELH*, 12 (1945), 165; Douglas Bush, 'Marlowe and Spenser', *Times Literary Supplement*, (Jan 1, 1938), 12; Georg Schoeneich, *Der litterarische Einfluss Spensers auf Marlowe* (Halle: Diss., 1907); John Bakeless, *The Tragical History of Christopher Marlowe*, 2 vols (Cambridge, MA: Harvard University Press, 1942) summarises Schoeneich at 1:205–8. Gill in *SpEncy* adds the following: *ITamb* 5.2.6, *FQ* I.vii 43, 5.2.196 and I.vii.22; *IITamb* 4.3.112 and *FQ* I.iv.4, 5.2.26 and II.vii.13. Also *ITamb* 1.2.173 and *FQ* VI.xii.35 may show Marlowe's influence on Spenser, since *FQ* VI is believed to have been written after *Tamb*, see Jump 1964, above); Charles Crawford, 'Edmund Spenser, "Locrine", and "Selimus"', *Notes and Queries*, 9th series, 7 (1901), 61–3, 101–3, 142–4, 203–5, 261–3, 324–5, 384–6. And a new book: Robert A. Logan, *Shakespeare's Marlowe: The Influence of Christopher Marlowe on Shakespeare's Artistry* (Aldershot: Ashgate, 2007).

[36] Though as always there were doubtless other contributing factors, one of these being the possibility that before or during the composition he had been reading *The Faerie*

a sufficient explanation, but it is one important contributory factor. For the poetry of *The Faerie Queene* is very heavily end-stopped, and not simply by the insertion of stops at line-end, but in the syntactical (and rhetorical) structures and their arrangements relative to the line. Just as important is the fact that Spenser accentuates the line as a unit of composition, syntactically and with his peculiar method of rhyming.[37] So that even where the lines are not end-stopped by punctuation there is very little genuine enjambment, the lines being in effect end-stopped by syntax. The clause structures, the order of words (syntax in the narrow sense) and their relations to the sentence or stanza, do not tend to force one line onto the next. Spenser gets his marked forwards movement in other ways. Consider the following lines from *Tamburlaine II*:

> AMYRAS. Now in their glories shine the golden crowns
> Of these proud Turks, much like so many suns
> That half dismay the majesty of heaven.
> Now, brother, follow we our father's sword,
> That flies with fury swifter than our thoughts
> And cuts down armies with his conquering wings.
>   (IV.i.1–6)

In this speech of Amyras, these opening six lines have a stanzaic ring to them; the last line is alexandrine in its effect. Following the syntax, we

---

Queene, whereas it is possible that by three or four years later, the immediacy of the memory had subsided. Is it also possible that Marlowe felt safer pillaging an unprinted work, whereas by Shakespeare's time, *The Faerie Queene* had been printed?

[37] On conversational rhythm and word-order, see George Young, *An English Prosody on Inductive Lines* ([Cambridge: Cambridge University Press, 1928] New York: Greenwood Press, 1969), see Index s.v. 'Spenser' and *Faerie Queene*; on Marlowe and Peele, 148–54. Also, Paul Alpers, 'Style', in *Spens. Enyc.*; Russ McDonald, 'Marlowe and Style' in *The Cambridge Companion to Christopher Marlowe*, ed. Patrick Cheney (Cambridge: Cambridge University Press, 2004), 55–69; Joseph B. Mayor, *Chapters on English Metre*, 2nd ed. (Cambridge: Cambridge University Press, 1901). Derek Attridge, *The Rhythms of English Poetry* (London: Longman, 1982), Chapter 5 'The Five-beat Rhythm' should be consulted. George Saintsbury notes that while 'the Marlowe-and-Peele or Peele-and-Marlowe group, great as was the advance which they made, never quite achieved that combination of internal dissimilarity and external communication which is necessary for the triumph of the vehicle', George Saintsbury, *A History of English Prosody from the Twelfth Century to the Present Day*, 3 vols, 2nd ed. ([1908] London: Macmillan, 1923), II.5. On Shakespearean blank verse, see II.3–65, where he speaks of the 'tendency [in these poets] to make line and clause coincide' (II.5). I cite this because Eliot alters 'clause' to 'sentence', an awkward change leading to confusion over enjambment: 'The verse accomplishments of *Tamburlaine* are notably two: Marlowe gets into blank verse the melody of Spenser, and he gets a new driving power by reinforcing the sentence period against the line period' (104). T.S. Eliot, 'Christopher Marlowe', in *Selected Essays*, new ed. (New York: Harcourt, Brace & Co., 1950), 100–106. On the Sonnets, Saintsbury writes of 'that same extraordinary symphonising of the prosodic effects of individual and batched verses, which was his secret in blank verse itself' (II. 59). See also Marco Mincoff, *Shakespeare, the First Steps* (Sophia: The Bulgarian Academy of Sciences, 1976) on the development of Shakespeare's style.

find that the first line is self-contained as a clause; that while the genitive in the first part of the second line is not independent, being dependent on the previous clause, the second clause ending with the line is, or at least appears to be, independent (it is self-contained and comes to an end at line-end), and the third line is a single relative clause.[38] In the second three lines we find Marlowe's default rhythm of one clause filling out the whole line and the line thus end-stopped. The closing pair have no punctuation to separate them; but this is a poor way to count end-stopping, since in the first place we can have no confidence in the provenance of the punctuation and secondly there are more important ways of stopping a line than simply affixing a greater or lesser stop to its end. In this case, the 'And' in the following line breaks the clause, and provides a re-beginning, a complete line-long sub-clause added to the previous complete line-long sub-clause in coordination rather than dependence: the sword of line four, flies and cuts (though this gives the sword wings rather than, as one might expect, the father); the sentence could just as easily stop after 'thoughts' as after 'wings'.

I have picked these lines quite at random, but they are typical of Marlowe's style, especially in *Tamburlaine*, though he has not quite grown away from it by the time he comes to *Faustus* or *Edward II*. Even in this short passage, moreover, one can sense the stanzaic nature of much of Marlowe's *Tamburlaine* poetry: the rhythms of the lines lengthening towards the ends of the speeches, so that a final line, as here, often has something of the retarding effect of an alexandrine close to a Spenserian stanza. In the following speech this effect turns the whole into a self-contained lyric:

> Proud fury and intolerable fit,
> That dares torment the body of my love
> And scourge the scourge of the immortal God!
> Now are those spheres, where Cupid used to sit,
> Wounding the world with wonder and with love,
> Sadly supplied with pale and ghastly death,
> Whose darts do pierce the centre of my soul.
> Her sacred beauty hath enchanted heaven,
> And had she lived before the siege of Troy,
> Helen, whose beauty summoned Greece to arms
> And drew a thousand ships to Tenedos,
> Had not been named in Homer's Iliads;
> Her name had been in every line he wrote.
> Or, had those wanton poets, for whose birth
> Old Rome was proud, but gazed a while on her,

---

[38] Note that hardly ever do speeches in *Tamburlaine* begin or end in mid line. The main document for consideration of end-stopping and related phenomena is Ants Oras, *Pause Patterns in Elizabethan and Jacobean Drama; an Experiment in Prosody* (Gainsville: University of Florida Press, 1960).

> Nor Lesbia nor Corinna had been named;
> Zenocrate had been the argument
> Of every epigram or elegy.   (*Tamb* II: II.iv.178–95)

Particularly in the closing five lines, which read like the culminating quatrain of a Shakespearean sonnet, one can feel that the whole is coming to a conclusion, and the final pair of lines suggests quite strongly the closing couplet of a sonnet, or the rhythmical equivalent of the alexandrine in Spenser's stanza. That is to say, the speeches are paragraph-stopped as well as end-stopped in the line. Marlowe is still so influenced by stanzaic verse that he sometimes writes virtual stanzas.[39] The speeches often do not follow each other from the necessities of conversation, but by verbal, syntactical or rhetorical legerdemain, much in the way that Spenser's stanzas in *The Faerie Queene* follow one another. In this passage every line is end-stopped, as much self-contained as Spenser's ringing bars of gold,[40] except for 823–4, which appears to have a true enjambment: though weak, since while 'Old Rome was proud', is the subject of the clause 'For whose birth ... proud', it is still in itself a full clause, though dependent.

All this means that in Marlowe's verse, there is already room, there is already the requisite shape to the line and the paragraph or group of lines, for Spenser's stanzaic verse to be slotted in—if need be, by the stanza-full, as in the famous 'Selinis' borrowing mentioned above and discussed below. Marlowe's dramatic poetry is far more capable of absorbing chunks of *The Faerie Queene* without alterations so drastic as to disguise the borrowing, than Shakespeare's. Even Shakespeare's earlier

---

[39] In this next passage for instance, Marlowe has written a fairly neat blank verse sonnet, with a half-rhyme couplet to conclude: though the first quatrain has five lines, and the third only three (approaching, already overgoing, the Miltonic sonnet). Is it significant that when Byron filched from this passage he, too, was writing Spenserian Stanzas—although with very different linear rhythms to Spenser? (*Childe Harold*, III.97, with 'word' for Marlowe's 'period'.)

> What is beauty, saith my sufferings, then?
> If all the pens that ever poets held
> Had fed the feeling of their masters' thoughts,
> And every sweetness that inspired their hearts,
> Their minds, and muses on admired themes;
> If all the heavenly quintessence they still
> From their immortal flowers of poesy,
> Wherein, as in a mirror, we perceive
> The highest reaches of a human wit;
> If these had made one poem's period,
> And all combined in beauty's worthiness,
> Yet should there hover in their restless heads
> One thought, one grace, one wonder, at the least,
> Which into words no virtue can digest.
>   (*ITamb*. V.i. 160–73).

[40] W. B. Yeats, *Essays and Introductions* (New York: Collier Books, 1968), 379.

plays are at least one step further away from the end-stopped line than Marlowe in *Tamburlaine*; and by the time he gets into his stride, Shakespeare's poetry not only overflows the line end, but is plastic in ways which neither Marlowe, nor Spenser ever dreamed of—and perhaps didn't wish at all to achieve.[41]

Turning to Shakespeare, it will be best to take him at his most plastic—in *Macbeth*. I wish only to recall in the present context how the line as a unit of composition is firmly and consistently subordinated to the sentence and where clause-end and line-end do not at all habitually correspond, and how the impression of the everyday speaking voice is everywhere apparent, enabled by the subordination of the line-clause coincidence. The line is there to be used, it structures the verse, it has not yet broken down, but Shakespeare writes in sentences not lines, just as one does in a common-or-garden speech-situation. Take Macbeth's aside in Act I, scene iii:

> Two truths are told,
> As happy prologues to the swelling act
> Of the imperial theme.—I thank you gentlemen.
> This supernatural soliciting
> Cannot be ill; cannot be good. If ill,
> Why hath it given me earnest of success,
> Commencing in a truth? I am Thane of Cawdor.
> If good, why do I yield to that suggestion
> Whose horrid image doth unfix my hair
> And make my seated heart knock at my ribs,
> Against the use of nature? Present fears
> Are less than horrible imaginings:
> My thought, whose murther yet is but fantastical,
> Shakes so my single state of man that function
> Is smother'd in surmise, and nothing is
> But what is not.
> (1.4.127–42)

The first thing to notice is that the speech begins half-way through a line, completing Banquo's 'Cousins a word I pray you'. The main stops, syntactically speaking are almost all of them in mid-line: 'imperial theme'; 'cannot be ill'; 'in a truth'; 'the use of nature'. Perhaps this is one reason why Shakespeare's lines seem so much shorter than Marlowe's; another reason would be the high density of monosyllabic words, not typical of Spenser or Marlowe—though this is not a whole explanation, and Shakespeare has managed to completely fill a line with only three words in 'This supernatural soliciting'. The syntax helps the forward movement, which is very noticeable in *Macbeth*—so that, to exemplify

---

[41] I do not wish to suggest the simplistic notion that there was a steady movement away from *Gorboduc* to *Macbeth* on all fronts by all dramatists, and certainly not self-consciously.

one technique, notice how the line 'My thought ... ' begins a clause, of which the conclusion, obviously to come, is deferred to the next line by the intervening parenthetical, qualifying relative clause, 'whose murther yet is but fantastical ... '; and we wait for the verb, which we are *expecting*, to which 'my thought' is the subject—and it comes in the next following clause, '*Shakes* so ... '. But this clause is built, again, so that it is evidently only prelude to another, depending on the 'so', which is not fulfilled with its 'that', until the next line again: '*That* function is smothered in surmise'. This is not writing-by-line, but by paragraph. Many of the lines are end-stopped, but their rhythm is forced over the ends, stops or no, by syntactical dependencies and postponements, and the main stops are mid-line. But still this is recognisably a structure of normal speech—more so than in Marlowe. Such syntax and its relation to the line would make it, far from impossible, but more of a difficulty than for Marlowe, to lift something straight from *The Faerie Queene*, which is so lineal in construction, and so far removed from spoken syntax and rhythm. Moreover, one writing like this might very well not feel the need or the desire deliberately to borrow from a poet whose syntax (and density) is so very different.[42]

Shakespeare's poetry, even in *Richard II* and *Romeo and Juliet* and the other lyrical plays is denser than Marlowe's. In the late plays we can assume that this is a result of many years' experience. But after the false starts of *Titus Andronicus* (probably co-written in any case) and the *Henry VI* trilogy, Shakespeare is less interested in mere effect than Marlowe, much of whose mighty line serves the purpose of might rather than subtlety of insight and detail of individuation. Marlowe has thus more room in his line for substantial borrowing of the cut, paste and edit variety. He shares with Spenser that the occasional line or phrase can be substituted without great loss. That is, Marlowe has more Spenserian room in the line and paragraph than Shakespeare.

What this suggests is that when Shakespeare borrows, the borrowing is likely to be broken into small segments, perhaps very small, fit for a line where space is very tight; that Shakespeare's borrowing is likely to be single-word intensive. Of course, such an observation would be to some extent capable of generalisation over the whole of Shakespeare's borrowing, and we could control the observation by judicious comparisons of his borrowings from other sources. But I should argue that these points have greater force when the loan poet is a writer such as Spenser (or Marlowe for that matter, making due adjustment in the claim), writing in heavily end-stopped lines, rhyme, stanza and in a style not characterised by dramatic density or the rhythms of ordinary

---

[42] We should, as it were in fairness to Marlowe, notice that the three lines beginning 'Or had those poets ...' employ a very similar technique to the 'My thought ...' lines; not, however, Marlowe's default mode.

speech. A good example of what I mean would be Lear's 'Singe my white head' speech, partly because it is touched by a passage in *Tamburlaine*.

> You cataracts and hurricanoes, spout
> Till you have drench'd our steeples, drown'd the cocks!
> You sulph'rous and thought-executing fires,
> Vaunt-couriers of oak-cleaving thunderbolts,
> Singe my white head! And thou, all-shaking thunder,
> Strike flat the thick rotundity o' th' world!
> Crack nature's moulds, all germains spill at once
> That makes ingrateful man! (3.2.2–9)

> So burn the turrets of this cursed town,
> Flame to the highest region of the air,
> And kindle heaps of exhalations
> That, being fiery meteors, may presage
> Death and destruction to th' inhabitants!
> Over my zenith hang a blazing star,
> That may endure till heaven be dissolved,
> Fed with the fresh supply of earthly dregs,
> Threatening a death and famine to this land!
> Flying dragons, lightning, fearful thunderclaps,
> Singe these fair plains, and make them seem as black
> As is the island where the Furies mask,
> Compassed with Lethe, Styx, and Phlegethon,
> Because my dear Zenocrate is dead.
> (Tam. II, III.ii)

If we ignore punctuation and attend to syntax, we can see that of Marlowe's lines here, only the fourth ('That, being fiery'), and the eleventh ('Singe these fair plains') are stopped at mid-position; whereas in the Shakespeare, four of the lines break at the mid-position.[43]

Perhaps a word or two more will help elucidate the points I am making. Notice that Marlowe's 'Flame', a verb, has no subject, and that it is very difficult to assign a satisfactory one if we argue that the subject is merely implied.[44] The fourth line forces a dreadful break into the proceedings, with its parenthetical clause quite unnecessarily imposed on the construction; the exact meaning and purpose of 'zenith',

---

[43] The figures for the 'Two tales are told' passage quoted above are in the same proportion, with eight lines mid-stopped, and eight not so. In other words, the lines without mid-position break are full clauses; there are three genuine enjambments. In the 'Ah fair Zenocrate' partially quoted above, the figures are of 38 lines, only six broken at mid-position. For these numbers, the special case of mere lists, such as Marlowe's 'Flying dragons, lightning, fearful thunderclaps', is not considered as breaking the line.

[44] We may supply 'them', i.e., the turrets, and this seems the best choice, but it is nevertheless syntactically very awkward.

especially with 'my' (since the reference seems not to be to a physical location on the earth, nor to Tamburlaine's prime), is unclear. I say these harsh things only to highlight more clearly how the speech flows on with Marlowe's usual and splendid, rolling might, despite rhythmical and syntactical infelicities which would have stopped a lesser poet dead in his tracks. But withall, we should notice that the speech rolls on its unstoppable way, not through syntactical means, but by a certain amount of bullying, from which Marlowe never quite manages to rid himself. This is particularly the case with the last two-and-a-half lines which produce the effect of a run-on sentence. They are a perfectly gratuitous addition, and do not arise from syntactical pressure (the sentence is complete after 'mask' for instance)—we are simply bullied into rounding out the speech in this manner by the force of personality, by the richness of the language and by the forwards momentum already generated. But it is fudged at crucial moments: is the island or are the Furies 'Compassed'? And what is the case or should happen because Zenocrate is dead—is it the blackness of the island (the island should be made black because Zenocrate is dead), or the singeing (singe these plains because Zenocrate ...), or do the Furies mask because Zenocrate is dead? Of course, this is part of the secret of Marlowe's success, and while Tamburlaine is not the only one who speaks like this, still, it suits his superb (*superbos*) nature.

Of course we all speak like this all of the time, and so they did in Shakespeare's day: broken sentences, run-ons (in particular), verbs without subjects or objects, sentences without verbs—but to reproduce this, except in exceptional circumstances, would be a step too far; the stage-speech must sound like, not necessarily be an anthropological reproduction of, common-or-garden speech.

There are moments such as this in Shakespeare, too. In *Romeo and Juliet* for example, where Romeo says, 'thou art / As glorious to this night, being o'er my head ...' (2.2.26–7), he uses a typical, Marlovian construction ('That being fiery meteors ...') complete with the stumble over the syntax; and when he continues 'As is a winged messenger of heaven .../ When he bestrides the lazy [pacing] clouds ...', we are just as much in awe, just as ravished as by Marlowe's syntactically similar exhalations, only it is the sheer lyricism who is the bully here—and of course such stuff *characterises* Romeo, who soon grows out of this sort of irresponsible effusion, which is not shared by Juliet. (At least in *The Faerie Queene*, Spenser will have nothing of this; one of the pleasantest miracles of that poem is Spenser's absolute control over his very different syntax.) Shakespeare in the *Lear* passage cited here for comparison, generates his forwards movement, his power, syntactically. The speech is under very tight control: 'You cataracts ... spout', 'You ... fires ... Singe'; 'and thou ... thunder, Strike ..., Crack ... spill', plus a brief adjectival clause defining 'germains'.

Lastly in this connection, a word about Shakespeare's sheer ordinariness. Consider again *Macbeth*, Act I, scene iv. What could be more ordinary or common-or-garden than 'is execution done on Cawdor'; 'I have spoken / with one who saw him die'; 'very frankly he confessed his treasons / Implored your highness pardon, and set forth / A deep repentance'? Or indeed than the famous lines that follow. It would be very difficult to order a cup of coffee in Marlowe's idiom, easy in Shakespeare's, perhaps one reason why Shakespeare goes so easily and well into modern dress and location, both on stage and screen. Spenser makes no effort to capture, and perhaps every effort to avoid, the conversational, the ordinary—and above all in his syntax (and diction, but that is not under direct consideration here). The speeches in *The Faerie Queene* are many of them marvellous things, but they, nor anything like them, would hardly be spoken, as it were, off the stage, let alone on it. Whereas Shakespeare, even at his most poetical, always manages to convey the impression that this is natural speech. The secret lies less in the diction than in the syntax (meaning here both the arrangement of clauses, and the order of words within them) and the units of composition.

Spenser's dependence on the line and an intricately rhymed stanza lead him far away from ordinary speech.[45] So that we have a great many words and phrases in Spenser which work only to complete or fill a line, or to provide a rhyme, or to pad out the stanza.[46] This is a neglected aspect of Spenser's poetry in *The Faerie Queene*, which would reward prolonged and systematic study. I have already instanced FQ II.viii.5, but repetition occurs over longer scales, as in the stanzas on Pride:

> By them they passe, all gazing on them round,
> And to the Presence mount; *whose glorious vew*
> *Their frayle amazed senses did confound:*
> In liuing Princes court none euer knew
> Such endlesse richesse, and so sumptuous shew;
> Ne Persia selfe, the nourse of pompous pride
> Like euer saw. And there a noble crew
> Of Lordes and Ladies stood on euery side
> Which with their presence faire, the place much beautifide.
>
> High aboue all a cloth of State was spred,
> And a rich throne, *as bright as sunny day,*

---

[45] Not that a complex stanza has to lead that way: 200 years later, Byron, again, was to subject another only slightly less complex stanza ferociously to the rhythms of ordinary colloquial speech with comic effect, in *Don Juan*. I do not mean to suggest that Spenser was trying or should have liked to try and write in those rhythms.

[46] Sale is good on this subject, *Reading Spenser*, especially Chapter II, 'Spenser's Undramatic Poetry'.

> On which there sate most braue embellished
> With royall robes and gorgeous array,
> A mayden Queene, *that shone as Titans ray,*
> In *glistring* gold, and peerelesse pretious stone:
> Yet *her bright blazing beautie* did assay
> To dim *the brightnesse of her glorious throne,*
> As enuying her selfe, *that too exceeding shone.*
>
> *Exceeding shone,* like Phoebus fairest childe,
> That did presume his fathers firie wayne,
> And flaming mouthes of steedes vnwonted wilde
> Through highest heauen with weaker hand to rayne;
> Proud of such glory and aduancement vaine,
> While flashing beames do daze his feeble eyen,
> He leaues the welkin way most beaten plaine,
> And rapt with whirling wheeles, inflames the skyen,
> With fire not made to burne, but fairely for to shyne.
>
> *So proud she shyned* in her Princely state,
> (I.iv.7–10)

How many times are we told that the palace, the room, the throne, the woman on the throne were bright, very bright, exceeding bright?[47] This would be an intolerable effect on the stage, no audience would choose to sit through all this, realising at once that it could be done far more efficiently: not even Gorboduc is so undramatically verbose, so undramatically dispersed. It wastes the dramatic resources of language; Spenser has made it part of the Epic-Romance resources of language.[48]

There is a further important point to make here and that is that this passage as most passages in *The Faerie Queene* is very highly allegorical, most obviously the epic similie of Phaeton (stz. 9) and it is partly this that justifies what from the dramatic point of view would be digressive and repetitious. Spenser is allegorical rather than dramatic, both in

---

[47] I have italicised some of the more direct statements. In the preceeding stanzas Spenser has made the point repeatedly, and in the following pair does so again.

[48] Having quoted Spenser in this context, we should notice that his ringing lines are sometimes more apparent than real—in the stanza above for example, each line is complete, and gives the impression of being laid down course on course, which Yeats, Alpers and Sale have noticed, an effect of Spenser's peculiar rhyming technique and very frequent end-stops. But also, that lines 2, 3, 5 and 9 are broken syntactically at mid-point. But again, very often lines broken at mid-point are re-unified by one side's completing a rhetorical figure or trope begun in the first half. Thus in the second line the second half is a simile expanding 'throne' (adjectival, relative, clause), and the same phenomenon occurs in line 5, though this is not the case with the third line which also contains a true enjambment, nor line 9 where the second half is again a relative clause. So that Spenser is a master of the mid-line pause, and, as Milton certainly did, Shakespeare may have learned this from Spenser; so that where Marlowe seems to have followed the line in Spenser, Shakespeare, perhaps seeing more, perhaps seeing differently in the light of Marlowe and the experiments of other playwrights, seems to follow rather the Spenserian mid-line pause.

structure, and here this is more important, in detail; I do not intend to oppose allegory flatly against drama;[49] but Spenser's verse is allegorical in a way that Shakespeare's is not (and hence the perceived abstraction in Spenser), and this is an important difference between the two poets, even while, as more than one of the papers in this collection show, Shakespeare is also in his way allegorical and perhaps under the influence of Spenser, and this is a new thought only now being thoroughly worked out and explored. But Shakespeare's poetry *per se* is not fundamentally allegorical, but dramatic; Spenser's poetry *per se* is not dramatic but fundamentally allegorical. Allegory in *The Faerie Queene* is pressed into every rift, nook and cranny, at every chance. Shakespeare represents jealousy by having Othello *be* jealous; Spenser represents jealousy by analysing its characteristics and setting them forth systematically, by having Malbecco *represent* jealousy—in concrete images sure enough, but with abstraction and generalisation as guiding principles. But again, this does not rule out borrowing, and Malbecco is a good example because Shakespeare does borrow, quite extensively actually, from this highly allegorical passage, but not for the same allegorical purposes as Spenser; Malbecco is not merely allegory—as if allegory were somehow medium-less—but allegory is written in verse and poetry.[50]

These, then are some of the reasons why we have justifiably felt that Shakespeare did not borrow over-much from Spenser, and why he was not likely to have done so.

There are others, Hieatt mentions temperament, for instance, and Mayhall, tone and movement and imagery;[51] but at any rate these, so far as they go, show only why Shakespearean borrowings from Spenser are heavily re-worked, must be heavily re-worked, and thus harder to locate than those of, say Marlowe. So that insofar as Shakespeare went to *The Faerie Queene* for phrases of varying lengths to borrow (to put it crudely), he would have found that, borrow as he might, the rephrasing required would possibly either hide the source—reducing it to clusters of shared diction or re-phrased images,[52]—or make *The Faerie Queene* less helpful as a source, than, say, Holinshed's prose, which he could put into verse with far greater freedom. Also, voiding Spenser's rhyme would also inhibit direct and easily visible borrowing. We shall see presently how Marlowe solved this particular difficulty. But none

---

[49] See Judith H. Anderson, 'The Conspiracy of Realism: Impasse and Vision in *King Lear*', *Studies in Philology*, 84 (1987), 1–23, and her paper in the present volume; together with those of Anne Lake Prescott, Rachel E. Hile, Susan Oldrieve and Ronald Horton, also in the present volume.

[50] See J. J. M Tobin, 'Spenserian Parallels', *Essays in Criticism*, 29 (1979), 264–9, and 'Malbecco, Yet Again', *Notes and Queries* 32 (1985), 478–9, and Martin Coyle, '*King Lear* and *The Faerie Queene*', *Notes and Queries* 31 (1984), 205–7.

[51] See note 3 above.

[52] As in Sonnet 106—see below.

of this implies or entails that Shakespeare could not and did not borrow from Spenser. Both were poets. The age borrowed and pilfered, even begged, copiously and as a matter of course; Shakespeare required vocabulary, linguistic ideas, images, to say nothing of poetic resources of prosody, the cunning deployment of the mid-line pause, and above all the facility of vocal movement from one word to another which was once much spoken of in praise of Spenser, and which Shakespeare fully possesses.

The differences I have outlined do not amount to a demonstration that Shakespeare could or did not borrow, in whatever ways writers do borrow from one another, consciously or otherwise, deliberately or not; nor to an explanation as to why Shakespeare did not borrow from Spenser—because he did borrow, despite all this. I am not arguing that poets such as Shakespeare cannot, or do not, borrow from poets such as Spenser; but given that while Marlowe helps himself sometimes to great mouthfuls, Shakespeare nibbles but morsels, though perhaps very frequently—given this, I am looking for some potential explanation of this which might also guide us in the further search for the linguistic presence of Spenser in Shakespeare. Spenser and Shakespeare are undoubtedly apples and oranges,[53] but that does not mean that Spenser could not or did not cross-fertilise Shakespeare. These comparisons are worth making, or re-making and in detail; they indicate the special qualities of each poet and thus the nature of what each is doing—one of the primary purposes of comparative criticism. What do they know of Shakespeare or Spenser or Marlowe who only Marlowe or Spenser or Shakespeare know? The only route to knowledge is difference—as our discipline hardly needs reminding.

V

In the belief (already alluded to above) that linguistic borrowing is important to the broader concerns and that we have not yet exhausted the question, I want now to examine some obvious and well-known borrowings from *The Faerie Queene* by Marlowe, to see whether we might find some hints in Marlowe's as to Shakespeare's borrowings and how then to bring them out. *How* does Marlowe borrow from Spenser, what does he borrow and what does he do with it? To see what sort of borrowing goes on, we need a clear and preferably lengthy example. We shall concentrate on the very well-known borrowings in this passage of *Tamburlaine* Part II:

> Then shall my native city Samarcanda,
> And crystal waves of fresh Jaertis' stream,

---

[53] See Robert L. Reid's opening remarks in his paper in the present volume.

> The pride and beauty of her princely seat,
> Be famous through the furthest continents;
> For there my palace royal shall be placed,
> Whose shining turrets shall dismay the heavens
> And cast the fame of Ilion's tower to hell.
> Thorough the streets, with troops of conquered kings,
> I'll ride in golden armour like the sun,
> And in my helm a triple plume shall spring,
> Spangled with diamonds, dancing in the air,
> To note me emperor of the threefold world;
> Like to an almond tree y-mounted high
> Upon the lofty and celestial mount
> Of evergreen Selinus, quaintly decked
> With blooms more white than Erycina's brows,
> Whose tender blossoms tremble every one
> At every little breath through heaven blown.
> Then in my coach, like Saturn's royal son
> Mounted his shining chariot gilt with fire,
> And drawn with princely eagles through the path
> Paved with bright crystal and enchased with stars,
> When all the gods stand gazing at his pomp,
> So will I ride through Samarcanda streets,
> Until my soul, dissevered from this flesh,
> Shall mount the milk-white way, and meet him there.
> To Babylon, my lords, to Babylon!
>
> (107–33)

Here is the first of the passages from *The Faerie Queene* on which this Marlowe is based:

> His haughtie helmet, horrid all with gold,
> Both glorious brightnesse, and great terrour bred;
> For all the crest a Dragon did enfold
> With greedie pawes, and ouer all did spred
> His golden wings: his dreadfull hideous hed
> Close couched on the beuer, seem'd to throw
> From flaming mouth bright sparkles fierie red,
> That suddeine horror to faint harts did show;
> And scaly tayle was stretcht adowne his backe full low.
>
> Vpon the top of all his loftie crest,
> A bunch of haires discolourd diuersly,
> With sprincled pearle, and gold full richly drest,
> Did shake, and seem'd to daunce for iollity,
> Like to an Almond tree ymounted hye
> On top of greene *Selinis* all alone,
> With blossomes braue bedecked daintily;
> Whose tender locks do tremble euery one
> At euery little breath, that vnder heauen is blowne.
>
> (I.vii.31–2)

The first thing to notice is that there are direct quotations: Marlowe's 'Like to an almond tree y-mounted high' quotes Spenser's 'Like to an Almond tree ymounted hye', the line being simply lifted from one poem into another.[54] Two further lines are virtually direct quotations:

> Whose tender blossoms tremble every one
> At every little breath that through heaven is blown.
> (*Tamb*)

> Whose tender locks do tremble euery one
> At euery little breath, that vnder heauen is blowne.
> (*FQ*)

Marlowe's 'thorough' is here di-syllabic, Spenser has the di-syllabic 'under'. In Marlowe's first line we have a single di-syllabic word, 'blossomes'—not always di-syllabic at the time in this spelling—replacing two monosyllables 'locks' and 'do' from Spenser. Marlowe's 'blossomes' comes, however, from the same passage in *The Faerie Queene*: 'With blossomes braue' (stz. 32.7), so that we have one of Spenser's expressions replaced with another also occurring locally. 'Blossomes' is a common enough word of course. Spenser's 'On top of *greene Selinis* all alone' becomes: 'Upon the *lofty* and *celestial mount* / Of evergreen Selinus, *quaintly decked*'. The additions are also from Spenser's passage, occuring locally. 'Lofty' occurs in 'upon the top of all his *lofty* crest'; 'decked' from 'bedecked', while 'quaintly' is suggested by Spenser's local 'daintily'; 'evergreen', comes of course from 'green', and is disyllabic presumably because Spenser's 'On top of' wastes resources, having already been implied by his 'ymounted high' and by Marlowe's 'Upon the lofty'.[55] Marlowe's 'And in my helm a triple plume shall spring' is partly built from Spenser's 'helmet', with 'plume' for 'crest'.[56] Marlowe's 'I'll ride in golden armour like the sun', is perhaps a coalescence of two Spenserian moments, one of which is barely

---

[54] Crawford shows that there are plentiful borrowings in *Locrine* and *Selimus*, heavily and verbatim at times, of the same wholesale variety I attend to here, and for much the same reason—these early plays have not yet broken away from end-stopped, stanzaic poetry; additionally, Crawford shows that both plays also borrow from *Ruines*, *Visions* and *Tears*. The latter is particularly interesting as adding an ounce of wieght to Hieatt's argument: that the sequences were obviously popular and mined by others makes it more, not less likely that Shakespeare should follow suit, though of course it complicates the lineage in that Shakespeare may have taken certain phrases and themes from a borrower and not necessarily from the source. Charles Crawford, 'Edmund Spenser, "Locrine," and "Selimus"', *Notes and Queries* 9th ser., 7 (1901), 61–3, 101–3, 142–4, 203–5, 261–3, 324–5, 384–6.

[55] The addition of 'quaint' in Marlowe is possibly not from Spenser; 'quaint' only occurs nine times in *The Faerie Queene*, quaint = 3, queint = 5, and quyent = 1, not all of them with Marlowe's meaning here.

[56] Spenser uses 'plume' frequently, including in this suggestive line: 'Decked with diuerse *plumes*, like painted Iayes', II.viii.5. Others are I.x.39: 'The *plumes* of pride, and wings of vanitie', I.xi.9: 'His aery *plumes* doth rouze, full rudely dight', I.xi.34: 'Where he hath

suppressed in the Seline passage: Arthur's 'haughtie helmet, horrid all with *gold*' breeds 'glorious brightness'—like the sun—and the crest is not only sprinkled with pearle but also with '*gold* full *richly dressed*', as Tamburlaine will be (richly) dressed in golden armour—Marlowe overreaching Spenser. Notice that 'haughtie' in Spenser does not have the same meaning as implied by the passage in Marlowe. Then, if we back up along this same passage from *The Faerie Queene*, we can find other pieces of the puzzle to slot in—stanzas 29 and 30 have more gold. And in another passage of importance to Marlowe here (see below) we find one source at least of 'I'll ride ... like the sun'. Saturn's royal son in his coach, reminds us of another god's royal son in a shining chariot gilt with fire. Indeed, Phoebus appears in Stz. 29 and again at 34—and elsewhere. Marlowe's 'whose tender blossomes ...' appears at *The Faerie Queene* II.viii.5 (and VI.2.31). Marlowe's expression drops the metaphor in 'locks'.

The question we are driving towards is what has Marlowe done to the stanza from which he borrows so extensively? First he has taken out the rhyme, except for the concluding line, 'one' and 'blown'. 'Crest' is gone for 'plume'; 'diversely' is gone; 'drest' is gone, but its implied state remains; 'jollitie' is gone and with it the tone of Spenser's version; 'hye' remains and on the same line-end position, the line being lifted without change; 'alone' is gone, though the idea remains in that Tamburlaine is setting himself up here as without compeers; 'daintily' is gone for 'quaintly'– in this case, Spenser's verb+adverb construction is replaced with the more directly spoken adverb+verb construction: 'bedecked daintily' with 'quaintly decked'. Marlowe has weakened Spenser's modal 'do' inversions: Spenser's 'Vpon the top .../ Did shake', with 'did shake' for 'shook', a very common rhyme-device in Spenser,[57] becomes in Marlowe the orally normal 'shall spring'. Spenser's 'do tremble' is eliminated by replacing the mono-syllabic 'locks' with the di-syllabic 'blossomes', but the grammatical effect is the same: the replacement of the modal construction in Spenser's epic, with a more dramatic (not to use the word 'active' here) lexical verb in Marlowe's drama. Further along these lines, Spenser's 'seem'd to daunce for iollity' is gone; it is undramatic in that it potentially suggests that no dancing took place, and Spenser's infinitive 'to daunce' is

---

left his *plumes* all hoary gray', II.iii.6: 'As Peacocke, that his painted *plumes* doth prancke', II.iii.36: 'She her gay painted *plumes* disorderid', II.vi.31: 'That quite it cloue his *plumed* crest in tway', II.xi.11: 'Some like to Puttockes, all in *plumes* arayd', III.xii.8: 'But painted *plumes,* in goodly order dight', III.xii.8: 'As those same *plumes*, so seemd he vaine and light', V.iii.20: 'That hast with borrowed *plumes* thy selfe endewed', VII.vi.17: 'The wingd-foot God, so fast his *plumes* did beat'. Very interesting here is the spread of the occurances: 3 in Book I, 5 in Book II, 2 in Book III, and only one in Books IV–VI and one in the later *Cantos of Mutabilitie*.

[57] See, e.g., Addison, 'Little Boxes' and 'Against the Grain'.

replaced with Marlowe's activated participle 'dancing'. This makes the phrase more dramatic, or at least dramatically stronger. Marlowe has, then, relaxed towards spoken modulations Spenser's formal and artificial, or literary, epic syntax; ridded himself of the rhyme, and adjusted the diction—of course making additions of his own. These observations point to the *hiding* of some of Spenser's most characteristic qualities in bringing the verse, even this bodily, into dramatic poetry, and we are fortunate to have so blatant a borrowing to judge from. Also, in borrowing wholesale, Marlowe uses other locally occurring words, and one of them, 'tender blossomes', suggested by the immediate passage, is possibly borrowed from elsewhere in *The Faerie Queene*, and it is possible that the same can be said of 'plumes'.

But there are other things to say on Marlowe's borrowings in this passage, important for a method of hunting for Spenser in Shakespeare, and of these the most enlightening seems to be that in the same passage where the Selina borrowing occurs, Marlowe borrows other things from elsewhere in *The Faerie Queene*. Reasonably obviously, concepts and some diction from Spenser's surrounding stanzas—in this case the same single episode or description—stuck to Marlowe's mind, like crumbs to sticky fingers. We can reverse the direction of approach and see that Marlowe plunders from different parts of *The Faerie Queene*, though in the same Book, in this same speech of Tamburlaine in the lines before and after the almond tree simile. The use of Arthur is sandwiched between two reminiscences of the House of Pride. That is, Spenser was in Marlowe's mind—or open upon his writing table—and we might legitimately and *a priori* suspect further borrowings in this same passage.

And these seem to me to be less directly deliberate borrowings, although in this proudful, hubristic speech, with Phaeton hovering just out of sight, though not out of mind, it is hardly surprising. The second of the two borrowings from the House of Pride is almost as well known as the Almond tree appropriation:

> Then in my coach, like Saturn's royal son
> Mounted his shining chariot gilt with fire,
> And drawn with princely eagles through the path
> Paved with bright crystal and enchased with stars,
> When all the gods stand gazing at his pomp,
> So will I ride through Samarcanda streets,
> Until my soul, dissevered from this flesh,
> Shall mount the milk-white way, and meet him there.

This from *The Faerie Queene* I.iv.16–17.

> Suddein vpriseth from her stately place
> The royall Dame, and for her coche doth call:
> All hurtlen forth, and she with Princely pace,

> As faire *Aurora* in her purple pall,
> Out of the East the dawning day doth call:
> So forth she comes: her brightnesse brode doth blaze;
> The heapes of people thronging in the hall,
> Do ride each other, vpon her to gaze:
> Her glorious glitterand light doth all mens eyes amaze.
>
> So forth she comes, and to her coche does clyme,
> Adorned all with gold, and girlonds gay,
> That seemd as fresh as *Flora* in her prime,
> And stroue to match, in royall rich array,
> Great *Iunoes* golden chaire, the which they say
> The Gods stand gazing on, when she does ride
> To *Ioues* high house through heauens bras-paued way
> Drawne of faire Pecocks, that excell in pride,
> And full of *Argus* eyes their tailes dispredden wide.
> (I.iv.16–17)

Whether this is direct, and Marlowe either deliberately copied from memory, or sought out the passage from a manuscript copy of *The Faerie Queene*, or only a vaguer hovering memory is, naturally, hard to say. Certainly the borrowing is less specific and direct than the Almond tree borrowing, though it may seem to have deliberately occurred; it is at least a shaping influence on this passage.

The image of Phaeton we have already seen, perhaps comes from this same episode.

> Exceeding shone, like *Phoebus* fairest childe,
> That did presume his fathers firie wayne,
> And flaming mouthes of steedes vnwonted wilde
> Through highest heauen with weaker hand to rayne;
> Proud of such glory and aduancement vaine,
> While flashing beames do daze his feeble eyen,
> He leaues the welkin way most beaten plaine,
> And rapt with whirling wheeles, inflames the skyen,
> With fire not made to burne, but fairely for to shyne.
> (I.iv.9)

There are other echoes of *The Faerie Queene* in Marlowe's lines. The first thing to notice, is that in the opening of the House of Pride episode, we have other echoes of the Almond tree passage, as it occurs in Spenser and Marlowe.

> ... it mounted was full hie,
> That euery breath of heauen shaked it   (*FQ* I.iv.5)

So that there is an overlap of borrowings—Marlowe borrows from a passage which repeats in the source.[58] The image common to both pas-

---

[58] Hieatt notes the importance of this phenomenon in 'Genesis'.

sages is important since it links the two passages at least in the memory of the attentive reader we suppose Marlowe to have been. Next there is plentiful shared diction: in Spenser we have 'mightie Prince' (I.4.2), in Marlowe 'princely seat'; 'stately palace' (stz 4), 'palace royal'; 'loftie towers'(stz 4), 'lofty eyes' (stz 14), 'Ilias's tower' (which is lofty—'topless towers of Ilium' *Faustus*, V.i.)—and so on. And there are longer echoes:

> That purest skye with brightnesse they dismaid (I.iv.4)
> Whose shining turrets shall dismay the heavens (1932)

where it is the walls of Pride's palace which shine. Further, not only does Marlowe's 'When all the gods stand gazing at his pomp', (129) echo Spenser's 'The Gods stand gazing on, when she does ride' (I.iv.17), it echoes, too, this from earlier in Spenser's description: 'By them they passe, all gazing on them round' (I.iv.7). The typical doubling of phrase and incident in *The Faerie Queene* apparent here, is important to bear in mind, because it would help to fix an image or phrase in the borrowing poet's mind.

Marlowe's 'pomp' was possibly suggested by Spenser's 'pompous', particularly noticeable in Marlowe's context for its relevant link with 'Persia':

> Ne *Persia* selfe, the nourse of *pompous* pride (I.iv.7)

Tamburlaine's golden armour—'I'll ride in golden armour like the sun'—is perhaps tributary to, or reinforced by Lucifera's state and robes:

> And a rich throne, as bright as sunny day,
> ....
>   that shone as *Titans* ray,
> In glistring gold,
>   (I.iv.8)

And the sun's brightness occurs again in the following stanza:

> Exceeding shone, like *Phoebus* fairest childe, (I.iv.9)

Also Lucifera's 'brightnesse brode doth blaze' like the sun, from which the image is presumably taken by Spenser. The immediately following lines provide another Marlovian phrase:

> The heapes of people thronging in the hall,
> Do *ride* each other, vpon her *to gaze*:
> Her glorious glitterand light doth all mens eyes amaze.
>   (I.iv.16)

> I'll *ride* [in golden armour] ...
> So will I *ride* ... ,

where Marlowe again lexicalises Spenser's modal form ('do ride', becomes 'I'll ride'). And this points us forward to the second passage I mentioned just now.

All of this is fairly commonplace, oft-repeated in *The Faerie Queene*. Also, fairly obviously applicable with or without *The Faerie Queene* to Tamburlaine: golden armour for example is not new with him. But commonplaces come from somewhere—and in this case, apparently, the immediate source of some of the Marlowe, a fairly obvious contributory source, is this passage in *The Faerie Queene*.[59] That is, we have corollary evidence that this specific instance of a commonplace was suggested by the similar commonplace in Spenser. To the question, why this passage instead of others? a superficial answer at least is not hard to find: Marlowe was writing about a proud, even arrogant overreacher, and just such a one is Lucifera:

> For to the highest she did still aspyre,
> Or if ought higher were then that, did it desyre.
>
> And proud *Lucifera* men did her call,
> That made her selfe a Queene, and crownd to be
> (I.iv.11–12)

And note how often the very word 'pride' occurs in this passage: emphasised and over-emphasised as we have seen. But naturally there are other reasons as well. Pride's coach is 'Adorned all with gold' (I.iv.17.2)—and this may well be transferred to Tamburlaine's armour (Marlowe's 'arrayed' can also mean 'dressed') and might have suggested, or helped to suggest the golden armour to Marlowe. We find 'royal' again at I.iv.17.4 for Tamburlaine's 'palace royal'. Then the well-known borrowings already cited (I.iv.17.6, yielding line 129), where Tamburlaine's chariot is drawn by eagles and not peacocks; but then his image differs from Spenser's in that Spenser has Juno's chariot and the peacock is Juno's bird, where for Marlowe's Jove, the chariot is quite correctly drawn by eagles which are Jove's birds; there is a change of gender from feminine to masculine throughout the imagery. The 'pomp' is also in Spenser, at I.iv.7, quoted above and again in the same episode at v.5 'With royall pomp and Princely maiestie' (I.v.5).[60]

There are parallels we shall pass over here. But two more do require notice. Tamburlaine will ride through the streets 'with troops of conquered kings'—and so in a manner does Lucifera. Una's dwarf, there in

---

[59] Hieatt claims that the commonplaces are quite different from correspondng commonplaces elsewhere—these are commonplaces, but the *application* of them is different: 'the evidence seems decisive that they arrived in *Sonnets* saturated in the medium that Du Bellay and Spenser had created for them' ('Genesis', 802).

[60] And again in the description of the proud brought low in Lucifera's dungeon: 'In princely pompe, of all the world obayd' (I.v.48).

the castle with Redcrosse, stumbles across them all 'in a dongeon deepe' (I.v.46), and they are all there:

> There was that great proud king of *Babylon*,...
>
> There also was king *Croesus*,
> And proud *Antiochus*, the which aduaunst
> His cursed hand gainst God,...
>
> And them long time before, great *Nimrod* was,
> ....
> And after him old *Ninus* farre did pas
> In princely pompe, *of all the world obayd*;
> There also was that mightie Monarch layd
> Low vnder all, yet aboue all in pride,
> That name of natiue syre did fowle vpbrayd,
> And would as *Ammons* sonne be magnifide ... .
> (I.v.47–8)

A veritable 'troop' of conquerored kings. Secondly, there is a line in this passage on Pride-Lucifera which Marlowe used more than once elsewhere in Tamburlaine:

> That seemd as fresh as *Flora* in her prime,[61]

We find that Marlowe's borrowings from Pride's Palace of Book I are taken apart and put back together differently: Saturn's son for Juno, Peacocks for eagles and so on. Spenser is somewhat distributed here.

The obvious borrowings which Marlowe makes from *The Faerie Queene* are instructive in several ways. Firstly, we see that one borrowing from *The Faerie Queene* has provoked others in the same speech,[62] but from different passages in *The Faerie Queene*; secondly, we find the passages both quoted at length, with more or less variation insufficient to hide their source, and broken up so that the borrowing is thematic and characterised by the use of phrases and single words drawn from both local and distant places in the source. We find that even commonplaces are sometimes derived, or encouraged, or reinforced at least, from definite places in the source. So that these observations might serve to assist the search for borrowings, for the influence of *The Faerie Queene* in the more difficult case of Shakespeare. We should expect, from what I have re-presented in the first parts of this Introduction, that the borrowings will be yet more fragmented in the case of Shakespeare, thus harder to find. But we should also now have some principles to help us. Of

---

[61] I.iv.17. See also: *FQ*. I.i.48, II.ii.6 and II.xii.50 (another passage Marlowe found attractive), and *I Tamb*. V.i.140 and *II Tamb*. II.iii.23.

[62] Of course we do not know the order of events in Marlowe's mind—but from the point of view of the source-hunter, this is a convenient and harmless way of putting it.

course, Shakespeare is not Marlowe, and differences will abound, but we might now suspect that the primary remains or traces, of Shakespeare's undoubted, careful and close reading of *The Faerie Queene*, are the single words, sometimes taken with relation to theme, but sometimes not. This latter point, that sometimes theme is irrelevant to the borrowing is a step forward in the hunt for sources which has usually, and, as far as it goes, rightly, been confirmed by thematic similarities, which, it is argued, suggest shared diction and image and so on. Leaving this conservative principle of safety and hygene is hazardous but necessary, if, as I am arguing, the Shakespeare's borrowings are hidden among the single words and not necessarily tied to shared thematic interests.

VI

As it happens, there are two papers, one by Patrick Cheney, and one by A. Kent Hieatt that examine Shakespeare's Sonnets rather along these lines, and they make a good test-case for the following principles: Scattered throughout the Sonnets, one borrowing from Spenser in one place in the Sonnets suggests that others might also be found locally in the Sonnets; one borrowing from one place in the Spenser-source suggesting other borrowings elsewhere in the Sonnets but from the same source-locality; that what remains after all the necessary adjustments is largely single words; and that we recognise these single words in certain systematic (but not fool-proof) ways.

What we shall find, is that despite the manifold uncertainties inherent in source-hunting and in the nature of this particular case, we have not only a perilous method for tracing Spenser in Shakespeare, but also at the same time, and arising from the same methods, some controls.

Before we turn briefly to Hieatt and his collaborators who have led the way in refining techniques to discover very small traces of Spenser in Shakespeare, I want to examine more briefly than it deserves a paper by Patrick Cheney that performs a valuable service in its attempt to locate some very small traces, words and isolated phrases in Sonnet 106 that appear to have their sources in *The Faerie Queene*.

There are, so far as I know, no borrowings from Spenser in Shakespeare nearly so open as these we have looked at in Marlowe, though there are agreed borrowings enough in Shakespeare, and less obvious borrowings in Marlowe. Yet sometimes we find something in Shakespeare which appears to come from, or *to have* come from, Spenser, but the reason why we feel this is hard to pin down, and if my earlier arguments have any force, it is not surprising that it should be so. One such case is Sonnet 106, where we are fortunate to have a thorough paper by Cheney which goes some way to illuminating the mystery, and we need to consider it.[63] Cheney argues that Sonnet 106 ('When in the chronicle of wasted time ...') is not only influenced by Spenser, but is about Spenser; the second part of the thesis does not concern us here; but Cheney's discussion of the presence of *The Faerie Queene* in Sonnet 106 can be turned to good account here.

We can present Cheney's argument, slightly against the lay of its coat, as suggesting that Shakespeare is 'brooding' (362) over Spenser's poetry in this sonnet, and as giving us some reasons, that is justification though not proof, for thinking so, and as helping us to some understanding of the *manner* in which it is done. Cheney considers the following words, singly and in phrases, to have a Spenserian provenance: 'chronicle', 'wasted', 'wights', 'rhyme', 'In praise of ladies dead and lovely knights', 'blazon', 'antique pen', 'praises', 'prophecies', 'prefiguring' and 'divining'. All these terms appear in *The Faerie Queene*, and I shall spend some time reviewing the main relevant portions of Cheney's arguments.

'Chronicle' appears twice, once in the argument to II.x, 'A chronicle of Briton kings', and once in I.v.3: 'And many Chroniclers, that can record / Old loues, and warres for Ladies doen by many a Lord' (Cheney, 343). And this in turn, with its 'Old loues, and warres', echoes 'Fierce *warres* and faithfull *loues* shall moralize my song' (I.Pr.1)—where it is not only the simple repetition of key terms that counts, but their repetition to describe 'Chronicles', and Spenser's own poem, thus linking the two and with that linking to the first quatrain of Sonnet 106. This one echo, curious as it is, is obviously not capable of standing seperately on its own two feet, but it is part of a cluster, which *qua* cluster is at least suggestive.

'Wasted time' 'has no equivalent in Spenser' (344), but 'wasted' and its variants occurs 129 times in the canon, and it is linked with 'time' 31 times, three of those in one line (*MHT* 75, *RT* 119 and *FQ* IV.ii.33). On this Cheney comments:

> None of this [on 'wasted'] is particularly decisive, but coupled with what we have compiled for 'chronicle', we can at least prepare ourselves to look at the sonnet's second line, where the editors do find Spenser. (344)

This is a sound principle and points us forward to 'fairest wights' in the sonnet's second line.

'Fairest wights' occurs in that form four times in *The Faerie Queene*, once in *Muioptomos*. One of these examples occurs in the Malecasta and Britomart episode—III.i.47 'so faire a wight'. Cheney notes (345n40) that 'critics agree that Shakespeare in *Venus and Adonis* has his eye on the

---

[63] 'Sonnet 106'. The opening pages give a very valuable brief history of criticism relating Shakespeare and Spenser.

tapestries of Malecasta', something which constitutes important collateral evidence. It shows that Shakespeare read the passage, put it to good use, and again, in other circumstances, looked it up, or recalled it. We have seen how Marlowe, having once borrowed from a particular passage returns to it in other contexts.

'Rhyme' occurs 44 times in Spenser, and 24 of those refer to Spenser's own poetry. Cheney remarks that 'in most of the authorial insertions' in *The Faerie Queene* Spenser uses 'rhyme' to refer to his own poem. The wide-spread use of 'rhyme' as synecdoche for 'poem' or 'poetry' among other poets, is not insignificant, however.

The line 'In praise of Ladies dead and lovely knights' echoes Spenser's 'And sing of Knights and Ladies gentle deeds' (I.Pr.1). There is usually remarked a borrowing from Daniel here, but in fact, apart from the fact that Daniel is himself probably borrowing from Spenser, the Spenser line, especially considered in relation to further evidence below, is closer to Shakespeare's than Daniel's (349). 'Ladies dead' could well refer to Elizabeth, whose death is perhaps mentioned in the next sonnet, 107 ('The mortal moon hath her eclipse endur'd', 349), and if so, would strengthen the Spenser connection, in that the relevant occurrences in Spenser also directly or indirectly refer to Elizabeth. The main point, however, is that Shakespeare's use of 'dead' here is Spenserian, as Cheney's examples show:

> Sir knight, mote I of you this curt'sie read,
> To weet why on your shield so goodly scord
> Beare ye the picture of that Ladies head?
> Full liuely is the semblaunt, though the substance *dead*.
>
> Faire Sir (said he) if in that picture *dead*
> Such life ye read, and vertue in vaine shew,
> What mote ye weene, if the trew liuely-head
> Of that most glorious visage ye did vew?
>   (*FQ* II.ix.3–2.)

It is not only the echo, perhaps very faint, of a Spenserian 'dead' in Sonnet 106, but the fact that directly in this instance, and indirectly in the next, Spenser is specifically using his 'dead' in passages which make the dead types of or for the living, and that those of whom Spenser is writing literally, not their allegorical counterparts, are in fact dead: in this case ladies. So that in this next example, a comment on Belphoebe addressed to the present, the point is explicit:

> To youre faire selues a faire ensample frame,
> Of this faire virgin, this Belphoebe faire,
> To whom in perfect loue, and spotlesse fame
> Of chastitie, *none liuing may compaire:*

> Ne poysnous Enuy iustly can empaire
> The *prayse* of her fresh flowring Maidenhead;
> For thy she standeth on the highest staire
> Of th'honorable stage of womanhead,
> That Ladies all may follow her ensample *dead*.
> (III.v.54)

Cheney seems to follow Hamilton in glossing this expression as 'when she is dead', and adds that it might be that 'dead' in crucial instances in *The Faerie Queene* refers to art, to fictive persons, to representations of Elizabeth specifically, Spenser making a distinction between the real and the fictive queen (350-1). Possibly, but I should have thought that the gloss provided by the Yale editors which Cheney notes of a similar expression in *Amoretti* 33—'that mote enlarge her living praises *dead*', ought also to be thrown into the scales here as an example of a Spenserian use of 'dead' echoed in Shakespeare's sonnet—as 'her posthumous fame' is closer to the mark; better would be 'when she is dead'; or, since Spenser wrote for eternity, 'now that she *is* dead'. So that the impact of the Belphoebe passage is that 'This dead lady is a good example to all'. The word refers to the shield and to a *mere* representation (i.e., 'dead') in the passage between Guyon and Arthur, whereas Belphoebe is, in fact, dead.

An important point is that these references refer directly or indirectly to Elizabeth (Spenser encourages Elizabeth to see her chastity in Belphoebe at III.Pr.5, and explicitly in the *Letter*). And in the light of the possiblities of Sonnet 107, this 'dead' in 106 might have been prompted, perhaps at some remove, by the 'dead' of Spenser, if Shakespeare is also thinking here of Elizabeth, and he may well be in Sonnet 107.

'"Lovely knights" is another Spenserian repetition' (351), from V.iii.40:

> Fit for such *Ladies* and such *louely knights*

'Lovely knights' is, at least to us, a striking phrase, and here it groups with 'ladies', as in the Shakespeare line. Cheney points out that this is another 'authorial stanza'. Spenser has no compunction about calling men and boys 'lovely' as well as ladies, and does so nine times, four of them being 'lovely boy' (I.vi.17, III.ix.36, III.xiii.7, IV.vii.23). The conjunction of 'ladies and knights' is used 19 times (351-2). One of those Ladies and Knights passages we have already cited:

> And sing of Knights and Ladies gentle deeds;
> Whose prayses hauing slept in silence long,
> (I.Pr.1)

where 'prayses' is also a key word in Sonnet 106: 'in *praise* of . . .', and 'so all their *praises*', and 'lack tongues to *praise*'. (Notice, however, that 'lovely' is less a description of the beauty of the men and women involved, but an adjective indicating ready to love, or worthy to be loved.)

Cheney is aware that Spenser is not the only one to use phrases combining knights and ladies in the period, but the phrases are typical of Spenser, and he was the only one to write a 'romantic epic in praise of knights and ladies', and in connection with all the other possibilities, and thus it becomes 'likely that Shakespeare is glancing at it in Sonnet 106' (352). Of course, we cannot exclude the possibility that Shakespeare, who certainly knew the Mediaeval romances, is referring more generally to poems about knights and ladies.[64] But once again, we should recall that commonplaces come from somewhere.

In the light of more likely borrowings, other indefinite, inconclusive echoes acquire new strength and significance. So from tiny hints, Cheney comes to say: 'Consequently, we may wish to read into Shakespeare's "blazon of sweet beauty's best" another echo' of Spenser (356). Spenser uses 'blazon', as a verb, three times; most importantly, in the opening stanza of *The Faerie Queene*, which it has already been suggested Shakespeare had his eye on.

> To *blazon* broad emongst her learned throng:
> Fierce warres and faithfull loues shall moralize my song.
> (I.Pr.i)

One of the most significant facts about these lines is that we have two apparent, or possible, borrowings close together in the loan text, a point which adds to the likelihood of a genuine borrowing. By itself the 'blazon' is probably not terribly convincing as a borrowing or echo; it does occur in that form in *The Faerie Queene*, and only here in the Sonnets. We are in the same position as with 'wights', where the borrowing is only a mere possibility, a shadow perhaps, cast as Shakespeare 'sate brooding on the waters'. However, we not only find several of these accumulating in Sonnet 106, but some of them come from closely related passages in *The Faerie Queene*. For example, several from the first Proem.

Similarly and for the same reason—that faint echoes are audibly accumulating—Cheney remarks that 'Spenser's recurrent presentation of himself as a poet of antique times makes Shakespeare's phrase "antique pen" another apt synecdoche for Spenserian Epic', and goes on in

---

[64] On the presence of the Romances in Renaissance England, see Michael L. Hays, *Shakespearean Tragedy as Chivalric Romance: Rethinking 'Macbeth', 'Hamlet', 'Othello', and 'King Lear'* (Cambridge: D.S. Brewer, 2003); Helen Cooper, *The English Romance in Time: Transforming Motifs from Geoffrey of Monmouth to the Death of Shakespeare* (Oxford: Oxford University Press, 2004), and Andrew King, *'The Faerie Queene' and Middle English Romance: the Matter of Just Memory* (Oxford: Oxford University Press, 2000). Cheney takes it that the 'chronicle' refers to one specific poem, since it is singular—he notes the possibility or a plural use, which is probably more compelling. The singular possibility is used to strengthen Cheney's argument; I have presented a somewhat weaker version.

the light of these hints, to 'resurrect' Sidney Lee's argument that Shakespeare turns Spenser's dedicatory sonnet to Admiral Charles Howard 'to splendid account':

> And ye, brave Lord, whose goodly personage,
> And noble deeds each other garnishing,
> Make you ensample *to the present age,*
> Of th' *old* Heroes, whose famous ofspring
> The *antique Poets* wont so much to sing
> (Emphasis Cheney's)

(We may add to this the content-specific relevance to the Sonnets in 'goodly personage', 'Make you ensample', and 'ofspring'.) Cheney reminds us that the sonnet is in fact part of the book printed as *The Faerie Queene* in 1590.

On 'antique pen' Cheney says it 'acquires Spenserian resonance' owing to the quantity of related phrases in *The Faerie Queene* (356). Cheney gives the figures: 'antique' 52 times, including 'antique poets', 'antiquities' three times and 'antiquity' ten. A total of 65 times.[65]

'Of Shakespeare's three words for the typological principle, the first and the third have Spenserian resonance' (359): 'prophecies', 'prefiguring', 'divining'. While Spenser does use 'prophet' and cognates (ten times according to Cheney), in particular Cheney considers 'divining' to be Spenserian for the reasons that Spenser uses it in various forms 66 times. (359) More importantly, Spenser uses the term in the *Letter* 'recoursing of things forepast, and *divining* of things to come', and of course Spenser, as an accomplished allegorist, uses at least a form of the principle of typology. In this case, however, I am inclined to think that it would be better to treat the term in the Sonnets as simply a linguistic recollection or stray, independent of its contexts in Spenser, since it is used in a very different manner in *The Faerie Queene*. and we must bear in mind that typology was very well-known and often rehearsed among Shakespeare's contemporaries, all of whom would have had live memories of the Bible, the Book of Common Prayer, and the Homilies, to say nothing of occasional sermons. On the other hand the presence of a vast and respected and self-conscious allegory at Shakespeare's elbow would surely add pressure to the uses of typology in the Sonnets.

Spenser, too, avails himself of the topos of comparing the present days to the past age (the 'wasted time'), not of course a rare topos. Shakespeare's 'present days' recalls the 'present age' of the Howard sonnet, and Cheney cites *The Faerie Queene* V.Pr.1:

> So oft as I with state of *present time,*
> The image of the *antique world* compare,

---

[65] Hieatt, 'Genesis', is cited here.

> ....
> Such oddes I finde twixt those, and these which are,
> ....
> I doe not forme them to the common line
> *Of present dayes*, which are corrupted sore,
> But to the *antique vse*, which was of yore,
> (V.Pr.i)

'Here Spenser anticipates Shakespeare in his comparative meditation on the relation between past and present' (361)—but this meditation is a commonplace. More to the point in this shared meditation are the phrases italicised, particularly 'of present dayes', which, commonplace though it is, still, it is shared with the sonnet 'these present days' (ln 13).

I have given the main headings of Cheney's argument as they relate to a particular cluster of possible linguistic influences; there is much which I have left out. What I should wish to do now is to consider the type of thing which occurs in his paper.

The first point to make is that none of these parallels or analogues are individually convincing as *evidence* of direct and deliberate borrowing; even in the mass they leave, still, somewhat to be desired. But, secondly, they do accumulate to something: scrape the barrel long enough and you find yourself with a small meal. So that Cheney's paper may be seen as a good piece of *criticism* in that it brings us to see more clearly something that we have sensed more dimly—that somewhere, somehow, Spenser has a presence, distant though it may be, in this Sonnet. At the very least, Cheney gives us some reasons why we seem to sense Spenser's presence, even if it does not add up to evidence that Spenser's presence is originary, that Shakespeare is directly or indirectly borrowing or alluding here (Cheney has other arguments for seeing *allusion*). And the nature of that presence would be in any case open to dispute. It is natural that it should be so, because many things come between we who read now and the sonneteer who recalled Spenser then. Evidently we do not have a direct borrowing here even remotely approaching to the type of Marlowe's borrowings, but something much more subtle, more distant. But we do seem to have enough pressure to suggest that perhaps Shakespeare was recalling (to himself if not to the reader) Spenser as he wrote this sonnet. Cheney uses the phrase 'Shakespeare brooding' over Spenser (362), capturing just the indirectness of the presence invited, allowed or recalled, into the sonnet. It is possible to wonder whether Shakespeare was originally recalling Spenser, maybe quite directly and deliberately, but was, perhaps in revising, led away from more direct use in an earlier version by the desire for a better poem in a later version; from one that alluded to, or made more obvious, or closer use of some of Spenser's phrases and ideas, to one that used those materials to make a unique poem to Shakespeare's satisfaction; so that he altered certain key words and phrases, ablating from Spenser in the name of local perfection, so to speak; or, that, revising the sonnet long after it was written, his original borrowing, or the original unconscious recollections, had weakened; or that his memory of exact details, phrases, words, contexts, played him false in the first place.[66] There are countless possibilities. But if Shakespeare were borrowing from Spenser, even deliberately, without necessarily intending to allude publicly to him—as he evidently borrowed, and more directly borrowed, from Constable, for instance, here and elsewhere—but got the words wrong, for after all he was not a scholar checking his quotations, but a poet brooding over materials to hand for his own purposes, and in his own medium, both very different from those which manufactured the materials in the first place—if any of this were the case, we should never know, nor be able to judge; it is part of the mystery, the transfiguration of eyes to pearl fathoms deep in a poet's mind.[67] But, yet, nevertheless: we might still sense the pressure of the original attempt, or the originary memory, inaccurate or not, conscious or not; it would leave an impression, an impress, which careful criticism based on careful scholarship might be able to to sharpen slightly—as when a slide of botannical tissue is stained to reveal structures invisible to naked eye-sight—even while, with the best will in the world, it might not be possible to actually demonstrate the original owner of the impress. And apart from methodological gains, this is where Cheney's paper has its importance. There is a great deal in *criticism* which is not susceptible of proof; it is right that it should be so, and no grounds for general scepticism; criticism is not physics. Of course I am not suggesting an excuse for sloppy work or wild speculation; there are justification and reason enough to the careful critic to enable us to argue rigorously and persuade fairly without having to reject everything that cannot be actually proven. The element of subjectivity is inescapable; but subjectivity is not identical with solipsism.

And even while what might be clear to a scholar by way of finefooting, might not be clear to the more casual reader; and even while there is always the danger that it might be more clear to a hunter who hopes to find it than to a more disinterested reader—still, the *mystery* in

---

[66] On the revisions to the *Sonnets*, see Katherine Duncan-Jones, 'Was the 1609 Shake-Speares Sonnets Really Unauthorized?', *RES* 34 (1983), 151–71, Hieatt et al, 'Rare Words' and 'When Did Shakespeare Write', and the various editions.

[67] To anticipate and quote Hieatt here: 'in spite of Shakespeare's extreme Elizabethan facility in seeing one order of phenomena in another, there is something mysterious in the prolonged change of key between Ruines and Sonnets, unexampled in his use of other sources.' Hieatt writes of Shakespeare's 'initial interest in *Ruines* which appears ultimately to have led him to celebrate his beloved in words and themes modulated out of a celebration of the Roman city and nation' ('Genesis', 802).

one poet's use of another, what we might call the strong use, as here, where Marlowe's use of Spenser, or Shakespeare's use of North in Enobarbus' speech in *Anthony and Cleopatra* would be a weak use, should not be ignored even while we seek for futher definition and develop tools specifically designed for de-mythologising mystery.[68]

Now Cheney wants to put the presence of Spenser in Sonnet 106 to historical use, as an historical fact to be used as *evidence* in assessing the relations of the two poets (a project continued in his paper in the present volume). This is the ideal to aim at. A caveat must be entered here, however: any historical conclusion is no stronger than the strength of its weakest evidence; but accumulation plays its part; and we have now a substantial accumulation of justification for the presence of Spenser in the Sonnets as elsewhere. In Cheney's case the argument would probably be this: we find Spenser in the Sonnets in general; it is not unlikely that we find him here then; there is an accumulation of possibility which adds up to a probability, even while no one example is conclusive. (As to the question of specific *allusion*, I suspect that we should continue to seek for corroborating evidence for this specific case.)

But it is not simply an either-or question of borrowing or not—there is at one extreme allusion, at the other extreme the common use of common-places, or the common use of common sources. There is, in between, a range of possibilities, and we must keep them sorted if we are to make historical use of the claimed borrowing. In the case of Sonnet 106 we appear to have a case of Spenser re-worked; it seems clear that Spenser is in the background somewhere, but transmuted into something Shakespeare's own. This is to be expected; lifting Spenser is difficult to the sort of verse Shakespeare is using, and also Shakespeare transmutes his borrowings—though not invariably out of immediate recognition. But in the Sonnets, though we can't be certain, Spenser does seem to be present, although at one remove, in detail and mass.

Whatever we make of these waifs in and not quite in the Sonnets, it remains the case that they are based on intuition, rounded out with careful reading, some work with various concordances, the OED and on our knowledge of other poetry as a control device. They are, in a word, somewhat amateurish in the best tradition. This should not be taken as perjorative, much of our best criticism is amateurish in the best sense (think of Arnold, Eliot, Leavis for instance). But even while insight, educated and experienced intuition, taste and a feel for poetry are a *sine qua non* of good criticism, and even while reading the poems

---

[68] See, Hunt, 'Wrestling', 35: 'Shakespeare's Lockean imagination subliminally assembled ...', referring to Edward A. Armstrong, *Shakespeare's Imagination: A Study of the Psychology of Association and Inspiration* ([1946] Lincoln: University of Nebraska Press, 1963).

qua poetry is a *sine qua non* of useful work with the concordance,[69] yet there remains scholarship, which is not identical to criticism, and there remains the subjective factor, which is of importance if we wish to do literary history in a solid and reliable manner, and to produce results that will stand the test and the tests of time.

We should like to know for example, whether in all the small indications we have that Shakespeare read and used *The Faerie Queene*, we have any real, positive evidence that could, for instance, be definitively falsified. There are other methods—tools, rather, which extend method—available which have not yet been widely applied to the question of Shakespeare's use of Spenser, and it is to these that we now turn.

So far as I am aware there has been only one sustained attempt to place on a systematic and reliable footing the question of Shakespeare's indebtedness to Spenser, that of A. Kent Hieatt and his collaborators. And it is his methods, and the eventual results of them, that I wish to describe, though briefly, here. These form a useful contrast to those just described, filling out some of their weaknesses and extending the possibilities in the direction of great elaboration and rigour of evidence, possibly too great a rigour.

Hieatt and his collaborators have utilised the statistics and the computer. Since their work much has been accomplished in this respect, but I shall stay with the Hieatt team since some of their work has been on Spenser's presence in Shakespeare's Sonnets.[70] Hieatt's method has two facets, the first implying the second. The first is that what is common to Shakespeare and Spenser, but not to other poets, or not so common in other poets as to Spenser and Shakespeare, can be assumed to come from Spenser to Shakespeare, perhaps interfered with *en route* by the static of other sources, and by the use to which Shakespeare puts his borrowings, uses which naturally distort the borrowing.[71] This implies both searching other poets for phrases which have first caught the eye

---

[69] See nn75 and 74 below.

[70] 'The Genesis of Shakespeare's Sonnets: Spenser's *Ruines of Rome: By Bellay*', *PMLA*, 98:5 (1983) 800–814; Gary Schmidgall and A. Kent Hieatt, 'Shakespeare's Sonnets', *PMLA*, 99.2 (1984), 244–5; Anne Lake Prescott and A. Kent Hieatt, 'Shakespeare and Spenser', *PMLA*, 100.5 (1985), 820–2. The method is pursued in A. Kent Hieatt, T.G. Bishop and E.A. Nicholson,'Shakespeare's Rare Words: "Lover's Complaint", *Cymbeline*, and *Sonnets*', *Notes and Queries*, 34 (1987), 219–224, and in Hieatt, '*Cymbeline* and the Intrusion of Lyric into Romance Narrative: *Sonnets*, "A Lover's Complaint", Spenser's *Ruines of Rome*', in *Unfolded Tales: Essays on Renaissance Romance*, ed. George M. Logan and Gordon Teskey (Ithaca: Cornell University Press, 1989), 98–118; A. Kent Hieatt, Charles W. Hieatt, and Anne Lake Prescott, 'When Did Shakespeare Write Sonnets 1609?', *Studies in Philology*, 88.1 (1991), 69-109.

[71] 'Here I am following the obvious, commonsense rule that shared verbal phenomena suggest a special connection between two works if these phenomena are scarce or absent incomparable works.' (Hieatt, 'Genesis', 800). The samples presented occur rarely and in-

by being unusual and common to both Spenser and Shakespeare; and the assessment of the quantities of these common phrases in relation to other works in the canon of each of Spenser and Shakespeare.[72] Where, for example a phrase is evenly spread over the whole of Shakespeare's works it is less likely to have been prompted by a reading of Spenser at only one time in the writing of those works: time is an essential factor here, and the chronology of each poet assumes importance. This implies in turn the search for phrases which are rare in each author, rare in the overlap, and rare in the period. All this can be much enhanced by the application of the computer's ability to locate rare, repeated and shared phrases far more effectively than the human eye and memory, if need be in very complicated searches including proximity and so on; and by the presence and continued growth of a corpus of reliable digitised texts as raw material for the computer to process. There is in principle nothing here that cannot be done with a good memory, very wide reading and a pencil and paper; but naturally, once fed the texts, a computer is very much more effective in conducting the original searches; there is a *quantitative* increase. The growth in the numbers of responsibily digitised texts, implies, however a *qualitative* addition, since it enables the critic to eliminate counter-possibilities (as far as the corpora reach), whereas with the memory the process is never so foolproof. This places the effort of finding borrowings, or swappings, on a different footing, changing the status of the work from what I have called the amateur to the professional. I should say at once that I am in complete agreement with scholars such as Hieatt and Brian Vickers who admonish us that the computer, however useful, even essential, is in itself insufficient and that the relevant works must be read and understood before the computer results can be responsibly deployed; indeed, I should go further and say that the works must be read and understood before the right questions can be asked of the computer. Not every phrase which occurs only in Spenser and then in Shakespeare can

---

consistently in other sonnets, and in Shakesepeare's vocabulary outside the Sonnets (802) and not significantly elsewhere in the received corpus—here of course one is perpetually open to challenge, and it was duly forthcoming: see Prescott and Schmidgall.

[72] Spenser uses 'antique' and 'antiquities' 'considerably more often in *Ruines* than in any other of his works (in nos. 1, 2, 4, 17, 19, 25, 27, and 32). Shakespeare uses 'antique' 'antiquities,' and 'antiquity' seven times in the *Sonnets* (in nos. 17, 19, 59, 62, 68, 106, 108) . . . far more often in *Sonnets* than in any other single work . . . and twenty-five times more often than in all his other works', Hieatt, 'Genesis', 801. Of 'antique' etc. in *The Faerie Queene*, Hieatt shows that the proportion is much less than in *Ruines*: 1:81 (*Ruines*) vs 1:c. 530 (*FQ*)—but these figures are less than helpful if they are designed to show what Shakespeare *may have noticed*—other factors must be included, the prominence for example of the words and concepts, their local repetition and so on. And so many of Spenser's uses in *The Faerie Queene* are very prominent, in the Proems, invocations at the beginnings and ends of cantos, particularly those we know on independent grounds that Shakespeare read—e.g. the Alma's Castle chronicles.

be said to have arrived at the latter by means of the former—just for instance.

Methods such as those are assisted by tools which are not made redundant by the computer, such as the *Shakespeare Lexicon*,[73] analytical concordances, analyses of pause patterns and enjambments, and lists of rare words[74] as well as of course earlier source-studies; many of these tools do not yet exist for Spenser's works.

This is not the place for a thorough analysis of Hieatt's methods and conclusions, the papers are well-known and widely cited; Hieatt is just in his assessment of the strengths of his evidence and arguments; his methods have been developed by others in slightly different directions and put to different purposes. There is a great opportunity for more of the same, and since those papers were published (the last of them several years ago), much has been accomplished in the creation of digitised texts and development of methods and specific studies, not all of it uncontroversial.[75]

One important step forwards needs to be mentioned here, however, and that is the tendency occasionally to disassociate word and phrase from theme in assessing borrowing.[76] This is essential, if, as seems likely,

---

[73] *Shakespeare Lexicon and Quotation Dictionary: A Complete Dictionary of all the English Words, Phrases and Constructions in the Works of the Poet*, Alexander Schmidt, 3rd ed. revised and enlarged by George Sarrazin, 2 vols (Berlin, 1902; New York: Dover Publications, 1971, often reprinted).

[74] A. Kent Hieatt, T.G. Bishop, E.A. Nicholson. 'Shakespeare's Rare Words: "Lover's Complaint," *Cymbeline*, and *Sonnets*, *Notes and Queries* 34.2 (1987), 219–24; W. E. Y. Elliott, 'A Touchstone for the Bard', *Computers and the Humanities*, 25 (1991), 199–209, here 199) and a shorter article concentrating on the Earl of Oxford's claim (in *Notes and Queries*, December 1991); G. Sarrazin, 'Wortechos bei Shakespeare I', *Jahrbuch der deutschen Shakespeare-Gesellschaft* (1897), 121–65, and 'Wortechos bei Shakespeare II', *Jahrbuch der deutschen Shakespeare-Gesellschaft* (1898), 119–69; Alfred Hart, 'The Growth of Shakespeare's Vocabulary', *Renaissance English Studies* 19 (1943), 242–54, and 'Vocabularies of Shakespeare's Plays', *Renaissance English Studies* 19 (1943), 128–40. See Brian Vickers, strictures in *Shakespeare, 'A Lover's Complaint', and John Davies of Hereford*, (Cambridge: Cambridge University Press, 2007), 212–13.

[75] Add that statistical studies is not an easy field and provides no ready-made answers, before entering the field, one might do well to read the works by Hieatt et al, and the works by Slater and the criticism of them by M. W. A. Smith, as well as these by Brian Vickers which provide among other things an education in the field: *Counterfeiting Shakespeare: Evidence, Authorship, and John Ford's 'Funerall Elegye'* (Cambridge: Cambridge University Press, 2002), *Shakespeare, Co-Author: A Historical Study of Five Collaborative Plays* (Oxford: Oxford University Press, 2002), and *Shakespeare, 'A Lover's Complaint' and John Davies of Hereford* (Cambridge: Cambridge University Press, 2007).

[76] On this point, see Hieatt 'Rare Words', 220—there is not necesarily any thematic or narrative connection between pairs or rare words in various of Shakespeare's works. Naturally, theme is also put to use in the assessments: 'In both sequences the authors frequently communicate physical transience through allusion to the decay of man-made structures, and both use oceanic images and synecdochic terms—"pencil" in *Ruines*, "pen" and "pencil" in *Sonnets* in expressing inferiority to others poets and a desire for these poets' powers' ('Genesis', 801). 'It is the accumulation of similar themes that seems significant'

Shakespeare either re-worked his writing at various periods, as seems to be the case with the Sonnets; and if as also seems likely, there was a time when, reading or having newly read, say, *The Faerie Queene*, it later on continued to influence him, but in more distant ways, less directly; additionally, if, as I have argued above, Shakespeare would have found it if not difficult, at least uncongenial to bite off Spenser whole, in the Marlovian manner, and the borrowing (of what ever sort) is primarily of phrases and words. Great caution must be exercised of course in thus separating shared theme from diction in the assessment of borrowing or influence, for shared theme among potentially shared diction has always been a confirmation of the claim that Spenser has a presence in this or that moment of Shakespeare. But there is no intrinsic reason why we should not claim that presence if other justifications are provided. Cheney occasionally avails himself of this dangerous freedom, and to good effect, in the paper we have examined above. Finally, Hieatt draws on the fact that the key terms he is assessing specifically *cluster* in the two works, and the density of the clustering is an important piece of evidence.

Nevertheless, in the light of the analyses presented in this Introduction, it needs to be added that the tests Hieatt applies are in one sense too strong. His control is summed up thus: 'the test of near exclusion both from the corpus of sonnets and associated lyrics and from the vocabulary of Shakespeare's other works' ('Genesis,' 803), as well as from potential common sources in other languages, in this case of Du Bellay. This control is open to breakage by readers who find any of Hieatt's key expressions used earlier than either Spenser or Shakespeare, and Anne Prescott and Schmidgall duly obliged.[77] Naturally, this is important evidence and qualifies the certainty of the results. But Hieatt's printed response to these findings goes too far: 'obviously breaks my method'. It may weaken the conclusion, but it does not break the method. Essentially the point remains that *Ruines* appear to have been part of the ingredients of *Sonnets*. Less so than at first expected perhaps, but it would take more than two counter-citations to break the argument completely. Hieatt seeks something very close to proof, and this is unlikely to be found given the nature of the beast; but while we cannot relax a vigilant look-out for slack work, and while we cannot afford to relax the vigilance of our assessment of the strengths and weaknesses of arguments, and while there is plenty of room for disagreement, Hieatt's paper amounts, even while it is looking at tiny traces of evidence, to a reasonable justification of his thesis—we are dealing with criticism not

---

('Genesis', 802).

[77] However, see Martin Dzelzainis, '*Antony and Cleopatra*, I.iii.102-5 and Spenser's *Ruines of Rome*' NQ 45 (1998), 345–6. Robert Ellrodt in *Cambridge Companion to Shakespeare Studies*, 'Shakespeare the non-dramatic poet', 41, 47, thinks Hieatt has over-stated his case; Cheney appears to endorse Hieatt's view.

mathematics. Of course, to base an interpretation of the Sonnets on Hieatt's paper would mean that the interpretation were only as strong as the justification of Hieatt's thesis. Additionally, Hieatt is not alone in seeing traces of Spenser in the Sonnets, and the arguments begin to accumulate to something like the presence I suggested above, if not more. At any rate, and this is one of my points, there is plenty enough justification to continue the search for more.

And there with Hieatt and Cheney the matter appears to have rested. The resources available to us now are, however, considerably greater than in the eighties and while source-hunting has had a great deal of bad press in the intervening years, perhaps we can adventure more now. As with all treasure-hunting, the potential reward is as high as the real risk.

As to computer analysis, it is indeed proving fruitful, though as with any tool, a printed word-list or a printed concordance, no work is done merely by the tool itself.

With Hieatt and Cheney, we seem to have gone, methodologically, in the direction of particle criticism perhaps as small as we can; and it is my belief that these methods will uncover more linguistic borrowing of various types than we have suspected. There remains macro-criticism, not the hunt for sources with ever more refined techniques (running the dangers of over-refinement), but, given the linguistic presence of Spenser in Shakespeare's works, what then of other sorts of influence might there be? And what to make of those influences?—It would be too much to expect that Shakespeare read Spenser with such care in the detail and escaped unscathed in other manners, even from a poet whom we might normally be tempted to say is so very different to him, if not exactly alien. And might these more galactic gravities perhaps draw us to an opportunity to learn more about the inexaustible Spenser and Shakespeare? The tiny hints we have been dwelling on that Spenser is in the Sonnets leads us quite naturally to other forms of presence besides, or beyond the linguistic, which are equally difficult to pin down exactly, but which are also likely, and in the light of the less tiny and better established linguistic links attested by many, if not all, of the items in the bibliography at the back of this book, there to be worked on; the results of the hunt are there to be put to use. That is to say, it brings us to the types of relations between Spenser and Shakespeare examined in the papers presented in this volume, and the best way to describe and assess these presences and the critical possibilities they suggest is to turn to the papers themselves.

VII

The rather limiting clean opposition between Spenser and Shakespeare is everywhere challenged in this volume. Judith Anderson continues the sterling work[78] of testing to destruction the opposition between allegory and embodied drama, a task specifically furthered by Anne Lake Prescott, Ronald Horton, Rachel Hile and Susan Oldrieve here in this volume. But there are also productive oppositions or at least departures—it would be a mistake to make the one author into the other—and the oppositions are productively brought together in papers by Robert Reid, Michael Hays, Patrick Cheney and Karen Nelson. And the fruitfulness of the exercise might be judged by the fact that this pair of listings could just as easily, from a slightly different standpoint, be reversed.

What brings the papers together is that they explore the large-scale *interplay* of relations between Spenser and Shakespeare—both historically, seeing Shakespeare as a reader of and responder to Spenser (Anderson, Prescott, Cheney, Hile, Horton and Reid), and critically, bringing out the shared elements (Nelson, Hays, Oldrieve and Reid) to mutual enlightenment; specific participation in the same conversation, more intimate than we have hitherto realised, even while the interlocutors adopt opposing or better, complementary positions; of course, some of the insights promulgated and suggestions bruited arise simply from the art of bringing the two writers of the same generation together; but others arise in the conviction (demonstrable) that Shakespeare specifically *engaged* Spenser.

One theme that weaves in and out of the papers is that both artists were too copious, too good as observers of the human and intellectual realms, to be cabined or cribbed into confining artificial oppositions; each overspills the generic categories we conveniently manipulate them with. This point is made in several of the papers and made possible by the presence of Spenser in Shakespeare, his apparent opposite, prompting a closer look at the techniques, generic variety and attitudes of each. For all that Spenser is very different to Shakespeare, that does not imply that he was inimical to him.

Judith Anderson, whose papers are foundationally cited in almost all the essays here summoned, pursues the task of breaking away from the restrictive belief that Shakespeare was not allegorical, did not use allegory as a technique, and that we should not use it as a reading concept either. Her paper shows that a rejuvenated notion of allegory brings out things otherwise hidden, showing just how friable the no doubt useful but petrifying binaries of our all-too-easily labelled concepts, concepts not necessarily found in the works under consideration (54 below) such as gender (hermaphroditism), love and death, and above all, because the key to that process, the generic concepts of allegory and drama are relentlessly crossed over. Such a reassessment has implications for Spenser, too, and Anderson points out that the reading of Shakespeare

---

[78] Begun in 'Conspiracy of Realism'.

healthily affects the reading of Spenser (58 below). This is effected by and suggests a reading of the 'deaths of Anthony and Cleopatra in ways that intersect with' the Garden of Adonis (70), a passage Shakespeare knew and used elsewhere (see also the paper by Anne Lake Prescott in this volume).

It would be wrong of course to turn Shakespeare into Spenser or Spenser into Shakespeare, and Robert Lanier Reid's paper enters a wholesome caveat.

Reid shows how important forms of self-love are to both writers in their very different ways, en route giving a very timely reassessment of the unfinished state of *The Faerie Queene* (Spenser's art is holistic), Spenser inclining to a more Protestant, Shakespeare to a more Catholic version: but the poets meet in the pursuit of the patronage of Essex, and in Shakespeare's use of Book I, and in particular of Una, in *A Midsummer Night's Dream* where it seems likely that Shakespeare is speaking to Spenser.

Neither Spenser nor Shakespeare is one-sided in their manner or their general ideas, but they privilege different poles (81). Overly simplistic though divisions such as Dionysian and Apollonian are, there are hints in the reception of the poets by their contemporaries, that they were seen as opposites, Spenser as the English Virgil, Shakespeare as the English Ovid (80), in this of course Reid engages a long-standing argument of Patrick Cheney's.

Nevertheless, as these oppositions are followed through, it becomes clear that Shakespeare was profoundly influenced by Spenser: not only standing him on his head in *Midsummer Night's Dream*, perhaps putting him back on his feet again in *The Tempest*, but also in the 'gleam of moral-religious allegory' (97), emerging in Portia and deepening in the tragedies and romances.

Anne Lake Prescott pursues Venus, Adonis and their boar through their cosmological significance, and Shakespeare's well-attested attention to the Garden of Adonis, to which she adds her own testimony, both in his *Venus and Adonis* and *Richard III*. Again, a protest is lodged against the allegory-in-Shakespeare-denigrators, and again a productive engagement with Spenser illustrates the inadequacy of opposing drama to allegory; there is more to allegory than inept moralising, and the myth itself was read also as calendrical, 'as much a matter for almanacs as for moralists' (174). Shakespeare seems to have listened to these aspects of Spenser's Garden, Adonis, and his toothed boar as returning with the cycles of the seasons—and these chimes play among the darkening ironies of *Richard III*.

Ronald Horton, in one of two 'white papers' in the volume,[79] suggests that Shakespeare's post-*Hamlet* tragedies might be built, program-

---

[79] An expression of Michael Hays', 228 below.

matically, upon versions of the seven vices, so memorably displayed in Book I of *The Faerie Queene*. And besides the intrinsic merits of this suggestion, Horton's paper is interesting for the weight it throws on the mediaeval presences in Shakespeare (an area of growing interest as his notes also show), and on Shakespeare's attitude to specific and deliberate moral teaching in drama.

Patrick Cheney sees *The Winter's Tale*, a play in which Shakespeare borrows much from Spenser, most importantly in the figures of the Spenserian Perdita and the poet-laureate of the final scene, as offering, certainly as thematising (might one say 'allegorising' in Horton's manner?) Spenser's authorship as a 'counter' to Shakespeare's own. Cheney is adding an important piece to the vast jigsaw puzzle he is setting out of the inter-relations, usually competitive, between Spenser, Marlowe and Shakespeare and their classical career-models, a scheme which involves the recognition, too long suppressed, that Shakespeare was at least also, if not first and foremost in his day, and self-consciously, a poet. Once again, large-scale borrowings, in very various modes, interpret cruces; even while Shakespeare is using his borrowings, here interpreted as positive allusions, partly to distance himself from his older contemporary, while simultaneously acknowledging his debt to him.

Of course, one must be careful not to spread the term 'allegory' so thinly that it covers nothing adequately; but if we can bring the embodied or incarnational, highly individual Shakespearean drama into play with the more intellectual and generalising, abstractive tendencies of Spenserian allegory, so much the better for both. Neither need be destroyed in the process; but both Anderson and Horton, and in a different way Oldrieve suggest ways how the allegorising tendencies in Shakespeare underpin the dramatic, giving it strength in the foundations, and going some way to explain its strength, its enduring strength in the reading and watching. It works about-face, too: taken as a whole the papers here also issue a challenge to the rather wooden notion that Spenser's allegory is fixed, single, abstract. These things need to be said and re-said, shown and shown again in and for each generation.

There are productive oppositions, too, explored in this collection. Michael Hays' 'white paper' makes the striking and fertile suggestion that it was Shakespeare who affirmed chivalric values (*Lear* being the test-case), and Spenser who stood them on their head (Book I being the test case), possibly even rejecting them, and following a long religious tradition in doing so. Hays quite unmistakably throws down a gauntlet. Pointing to the wide-spread, but critically underrated, presence of Chivalric Romance in Shakespeare's day, Hays offers a bracingly astringent sketch of his texts in that broader, *shared*, context.

Essex also appears on stage in Rachael E. Hile's paper, which argues that the beast imagery in *Hamlet* strongly suggests that Polonius and Osric are satires highly critical of Cecil—a dangerous man to satirise in those days. But this satire is not only brought to the attention of a critic, again by textual cross-overs between the play and Spenser, *Mother Hubberd's Tale* this time, but the satire is made possible through reference to that poem in the micro-tradition that it initiates. Incidentally, in the process adding to the growing weight of evidence that Shakespeare read the *Complaints* volume with unusual care.

Susan Oldrieve begins with the allegory we find in Shakespeare, and asks how to account for the sense we have that the plays go 'beyond allegory to involve us in the realities of human experience' (201). Her answer begins in the Renaissance commentaries on Aristotle's *Poetics* and *Rhetoric*, and in Sidney's *Arcadia*, between allegorical characterisation as metaphor, as example and the wonder that results from thickening the specific textures of (Spenserian) metaphor and example, fusing them until they 'explode' the form into wonder. Oldrieve lights on the presence of Ruddymane's bloody hands in *Macbeth*, and follows the allegory into *Lear* ('Lear is his own Ruddymane to his own Amavia', 217), Shakespeare 'transporting' a Spenserian figure and ringing variations.

Karen Nelson lays side-by-side Spenser and Shakespeare's (with Lodge in a supporting rôle) shared uses of the pastoral as vehicle of religio-political commentary, and their common interest in hermits, exile and sacrifice, as 'figuring forth' issues of communion each after his own conviction. The comparison sheds light on the resolutions each writer offers and their differing responses to closure. Nelson treats Spenser and Shakespeare, however, not as authors of polemic but of literature, and as such as having the freedoms and luxuries of literature, playfulness, for instance in expounding points of view, various, contradictory and hyperbolic.

All the papers here begin with the assumption that Shakespeare read Spenser, remembered what he read and put it to good use; and that there are also influences on the large scale—not borrowings only, where Shakespeare uses a Spenserian moment or technique—but also occasions where Shakespeare begins at the point Spenser left off, or develops his own agenda in specific response to Spenser's; or develops his own positions or techniques in specific rejection of some one or another of Spenser's; or, as with Spenser before him, from tiny details to large schemes, Shakespeare's fecund creativity gathered Spenser to him as it did so many other writers. That all this was not obvious long ago would itself be a useful question for research.

So that we have the historical claim: that Shakespeare is responding to Spenser. But also, in bringing the pair together, a pair more closely connected than we should have thought some few years ago, new things are seen in both, particularly in Shakespeare: so that new interpretations, new critical insights, result—to be weighed and sifted as our conversations continue. There is a great deal more which could be done. And one might be forgiven for hoping that now we can say with some assurance that Shakespeare read Spenser carefully and remembered what he read, now that we have an accumulation of evidence which can hardly be ignored (both in the accompanying bibliography, and of course in these papers themselves), and that perhaps what has been begun here will be taken up by others.

Beyond Binarism: Eros/Death and Venus/Mars in Shakespeare's *Antony and Cleopatra* and Spenser's *Faerie Queene*

Judith H. Anderson

Shakespeare's *Antony and Cleopatra*, like his earlier *Venus and Adonis*, is known to be generically mixed and even anomalous in the extent and degree to which it combines tragedy, comedy, and romance with lyric, allegory, myth, and history.[1] This is the first of several analogies I would draw between Shakespeare's play and Spenser's *Faerie Queene*, that hobgoblin's garland of epic, romance, lyric, allegory, myth, history, and more. The breaking of formal conventions beyond their generic variousness also connects these works. In Ania Loomba's view, for example, the non-teleological form of *Antony and Cleopatra* resists closure, and in Margot Heinemann's, this play refuses 'a single historical or ethical center'.[2] Together, these defining characteristics correspond to what Jonathan Goldberg, quoting Spenser, has described as the 'endlesse worke' of *The Faerie Queene*, an endlessness more readily associated with romance and historical narrative than with classic drama.[3] Thoughout Spenser's six books, refracting figures and events and reverberating words and phrases develop, modify, parody, or reverse perspectives and once stable-seeming points of reference.[4]

Like Spenser's poem, Shakespeare's play is also in good part about gender. It focally concerns one infinitely various female persona, a dramatized conception that can itself be seen as a variation on Spenser's multiple, refracted female figures. Shakespeare's leading male persona,

---

[1] On genre, see Sara Munson Deats, 'Shakespeare's Anamorphic Drama: A Survey of *Antony and Cleopatra* in Criticism', in *Antony and Cleopatra: New Critical Essays*, ed. Deats, (London: Routledge, 2005), 1–93, here esp. 12–14. Deats's review of ethos (Rome/Egypt), characters (Cleopatra, Antony, Octavius Caesar), and performance is also excellent. For discussion of *Antony and Cleopatra* as mannerist, anamorphic tragi-comedy, see Pauline Blanc, '"All Joy of the Worm": Tragi-Comic Tempering in Shakespeare's *Antony and Cleopatra*', *Q/W/E/R/T/Y*, 10 (2000), 5–18.

[2] See Jyotsna G. Singh, 'The Politics of Empathy in *Antony and Cleopatra*: A View from Below', in *A Companion to Shakespeare's Works*: Vol. I: *The Tragedies*, ed. Richard Dutton and Jean E. Howard (Oxford: Blackwell, 2003), 411–29, here, 413, 419–20: Singh quotes Loomba, '"Travelling Thoughts": Theatre and the Space of the Other', in *New Casebooks: Antony and Cleopatra*, ed. J. Drakakis (London: Macmillan, 1994), 279–307, here, 281; and in the same volume, Heinemann, '"Let Rome in Tiber Melt": Order and Disorder in *Antony and Cleopatra*', 166–81, here 177.

[3] *Endlesse Worke: Spenser and the Structures of Discourse* (Baltimore: Johns Hopkins University Press, 1981).

[4] *Spenser: The Faerie Queene*, ed. A. C. Hamilton, 2nd ed., with text edited by Hiroshi Yamashita and Toshiyuki Suzuki (Harlow: Pearson, 2001). Unless otherwise specified, reference to Spenser is to this edition.

again like Spenser's cast of refracting male figures, is also complementarily various to an extent less appreciated, I suspect, because harder to assimilate to still-conventional notions of gender. In my view, *Antony and Cleopatra* is also the pure embodiment of excess: by *pure* I mean 'crystalline' or 'distilled', and 'concentrated absolutely', hence 'conceptual'. *Excess*, as I use the term here, refuses containment by the quotidian, containment understood only as limitation and not as inclusion. Virtually by definition excess inheres in passion and multiplicity, and, therefore, like the imagination itself, has its basis in earthly materials. *Pure excess*, itself oxymoronic, refuses categorization and centering, and the most relevant native antecedent of Shakespeare's play that I see, besides the playwright's own *Venus and Adonis*, which is itself related to *The Faerie Queene*, is Spenser's romance epic.

First to basics: dates and details pertaining to the plausibility of significant intertextual relations between *Antony and Cleopatra* and *The Faerie Queene*. Citations of, and allusions to, Spenser's third Book in Shakespeare's *Richard III*, a play written approximately when *Venus and Adonis* was, establish Shakespeare's close, imaginatively processed knowledge of Spenser's 1590 volume. Evidence in *King Lear*, written relatively near but before *Antony and Cleopatra*, similarly establishes Shakespeare's reading of Spenser's second three books of 1596.[5]

As recently as 2003, I have argued that Shakespeare's *Venus and Adonis* is 'a seriocomic meditation on the landscape of desire and the kinds of figures it generates in Book III of *The Faerie Queene*', and I have joined earlier critics in suggesting that Shakespeare's Venus anticipates his Cleopatra. More exactly,

> Shakespeare's recreative poem explores the effect of transforming a number of Spenser's allegorical figures into a *relatively* more realized character—what would result from the folding of its unfolded refractions into a more fully fleshed out version.[6] At the

---

[5] Further evidence exists in other plays, *Midsummer Night's Dream* being an obvious candidate. I cite here the evidence I have investigated or discovered to my own satisfaction. See my *'Venus and Adonis*: Spenser, Shakespeare, and the Forms of Desire', in *Grief and Gender, 700–1700*, ed. Jennifer C. Vaught with Lynne Dickson Bruckner (New York: Palgrave, 2003), 149–60, here 150–2; 'The Conspiracy of Realism: Impasse and Vision in *King Lear*', *Studies in Philology*, 84 (1987), 1–23, esp. 11–22; *Biographical Truth: The Representation of Historical Persons in Tudor-Stuart Writing* (New Haven, CT: Yale University Press, 1984), 118–20. On dating, I have followed *The Riverside Shakespeare*, ed. G. Blakemore Evans et al., 2nd ed. (Boston: Houghton Mifflin, 1997), 78–87; supplemented by reference to Antony Hammond, ed. *King Richard III* (London: Methuen, 1981), 54–61; John Roe, ed. *The Poems* [of William Shakespeare] (Cambridge: Cambridge University Press, 1992), 1, 12–15; David Bevington, ed. *Antony and Cleopatra*, updated ed. (Cambridge: Cambridge University Press, 2005), 1–2; and John Wilders, ed. *Antony and Cleopatra* (London: Routledge, 1995), 69–75.

[6] On the surface, Pauline Kiernan's view in *Shakespeare's Theory of Drama* (Cambridge: Cambridge University Press, 1996) resembles mine: Shakespeare's 'narrative poems are

same time, however, Spenser's interlaced refractions represent a variety that actually exceeds and challenges such a concentration, defying containment by it, at least until Shakespeare's creation of the infinitely various Cleopatra, in whose figure I would discern a memory of his Venus, albeit further modified in both a testimony to the poet-dramatist's own development and to that of the developing taste of the early Jacobean period.[7]

Aside from occasional overlaps in phrasing and imagery, the relationship between *Venus and Adonis* and *The Faerie Queene* mainly involves Spenser's Garden of Adonis and his strikingly thematized, recurrently refracted figure of a female bending over a recumbent male. This silhouetted pietà includes not only Acrasia in Book II, but in Book III also Venus (twice), Cymoent, Belphoebe, Argante, and Britomart (twice). Perspectivism, versionality, and gender are memorably written into the refractions of this figure: variously, lover, mother, virago, enchantress or witch, queen, and numerous aspects of Venus—*virgo, armata, genetrix, vulgaris*. All these topics and forms, rather than simply the focal, refracting image of the pietà itself, bear most significantly on both *Venus and Adonis* and *Antony and Cleopatra*, although this image notably occurs in the epyllion, as it does in Cleopatra's final scene with the mortally wounded Antony.

The further relation of *Antony and Cleopatra* to *Venus and Adonis* is well attested in critical studies and ranges from specific verbal echoes and rhetorical motifs to character and theme. For example, W. B. C. Watkins notes the extensive connection between the memorably striking 'jennet and courser incident' in the epyllion and Cleopatra's imagining herself as the 'happy horse, to bear the weight of Antony', an equine image of passion variously recurrent in the play.[8] Watkins also judges Antony's and Cleopatra's love an 'obsessive disease' before describing it in phrases that suggest the Garden of Adonis, as well as other texts, since their love, like Venus', 'can exist only by denying this world and creating a romantic paradise "where souls do couch on flowers", eternally consuming each other rather than consummating something of greater importance than either' (35). Watkins' conclusion cites Antony's urgent, if somewhat desperate, vision—souls couching on flowers—prior to his near suicide and brief reunion with Cleopatra. It is worth note that Watkins' seemingly clinical judgment, an 'obsessive disease', is basically the same as Octavius Caesar's.

---

a dramatist's way of working out his relationship to non-dramatic poetry' (24). In some areas Kiernan has excellent insight, but her notions of mimesis, invention, and fiction are neither historical nor complex, and her idea of rhetoric is unfathomable to me.

[7] With slight changes, taken from my 'Forms of Desire', 160.

[8] E.g., I.v.22, cf. III.vii.7, x.10–15, IV.viii.14–16: for *Antony and Cleopatra*, unless otherwise specified, I cite the third Arden edition of John Wilders. Watkins, *Shakespeare and Spenser* (1950; rpt. Cambridge, MA: Walker-de-Berry, 1961), 25.

More extensive connections between play and epyllion can be found in essays in the 1960s by J. W. Lever and Adrien Bonjour.[9] Highlights of Lever's essay include Lucretian fertility (with reference to Spenser's Temple of Venus), the striking fish imagery in *Venus and Adonis* (Adonis as immature fry) and in *Antony and Cleopatra* (angling as seduction, the salt fish on Antony's line), the pointed invocation of Venus and Mars, and the heightened antinomies, such as love and death, beauty and destruction, and creation and chaos (83–4, 87). Like other insistently thematized binaries—most obviously, Rome and Egypt, measure and measurelessness, spirit and body, eternity and time, male and female, together with the attributes conventionally associated with either—such initially seeming opposites mirror the constructs of allegorical vision, albeit not the narrative process of allegory itself, which modifies and sometimes merges these binaries.[10] Bonjour, invoking specific verbal and rhetorical similarities, also relates the text of *Venus and Adonis* persuasively to Enobarbus' celebrated description of Cleopatra's barge and beyond this, to the crucial conception of her 'infinite variety' (73, cf. 79).

The final piece of background I need is the already acknowledged relation of *Antony and Cleopatra* to *The Faerie Queene* within modern critical studies. This relation is everywhere a point of reference in Janet Adelman's masterful study *The Common Liar* and implicitly in her use of the myth of Isis and Osiris in *Suffocating Mothers* as well.[11] Adelman, an avowed admirer of Spenser's romance epic, refers often, at length, and in detail to Spenser's Books I through V, including the significant occurrence of the River Nile and the related imagery of serpents, crocodiles, and fertile flooding; the enchanting figure of the Fairy Queen herself; the sensuous, dominant, Venerian Acrasia and her enchanted, feminized lover Verdant; the emblematic figure of Concord, flanked by Love and Hate, and the hermaphroditic Venus in her eponymous Temple; Spenser's versions of Mars and Venus, of *Venus armata* (especially Britomart), of Isis and Osiris, and of Hercules, particularly as feminized by Omphale (a mythic precursor of Radigund); and Spenser's treatment of

---

[9] Respectively, 'Venus and the Second Chance', *Shakespeare Survey*, 15 (1962), 81–8; and 'From Shakespeare's Venus to Cleopatra's Cupids', *Shakespeare Survey*, 15 (1962), 73–80.

[10] On the constructs of allegorical vision, Paul de Man's seminal essay 'The Rhetoric of Temporality' remains useful: *Interpretation: Theory and Practice*, ed. Charles S. Singleton (Baltimore: Johns Hopkins University Press, 1969), 173–209.

[11] Respectively, *The Common Liar: An Essay on 'Antony and Cleopatra'* (New Haven, CT: Yale University Press, 1973); and *Suffocating Mothers: Fantasies of Maternal Origin in Shakespeare's Plays, 'Hamlet' to 'The Tempest'* (New York: Routledge, 1992); see also Barbara J. Bono, *Literary Transvaluation: From Vergilian Epic to Shakespearean Tragicomedy* (Berkeley: University of California Press, 1984), 176–82. On the various mythic associations of Cleopatra and Antony, see also Deats's survey, 20–1, 29–33.

the virtue of Temperance.[12] Yet the characterizing appositive Adelman uses to describe Spenser's 'Palmer, that repository of common knowledge', is indicative of her carefully restricted, rather flat approach to the relation of the two works (123).

For a reader who knows Spenser well, some of Adelman's insight into *Antony and Cleopatra* actually seems to derive from her reading of *The Faerie Queene*. Yet these two works, connected by numerous common texts and commonplaces, in Adelman's seminal book also seem *merely* products of the same rich culture, as to an extent they surely are. It is finally as if even Adelman, appreciative but leery of further relation, is all too aware of critical resistance to the contamination of 'poetry', particularly but not exclusively allegorical poetry, that is felt by some articulate *aficionados* of stage plays even in so egregiously anomalous a tragedy as *Antony and Cleopatra*. Adelman's phrase in *Suffocating Mothers* to describe *Timon of Athens*, namely 'an almost allegorical purity', is revealing (165). I am not sure what Adelman means by 'allegorical purity', but I suspect an assumed identification either between *allegorical* and *moral* or, more likely, between *allegorical* and *abstract* in the phrase. As elsewhere, I question such equations and assert that allegory, in its defining form, is never unmixed or internally unchallenged.[13] Abstraction, as well as morality, is formally *other* to pure, or real, allegory, which not only has a material base but also inheres in narrative process.

More recently and perhaps more notoriously, Camille Paglia has coupled *Antony and Cleopatra* and *The Faerie Queene* in separate but adjoining chapters as expressions of Dionysian and Apollonian art, body and mind, passion and form, dissolution and definition, respectively. Paglia's broad-brushed observations deliver insight energetically, particularly regarding Cleopatra's 'robustly half-masculine' persona and Shakespeare's Egypt as 'Spenser's Bower of Bliss'.[14] 'Adorne[d] with all variety', the kinetic, synaesthetically sensuous depiction of Acrasia and her Garden is remarkably, imaginatively close to Enobarbus' vision of Cleopatra at Cydnus (II.xii.59). But Paglia's Dionysian-Apollonian binarism suffers from the kind of neat opposition that Spenser's poem and Shakespeare's play alike profoundly challenge: Apollo and Diony-

---

[12] *Common Liar*, e.g., 62, 65–6, 83–8, 90–3, 123; on Isis and Osiris, although not Spenser, cf. *Suffocating Mothers*, 183–4. Katherine Eggert compares Cleopatra to Acrasia in order to differentiate them: *Showing Like a Queen: Female Authority and Literary Experiment in Spenser, Shakespeare, and Milton* (Philadelphia: University of Pennsylvania Press, 2000), 144, 153. Adelman wittily characterizes her academic life as a Shakespearean as 'a kind of forty-year-long hiatus from Spenser': Hugh Maclean Memorial Lecture: 'Revaluing the Body in *The Faerie Queene*', *The Spenser Review*, 36 (2005), 15–25, here 15.

[13] For a sophisticated discussion of allegory, see Carolynn Van Dyke, *The Fiction of Truth: Structures of Meaning in Narrative and Dramatic Allegory* (Ithaca, NY: Cornell University Press, 1985), 15–46.

[14] *Sexual Personae: Art and Decadence from Nefertiti to Emily Dickinson* (1990; rpt. New York: Random House, 1991), 213, 216–19.

sius can no more be kept neatly apart in the end (and long before the end) than can Rome and Egypt, Mars and Venus, the various forms of Venus, or, indeed, even Guyon and the Bower of Bliss—again, just for starters. If early in the play, Egypt recalls the Bower, where 'nature ... ensude / Art, and ... Art at nature did repine', at the end it looks more like Spenser's Garden of Adonis, an earthly, mythic place 'So faire ... as Nature can deuize', where art itself is natural.[15]

The limitations, as well as the heightened perceptions, of Paglia's discussion can be instanced in her remark that *Antony and Cleopatra* is 'the most thorough of Shakespeare's replies to Spenser' or in her contrast between 'the frozen iconic entrance' of Spenser's Belphoebe and Enobarbus' 'answering' *depiction* of Cleopatra in her barge, the latter 'Venus in motion' (213, 223). To the first, one response might be to question—as I have in my essay on Shakespeare's *Venus and Adonis* and elsewhere—the reigning assumption that the only relationship possible between writers is mocking rivalry. This assumption is simplistic, naively and narrowly gendered, and unhistorical, to boot. It often results from the habit of excising words, phrases, and short passages from their larger contexts to find quantifiable, 'hard' evidence of 'influence' and from the desire of an older criticism to base intertextual relationship only on a writer's deliberate and specific *linguistic* allusions.

A sufficient response to Paglia's second claim would involve detailed discussion of the unfolding, fluidly perceptual description of Belphoebe, whose hair waves 'like a penon wyde dispred':

> And whether art it were, or heedelesse hap,
> As through the flouring forrest rash she fled,
> In her rude heares sweet floures themselues did lap,
> And flourishing fresh leaues and blossomes did enwrap.
> (II.iii.30)[16]

A response would also involve the relation of the description of Belphoebe to the numerous versions of Venus-Virgo to which it alludes both immediately and within the poem as a whole. Finally, it would

---

[15] II.xii.59, III.vi.29. In the Garden, the arbor on the Mount is 'not by art, / But of the trees owne inclination made' (III.vi.44). Aside from the fact that the inclination of the trees is naturally artful, the whole Garden canto is egregiously so. It is a lyrical myth that includes the generativity of art and specifically the mythic transformations to which 'sweet Poets verse hath giuen endlesse date' (45). Acrasia's art is artificial in a sense that a reader of Baudrillard might appreciate.

[16] The waving of Belphoebe's hair 'like a penon wyde dispred' irresistibly calls to mind the illustration of a title that is 'deformed in such a way as to give the impression that a wind is blowing the flat surface on which they [the letters in the title] are written', which Jean-François Lyotard uses to suggest 'how language, at least in its poetic usage, is possessed, haunted by the figure': 'The Dream-Work Does Not Think', trans. Mary Lydon, in *The Lyotard Reader*, ed. Andrew Benjamin (Oxford: Blackwell, 1989), 19–55, here 27, 30.

involve enough contextualizing of the barge speech to understand its nature (in both generic and specific senses) and its function in the play, which, in an understatement, have been variously received.[17]

I turn next to a recent example of reception advocating that highly rhetorical poetry and embodied drama are inimical, existing in a relation of simple, radical opposition and thereby opposed to my present argument. While not treating *The Faerie Queene* directly, *Shakespeare's Theory of Drama*, by Pauline Kiernan, considers *Antony and Cleopatra* a direct repudiation of the golden world of Sidney's *Apology for Poetry* and, correlatively, an endorsement of the real, brazen world of plain speech and physical bodies. As a rejection of highly rhetorical poetry—'written poetry's ... excesses'—related to *Venus and Adonis*, Shakespeare's play becomes implicitly an attack on any such poem as *The Faerie Queene* and particularly on Spenser's poem, insofar as it is the conspicuously rhetorical, major non-dramatic written work of the English High Renaissance, one to which Sidney's theory of poetry is strikingly apposite.[18] Kiernan's perception of 'the difference between a poetry bred by a union with the rhetorical past which is doomed to perish, and a poetry that is self-created and uncontaminated by such rhetoric' is linguistically naive and fantastically utopian. Nonetheless, it can as readily and ironically be related to the bejeweled vines and 'christall running by' of Acrasia's wicked Bower as to the 'ivory in an alabaster band' that, in Kiernan's view, Shakespeare's Adonis ironically becomes within the 'circuit of ... ivory' of the goddess Venus' embrace.[19] If Shakespeare is engaged in rhetorical parody in *Venus and Adonis*, he faithfully follows in Spenser's Acrasian footsteps. These steps would also have led him to the witch's creation of False Florimell in Book III (viii.6–8), a walking parody of the sonneteer's idolized Beauty that is garnished with actual wires rather than hair and thereby a precursor of Shakespeare's parodic sonnet 130: 'My mistress' eyes are nothing like the sun; ... If hairs be wires, black wires grow on her head'.

Kiernan's argument stakes out theoretical ground that is either unspoken or spoken less provocatively in other discussions, and for this reason, I want to consider it further. Whereas Adelman discovers in

---

[17] The indispensable place to start a consideration of the description of Belphoebe remains Harry Berger, Jr.'s detailed analysis in *The Allegorical Temper: Vision and Reality in Book II of Spenser's 'Faerie Queene'* (New Haven, CT: Yale University Press, 1957), 120–49.

[18] 174; cf chaps. 2–3. Patrick Cheney, while acknowledging that Goddard might not have 'quite got the "story" right' in asserting, a '"gradual subjection of the theatrical to the poetical"' in Shakespeare's plays, embraces Goddard's view if poetry is understood as lyric or song: *Shakespeare, National Poet-Playwright* (Cambridge: Cambridge University Press, 2004), 275–6; Harold C. Goddard, *The Meaning of Shakespeare* (1951; rpt. Chicago, IL: Chicago University Press, Phoenix ed., 1960), II, 203.

[19] Kiernan, 47, 51; *The Faerie Queene*, II.xii.54–5, 58; cf. 'sparkling [or crystallizing] face', xii.68; *Venus and Adonis*, 230, 363 (passages in the epyllion referenced by Kiernan). For Shakespeare's writings other than *Antony and Cleopatra*, I cite *The Riverside Shakespeare* unless otherwise specified.

Cleopatra's realization, 'I am again for Cydnus', a return 'to no literal Cydnus but to the Cydnus of Enobarbus' description', Kiernan finds rejection of the latter—a 'triumph over' its insubstantial rhetoric (V.ii.227).[20] What we have instead at the end is 'Cleopatra's body, standing on a bare stage'; it is this that is 'nature's piece, 'gainst fancy, / Condemning shadows quite' (190). While Kiernan's distinction between Cleopatra's literal, physical absence in the barge speech and her presence in voicing her last, imagined destination is certainly valid in part, a single-minded focus on Cleopatra's body—her staged, boy'd presence—discounts her words and finally leaves us with a richly costumed corpse.[21] Missing from the equation of nature and body is quite simply the mind's productions and here more exactly those of the related functions of memory and imagination—the mnemonic imagination, if you will. To invoke a very different, modern context, a description of Proust that shares much with Renaissance Neoplatonism and Augustinism, 'memory is active and human, at the place between fiction and desire, experience and imagination, poetry and history'.[22] The functions of the mnemonic imagination are properly, if also precariously, distinguished from the delusions of *mere* fancy in sixteenth-century theories of poetry, whether dramatic, epic, or lyric. Variously conceived as the mind's eye, the sight of the soul, the icastic imagination, poetic wit, constructive invention, and so on, such insight is *natural* to human beings within both Aristotelian and Neoplatonic traditions of the time.[23] In Cleopatra's correction of Dolabella's commonsensical

---

[20] Adelman, 150; cf. 161; Kiernan, 190. Cf. Marguerite A. Tassi, 'O'erpicturing Appelles: Shakespeare's *Paragone* with Painting in *Antony and Cleopatra*', in Deats, ed. 291–307, here 303–4. Also Philippa Berry, *Shakespeare's Feminine Endings: Disfiguring Death in the Tragedies* (London: Routledge, 1999), 87: 'the enigmatically obscure spectacle of Cleopatra on Cydnus reminds us' that tragedy directs 'our attention precisely towards those aspects of experience which elude absolute comprehension'.

[21] A more persuasively balanced antecedent of Kiernan's argument is W. B. Worthen's essay, 'The Weight of Antony: Staging "Character" in *Antony and Cleopatra*', *Studies in English Literature*, 26 (1986), 295–308, esp. 301–3, 305. Referring to Cleopatra's return, as it were, to Cydnus, Worthen argues that 'the play forces us to negotiate the difficulties of its own representation, the "restoration" of an inaccessible, nearly unimaginable greatness—one known to us only through words, as a text—to the stage .... [where] there will be no barge burnishing, no music, no Cupids and Nereides, only a barren platform and two weeping servants' (305). A successful negotiation, he adds, will accept Cleopatra's rhetoric and staged pathos as efficacious play. See also Carol Cook, 'The Fatal Cleopatra', in *Shakespearean Tragedy and Gender*, ed. Shirley Nelson Garner and Madelon Sprengnether (Bloomington: Indiana University Press, 1996), 241–67, here 245: in V.ii, the 'boy actor, speaking the lines of the male playwright, draws our attention to the absence of Cleopatra from this scene, the absence which constitutes Cleopatra, constitutes the unrepresentable woman, the unassimilable other'. Cook's Irigarayan reading of the play rightly places a high value on fluidity. A more postive balance to Cook's not-thereness might be found in the thoughtful discussion of early modern 'vitalism' by Berry, *Shakespeare's Feminine Endings*, 12–20, esp. 13–14.

[22] Mary Orr, *Intertextuality: Debates and Contexts* (Cambridge: Polity Press, 2003), 57.

[23] Imprecise or unstable terminology obscures similarities and differences, but a selection of relevant views can be found in Sir Philip Sidney, *An Apology for Poetry*, ed. Geof-

assessment of her vision—if not her waking dream—of Antony, imagination is precisely the faculty she invokes in the line above Kiernan's citation: 't'imagine / An Antony were nature's piece 'gainst fancy', quite a different piece from a body on a bare stage and necessarily, by Sidney's identification of poesy with fiction, a poetic piece realized in rhetorical language (V.ii.97–8: my emphasis).

Essentially, Cleopatra's affirmation is Sidney's position in his *Apology*, where the creative wit of the poetic maker exceeds the limits of the merely natural world, the physical 'stuff' of nature, but where this human maker is also a piece of the nature that God has made. The fact of going beyond physical nature, whether by transcendence, excess, supplementation, sublation, recombination, distortion, or even reduction—'Heroes, Demigods, Cyclops, Chimeras, Furies and such like'—is basically what defines Sidney's view of the poetic imagination (100). At issue in Kiernan's theory of Shakespeare's drama are conceptions both of nature and of mimesis and fiction, and these bear on her radical opposition not only between written poetry and embodied action but also between rhetoric and plain speech, the latter at base an opposition between figurative and literal dimensions that many of Shakespeare's writings engage deeply and as wholes. Kiernan's argument exposes issues that currently underlie any attempt intertextually to align Spenser's epic romance with *Antony and Cleopatra*. These include those coded 'stage and page', voice and writing, 'honest kersey noes' and 'Taffata phrases', or, indeed, the 'Three-pil'd hyperboles', that, along with paradox, Adelman sees definitively shaping form and content in *Antony and Cleopatra*.[24]

Strategically, Kiernan explains, 'In the mimesis concept of art, the ideal is a skilled imitation of nature that is so life-like we are deceived

---

frey Shepherd (1965; rpt. Manchester: Manchester University Press, 1973), 125; George Puttenham, *The Arte of English Poesie* (1589; rpt. Kent, OH: Kent State University Press, 1988), 34–5; Allan H. Gilbert, ed. *Literary Criticism: Plato to Dryden* (1940; rpt. Detroit, MI: Wayne State University Press, 1962), 305–7, 312, 324 (Castelvetro); 360–2, 367–70, 386–8 (Mazzoni); 472, 474, 476–81, 492–4 (Tasso). On Tasso's views, see also the discussion of Mindele Anne Treip, *Allegorical Poetics and the Epic: The Renaissance Tradition to 'Paradise Lost'* (Lexington: University Press of Kentucky, 1994), 45–9 and chaps. 5–8, esp. 67, 74–9, 82–5, 91–4. While the Aristotelian Pietro Pomponazzi does not address poetics in his treatise *On the Immortality of the Soul*, his argument that 'in all cognition, however far abstracted, we form some bodily image', or, as Aristotle himself had put it, ' "knowing is either imagination, or is not without imagination" ', is likewise suggestive regarding the status of poetic imagery: *The Renaissance Philosophy of Man*, ed. Ernst Cassirer, Paul Oskar Kristeller, John Herman Randall, Jr. (1948; rpt. Chicago, IL: University of Chicago Press, 1956), 257–381, here 305, 319.

[24] Adelman, 121–2. *Love's Labor Lost*, V.ii.406–7, 413. On stage and page, see Harry Berger, Jr., 'Bodies and Texts', in *Situated Utterances: Texts, Bodies, and Cultural Representations* (New York: Fordham University Press, 2005), 99–128; also his *Imaginary Audition: Shakespeare on Stage and Page* (1989; rpt. Berkeley: University of California Press, 1991). Cf. Kiernan, 10–11, 15, for example.

into thinking the imitated subject is the real thing' (8). This reductive definition of mimesis is hardly that of an early modern Neoplatonist, let alone that of a true Aristotelian. If it is arguably Platonic, it is also already in opposition to the Platonic 'ideal', and from this perspective, self-canceling. Kiernan's mimesis is a concept Spenser's Acrasia might endorse (even while seductively and subversively contesting the definition of 'nature'), but, as Kiernan knows, it also opposes the mimetic conception of dramatic art in Shakespeare's *Hamlet*, where the mirror—'as 'twere', or 'as if it were', and thus already a metaphorized, counterfactual surface—that is held up to 'nature' registers such perceptual, interpretative, and questionably substantial characteristics as 'form', 'pressure', 'feature' and 'image' (III.ii.22–4).[25] Such characteristics are variously to be found in the mirror that Spenser offers his age and country, as well. Mirroring and techniques of mirroring, such as doubling, are everywhere in *The Faerie Queene*, conspicuous in both Proems and narrative.

Consider in response to Kiernan's definition, a relevant objection to the naively photographic conception of mimesis by the modern Aristotelian Paul Ricoeur:

> If we continue to translate mimesis by 'imitation', we have to understand something completely contrary to a copy of some preexisting reality and speak instead of a creative imitation. And if we translate mimesis by 'representation' ... we must not understand by this word some redoubling of presence, as we could still do for Platonic mimesis, but rather the break that opens the space

---

[25] The phrase 'as 'twere' conceivably can be taken either with the verb 'hold' that precedes it or, more likely, with the 'mirror' that follows it: the purpose, or end, of playing is 'to hold as 'twere the mirror up to nature'. Either way, the statement is counterfactual and the act of holding or the reflecting surface is conceived metaphorically. On this speech by Hamlet, cf. Robert Weimann, 'Mimesis in *Hamlet*', in *Shakespeare and the Question of Theory*, ed. Patricia Parker and Geoffrey Hartman (New York: Methuen, 1985), 275–91, esp. 278–80: Shakespeare's 'uses of mimesis cannot be formulated in (let alone reduced to) either a representational or nonrepresentational theory of dramatic language' (278). Cf. Also Weimann's 'Towards a Literary Theory of Ideology: Mimesis, Representation, Authority', in *Shakespeare Reproduced: The Text in History and Ideology*, ed. Jean E. Howard and Marion F. O'Connor (1987; rpt. New York: Routledge, 1993), 265–72, here 268. In this relatively more recent essay, Weimann's observation that 'there is no point in minimizing the actually existing contradiction between mimesis and the sign', true as it is, reflects his apparent identification of mimesis with referentiality and of signification with semiotics (266). Dichotomous terminology, while clear, seems inescapably problematical. I doubt Aristotle meant mimesis in as limited a sense as Weimann's here, but my doubt immediately opens the meaning of referentiality to question, as does Weimann's own discussion of *mimesis* in his distinguished *Shakespeare and the Popular Tradition in the Theater: Studies in the Social Dimension of Dramatic Form and Function*, ed. Robert Schwarz (Baltimore: Johns Hopkins University Press, 1978), 2–3: here, while he emphasizes the interpretive role of the actor (*hypokrites*), for whom the Ionian equivalent was *exegetes* (exegete), he notes, from earliest times, basic aspects of *mimesis* not derived from the object imitated: so how do we distinguish the dancer from the dance?

for fiction. Artisans who work with words produce not things but quasi-things; they invent the *as-if*.[26]

Kiernan presumably offers her naive definition of mimesis in order to accommodate the primacy she claims for fiction to that she claims for staged embodiment in Shakespeare's plays: Shakespeare's embodiment is not mimetic, she would argue, in order to prove it at once embodied *and* fictive. But this 'no brainer' signals another purpose. In conflating the fictive with embodiment, Kiernan also attempts to claim authentic, substantial, or real fiction exclusively for voice, body, presence, and stage. Written, notably rhetorical poetry is in contrast disembodied absence. Thus Kiernan further complicates these theoretical binaries by trying, via transcoding to equate embodied presence with the plain, worldly speech of Sidney's brazen world. All these distinctions and equations are bound for trouble, as a final example will demonstrate.

Kiernan draws the following contrast between Sidney's *Apology* and Shakespearean drama and in doing so identifies fiction with untruth, precisely the puritanical position that Sidney rejects:

> Sidney claims that the poet 'nothing affirms, and therefore never lieth'. Shakespearean drama declares itself unabashedly a liar in order to affirm one unassailable truth, which is the impossibility of determining the truth. It is for this reason that its fictitiousness is the foundation for all that it attempts to achieve. (12)

Sidney, of course, refers to fiction, for which his name is poesy, when he claims that the poet does not lie, and Shakespearean drama certainly more often declares its own ambiguous fictiveness than its falsehood, the latter the province of 'the common liar' in *Antony and Cleopatra*.[27] Moreover, such a declaration, indeed such interrogation and exposure, of fiction is readily aligned in Spenser's non-staged poetry with issues of representation and beyond this concern, even more self-consciously with its own performance of representation, which any reading, necessarily temporal, recaptures. For a start, consider the difference between the symbol of Christianity, the red-crossed armor at the very outset of the first canto of *The Faerie Queene*, the most obvious, trustworthy symbol imaginable, and Archimago's donning this symbolic armor early in the second canto, where the now-mock-innocent narrator's conclusive phrasing, 'Full iolly knight he seemde' exactly replicates, not to say mirrors, his initial description of Redcrosse (I.i.1, ii.11). Shakespearean drama does not declare itself an unabashed, or common, liar, but like

---

[26] *Time and Narrative*, I, trans. Kathleen McLaughlin and David Pellauer (Chicago, IL: University of Chicago Press, 1984), 45. See also Orr, chap. 3: 'Imitation', esp. 96–106.

[27] Sidney, 123; Shakespeare, I.i.61.

other contemporary poetic writings, and most massively, conspicuously, and relevantly *The Faerie Queene*, it raises issues everywhere about truth, about representation, and about the unstable relation between them.

Kiernan's notion of Orphic poetry, which, in the words of Gerald Bruns, 'seeks its transcendence not in isolation but in relation to the world of natural things', is suggestively close to Wolfgang Iser's conception of the fictive, which is not tied to 'the old fiction/reality dichotomy'.[28] Instead, Iser's fictive 'keeps in view what has been overstepped', while it is nonetheless 'an act of boundary-crossing' that at once 'disrupts and doubles the referential world'. The irony of my invoking Iser in responding to Kiernan is that his theory of the fictive and imaginary specifically references, thus privileging, Sidney's pastoral *Arcadia*—prose fiction, yet still 'poesy' in Sidney's lexicon, insofar as 'it is not rhyming and versing that maketh a poet' (103). Shakespeare, I suspect, would have accepted this analogy for his plays and with it the intertextual, imaginative affinity of his work with both Sidney's and Spenser's.

Turning more directly to the relation of *Antony and Cleopatra* to *The Faerie Queene*, I want to argue an imaginative affinity between them that their common cultural sources undergird—as more specifically does the combined relation of the play to *Venus and Adonis* and of this epyllion to Spenser's epic romance—but that these common cultural sources fail to account for credibly and sufficiently. This affinity is overwhelmingly thematic, although its themes extend to subtler and more specific effects: for example, in Adelman's thoroughly Spenserian word-concept, the 'fusion' of Antony and Cleopatra in the end extends to the exchange of characterizing words and phrases, the symbolic blending of character that is basically allegorical in conception and a defining characteristic of *The Faerie Queene*.[29] The thematic ties that conspicuously bind these works include language and representation, as well as infinite variety, versionality, and endlessness, as I have already indicated.[30] In

---

[28] Kiernan, 13; Kiernan cites Bruns, *Modern Poetry and the Idea of Language: A Critical and Historical Study* (New Haven, CT: Yale University Press, 1974), 1–5. Iser, *The Fictive and the Imaginary: Charting Literary Anthropology* (Baltimore: Johns Hopkins University Press, 1993), xiv–xv. On the relation of Sidney's *Apology* to *Antony and Cleopatra*, see also Bono, *Literary Transvaluation*, 141, 150–1, 219.

[29] *Suffocating Mothers*, 189, *Common Liar*, 161. On the blending of character in Shakespeare and Spenser, see my examples in 'Conspiracy of Realism', 7–8 (*King Lear*), and *Translating Investments: Metaphor and the Dynamic of Cultural Change in Tudor-Stuart England* (New York: Fordham University Press, 2005), 29–30 (*1* and *2 Henry IV*). Early instances of the merging of different speakers' statements can be found in the Despair and Contemplation episodes of Spenser's first Book (I.ix.41–2, x.62) and in the replies of the Palmer and Guyon to Atin in Book II.iv.44.

[30] James Hirsch remarks the Egyptian, or infinitely various, structure of this play, whose scenes number more than forty, some 'absurdly brief': 'Rome and Egypt in *Antony and Cleopatra* and in Criticism of the Play', in Deats, ed. 175–91, here 189. Hirsch's re-

addition, they conspicuously include hermaphroditism and analogous composites or mergings, as opposed to, undermining, and exceeding binarism. Egregious among these composites is the oxymoronic linkage of eros and death—Spenser's Verdant and Mortdant, or fertile springtime and mortality (in both senses of this word). Another, related instance of this oxymoronic coupling in Spenser occurs in Amavia and Mortdant ('lovelife' and 'death giving'), a pair impinging openly on the pun that unifies sexual and deathly dying. In terms I have used elsewhere, these thematic ties extend to the organizing, symbolic referents of Spenser's third Book, the Venerian flower and the Martian boar, and recurrently and insistently as well—Watkins might say obsessively, and Angus Fletcher 'allegorically'—to thematized questions regarding the source and nature of vision.[31]

Introducing *Metaphor and Belief in 'The Faerie Queene'*, Rufus Wood instances Antony's definition of the crocodile as 'a telling critique of the imaginative sterility of non-metaphoric language'.[32] In response to Lepidus' question, 'What manner o' thing is your crocodile?' we find the following:

> ANTONY: It is shaped, sir, like itself, and it is as broad as it hath breadth. It is just so high as it is, and moves with its own organs. It lives by that which nourisheth it, and the elements once out of it, it transmigrates.
> LEPIDUS: What colour is it of?
> ANTONY: Of its own colour too.
> LEPIDUS: 'Tis a strange serpent.
> ANTONY: 'Tis so, and the tears of it are wet.
> (II.vii.41–50)

For Wood, this comically absurd exchange is directed less at the drunken Lepidus than at the literalism of Roman values and the perceptions of 'things' informed by them. For me, it could not contrast more openly with Enobarbus' description of Cleopatra in her barge only five scenes earlier or more pointedly raise the issue of representation in language and specifically question the values of rhetoric and literalism, not

---

view of the Rome/Egypt binarism in criticism of the play nicely supplements Deats's survey (n1, above). On the spatial politics of the play, see also Ania Loomba, 'Theatre and the Space of the Other in *Antony and Cleopatra*', in Susanne L. Wofford, ed. *Shakespeare's Late Tragedies: A Collection of Critical Essays* (Upper Saddle River, NJ: Prentice Hall, 1996), 235–48, here 237–40.

[31] In *Allegory: The Theory of a Symbolic Mode* (Ithaca, NY: Cornell University Press, 1964), Fletcher aligns allegory with obsessive-compulsive neurosis: chap. 6. His argument merges individual with broadly historico-cultural explanation and medical pathology with ideological hegemony.

[32] (Houndmills, Basingstoke: Macmillan, 1997), 2–3.

to say of imagination and thing.[33] To remark that the same issue occurs relevantly in *The Faerie Queene* seems almost superfluous, but the significant contrast in Book II between the rhetorically heightened, sensuous Bower of Bliss and the heightened abstraction of the Castle of Medina comes readily to mind, as do the strains 'between metaphorical and material dimensions of meaning, between concept and history, and between words and things' that are thematic throughout Book V.[34] Along with other memories of contrast between the true and artificial Florimells in Books III to V, the metamorphosis of Malbecco in Book III (x), an alteration which subverts his humanity (specifically his manhood) into the monstrous figure Jealousy made by his own mind, highlights the central concern of this book with the making of metaphors. Still more to the point is the contrast between the cannibalistic literalizers of the blazon who capture Serena and the rhetorical values of Mount Acidale, both instances in Book VI that openly, problematically, and relevantly engage the inseparability of vision from desire. Additional contrast between epic and other values significantly embodied in form comes in recurrences of pastoral (and even Langlandian) moments—for example, the future Redcrosse's being found in a furrow by a plowman or the gnats that recurrently annoy the Faerie fields; these are Spenser's nods to 'russet neas' and 'kersey noes', as any Elizabethan or Jacobean with a grammar school education would have recognized, thereby avoiding confusion of such incursions of the low style with literalism.

More tellingly, however, the focusing of the issue of representation in language explicitly and insistently on the necessity, inescapability, and creative-destructive, illusory-insightful potential of metaphor is a denominator considerably closer to what ties Shakespeare to Spenser than are the common myths, as such, that they inherit. Likewise closer is the issue of moral framing, another matter of representation and interpretation. The insufficiency of such Octavian framing may need little urging in Shakespeare's play, but it should be noted that signs of it are famously numerous in Spenser's Bower as well, including the ambivalent narrator, Guyon's violence, the nature of this Knight's relation to the Bower, and the nature of the Bower itself. The slippery, sliding, relation between Acrasian beauty and Guyonic waste, as later between

---

[33] The contrast is heightened by further parallels: Enobarbus describes from land a boat-scene, while Antony, situated on a boat (tenuously tied to land), describes an amphibian. What is striking about both is their amphibiousness. Cf. Cook, 'Fatal Cleopatra', 249, who reads the crocodile exchange as mockery of the Roman 'logic of identity', or sameness.

[34] Altering the conjunction 'or' to 'and', I quote from my *Words That Matter: Linguistic Perception in Renaissance English* (Stanford, CA: Stanford University Press, 1996), 168: this book is concerned throughout with the relations of words to things and therefore offers relevant cultural context.

Busiranic form and emptiness, and the persistence of Acrasia and Busirane in what follows their apparent captures is closer to Shakespearean versions of these than any notion of 'allegorical purity' would suggest.

Another denominator closer to what connects Shakespeare to Spenser than the rich archive of myths, the 'stuff', they inherit and distinctively employ, is what I have called the theme of hermaphroditism, of which the androgyne is a cultural and figurative variation not always distinguished clearly or consistently from the sexual hermaphrodite in this period.[35] No two other literary works in English in the period treat this theme more creatively, complexly, and to a more concentrated and focal extent than do the two writings in question. For Spenser, its focal treatment spans the cross-dressed Britomart's three books and then some, pertaining especially but not exclusively to her. In these books, namely III to V, it becomes evident that a binaristic conception of gender is simply inadequate; there are four terms, not two in play, or at least two in each of the major amatory players, Britomart and Artegall.

For Shakespeare, this doubling of gender involves Antony and Cleopatra equally. Consider a selection of familiar examples preceding their deaths: Antony's cross-dressing in Cleopatra's 'tires and mantles', while she wears 'his sword Philippan', one of several allusions to Venus and Mars in the play; or Cleopatra's startling desire that a message be 'Ram[med]' in her ears, a desire doubly gendered by her possession *and* expression of its violently forceful, imagistic rhetoric (animal, gun, vagina), and her transferential relish in using her bended hook to 'pierce / The ... slimy jaws' of fishes, each of them imagined an Antony; or her desire to 'Appear there for a man' in the first sea battle, 'for' hovering among 'as', 'instead of', and 'on behalf of'; or her marble-constancy, rock-hard, as death approaches.[36] Further highlighting hermaphroditic symbolism early in the play, Octavius memorably charges that the reveling Antony 'is not more manlike / Than Cleopatra, nor the Queen of Ptolemy / More womanly than he'; subsequently, Antony violates his 'manhood, honour' and suffers the figurative loss of his sword, or manhood, in the two battles at sea; he then dissolves or loses his firm shape even before determining on death, and dying he literally loses his sword, which is presented by one of Antony's men to Caesar, a passing of the phallus if ever there was one.[37]

---

[35] Background for my argument can be found in Thomas Laqueur, *Making Sex: Body and Gender from the Greeks to Freud* (Cambridge, MA: Harvard University Press, 1990), preface and chaps 1–2, e.g., viii, 8, 11, 30–1. Another important touchstone is Valerie Traub's thoughtful, precise introduction in *Desire and Anxiety: Circulation of Sexuality in Shakespearean Drama* (London: Routledge, 1992), 1–22.

[36] II.v.12–14, 21–4, III.vii.18; V.ii.239. On hermaphroditism and androgyny in relation to Cleopatra, cf. Michael Payne's 'Erotic Irony and Polarity in *Antony and Cleopatra*', *Shakespeare Quarterly*, 24 (1973), 265–79, esp. 271–4.

[37] I.iv.5–7, III.x.23, IV.xiv.10–14, 23, 113–14. Heather James perceptively treats another

As these samples suggest, instances of double gendering and cross-gendering accumulate in *Antony and Cleopatra*, and they also advance thematically as the play moves into its final Acts. Here also questions about the source and nature of vision become explicit, as they do with particular relevance in Spenser's Books III and VI, the latter taken as a whole that climaxes on Mount Acidale. Spenser's third Book centrally concerns the mind's—more exactly, the imagination's—power to project its own shapes on reality. Throughout this Book, the Venerian flower and the Martian boar, which I earlier aligned with eros and death and with fertility and mortality, symbolically frame the quest of Britomart, the focal *Venus armata* of the poem. In the middle of Book III rises the Garden of Adonis, an earthly site where life and death co-exist eternally and spring is 'Continuall' with harvest, 'both meeting at one tyme' (III.vi.42).[38]

In the Renaissance, a Garden of Adonis, from ancient times the term for a forcing bed or place of heightened fertility, became by etymological confusion of Adonis with Eden a 'ioyous Paradize', as Spenser calls it, and the seminary of all created things (III.vi.29).[39] At the center of Spenser's Garden is a *mons pubis*, and directly beneath it the sharp-tusked boar, a traditional symbol of aggression, sexual passion, chaos, winter, and death, is imprisoned in a cave.[40] The recycling babes returning through a gate of death 'in that Gardin planted bee agayne; / And grow afresh, as they had neuer seene / Fleshly corruption, nor mortall payne' (III.vi.33). On the Mount itself, Venus 'takes her fill' of Adonis' 'sweetnesse', and

> There yet, some say, in secret he does ly,
> Lapped in flowres and pretious spycery,

---

exchange of gender in Cleopatra's ambivalent observation that Antony is one way painted 'like a Gorgon', that is, like the female Medusa (II.v.116): 'The Politics of Display and the Anamorphic Subjects of *Antony and Cleopatra*', in Wofford, ed., 208–34, here 212.

[38] On the imagination's power to project its own shapes on reality and on the symbols of flower and boar in Book III, see my *Growth of a Personal Voice: 'Piers Plowman' and 'The Faerie Queene'* (New Haven, CT: Yale University Press, 1976), 98–113.

[39] See Hamilton, ed., 346nn30–50. Also John Erskine Hankins, *Source and Meaning in Spenser's Allegory: A Study of 'The Faerie Queene'* (Oxford: Clarendon, 1971), 277–86; and James Nohrnberg, *The Analogy of 'The Faerie Queene'* (Princeton, NJ: Princeton University Press, 1976), 516. Of course traditionally the Garden of Adonis also implied ephemerality and triviality: for example, see Nohrnberg, 493–4, who suggests that Spenser put the negative associations of the Garden of the Adonis into the Bower of Bliss. Kenneth Gross qualifies Nohrnberg's observation, maintaining that Spenser both cancels and preserves the negative associations within the Garden: *Spenserian Poetics: Idolatry, Iconoclasm, and Magic* (Ithaca, NY: Cornell University Press, 1985), 201–2.

[40] Traditionally the Garden Mount is considered a *mons veneris*, and it is this, although this is not all that it is. Elsewhere, I argue for the bisexuality of the Mount: 'Flowers and Boars: Surmounting Sexual Binarism in Spenser's Garden of Adonis', forthcoming, *Spenser Studies*, 23 (2008).

> By her hid from the world, and from the skill
> Of *Stygian* Gods.
> (III.vi.46)

Both in this passage and elsewhere in the Garden sex is collocated with death—much as in the pun on dying—and generation at once accompanies and alternates with exhaustion, even as spring with harvest and life with death. As Anne Prescott notes elsewhere in this volume, mythic time converges here with mortality. Here grows 'euery sort of flowre, / To which sad louers were transformde of yore', and Adonis, 'in euerlasting ioy', finds the continuity of dying with the perpetuation of life (III.vi.45–7, 49).[41] Here as well, the conventional gendering of the quotidian world is disrupted, if we believe the scholars who have studied this episode most closely and, indeed, our own commonsensical reading: Adonis lies passively and Venus takes her fill, and within his 'subiect[ion] to mortalie', he experiences life 'in eternall blis, / Ioying his goddesse, and of her enioyd' (III.vi.47, 48).[42] Understanding the Garden as an intense site of pleasure, knowledge, and power, Kenneth Gross describes it conclusively as at once 'an ear[th]ly paradise', 'an apocalypse that preserves rather than destroys the natural, and a vision of supernatural sources that survives being thrown into time, into the warring cycles of *eros* and *thanatos*' (209, cf. 200).

In the space remaining, I want to read the deaths of Antony and Cleopatra in ways that intersect with the Garden, as I have described this celebrated mythic place, which, it bears remembering, Shakespeare demonstrably knew.[43] In the fourth Act of *Antony and Cleopatra*, both after Mardian's false report of Cleopatra's death, as before it, what strikes me are Antony's repeated outcries: 'Eros!' Shakespearean criticism has surely noticed these—time out of mind, however. No one recently has

---

[41] On the dying Adonis, cf. Gordon Williams, 'The Coming of Age in Shakespeare's Adonis', *Modern Language Review*, 78 (1983), 769–76, here 770, 775. Nohrnberg, 532, aligns the combining of womb and tomb in the Garden with the act of sex when he observes, 'Although a man cannot re-enter the womb except symbolically, he can do so seminally'.

[42] On the subordination of Adonis to Venus, see the discussion of Jon Quitslund, *Spenser's Supreme Fiction: Platonic Natural Philosophy and 'The Faerie Queene'* (Toronto: University of Toronto Press, 2001), 211–19. For a historicist's approach to such subordination, see Lisa Celovsky, 'Early Modern Masculinities and *The Faerie Queene*', *English Literary Renaissance*, 35 (2005), 210–47, here 212–17. Further relevant are the differing analyses of the Garden canto by Harry Berger, Jr., 'Spenser's Gardens of Adonis: Force and Form in the Renaissance Imagination' (1961), in his *Revisionary Play: Studies in the Spenserian Dynamics* (Berkeley: University of California Press, 1988), 131–53, and 'Actaeon at the Hinder Gate: The Stag Party in Spenser's Gardens of Adonis', in *Desire in the Renaissance: Psychoanalysis and Literature*, ed. Valeria Finucci and Regina Schwartz (Princeton, NJ: Princeton University Press, 1994), 91–119.

[43] See my *'Venus and Adonis'*, 150–2, for Shakespeare's allusion to Spenser's Garden in *Richard III*. Shakespeare's *1 Henry VI*, I.vi.6 also refers to 'Adonis' garden', and the Riverside edition notes in this reference the possibility of another Spenserian allusion.

wanted to dwell on the obvious allegorical signal—'Eros!'—or to consider it the sign of a shift in register, a radical heightening of the mythic mode, one that is all the more noticeable for the practical Enobarbus' departure and replacement by Antony's freedman of this name.[44] That the name Eros exists in Plutarch, Shakespeare's major source, hardly diminishes the conspicuousness of this signal in his play, unless we want absurdly to pretend that Shakespeare copied history without imaginatively processing it.

To allude and refer to myth repeatedly in a play is one thing, but to bring it to life, embodying it in an actor on stage, is quite another. Antony's repeated outcries 'Eros' are the equivalent of pointing hands in the margin of a book to attract and direct our attention to something important: 'This grave charm ... Like a false gipsy hath at fast and loose / Beguiled me to the very heart of loss. / What, Eros, Eros! ... Ah, thou spell! Avaunt!'; 'Eros, ho! / The shirt of Nessus is upon me .... She dies for't. Eros, ho!'; 'Eros!—I come, my queen.—Eros!—Stay for me. ... Come Eros! Eros!' Raging like the Thessalian boar, Antony believes himself poisoned by a combination of love and betrayal, as was Hercules by the shirt of Nessus, but at the same time he turns in passionate desperation to Eros for some form of affirmation.[45] On his realization of Cleopatra's (feigned) suicide, his need quickly turns into a desire for mutual consummation. Traditionally, Eros is a god of death as well as of life, of *consummation* in both these uses of the word—*consummatum est*. In the lines I have cited, Antony's desire coincides with death, again as the pun on *die*, so dear to Elizabethans and Jacobeans, expresses this juncture.[46] Indeed, it is 'with a wound [that Antony] ... must be cured' (IV.xiv.79); with the reference to curing, one thinks both more readily

---

[44] Again, 'dwell': various recent commentators on the play mention allegory at this point but do little more with it. Coppélia Kahn, for example, confines it to a local effect, 'a signifier of love specifically between men': *Roman Shakespeare: Warriors, Wounds, and Women* (London: Routledge, 1997), 130. While astutely recognizing the allegorical binarism of other critics, James Hirsch remains suspicious of allegory itself: 'Allegorical figures usually represent fixed abstractions, whereas Cleopatra strives for variety, change, originality, and individuality. And yet there is something obsessive about this striving', and 'She, too, presents herself as an allegorical figure, although a paradoxical one, the embodiment of Infinite Variety, the antithesis of allegorical reductionism'. Similarly, for Hirsch, the individualized Antony is no Everyman, 'and yet, like a morality-play character, he does make a fateful choice between incompatible alternatives' (188). See also Cook, 253–4: '*Antony and Cleopatra* ... is in many ways closer to something like allegory or dialectic than to psychological drama'.

[45] IV.xii, 25–30, 42–9, xiii.2, xiv.51–5. In *Richard III*, Richard's heraldic device, a boar, presumably triggers Shakespeare's allusion to Spenser's Garden of Adonis. In the fourth Act of *Antony and Cleopatra*, while Antony's descent from Hercules triggers reference to the Thessalian boar, in the present context of love and death, memories of the boar beneath Spenser's Garden Mount are plausible as well. On the boar and the Garden, cf. Anne Prescott's paper in the present volume.

[46] Edgar Wind, *Pagan Mysteries in the Renaissance*, rev. ed. (Harmondsworth: Penguin, 1967), chap. 10: 'Amor as a God of Death'. John: 19.30.

of Adonis than Mars and more readily of Spenser's Adonis than Shakespeare's.

Although I am cautious, if not skeptical, of Christianizing efforts to associate Adonis with Christ in Spenser's Garden, such association certainly occurs in Christian appropriations of the classical myth and for Antony's words could provide another resonance that is shared by Shakespeare and Spenser.[47] Antony's curing by a wound surely glances at a sacrificial context of the sort Milton will invoke in his catalogue of devils: where 'smooth *Adonis* from his native Rock / [Runs] ... purple to the Sea, suppos'd with blood / Of *Thammuz* yearly wounded'. Thammuz-Adonis, also identified with Osiris, was treated as a fertility cult by numerous, relatively popular commentators contemporary with Spenser and Shakespeare, and as later for Milton, as for many other early moderns, pagan belief is typically a deceptive shadow of truth.[48] Again, such words as 'resonance' and 'glance' are appropriate to these mythic possibilities, whereas heavy-handed impositions of mythic equivalents are not. Their possible presence is as readily available to irony, moreover, as it is to the impulse of wish-fulfillment.

Antony's desire for consummation, as I have quoted it, actually frames the lines Watkins rightly, if inexplicitly, appears to have associated with the Garden of Adonis:

> Eros!—I come, my queen—Eros!—Stay for me.
> Where souls do couch on flowers we'll hand in hand
> And with our sprightly port make the ghosts gaze.
> Dido and her Aeneas shall want troops,
> And all the haunt be ours. Come Eros! Eros!   (IV.xiv.51–5)

As commentators on Antony's reference to the Elysian Fields have observed, his desire notably revises Vergil on Dido and Aeneas in the netherworld, where Dido shuns her betrayer, and I would suggest he does so via a fleeting Shakespearean memory of the Garden of Adonis,

---

[47] On the identification of Adonis with Christ, see, for example, Syrithe Pugh, *Spenser and Ovid* (Aldershot: Ashgate, 2005), 55–7; also Gross's precariously balanced assessment in which Adonis is at once 'the fallen Adam *and* the redemptive Christ', and yet however much he combines them, 'he sustains a crucial measure of difference from both' (197–8). Lisa Hopkins neatly sums up the many biblical associations of *Antony and Cleopatra*: 'Cleopatra and the Myth of Scota', in Deats, ed., 231–42, here 235. In the twentieth century, the association of Antony with Christ goes back at least to John Middleton Murry (1936), who took it seriously, and to Roy Battenhouse (1969), who thought it ironic: see Deats, 8, 28.

[48] *Paradise Lost*, I.450–2, in *John Milton: Complete Poems and Major Prose*, ed. Merritt Y. Hughes (New York: Odyssey, 1957): also 222–3nn446, 458–60. See as well Richard T. Neuse's discussion of *Adonis, gardens of* in *The Spenser Encyclopedia*, ed. A. C. Hamilton, et al. (Toronto: University of Toronto Press, 1990).

which commentary has otherwise also related to Vergil's Elysium.[49] In a line from the Garden earlier quoted, which Shakespeare had already remembered in *Richard III*, Adonis lies 'Lapped in flowres and pretious spycery'; and two stanzas later, 'There now he liueth in eternall bliss, / Ioying his goddesse, and of her enioyed' (III.vi.46, 48). Like the contrasting frame of summonses to Eros and the imagined site in Shakespeare's lines, Antony is caught more discordantly than ever before between fleshly consummation and mythic desire. Of course he is caught as well between homo- and heteroeroticism and between Roman and Egyptian allegiances.[50]

Shakespeare's character Eros kills himself out of love for Antony, a kind of total realization of his name. He becomes, like a simplified figure in allegory, exactly what he does. The sacrifice of Eros for Antony also frees, not to say forces, Antony to rise above his former self, if neither smoothly nor very effectively. In a speech initially addressed to the (allegorically) self-murdering Eros and then to himself, Antony resolves to commit suicide and then attempts it:

>   O valiant Eros, what
> I should and thou couldst not! My queen and Eros
> Have by their brave instruction got upon me
> A nobleness in record. But I will be
> A bridegroom in my death and run into't
> As to a lover's bed. Come then! And, Eros,
> Thy master dies thy scholar. To do thus
> I learned of thee.
>   (IV.xiv.97–104)

Antony wants to embrace death as a lover, indeed a bridegroom. Once again the culturally focal pun on dying is present, and he wants, in an absolute sense, to realize it. But the bridegroom Antony's running (or less climactically falling) on his sword, in view of the conspicuously phallic, often penile, symbolism of a sword in the play to this point, is remarkably hermaphroditic. If he is the bridegroom, here he is also the wounded bride.

Not surprisingly, while Antony does not finally fail to commit suicide, he certainly bungles its accomplishment in terms either of Octavian efficiency or Herculean strength. More figuratively, however, he

---

[49] Hankins observes the bearing of Vergil's Elysian Fields on Spenser's wheel of death and regeneration, 274. Also Nohrnberg, 503, 514, 517. In the November Eclogue of Spenser's *Shepheardes Calender*, E. K.'s gloss on line 179 describes the Elysian Fields as 'a place of pleasure like Paradise': *The Yale Edition of the Shorter Poems of Edmund Spenser*, ed. William A. Oram, et al. (New Haven, CT: Yale University Press, 1989), 198. Heather James, 229, considers Antony's seeming mistake regarding Dido a deliberate act of 'resistance to Caesar's ideological appropriation of him'.

[50] Quitslund coincidentally observes that Cupid's wanton play with Adonis in Spenser's Garden is homoerotic, keeping 'Venus's consort ready for her' (208).

reaches awkwardly, even with dramatic absurdity, to realize the complexity of an identity that has so far eluded him. This identity is a compound whole, a healing of systemic binaries, and of course it cannot be fully realized, as the pain of prolonged dying and the deflating falsehood of Cleopatra's feigned death cruelly bring home. As with so much in this play, however, the impossibility of such realization might be further challenged, and it is in Cleopatra's actual death. Although only Cleopatra can finish what Antony starts and close the wound he opens to view, a heightening of the mythic mode in his start is all the more emphatic precisely for its discord with physical reality, and it is also precisely what renders visible a significant, vital continuity between the two lovers' paired endings.

These endings are structurally analogous to those of *King Lear*. Antony's situation at the end inversely resembles the faux ending of *Lear*, where Edgar and Albany stand around moralizing about the justice of the gods and the wheel's coming full circle, only to have their vision shattered by that 'Great thing of us forgot!'—death, in effect, cruelly real, unjust death in the fate of Cordelia, then the death of Lear himself (V.iii.237). The morality-play feint of Edgar's and Albany's reflections only heightens the tragic questions that follow it in the actual ending of the play. Where a pious vision is shattered by the end of *Lear*, however, mythic vision is reaffirmed and dramatically realized at the end of *Antony and Cleopatra*, yet with this difference: whereas Antony collocates sex and death, only to be painfully reminded of the difference, Cleopatra, making the same connection, goes beyond it to figure death effectively as (re)generation.

Antony's collocation 'Eros!—I come, my queen—Eros!—Stay for me . . . . Come Eros! Eros!' cited out of its full context, is almost embarrassing, almost laughable, like his botched suicide. Perhaps another memory of *King Lear*, the notorious impulse to laughter noted at times by actors rehearsing it and by audiences in its actual performance, pertains here. Excess invites laughter and succeeds not despite but by co-operating with it, co-opting release and reality-check to vision. In this way excess can acknowledge the connection of vision with desire without simply being reduced to the latter and denying the creative value of fiction and figurative language—the as-if dimension of poesy. In effect, Antony's bungling runs interference for Cleopatra's vision by *constructive* contrast, both introducing a heightened mythic mode and providing a butt for realistic criticism that to an extent will deflect it from what is to come, even while paradoxically acknowledging the *connection* necessary to contrast, or meaningful difference.[51] Seen as deflection, Antony's death actually is sacrificial.

When the dying Antony is briefly reunited with Cleopatra, she bends in the familiar pietà posture over his recumbent body and wishes that he might 'Die when ... [he has] lived' and 'Quicken with kissing' (IV.xv.39–40). Apparently now ceding such myths to her, he asserts in his remaining breaths, 'Not Caesar's valour hath o'erthrown Antony, / But Antony's hath triumphed on itself' (IV.xv.15–16). His attention is again on Roman values. Or is it really? Given Antony's failure to commit suicide efficiently, his claim meets skepticism: his Roman valor has dubiously been reasserted.[52] We might even consider his claim delusive or merely pathetic. Yet it might also be asked whether Caesar's conception of valor and Antony's are still the same (if they ever were) or even whether and how a Roman conception and Caesar's are identical at this moment. With the deaths of Enobarbus and Eros and the self-seeking betrayals of other followers of Antony, the nature and value of Roman valor are surely in question, and the redefining process of the entire play bears on Antony's present sense of them. His dying claim can be read as an affirmation of the distinction between Caesarean valor and

---

[51] Related techniques occur in *The Faerie Queene*, for example, in the contrast, already mentioned, between the vision of sonneteering cannibals and that of Mount Acidale in Book VI. Another, analogous kind of example can be found in Spenser's basing Arthur's dream of the Faerie Queene on Chaucer's parodic *Sir Thopas* or the embedding of allusions to *Troilus* and to the Wife of Bath's Prologue in Arthur's account of this dream. Instead of destroying Arthur's vision, these allusions bring it momentarily into relation with other, less idealized realities. Their point is connection, not identity—difference and similarity at once.

[52] Shakespeare drops the word 'other' from Antony's ambiguous claim in North's Plutarch that he is 'a Roman by an other Romane' overcome, which could refer either to Antony himself or to Caesar, and instead has Antony assert that he is 'a Roman by a Roman / Valiantly vanquished' (IV.xv.59–60). Shakespeare thus rewrites Plutarch to emphasize Antony's valor, but simultaneously turns this valor in on itself, making it more clearly self-referential, rather than necessarily an affirmation of Roman identity, which in fact it succeeds in extinguishing: 'The Life of Marcus Antonius', from *Plutarch's Lives of the Noble Grecians and Romanes*, trans., Sir Thomas North, in *Narrative and Dramatic Sources of Shakespeare*, ed. Geoffrey Bullough (London: Routledge and Kegan Paul, 1964), V, 254–321, here 310. Plutarch's final evaluation of Antony's suicide is also mixed: Antonius 'slue him selfe ... cowardly, and miserably, to his great paine and griefe: and yet was it before his bodie came into his enemies hands' (321). Cf. Robert A. Logan's argument that Shakespeare, in contrast to Plutarch, his main source, gives more space to Antony's heroism: '"High Events as these": Sources, Influences, and the Artistry of *Antony and Cleopatra*', in Deats, ed., 153–74, here 159–61. For a sympathetic explanation of Antony's final actions, cf. also Jacqueline Vanhoutte, 'Antony's "secret house of death": Suicide and Sovereignty in *Antony and Cleopatra*', *Philological Quarterly*, 79 (2000), 153–75, esp. 160–1, 166–9, and Bono, *Literary Transvaluation*, 187. For a defense of Antony's stature and 'weight', or 'greatness', that is oriented to performance, cf. Michael Goldman, '*Antony and Cleopatra*: Action as Imaginative Command', in Wofford, ed., 249–67, here 255–7, 259–60; and for an unqualifiedly negative view of Antony's end, cf. Julia M. Walker, *Medusa's Mirrors: Spenser, Shakespeare, Milton, and the Metamorphosis of the Female Self* (Newark, NJ: University of Delaware Press, 1998), 139–41.

valor of another kind. Antony's valor is now expressed not in suicide *per se* but in *dying*, a word and reality he invokes four times in his last moments with Cleopatra. As the familiar pun, this word-concept has a long history in the play, and its double-edging not only lingers, perhaps ironically, in Antony's memorably repeated line 'I am dying, Egypt, dying', but in time it also merges with Cleopatra's own performance of death (IV.xv.19, 43).[53]

'Say I would die' is Cleopatra's message to Caesar once she has been captured and imprisoned in her monument, already, so to speak, a monumentalized prisoner of Roman history—unless, of course, she can find a way out of it (V.ii.69). This is the point at which she turns, as Antony did when he heard of her feigned death, to sleep and dreaming as the precursors of death and vision—on his part, a place 'Where souls do couch on flowers', and on hers, 'nature's piece' beyond 'the size of dreaming': for Antony's plenitude—'his bounty', as she imaginatively recalls it—'There was no winter ... ; an autumn it was / That grew the more by reaping'.[54] Once again, imagination's forms touch Spenser's Garden, where male and female, life and death, spring and autumn, eternity and mortality converge. The biting of the asp, as the comic countryman will pertinently tell Cleopatra, is 'immortal', a pun in which we will hear again both death and desire and with them the bonding of earthly and unearthly meanings (V.ii.245–6). Caesarean domination, which is necessarily hierarchical, fails to encompass potency: as Jean-Luc Nancy has tellingly observed, 'The *imperium* is not the divine power of the pharaoh—and that is why in the end it will have divided up not so much the world as, on the contrary, the duality of world and heaven, the separation and the rivalry between two kingdoms with different forms of omnipotence'.[55]

---

[53] Cf. Cook: Antony's loss of ' "visible shape" ... follows from the nature of his desire and seems requisite for its consummation .... The annihilation of separateness comes to entail the annihilation of bodies' (259, IV.xiv.14). Cook's comment pertains to Antony's desire before his attempted suicide, but it applies ironically here as well. Cf. also Lisa S. Starks, ' "Immortal Longings": The Erotics of Death in *Antony and Cleopatra*', in Deats, ed., 243–58: 'The death of desire' becomes 'the ecstatic *desire of death*, a longing beyond the pleasure principle, a fusion of the destructive and regenerative forces of Thanatos and Eros' (245).

[54] IV.xiv.36, 52; V.ii.85–7, 96, 98. Carol Thomas Neely (*Broken Nuptials in Shakespeare's Plays* [1985; rpt. Urbana: University of Illinois Press, 1993], 160) characterizes the 'reciprocal opposites' of male and female sexuality in the complementary visions of Enobarbus (of Cleopatra) and Cleopatra (of Antony) in terms that resonate with Spenser's Garden: 'infinite variety and eternal bounty, magnetic power and hyperbolic fruitfulness, stasis and motion, art and nature'.

[55] *The Ground of the Image*, trans. Jeff Fort (New York: Fordham University Press, 2005), 133; see also 137: 'The conjunction of power and *jouissance* corresponds to the withdrawal of the sacred foundation of authority: in the pleasure of power and in the power of pleasure— the chiasmus of a double autotelos—is indicated an unfathomable double secret that no sacred certainty can resolve. ... neither sovereignty nor love owes

'I have immortal longings in me', Cleopatra declares emphatically at the outset of her final speeches, which are punctuated by Iras' death and Charmian's choric responses (V.ii.280). While Cleopatra does not bungle her suicide, the interlude of Iras' sudden, unexpected expiration momentarily threatens the majesty of her performance, yet Cleopatra's spontaneous rescripting only enforces the easy, comic, natural nearness of life and death: 'If she first meet the curled Antony, / He'll ... spend that kiss / Which is my heaven to have' (V.ii.300–2). If this Cleopatra is newly ennobled, she is also familiar, comically human, and credibly continuous with her past—her passion to possess, however grand, little different from a milk maid's (IV.xv.77–9).

Cleopatra's words in these final speeches repeatedly imply the convergence of sex and death, recalling Antony's words when he, too, was resolving on suicide: 'Husband, I come!'; 'The stroke of death is as a lover's pinch / Which hurts and is desired'; 'As sweet as balm, as soft as air, as gentle— / O Antony!—Nay, I will take thee too'.[56] The last two lines might even seem to gesture toward an idyllic place where lovers couch on flowers. Cleopatra's maternal image of the deadly asp likewise belongs to the matrix of generation and death—'Dost thou not see my baby at my breast / That sucks the nurse asleep?' (V.ii.308–9). The phrase 'sucks the nurse asleep' can be read as 'sucks to sleep' and as 'sucks the nurse sleeping', either option making death gently and naturally, but only because also figuratively and creatively, continuous with life. Yet the baby's sucking the nurse sleeping is not so far removed from Acrasia's sucking Verdant's 'spright' as to cancel a momently glimpsed negative nuance, the acknowledged possibility of an insidiously deadly draining of vital forces, another realistic intonation contributing to Cleopatra's final accomplishment.

The maternal and the phallic further combine in Cleopatra's image of the sharp-toothed serpent, itself an attribute of the Goddess Isis keyed already to myth. Dressed ceremonially as Isis, Cleopatra, Antony's 'serpent of old Nile', figures the goddess identified by Plutarch as generation and mother of the world, whose moon-like nature is 'both male and female, as she is receptive and made pregnant by the Sun, ... [while] she herself in turn emits and disseminates into the air generative principles' (I.v.26).[57] Once again we are imaginatively and

---

anything to anyone or to anything other than itself, and this unparalleled sufficiency is also their extraordinary fragility. They are, each of them, what they are only inasmuch as they renounce their own ground and therefore are capable, ultimately, of renouncing themselves'. Nancy's essay treats images of Cleopatra, including Shakespeare's.

[56] V.ii.286, 294–5, 310–11.

[57] Plutarch, 'Marcus Antonius', 291: 'she did not onely weare at that time (but at all other [public] times els ...) the apparell of the goddesse Isis'. For the quotation about Isis' double nature, see Plutarch, *Moralia*, trans. Frank Cole Babbitt (1936; rpt. Cambridge, MA: Harvard University Press, 2003), V, 105 (368.43D). Bono, *Literary Transvaluation*,

conceptually very close to the Garden of Adonis.

Cleopatra, like Antony, is 'noble' in act at the end and perhaps finally truer than he to the old, '*high* Roman fashion'. More than he at the end, she is also 'marble-constant'—a phrase gendered stiffly, monumentally male, for she has 'nothing / Of woman' in her. Even here, however, the pun on 'nothing' is inescapably present—simultaneously a denial of female nature as inconstancy and a reassertion of its genital sexuality—as her climactic performance crosses the limits of sex and gender, together with those of life and death and myth and mortality.[58] Imaginatively, she meets not only Antony, but also the Venus and Adonis of Spenser's Garden.

202, and Kiernan, 177, also refer to this passage.

[58] IV.xv.90–1 (my emphasis), V.ii.237–9, 284. Berry (6, 17–18, 155) finds other sexual references and exquisite puns in Cleopatra's urging the asp to untie 'this knot intrinsicate' (V.ii.303) and, after Cleopatra's death, in Octavius' observation that she would 'catch another Antony / In her strong toil of grace'—that is, the grease of carnival pleasures, those genital in particular (ii.346–7)—and finally in other Romans' noting the 'vent of blood, and something blown' and the aspic's slimy trail in the scene of Cleopatra's suicide (ii.347–52). While assenting to these, I consider them less focal than the familiar pun on 'nothing'.

Spenser and Shakespeare: Polarized Approaches to Psychology, Poetics, and Patronage

Robert L. Reid

Long ago Arthur Kirsch warned me not to compare Spenser and Shakespeare—'apples and oranges'—their world-views not fluidly complementary but mutually exclusive. The fictions, genres, and aesthetic modalities of these preeminent English Renaissance poets exemplify distinct conceptions of human nature. Though many scholars still assume a single Renaissance psychology, one that privileges Aristotelian empiricism and Aristotelian structuring of faculties (often with the express goal of explaining Shakespeare's plays), we must cast the net elsewhere to reap the allegory of *The Faerie Queene*, for only a Christianized Platonic psychology that subordinates Aristotelian features can make sense of the three-part hierarchic pattern which informs Spenser's allegory, notably in Books 1 and 2: three rising phases of education in the House of Holiness and in Alma's Castle, which match the three progressive stages of temptation in Mammon's Cave and in the Bower of Bliss; the characters grouped in hierarchic triads (Redcrosse-Una-dwarf, Orgoglio-Duessa-monster, Mortdant-Amavia-Ruddymane, Artegall-Britomart-Talus, Eden's warriors-maidens-commoners).[1] Spenser depicts human

---

My thanks to those who helped shape this essay: J. B. Lethbridge, Ronald Horton, and members of the 2006 SAA 'Shakespeare-Spenser' seminar, especially Catherine Canino, Katherine Eggert, Kristen Olson, and Rachel Hile.

[1] On Spenser's subordinating Aristotelianism to Christian Platonism in his scheme of human nature, see Robert L. Reid, 'psychology, Platonic', in *The Spenser Encyclopedia*, ed. A. C. Hamilton et al. (Toronto: University of Toronto Press, 1990) [hereafter *SpEncy*]. Cf. Reid, 'Spenserian Psychology and the Structure of Allegory in Books 1 and 2 of *The Faerie Queene*', *Modern Philology*, 79 (1982), 359–75; 'Man, Woman, Child or Servant: Family Hierarchy as a Figure of Tripartite Psychology in *The Faerie Queene*', *Studies in Philology*, 78 (1981), 370–90; 'Alma's Castle and the Symbolization of Reason in *The Faerie Queene*', *Journal of English and Germanic Philology*, 80 (1981), 512–27. Herschel Baker in *The Image of Man* (New York: Barnes and Noble, 1952; orig. *The Dignity of Man*, Harvard University Press, 1947) is almost alone in surveying diverse sources of Renaissance psychology. On Spenser's use of Aristotle's ethics, especially via Aquinas, see W. F. DeMoss, *The Influence of Aristotle's 'Politics' and 'Ethics' on Spenser* (Chicago, IL: University of Chicago Press, 1920); Ernest Sirluck, '*The Faerie Queene*, Book II, and the *Nicomachean Ethics*', *Modern Philology*, 49 (1951), 73–100; Gerald Morgan, 'Spenser's Conception of Courtesy and the Design of the *Faerie Queene*', *Review of English Studies*, ns 32 (1981), 17–36; 'Holiness as the First of Spenser's Aristotelian Moral Virtues', *Modern Language Review*, 81 (1986), 817–37; 'The Idea of Temperance in the Second Book of *The Faerie Queene*', *Review of English Studies*, ns 37 (1986), 11–39; ' "Add faith vnto your force": The Perfecting of Spenser's Knight of Holiness in Faith and Humility', *Renaissance Studies*, 18 (2004), 449–74; and 'Aquinas in

identity in fixed visual iconic intellectualized epiphanies, grouped in thematic categories that sum up the literary-moral-religious authority of the past. In striking contrast, Shakespeare portrays human identity as ever-evolving in an immediate, protean, theatrical world of present experience, shaped in passional cycles around moments of self-discovery.[2]

A similar distinction between intellectual and emotional modes of epiphany is explored by Camille Paglia, who in *Sexual Personae* describes Spenser as Apollonian and Shakespeare as Dionysian,[3] a division that roughly resembles how contemporaries matched them with the most admired antique poets. Many English Renaissance literati agree that 'learned Spenser' is the 'English Virgil' (e.g., Nashe, Florio, Churchyard, Barnfield, Covell, Meres, Speght, Peacham, Daniel, Lodge, Fitzgeffrey, Harrington, Burton), and Watson is one of many who associate Spenser with Apollo, who 'Amongst the Muses hath a chiefest place' (20).[4] Shakespeare, on the other hand, is the 'English Ovid', whose pas-

---

SpEncy; Ronald A. Horton, 'Aristotle and his commentators', *SpEncy*.

Playing against my view of Spenser's Christianized Platonic hierarchy of human nature, which subordinated woman as passional heart to man as rational head, is the important work of Linda Gregerson and James Broaddus, exploring in Britomart's quest a movement toward a more egalitarian psychology of gender: see n62 below.

[2] See Robert L. Reid, *Shakespeare's Tragic Form* (Newark, NJ: University of Delaware Press, 2000), chap. 1: 'The Dramaturgical and Psychological Structure of Shakespeare's Plays'.

[3] Paglia, *Sexual Personae: Art and Decadence from Nefertiti to Emily Dickinson* (New Haven, CT: Yale University Press, 1991), chap. 6–7; 'The Apollonian Androgyne and *The Faerie Queene*', *ELR*, 9 (1979), 42–63; cf. Grace Tiffany, 'Shakespeare's Dionysian Prince: Drama, Politics, and the "Athenian" History Play', *Renaissance Quarterly*, 52 (1999), 366–83. For a different view of Paglia's overly simplistic dichotomy between Spenser and Shakespeare, see Judith Anderson's paper in the present volume.

[4] Thomas Watson, *An Eglogue Upon the Death of the Right Honorable Sir Francis Walsingham* (London, 1590), Sigs. C3v-C4, in *Spenser Allusions in the Sixteenth and Seventeenth Centuries*, ed. W. Wells (Chapel Hill: University of North Carolina Press, 1972). Contemporary literati matched Spenser with Homer (21, 28, 29, 48, 60, 116, 136) and Petrarch (19, 21, 29, 41) but mostly Vergil (28–9, 41, 48, 60, 62, 70, 85, 94, 112, 113, 116, 136). Like Watson, many allied Spenser with Apollo (20, 21, 34, 70, 145).

On the 'Vergilian career trajectory' as Spenser's model, building on important studies of Richard Helgerson, David A. Miller, William A. Oram, Richard Rambuss, and Joseph Loewenstein, see Patrick Cheney, *Spenser's Famous Flight: A Renaissance Idea of a Literary Career* (Toronto: University of Toronto Press, 1993), and M. L. Donnelly, 'The Life of Vergil and the Aspirations of the "New Poet"', *Spenser Studies*, 17 (2003), 1–35. Also, Merrit Y. Hughes, *Virgil and Spenser* (Berkeley: University of California Press, 1929); W. S. Webb, 'Vergil in Spenser's Epic Theory', *ELH*, 4 (1937), 62–84; James Nohrnberg, *The Analogy of 'The Faerie Queene'* [hereafter *Analogy*] (Princeton, NJ: Princeton University Press, 1976), 29–35 and passim; Michael O'Connell, *Mirror and Veil: The Historical Dimension of Spenser's 'The Faerie Queene'* (Chapel Hill: University of North Carolina Press, 1977), 4–7, 10–11, 23–40, 71, 76–8, 83, 90, 95, 101–3, 108, 120, 126, 141, 149, 175; Michael Murrin, *The Allegorical Epic: Essays in Its Rise and Decline* (Chicago, IL: University of Chicago Press, 1980), 3–25, 131–52; Andrew Fichter, *Poets Historical: Dynastic Epic in the Renaissance* (New Haven, CT: Yale University Press, 1982), 1–39, 156–206; William J. Kennedy, 'Virgil', *SpEncy*. Despite his central emulation of Vergil's moral rectitude, laureate artistry, and

sional metamorphoses celebrate Dionysus's power: 'the sweete wittie soule of *Ovid*', says Meres, 'lives in mellifluous & hony-tongued *Shakespeare*'.[5]

Each poet, of course, explores both rational and affective modes, but they privilege opposite poles. Shakespeare favors Antony's revelling, generous spirit over Octavius's prudent Apollonian control; Spenser, though sympathetic to both Belphoebe and Amoret, (both Diana and Venus, both chaste Britomart and Book 4's friendly knights) always prioritizes the 'hard' virtue.[6] Though both poets draw heavily on Ovid,

---

nationalist heroic image, Spenser no less than Dante indicates Vergil's limitations. For example, Duessa carrying Sansjoy's body to be sustained by Aesculapius in eternal joylessness parodies Aeneas's descent into Avernus. See A. C. Hamilton, *The Structure of Allegory in 'The Faerie Queene'* (Oxford: Clarendon Press, 1961), 70; Darryl J. Gless, *Interpretation and Theology in Spenser* (Cambridge: Cambridge University Press, 1994), 101–4; and Syrithe Pugh, n7 below.

On Shakespeare's resisting and curtly 'translating' Vergil, see Heather James, *Shakespeare's Troy: Drama, Politics, and the Translation of Empire* (Cambridge: Cambridge University Press, 1997), 119–50. See n49 below for studies of Shakespeare's fuller integration of 'sad' Vergil in *The Tempest*—though with lingering resistance (see James, *Shakespeare's Troy*: 'How Came That Dido in?').

For Ovid's influence on Shakespeare, see L. P. Wilkinson, *Ovid Recalled* (Cambridge: Cambridge University Press, 1955), 406–23; Douglas Bush, *Mythology and the Renaissance Tradition in English Poetry* (Minneapolis: University of Minnesota Press, 1932); rev. ed. 1964), chaps 4, 5, 7; William Carroll, *The Metamorphoses of Shakespeare's Comedy* (Princeton, NJ: Princeton University Press, 1985); Leonard Barkan, *The Gods Made Flesh: Metamorphosis and the Pursuit of Paganism* (New Haven, CT: Yale University Press, 1986), 243–88; A. D. Nuttall, 'Ovid's Narcissus and Shakespeare's Richard II: the reflected self', in *Ovid Renewed: Ovidian Influences on Literature and Art from the Middle Ages to the Twentieth Century*, ed. Charles Martindale (Cambridge: Cambridge University Press, 1988), 137–50; Elizabeth Truax, *Metamorphosis in Shakespeare's Plays: A Pageant of Heroes, Gods, Maids and Monsters* (Lewiston, NY: Edwin Mellen, 1992); Jonathan Bate, *Shakespeare and Ovid* (Oxford: Clarendon Press, 1993); M. L. Stapleton, *Harmful Eloquence: Ovid's 'Amores' from Antiquity to Shakespeare* (Ann Arbor: University of Michigan Press, 1996), 134 ff; *Shakespeare's Ovid: The Metamorphoses in the Plays*, ed. A. B. Taylor (Cambridge: Cambridge University Press, 2000); Lynn Enterline, *Rhetoric of the Body from Ovid to Shakespeare* (Cambridge: Cambridge University Press, 2000). On Spenser and Ovid, see n7 below.

[5] Francis Meres, *Palladis Tamia* (London, 1598), in A. Bruce Black and Robert Metcalf Smith, *Shakespeare Allusions and Parallels*, 2 vols. (Bethlehem, PA: Lehigh University Press, 1931).

[6] I do not minimize Spenser's attention to passion, central to Books 3 and 4, and crucial throughout the epic. Uncontrolled it distracts each knight, makes Britomart intensely ill, leaves a knife in the heart of Amavia and Amoret, but controlled brings fruitful union. In contrast to Shakespeare, however, Spenser seeks to contain passion in rigorously prudent intellectual order. On *The Faerie Queene*'s ethical and theological design, see A. S. P. Woodhouse, 'Nature and Grace in *The Faerie Queene*', *ELH*, 16 (1949), 194–228; Harry Berger, Jr., 'A Secret Discipline: *The Faerie Queene* Book VI' (1961), in *Revisionary Play* (Berkeley: University of California Press, 1988), 215–42; A. C. Hamilton, *The Structure of Allegory in 'The Faerie Queene'* (Oxford: Clarendon Press, 1961), chap. 3: 'The Architectonike of the Poem', 89–123; Donald Cheney, *Spenser's Image of Nature* (New Haven, CT: Yale University Press, 1966), 1–17; *'Eterne in Mutabilitie': The Unity of 'The Faerie Queene'*, ed. Kenneth John Atchity (Hamden: Archon Books, 1972); Judith Anderson, *The Growth of a Personal Voice: 'Piers Plowman' and 'The Faerie Queene'* (New Haven, CT: Yale Uni-

Spenser's strategy is containment: his chaste heroine is not seduced (just lightly wounded) by Malecasta's and Busyrane's erotic tapestries; and Spenser further contains Ovid-Bacchus by means of Neoplatonic and Christian allegory, as in the Garden of Adonis, where doctrinal logic channels passion, metamorphosis, and Mutability. Spenser does not, like Shakespeare, emphasize Adonis's *sensory being* and his *experiential passions* (though these elements are keenly evoked by implication) but rather Adonis's *intellectual function* and his *Godlike essence*: he is 'the Father of all formes' (*FQ*, III.vi.47).[7]

Paglia's use of Nietzsche's polarity is, however, simplistic—inattentive to the peculiar Christian-Classical synthesis in each poet's work. One desires a more comprehensive scheme for understanding their difference and their interplay. In *Modes of Being* Paul Weiss subsumes Nietzsche's duality in a four-fold ontology—Actuality, Ideality, Existence, and God[8]—a division which matches Aristotle's four causes, Blake's four zoas, Jung's four psychic types. The first two, Actuality and Ideality, assume transcendent form in the latter two, Existence and God. Shakespeare's art favors Actuality and Existence (material and efficient causes, Urthona and Luvah, Instinct and Emotion—*sensory being* and *experiential passions*), while Spenser favors Ideality and God (formal and

---

versity Press, 1976), comparing Spenser's three pairs of legends to stages of Piers' *visio* to disclose intellectual and theological dimensions of both poetic 'summas'; Nohrnberg, *Analogy*, 35–6, 58, 71–86, 655–733, 777–91; Ronald Arthur Horton, *The Unity of 'The Faerie Queene'* (Athens: University of Georgia Press, 1978); Gerald Morgan, n1 above; Darryl J. Gless, 'nature and grace', *SpEncy*; Sean Kane, *Spenser's Moral Allegory* (Toronto: University of Toronto Press, 1989), 3–30, 211–25.

[7] Quotations of *The Faerie Queene* are taken from A. C. Hamilton's edition (London: Longman, 1977). Hamilton surveys critical debate over this crucial line. On Spenser's containing Ovidian mutability in Neoplatonic and Christian allegory, see D. C. Allen, *Mysteriously Meant: The Rediscovery of Pagan Symbolism and Allegorical Interpretation in the Renaissance* (Baltimore: Johns Hopkins University Press, 1970), chaps 7–10; Nohrnberg, *Analogy*, 84–5, 141–3, 427–651; Michael Holahan, '*Iamque opus exegi*: Ovid's Changes and Spenser's Brief Epic of Mutability', *ELR*, 6 (1976), 244–70; Daniel Javitch, 'Rescuing Ovid from the Allegorizers', *Comparative Literature*, 30 (1978), 97–107; Barkan, *The Gods Made Flesh*, chap. 6: 'Fusions: Platonism and Spenser', 231–42; Colin Burrow, 'Original Fictions: Metamorphoses in *The Faerie Queene*', in *Ovid Renewed*, 99–119; Burrow 'Spenser and Classical Traditions', in *The Cambridge Companion to Spenser*, ed. Andrew Hadfield (Cambridge: Cambridge University Press, 2001), 217–36; Jon Quitslund, *Spenser's Supreme Fiction* (Toronto: University of Toronto Press, 2001), esp. chaps 4–7; in *SpEncy*: Supriya Chaudhuri, 'metamorphosis'; John Louis Lepage, 'mutability'; Holahan, 'Ovid'; Joan Larsen Klein, 'Bacchus'; Michael Pincombe, 'The Ovidian Hermaphrodite: Moralizations by Peend and Spenser', in *Ovid and the Renaissance Body*, ed. Goran V. Stanivukovic (Toronto: University of Toronto Press, 2001), 155–70; Heather James, 'Ovid and the Question of Politics in Early Modern England', in *Images of Matter: Essays on British Literature of the Middle Ages and Renaissance*, ed. Yvonne Bruce (Newark, NJ: University of Delaware Press, 2005), 92–122; Syrithe Pugh, *Spenser and Ovid* (Aldershot: Ashgate, 2005), a valuable study that overstates Spenser's identifying with exiled Ovid more than with Vergil's prudent support of empire.

[8] Paul Weiss, *Modes of Being* (Carbondale: Southern Illinois University Press, 1958).

final causes, Urizen and Tharmas, Reason and Intuition—*intellectual function* and *Godlike essence*).[9] Spenser's emphasis of intellect and conscience (the latter a mythic intuition of divinity) is evident in *The Faerie Queene*'s vast systematic foreconceit that thematically and teleologically defines and places each fiction in relation to all others. This *architectonike* structures the poem—and each character-grouping and sequence of events—by an absolute and ideal order: (a) the Platonic-Christian principle of tripartite hierarchy that informs humankind as an *imago Dei*, (b) the Empedoclean-Hippocratic-Aristotelean principle of antithesis and complementarity that shapes a quaternity of elements and of passional temperaments; (c) the packaging of storied language in a nine-line stanza, a twelve-canto legend, a twelve-legend epic; and (d) the mystic numerology that informs these orderings. In contrast to this overt intellectual shaping, Shakespeare conceals his dramaturgical structure—an intricate 2-1-2 sequence of acts, built upon expanding-and-contracting cycles of action and of relationship—that appear in careful reading but not in performance.[10]

Though each poet engages all four modes of being (the full range of causes, zoas, psychic types), they privilege contrary generic scenarios, contrary modes of psychic management. As we shall see, Spenser's art is universal and teleological: to understand each part we must intellectually ascertain the holistic end, synecdochally figured as a carefully-arranged iconic templar vision. In contrast, Shakespeare's art is particular and existential; though the end is always in doubt, characters (and audiences) are deeply engaged in each dynamic moment of the soul's naturally-unfolding, cyclic rhythm of emotive development. What we do not expect, however, is the profound degree to which Shakespeare's art was influenced by that of his laureate peer.

I. Envisioning Spenser's Plan

To create a definitive, authoritative form for each literary genre, Spenser plunders various cultural treasuries of story and myth. The progress of love in *Amoretti* and *Epithalamion* assumes universality as it builds a Christian-Platonic ladder of awareness and fulfils a calendrical cycle with epiphanies at high holy dates. The universality is enhanced, notably in *Epithalamion*, by a gorgeous lyricism that blends the riches

---

[9] The latter terms are transcendent versions of the former: Actuality becomes Existence, Ideality becomes God. Likewise, Instinct becomes Emotion, and Intellect becomes Intuition. And similarly, Material becomes Efficient Cause, as Formal becomes Final. In William Blake's epics, Tharmas should be the Godlike 'parent power' of intuition or conscience but is in fact the most disabled and formless zoa in the fallen world.

[10] See Reid, *Shakespeare's Tragic Form*, chap. 1.

of natural and social imagery with musical and metrical harmonies.[11] Spenser's most impressive use of this systematic and sacred art is *The Faerie Queene*, a *summa poetica* that teases us with only the first half of its ambitious design. Its comprehensiveness is suggested by (a) three pairs of virtues that descend through the three Christian-Platonic levels of human consciousness and (b) division of each pair into alternating conceptual modes: 'hard' and 'soft' virtues, briton and fairy protagonists, allegorical centers that disclose first a transcendent Judaeo-Christian revelation and then pagan deities that signify an immanent, less-fully-revealed spirit-power within nature.[12] This descent through the six wings of Ezekiel's cherub implies, subsequently, an inverse ascent.

A tragedy of modern criticism is the now-common view that *The Faerie Queene* is complete as it stands (a view ably summarized by A. C. Hamilton)[13]—ascribed to Spenser's realizing the original plan's tenuous relation to reality, or his discerning the metaphysical impossibility of closure. Some believe he intentionally narrowed his plan to six virtues, with the Mutability Cantos as coda: thus Justice ('Most sacred virtue she of all the rest, / Resembling God in his imperiall might', 5.Pr.10) and Courtesy ('Amongst them all growes not a fayrer flowre', spreading 'itself through all civilitie', 6.Pr.4) provide effective closure.[14] For

---

[11] See A. Kent Hieatt, *Short Time's Endless Monument: The Symbolism of the Numbers in Edmund Spenser's 'Epithalamion'* (New York: Columbia University Press, 1960); Alastair Fowler, *Spenser and the Numbers of Time* (London: Routledge & Kegan Paul, 1964); Fowler 'Numerical Composition in *The Faerie Queene*', *Journal of the Warburg and Courtauld Institutes*, 25 (1962), 199–239; Alexander Dunlop, 'The Unity of Spenser's *Amoretti*', in *Silent Poetry*, ed. Alastair Fowler (London: Routledge & Kegan Paul, 1970), 153–69; S. K. Heninger, Jr., *Touches of Sweet Harmony: Pythagorean Cosmology and Renaissance Poetics* (San Marino: Huntington Library, 1974), 351–7, 366–78, 388–93; Alexander Dunlop, 'The Drama of *Amoretti*', *Spenser Studies*, 1 (1980), 107–20; Carol V. Kaske, 'Spenser's *Amoretti* and *Epithalamion* of 1595: Structure, Genre, and Numerology', *ELR*, 8 (1978), 271–95; Maren-Sofie Røstvig, *Configurations* (Oslo, Copenhagen, Stockholm: Scandinavian University Press, 1990), 267–370; Røstvig, 'number symbolism, tradition of'; Alexander Dunlop, 'number symbolism, modern studies in', *SpEncy*.

[12] On Spenser's using pagan gods to figure Christian immanence, see Allen, *Mysteriously Meant*, chaps 1–2, 6–10; William J. Kennedy, 'Paynims', *SpEncy*; and n7 above. On the use of pagan gods to figure the prowess of Elizabeth and leading courtiers, see Paul F. Olson, 'A Midsummer Night's Dream and the Meaning of Court Marriage', *ELH*, 24 (1957), 95–119; Enid Welsford, *The Court Masque* (Cambridge: Cambridge University Press, 1927), 324–49; Allardyce Nicoll, *Stuart Masques and the Renaissance Stage* (London: George G. Harrap, 1937), 72–5, 177, 202–4; Stephen Orgel, *The Jonsonian Masque* (New York: Columbia University Press, 1967), 87–91; and in *SpEncy*: Thomas H. Cain, 'Elizabeth, images of'; William J. Kennedy, 'Diana'.

[13] Intro. to Book 6, *The Faerie Queene*, ed. Hamilton. I am obliged to Dr. Hamilton for generous response to my work and for guidance of modern research on Spenser, including *The Spenser Encyclopedia*, an invaluable aide.

[14] See Richard Neuse, 'Book Six as Conclusion of *The Faerie Queene*', *ELH*, 35 (1968), 329–53; Humphrey Tonkin, *Spenser's Courteous Pastoral: Book Six of 'The Faerie Queene'* (Oxford: Clarendon Press, 1972); Tonkin, 'The Faerie Queene, Book VI' in *SpEncy*; Su-

others, Spenser in despair abandoned his Vergilian laureate quest: the endless interruptions and failed closure of Book 6 show the Glorianadream succumbing to Mutability, as Elizabeth is unable to rectify Ireland, the court, and the patronage system, and as hopes fade for an adequate 'Arthur' to marry or to succeed her. For others, the 'endlesse worke' caused by historical mutability, human sin, and linguistic slippage make the completion of Spenser's allegory forever elusive.[15] As a result, few scholars join Tuve and Horton in aggressively seeking clues for the design of the final half.[16] Study of Classical and Medieval ethical systems indicates that 'Aristotle and the rest' were adapted to Spenser's own scheme, which subordinates Aristotle to Christian Platonism. But despite several superb foundational studies that give heavy attention to Platonism—Fowler's *Spenser and the Numbers of Time*, Nohrnberg's *The Analogy of 'The Faerie Queene'*, Quitslund's *Spenser's Supreme Fiction*— no one has discovered the structural principles for Spenser's 'twelve virtues'.[17]

---

sanne Woods, 'Closure in *The Faerie Queene*', *Journal of English and Germanic Philology*, 76 (1977), 195–216.

[15] In 'Spenser's Last Days: Ireland, Career, Mutability, Allegory', in *Edmund Spenser: New and Renewed Directions* (Madison: Fairleigh Dickinson University Press, 2006), 302– 36, J. B. Lethbridge concludes, 'Every bit of evidence we have suggests both that *The Faerie Queene* is not finished and that Spenser intended to go on with it' (303). Lethbridge's impressive analysis supports key ideas in my essay. Also on Book 6 as closure: Berger, 'Secret Discipline'; Sherry L. Reames, 'Prince Arthur and Spenser's Changing Design', in *'Eterne in Mutabilitie'*, ed. Atchity, 180–206; Nohrnberg, *Analogy*, 35–6, 58, 71– 86, 655–733, 777–91; David Lee Miller, 'Abandoning the Quest', *ELH*, 46 (1979), 173–92; Jonathan Goldberg, *Endlesse Worke: Spenser and the Structures of Discourse* (Baltimore: Johns Hopkins University Press, 1981), 1–30, 166–74; Jan Karel Kouwenhoven, *Apparent Narrative as Thematic Metaphor: The Organization of 'The Faerie Queene'* (Oxford: Clarendon Press, 1983), 1–71, 198; Stanley Stewart, 'Sir Calidore and "Closure"', *Studies in English Literature*, 24 (1984), 69–86; Balachandra Rajan, *The Form of the Unfinished: English Poetics from Spenser to Pound* (Princeton, NJ: Princeton University Press, 1985), 44–84; Rajan, 'closure' *SpEncy*; Richard McCabe, *The Pillars of Eternity: Time and Providence in 'The Faerie Queene'* (Dublin: Irish Academic Press, 1989), 15–54, 154–225; Paul A. Marquis, 'Problems of Closure in *The Faerie Queene*', *English Studies in Canada*, 16 (1990), 149–63; Maria R. Rohr Philmus, '*The Faerie Queene* and Renaissance Poetics: Another Look at Book VI as "Conclusion" to the Poem', *English Studies*, 76 (1995), 497–519; Michael F. N. Dixon, *The Polliticke Courtier: Spenser's 'The Faerie Queene' as a Rhetoric of Justice* (Montreal: McGill-Queen's University Press, 1996), chaps 7–9; Andrew Hadfield, ' "Who knowes not Colin Clout?" The Permanent Exile of Edmund Spenser', in *Politics and National Identity: Reformation to Renaissance* (Cambridge: Cambridge University Press, 1994), 170–201; Hadfield, *Edmund Spenser's Irish Experience: Wilde Fruit and Salvage Soyl* (Oxford: Clarendon Press, 1997), chaps 5–6.

[16] Rosamund Tuve, *Allegorical Imagery: Some Mediaeval Books and Their Posterity* (Princeton, NJ: Princeton University Press, 1966), 57–143; Horton, *The Unity of 'The Faerie Queene'*, 15–137, 177–84, and 'Virtues', *SpEncy*; Robert Cummings, 'Spenser's "Twelve Private Morall Virtues"', *Spenser Studies*, 8 (1990), 35–59.

[17] Fowler, *Spenser and the Numbers of Time*, 40–1, 51–9, 170n; Nohrnberg, *Analogy*, 35–6, 58, 71–86, 655–733, 777–91; Jon Quitslund, *Spenser's Supreme Fiction* (Toronto: University of Toronto Press, 2001), esp. 52–77, 133–83. On Spenser's Platonism, often without

Nor have critics fully assessed the implications of truncating the poem's grand foreconceit. First, as central protagonist, Arthur is incomplete. His receipt from Redcrosse of 'A booke, wherein his Saveours Testament / Was writt with golden letters rich and brave; / A worke of wondrous grace, and hable soules to save' (*FQ* I.ix.19), implies that Arthur, though wondrously empowered, is not yet fully Christian and, further, that he needs to be—needs deep refinement of his native gifts. He does not join Redcrosse in the rigorous enlightenment of the House of Holiness, though in Book 2 he does join Guyon in the tour and defense of Alma's Castle: thus in Books 1–6 Arthur knows himself *sub specie temporis*, but not *sub specie aeternitatis*.[18] Arthur's need for further enlightenment becomes acute in Book 6 (Cantos 5–8): his discomfiture at the shame of Timias and Serena, his astonishment at Turpine and Blandina's perfidy, his inability to rescue Mirabella from Disdaine. Arthur's confused ineffectiveness at the epic's midpoint duplicates the situation of Redcrosse and Una in Cantos 5 and 6 of Book 1, an impasse which suggests, not Spenser's despairing abandonment of the poetic quest, but preparation for Arthur's further growth.[19] Would he undergo

---

evaluating its alliance with Christian doctrine, see Alastair Fowler, 'Emanations of Glory: Neoplatonic Order in Spenser's *Faerie Queene*', in *A Theatre for Spenserians*, ed. Judith M. Kennedy and James M. Reither (Toronto: University of Toronto Press, 1973), 53–82; S. K. Heninger, Jr., *Touches of Sweet Harmony*, 351–7, 366–78, 388–93; David Burchmore, 'Triamond, Agape, and the Fates: Neoplatonic Cosmology in Spenser's Legend of Friendship', *Spenser Studies*, 5 (1984), 45–64, 273–87; Elizabeth Bieman, *Plato Baptized: Towards the Interpretation of Spenser's Mimetic Fictions* (Toronto: University of Toronto Press, 1988), 105–51, 212–43; Cummings, 'Spenser's "Twelve Private Morall Virtues"'. Cf. Roy W. Battenhouse, 'The Doctrine of Man in Calvin and in Renaissance Platonism', *Journal of the History of Ideas*, 9:4 (1948), 447–71.

[18] Arthur's partial engagement in Holiness contrasts with his full participation in Temperance (his tour and defense of Alma's Castle). As a Briton like Redcrosse rather than a fairy like Guyon, Arthur must receive fuller education and vision, but apparently not until the final half of the epic. On the complex and crucial issue of whether '*Arthurus est Christus*', see Tuve, *Allegorical Imagery*, 134–43; Anderson, *The Growth of a Personal Voice*, 159–84, esp. 160–2; Nohrnberg, *Analogy*, 35–58, 74–6, 85, 272–5, 317–31, passim; Gordon Teskey, 'Arthur in *The Faerie Queene*', *SpEncy*; Gless, *Interpretation and Theology*, 126–41. Kenneth Borris's compelling argument for the 'continued heroic allegorism' of Arthur's role in Book 6, with emphasis on 'Salvaging the State of Nature', reinforces our view that Courtesy is not the culminating virtue of *The Faerie Queene* but rather prepares for the nadir of the soul's 'dilation' or descent. See *Allegory and Epic in English Renaissance Literature: Heroic Form in Sidney, Spenser, and Milton* (Cambridge: Cambridge University Press, 2000), chaps 6 and 7.

[19] If Spenser had died after completing six cantos of Book I, one might argue that Redcross's defeat of Sansjoy in Canto 5 and Una's courteous civilizing of woodland creatures in Canto 6 form a suitable ending for 'Holiness'. Yet Redcrosse is dismayed by his inconclusive victory over Sansjoy (as the real-life Artegall knows the power behind the Souldan and Grantorto is still at large), dismayed by the House of Pride's false revels (as Artegall is dismayed by Envy and Detraction), and dismayed by 'huge nombers' of imprisoned 'wretched thralls' (I.v.45) (as unsettling as the legions slain by Talus): Holiness, at Canto 5, is as insecure as Justice in Book 5. In Canto 6 Una gains brief pastoral respite while struggling to enlighten pagan souls (as Pastorella inspires civility); but neither maiden

a humbling fall in Book 7, aid from other(s) in Book 8, rigorous enlightenment in Books 9–10 (escalating Book 2's tour/defense of the physical body), and confrontation of ever-grander foes who figure his deepest problems—in short, features comparable to the final half of Book 1?

Communion with Gloriana, the poem's titular subject and Arthur's goal, is equally unrealized. She is not just an Idea, an immaterial *visio*, but a potentially complex character who leaves vestigial traces ('pressed gras where she had lyne', *FQ*, I.ix.15) and achieves incarnation indirectly. Through her subsidiary types Gloriana encounters, like Arthur, increasing challenges in her own 'journey'—reflected negatively in Lucifera's vain self-mirroring and 'progress' but also positively in Una's 'errancy' (Book 1.ii–vi), in Belphoebe's errant relation with Timias (Books 3–4) and in Florimell's elusive flight, in Britomart's impassioned quest (which transfers to Gloriana a remarkable characterological complexity, Books 3–5), in Mercilla's quandary over costly wars and executing 'Duessa', and in the frustrated pastoral of Book 6, where Elizabeth is explicitly omitted from the vision on Acidale.[20] Instead of diminishing her allure, these growing restraints should set the stage for Elizabeth's own anagnorisis and gradual triumph over the enormous challenges to moral integrity which she faced throughout her reign.

Equally incomplete is Spenser's plan for the twelve-fold virtues of perfect gentility. The missing cardinal virtues—*Courage, Prudence*—could (like Temperance and Justice) occupy the center of each remaining triad of legends. The highest virtues of the perfect courtier—*Liberality, Magnificence, Magnanimity*—drawn from Aristotle and Cicero but refined by Platonic and Christian principles, could expand and perfectly contextualize the meaning of Courtesy (which, like Courage and Justice, depends on Magnificence).[21] Similar escalation of moral contexts could build Temperance into *Patience* (elaborating the house of Holiness's first stage of training), Chastity into *Charity* (elaborating the house of Holiness's second stage), Justice into *Sapience* (elaborat-

---

has at this point fulfilled a quest; each is disheveled by threats of rape and slander, despite the efforts of Satyrane and Calidore. One must not underestimate the achievement of Books 5 and 6, but neither Mercilla's Court nor Colin's Acidale vision resolves these dreadful problems. Justice and Courtesy can be secured only if reinforced by additional virtues—all integrated to form a perfect ring of twelve.

[20] On Elizabeth I's elusiveness and omission from Acidale, see Elizabeth J. Bellamy, 'The Vocative and the Vocational: The Unreadability of Elizabeth in *The Faerie Queene*', *ELH*, 54 (1987), 1–30; Marshall Grossman, *The Story of All Things: Writing the Self in English Renaissance Narrative Poetry* (Durham and London: Duke University Press, 1998), 126–37; Katherine Eggert, *Showing like a Queen: Female Authority and Literary Experiment in Spenser, Shakespeare, and Milton* (Philadelphia: University of Pennsylvania Press, 2000), 47–8, 217.

[21] Roger Kuin, 'The Double Helix: Private and Public in *The Faerie Queene*', *Spenser Studies*, 16 (2002), 1–22, says a Legend of Courage 'would go well in the middle of the third triad', but he rejects a Legend of Prudence for Book 11 (14–15). On magnificence as source of courtesy, courage, and justice, see *Speculum morale*, I.53–4; Hugh MacLachlan and Philip B. Rollinson, 'magnanimity, magnificence', *SpEncy*; and n59 below.

ing the house of Holiness's final stage): such additions would refine Arthur's character and elicit Gloriana's fuller presence. To encourage Arthur, the Palmer notes Gloriana's honoring of Sophy and Arthegall (II.ix.6), implying that Temperance and Magnificence will ally with Justice and Sapience.[22] This dialogue of Guyon, Arthur, and the Palmer before touring the 'House of Temperance' (II.ix.1–8) closely parallels that of Redcrosse, Arthur, and Una before the House of Holiness (I.ix.1–19): both focus on Arthur's search for Gloriana, the quest for glory that unites the 'goodly golden chayne' of virtues (I.ix.1). But we note distinctions between the two episodes: Redcrosse's nearly fatal distraction by Despair has no adequate counterpart in the parallel sequence of Book 2; and Una's rescue (and guidance to further training) far exceeds the Palmer's counsel. The holistic allegorical scope of Holiness systematically shrinks in subsequent legends—yet becomes pragmatically relevant to everyday life—as they descend ever deeper into material reality, a descent incorporating mind and spirit in actuality before re-ascending to fullest apprehension. This 'dilation' merits close study.[23]

Compared with Book 1, the allegory of Book 6 is oddly constrictive: Redcrosse's dreadful fall (his wretched bondage after disarmed dalliance with Duessa) shrinks to Calidore's ambivalent truancy with Pastorella; Arthur's heaven-assisted redeeming of Redcrosse from Orgoglio shrinks to Arthur's puzzled inability to rescue Mirabella from

---

[22] 'Sophy' as 'sophia' (sapience) or 'sophrosyne' (prudence) could be the eleventh virtue (central to the final triad), prior to the conclusive Magnificence/Magnanimity that completes Arthur's quest, congregating and integrating the twelve virtues. For a connection between prudence and sophia in *The Faerie Queene*, see Judith H. Anderson, 'Prudence and Her Silence: Spenser's Use of Chaucer's Melibee', *ELH*, 62 (1995), 29–46. On the Platonizing and Christianizing of prudence, see Helen North, *Sophrosyne: Self-Knowledge and Self-Restraint in Greek Literature* (Ithaca, NY: Cornell University Press, 1966), 1–31, 150–96, 312–86.

[23] Several critics have ingeniously explained Spenserian dilation ('by their change their being doe dilate: / And turning to themselves at length againe, / Doe worke their owne perfection', *FQ*, VII.vii.58), notably Nohrnberg, *Analogy*, 76–86, 325n, 729, 737–60; and Patricia A. Parker, *Inescapable Romance: Studies in the Poetics of a Mode* (Princeton, NJ: Princeton University Press, 1979), 54–63, passim. But no one has adequately explained the eventual *reversal of dilation* (whereby creatures 'turning to themselves againe' can 'worke their owne perfection'). Nohrnberg (*Analogy*, 655–733) envisions an abbreviated recovery, with Books 1 to 6 as a parabola: instead of three pairs of legends, he links Books 1 and 6, Books 2 and 5, Books 3 and 4.

If, however, Books 1 to 6 trace a continuous descent into fleshly temporality, then Books 7 to 12 would show the soul's inverse ascent through three pairs of polarized quests to renewed contact with spiritual purity and unity. That recovery is perhaps adumbrated by the incarnational events that consummate the three stages of training in the house of Holiness: in each, the soul imitates Christ by *accepting incarnation* and thereby *suffering passion* as a means of *union with God who is Love*: Fidelia's teaching ends in mortifying one's own bodily desires, Charissa's lesson ends in tending to others' afflictions through the life-cycle, Contemplation's vision of heaven ends in combating the Dragon of the false self (and accepting repeated self-mortifications) in order to redeem the Edenic body. See Robert L. Reid, 'holiness, house of' in *SpEncy*.

the similar but less-comprehensive giant Disdain;[24] Redcrosse's rigorous training in faith, charity, and contemplation shrinks to a simple blossoming of Calidore's innate gifts in the pastoral; Redcrosse's slaying the great Dragon, the abusive collective power of sin, shrinks to Calidore's briefly muzzling a bleating beast of discourteous backbiting. Within the purview of the Vergilian epic pattern and, more important, the Christian-Platonic allegorizing of that pattern, the action of Book 6 is the opposite of closure.

If Book 1 offers a microcosmic pattern for *The Faerie Queene*'s overall development, then the bitter aftertaste of Book 5 (Duessa's execution, Burbon's fickle ingratitude, the implicit persistence of England's political foes, Envy and Detraction's assault) resembles Redcrosse's post-victory dilemma in Book 1, Canto 5 (the illusory defeat of Sansjoy and his own residual joylessness);[25] and Book 6's inconclusive allegory similarly replays and elaborates the pastoral, half-pagan events of I.vi (Una's failure to enlighten fauns and satyrs, the impasse of Satyrane battling Sansloy). One must wonder if the heroes of Books 7–12 (after the insecure victories of Books 2–6) would be tested by foes of clearer, more comprehensive monstrosity (as the Sans-boys gave way to Orgoglio, Despair, and the Dragon). Would the protagonists of the final legends relate more fully to Gloriana's subtypes, and would Elizabeth realize fuller selfhood and destiny through those new mirrorings?[26] The disturbing quality of Books 5 and 6 (the poignancy of a literal sensory realm that prepares for the epic's nadir and peripety in the Legend of Constancy)[27] makes us yearn to see the challenges and revelations of the poem's second half, the missing chancel, choir, and rose window of this awesome literary cathedral.

---

[24] On Mirabella's endless penalty, see Tonkin, *Spenser's Courteous Pastoral*, 87–100, 204–5, 223–37; Anne Shaver, 'Rereading Mirabella', *Spenser Studies*, 9 (1991), 211–26.

[25] See Richard Mallette, 'Book Five of *The Faerie Queene*: An Elizabethan Apocalypse', *Spenser Studies*, 11 (1994), 129–59.

[26] On Gloriana, not Elizabeth I, as the essential subject of Spenser's epic, see Jeffrey P. Fruen, ' "True Glorious Type": The Place of Gloriana in *The Faerie Queene*', *Spenser Studies*, 7 (1987), 147–73; 'The Faery Queen Unveiled? Five Glimpses of Gloriana', *Spenser Studies*, 11 (1994), 53–88. Cf. Nohrnberg, *Analogy*, 40–60, 52–3 nn133–5; W. H. Herendeen, 'Gloriana', *SpEncy*.

[27] Books 5 and 6 represent a descent into material-historical-personal reality, presaging a temporary impasse in Book 7 (corresponding to captivity by carnal pride in I.vii). The quest for Constancy veils a Christian-Platonic anxiety over the impact on the soul of fleshly mutability—an anxiety Spenser voices with increasing urgency. In the literal-personal perspective of Justice and Courtesy, the antagonists are objectified as 'other', rather than as mirrors of the hero's own inner darkness, as in Book 1. On this problematic mirroring, contributing to the Spenserian hero's inconclusive quest, see Douglas A. Northrop, 'The Uncertainty of Courtesy in Book VI of *The Faerie Queene*', *Spenser Studies*, 14 (2000), 215–32; William A. Oram, 'Spenserian Paralysis', *Studies in English Literature*, 41 (2001), 49–70.

II. Shakespeare's Riposte

Spenser's grandiose intellectual epic, a vast moral and mythic tribute to Elizabeth and her aristocratic circle, posed an obstacle and challenge to Shakespeare's goals. In 1595–1596, as the English court awaited the second installment of Spenser's epic, Shakespeare in *A Midsummer Night's Dream* reduced Spenser's central trope to hilarious comedy: Gloriana's recondite mystery and virginal discreteness is displaced by the bodily-present emotional allure, the charismatic vanity, of Titania (titan-née), whose mating with ass-headed Bottom humorously reifies Elizabeth's claim to be married to *all* her people.[28] This brilliant rejoinder to Spenser's fairy queen must in part result from Shakespeare's reading of Book 1's most puzzling episode, Una's sojourn with satyrs and fauns. Spenser provocatively exposes Una (the holiest subtype of Gloriana) to the Ovidian-Dionysian energies that so attracted Shakespeare: 'old Sylvanus [...] wonders what them makes so glad, / Or Bacchus merry fruit they did invent, / Or Cybeles franticke rites have made them mad' (I.vi.15). In its richly sensual and mythic allure the episode recalls the seductive entertainments for the Virgin Queen in her early reign, such as Leicester's pageant at Kenilworth (which Shakespeare's Oberon wistfully recalls: *MND*, 2.1.148–64). But the resistance to theological truth by these 'salvage people', their distracted focus on immediate sensory things, suggests the energetic popular response of commoners to Elizabeth's mystique, a popular appeal that especially rivals Shakespeare's artistic interests. The stanza that must have toppled Shakespeare from his seat with laughter concerns Una's effort to Christianize these pagan/rustic creatures.

> [She] long time with that salvage people stayd, [...]
> During which time her gentle wit she plyes,
> To teach them truth, which worshipt her in vaine,
> And made her th' image of idolatryes;
> But when their bootlesse zeale she did restrayne
> From her own worship, they her asse would worship fayn.
> (I.vi.19)

Once while teaching this episode I noted that, instead of listening to Una's 'truth', the satyrs *worshipped her ass*. The resulting storm of hilarity was so vehement and unending, as my face reddened and authority vanished, that I dismissed the class. Since most of my lusty rustic-satyr students had not read the text, it was with great freshness

---

[28] See James P. Bednarz, 'Imitations of Spenser in *A Midsummer Night's Dream*', *Renaissance Drama*, 14 (1983), 79–102; Robert L. Reid, 'The Fairy Queen: Gloriana or Titania?', *The Upstart Crow*, 13 (1993), 16–32; Matthew Woodcock, *Fairy in 'The Faerie Queene': Renaissance Elf-Fashioning and Elizabethan Myth-Making* (Aldershot: Ashgate, 2004), 88–140.

that they caught both the pun[29] and my pedantic stupidity in stumbling into it. Perhaps it was these lines—indeed the whole episode of taming lavish Bacchic energies (Spenser parading an arsenal of legendary erotica to prove Una-Gloriana-Elizabeth's chaste 'truth')—that helped to inspire *A Midsummer Night's Dream*. Shakespeare reverses the loaded pun: the fairy queen (Una's parodic type) worships the ass!—but now it is the complexly subversive ass of Erasmus and Apuleius, consummately ignorant and implicitly priapic.[30] If Spenser is aware of the vulgar subtext, he treats it with masterful Apollonian-Christian aplomb: only the unthinking lewdness of satyrs can subvert the meaning of the lowly ass ridden to the Crucifixion, or the patristic allegory of humble clergy carrying the Word to the people.[31] Shakespeare, however, exploits the satyrs' mistake, stripping the ass of sacred allegory to reclothe it in allegory of a different sort, transforming it from a basis for holiness to base foolishness—'Bottom'—utterly self-delighted, eager to play all human roles and gain universal admiration, and ingenuously

---

[29] For Elizabethans, the pun yokes the holy biblical ass with the foolish ass of Erasmus, *In Praise of Folly*, and the priapic one in Apuleius, *The Golden Ass*, trans. William Adlington (London, 1566). According to the OED ('ass', I.1a, 1b, 'bottom', I.1b), Elizabethans did not yet know the lewder puns: ass (or bottom) = arse. If, however, this vulgar pun was available, Shakespeare seems more likely than Spenser to have exploited it, and in Bottom to have made an emblem of it.

[30] See J. J. M. Tobin, *Shakespeare's Favorite Novel: A Study of 'The Golden Asse' as Prime Source* (Lanham, MD: University Press of America, 1984); Tobin, 'Apuleius' *SpEncy*.

[31] See John M. Steadman, 'Una and the Clergy: The Ass Symbol in *The Faerie Queene*', *Journal of the Warburg and Courtauld Institutes*, 21 (1958), 134–7; Nohrnberg, *Analogy*, 207–22, 237–8; Douglas Brooks-Davies, 'Una', *SpEncy*, and *Spenser's 'Faerie Queene': A Critical Commentary on Books I and II* (Manchester: Manchester University Press, 1977), 60–9; Gless, *Interpretation and Theology*, 105–14. In Books 1 to 6 of *The Faerie Queene*, the impact of a 'salvage nation' on three different maidens clarifies the nature of the three stages of descent in the three pairs of legends. In Books 1–2 the satyr-savages, notably with Una in I.vi, subvert theological-philosophical truths accessible to Reason. In Books 3–4 the satyrs, especially with Hellenore (III.x) but also implicitly in events directed by 'Satyrane', distort passions of the Heart. In Books 5–6, which both concern the 'salvage Island' (V.xi.39; VI.i.9), the savages (no longer called satyrs) focus their idolatry and lust in cannibalism, treating Serena as nourishment for the Sensory Appetites (VI.viii). On identifying satyrs and savages in the Sixteenth century, see Richard Bernheimer, *Wild Men in the Middle Ages* (Cambridge, MA: Harvard University Press, 1952), 71; and Tonkin, *Spenser's Courteous Pastoral*, 61–2. In Andrew Hadfield's important 'The "sacred hunger of ambitious minds": Spenser's Savage Religion', in *Edmund Spenser*, ed. Andrew Hadfield (London and New York: Longman, 1996), 177–95, the shift from almost-redeemable savages who 'save' Una (I.vi) to unredeemables who would devour Serena (VI.viii) shows Spenser's hardening view of the Irish; in *Edmund Spenser's Irish Experience* (see n15 above) Hadfield's more extensive analysis of the 'salvage nation' also includes the savage/satyrs who cavort with Hellenore—contributing (I think) to the second in three stages of descent or 'dilation'. Kenneth Borris, in '"Diuelish Ceremonies": Allegorical Satire of Protestant Extremism in *The Faerie Queene* VI.viii.31–51', *Spenser Studies*, 8 (1987), 175–209, also gives a valuable context for viewing the satyrs—but only as Puritans, rather than, more broadly, as the exuberant half-bestial energies of the common masses in unillumined enjoyment of the natural world.

good-natured before Titania and Theseus. This wonderfully complex creature inspires (via a love-wounded flower) Titania's lusty idolatry and (via love-wounded 'art') Theseus's wry approval. An astonishing inversion of Spenser's 'asse'. Naturally Shakespeare deflected royal displeasure by separately praising Elizabeth (his only explicit flattery during her lifetime) with Oberon's exquisite mythic account of a beauteous virgin, impervious to Cupid's arrows, who is the Unmoved Mover of Love (*MND* 2.1.148–72). Shakespeare's comedy thus implicitly critiques Elizabeth as a willful fairy queen but also detaches her from Spenser's celebratory trope. The main target of the comic demiurge is not Elizabeth but Spenser's elitist, Petrarchan aesthetic.

Did Shakespeare intend simply to upstage the second installment of Spenser's epic, or did his parodic 'fairy queen' serve a deeper political agenda? Maurice Hunt elaborately reviews the possibility that Titania's dotage on Bottom alludes to Elizabeth's infatuation with the Duke of Alençon (later, Duke of Anjou) near the end of their decade-long marriage negotiations (1572–1581).[32] Many odd details invite this topical allegory: Bottom's eleven uses of 'monsieur'; Elizabeth's animal names for Anjou and his emissary Simier; the 'little Indian boy' as covert reference to James VI, child of Mary Queen of Scots, Elizabeth-Titania's 'votaress'; Oberon as Henry VIII or Leicester or Essex; the 'wounded flower' as Lettice Knollys Devereux Dudley, her love-wound dividing Leicester and Elizabeth, then in recompense inflicting Elizabeth's dotage.[33] Though such an allegory, sponsored by Essex's circle, could support the argument of my essay, I believe Shakespeare's glance at Elizabeth's disturbing infatuation is swallowed up in a populist wish-fulfilment that offers a more satisfying resolution for the fairy queen's errancy. The enthusiastic, loyal, rough-hewn artistry of Bottom and the rustics quaintly celebrates Shakespeare's own theatre, demonstrating its salubrious, well-intended impact on Elizabeth and England, far more than it mocks the queen's errancy with an unworthy French lord. The concluding play-within-the-play allows the commonest of players to upstage all aristocratic courtiers, whether French or English. Moreover, Bottom's good-natured crudeness provides a transition to Falstaff and other tavern idlers, who also evoke royal and universal infatuation before being invited into a brotherhood of holy warriors. Since the lyricism of *A Midsummer Night's Dream* dates it with *Richard II*, it seems both plays were intended to set the stage for a quite different English epic—namely, the populist, male-glorifying *Henriad*. Its 'all-humored' prince purposely associates with idling commoners as well as aspiring aristo-

---

[32] Hunt, 'A Speculative Political Allegory in *A Midsummer Night's Dream*', *Comparative Drama*, 34 (2000–1), 423–53, builds on scholarship of Rickert, Brooks, Taylor, Bednarz, and Reid.

[33] All Shakespeare quotations are taken from *The Complete Works of Shakespeare*, updated 4th ed. of David Bevington (New York: Longman, 1997).

crats, finally binding them in militant blood-brotherhood on Crispin's Day. The *Henriad*, moreover, exalts a prince who, like his usurper-father, claims the throne by clever self-fashioning, and (as a key element in Shakespeare's agenda) it ends with a glowing tribute to the Earl of Essex, comparing him to Henry V in heroic leadership, popularity, and monarchic potential (Falstaff's persistent 'when thou art king': *1H4* 1.2.16, 23, 55, 58, 60). Much of Shakespeare's idealizing of Hal seems designed to match Essex's celebrated virtues. In meticulous detail Paul Hammer recounts how Essex, to lead the Protestant cause, subjected his armies and enemy commanders to religious services, forbade immorality and pillage of the poor, and was widely praised for combining bravery with chivalric courtesy, decorous self-restraint, and piety.[34]

Certainly Essex's self-image matches Henry V as a 'mirror of all Christian kings' (*H5* 2.Pr.6) 'redeeming time when men think least I will' (*1H4* 1.2.213). The messianic-providential image of Henry V reflects an on-going Reformation debate over England's chronicles.[35] Edward Hall in *The Vnion of the two noble and illustre families of Lancastre and York* (1548) gave the idealizing nationalist view: Henry V is 'the blasyng comete', 'the myrrour of Christendome & the glory of his country', 'the floure of kynges passed, and a glasse to them that should succeed'. But Holinshed, influenced by puritans like Foxe who sought to repair Oldcastle's reputation and to desacralize Henry V, omitted the apocalyptic 'blasyng comete' and the idolatrous 'mirrour of Christendome'.[36] Shakespeare restores the exalted view of Henry's providential role, and apparently exploits Foxe's allusion to a false slander of Oldcastle as a 'greatpaunch glutton'. In the *Henriad* Shakespeare's affirmation of Henry's providential militarism[37] perfectly served the goals of Essex, who carefully cultivated his reputation as a holy warrior after scrutinizing English and ancient Roman history. Perhaps Essex's scholarly secretary Henry Cuffe offered the playwrights, especially Shakespeare and Daniel, this reading of Henry V and of Oldcastle, ancestor of Es-

---

[34] Paul E. J. Hammer, *The Polarization of Elizabethan Politics: The Political Career of Robert Devereux, 2nd Earl of Essex, 1585–1597*, vol.1 [hereafter *Polarization*] (Cambridge: Cambridge University Press, 1999), 120, 138–40, 161–2, 211–16, 225–6, 229–31, 268, 297–8, 302, 307–8, 315, 318, 326, 333 ff, 349, 358, 371–3, 380–1, 387, 393–4, 399 ff, 403–4. Cf. Annabel Patterson, *Shakespeare and the Popular Voice* (Cambridge, MA: Basil Blackwell, 1989), 92, 178n7.

[35] See R. M. Benbow, 'The Providential Theory of Historical Causation in *Holinshed's Chronicles* 1577 and 1587', *Texas Studies in Language and Literature*, 1/2 (1959), 276 ff; E. S. Donno, 'Some Aspects of Shakespeare's Holinshed', *Huntingdon Library Quarterly*, 50 (1987), 229–48; David Womersley, 'Why Is Falstaff Fat?', *Review of English Studies*, ns 47:185 (1996), 1–22.

[36] Edward Hall, *The Vnion of the two noble and illustre families of Lancastre and York* (1548), Sig. Nvii^v; Benbow, 'Providential Theory', 277–8.

[37] On Essex's rise to leadership of the 'Protestant cause', see Hammer, *Polarization*, 6, 39 ff, 51–2, 76, 107, 119, 143, 241 ff, 247, 260–1, 284, 393–4, 400.

sex's bitter enemy, Lord Brooke. After the miracle-victory at Agincourt, the Chorus reaffirms Henry V's saintly image: '*free from vainness and self-glorious pride*, / Giving full trophy [...] / Quite from himself to God' (5.Pr.20–2; italics mine).

Such perfect humility, however, sharply differs from Essex's vacillating behavior at this time. At first the exemplar of chivalry and courtesy, by 1597 Essex was maddeningly frustrated by the Council's opposition to his quest for honor, often as arrogantly self-promoting as Hotspur. Eric Mallin notes that *Troilus and Cressida* exemplifies Essex in moral opposites.[38] This ambivalent portrayal of the quest for honor in fact occurs in each play connected with Essex: in *1 Henry IV* he resembles both Hal and Hotspur; in *Julius Caesar*, both Brutus and Caesar; in *Hamlet*, both Hamlet and Laertes; in *Troilus and Cressida*, both Hector and Achilles. Wayne Rebhorn likewise observes that *Julius Caesar* is no simplistic *pièce à clé* but a complex anatomy of Essex's militaristic quest for honor and power, which became increasingly obsessive and self-destructive.[39] Shakespeare's depiction of Hal-Henry V as a good-humored, saintly king is thus wishfully proleptic with regard to Essex, inviting him to realize his greatness through imitating a fantasy-monarch (a 'Caesar') which is partly Essex's own creation.

> But now behold, [...]
> How London doth pour out her citizens!
> The Mayor and all his brethren ...
> Go forth and fetch their conquering Caesar in;
> As by a lower but loving likelihood,
> Were now the General of our gracious Empress,
> As in good time he may, from Ireland coming,
> Bringing rebellion broached on his sword,
> How many would the peaceful city quit
> To welcome him!
> (*Henry V* 5.Prol.20–34)

Thus, after *A Midsummer Night's Dream* comically deconstructs the literary hegemony of Spenser's 'fairy queen', Shakespeare offers his own

---

[38] Eric S. Mallin, 'Emulous Factions and the Collapse of Chivalry: *Troilus and Cressida*', *Representations*, 29 (1990), 145–79. On Essex's 'ambition of warre', political ruthlessness, and obsessive quest for honor, see Hammer, *Polarization*, 50–1, 62 ff, 71–5, 82–3, 88–90, 94–7, 103 ff, 111 ff, 118, 145–6, 199 ff, 208, 216 ff, 225 ff, 233–4, 249, 267–8, 297–8, 323, 367–8, 371–3, 386 ff, 393 ff, 399–401, 404. For speculation on Shakespeare's access to Essex House, see Martin Green, *Wriothesley's Roses in Shakespeare's Sonnets, Poems, and Plays* (Baltimore: Clevedon Books, 1993), 115–56, 201–11; see n87 below.

[39] Rebhorn, 'The Crisis of the Aristocracy in *Julius Caesar*', *Renaissance Quarterly*, 43 (1990), 75–111. For the philosophical and theological tradition of anti-militancy in relation to *Henry V*, see Harold C. Goddard, *The Meaning of Shakespeare*, vol.1 (Chicago, IL: University of Chicago Press, 1951), 215–68; Roy W. Battenhouse, 'The Relation of *Henry V* to *Tamburlaine*', *Shakespeare Survey*, 27 (1974), 71–9, and '*Henry V* in the Light of Erasmus', *Shakespeare Studies*, 18 (1985), 77–88.

irresistible epic, the *Henriad*, making Hal a populist prodigal turned holy prodigy who might be reincarnated in Essex. Shakespeare's control of this delicate material is subtle: he evokes riotous laughter at himself and his troupe as Peter Quince and the rustics, before creating in the *Henriad* a thrilling socially-inclusive theatrical epic to replace Spenser's refined intellectual allegory. Instead of 'fashioning gentlemen' of the privileged elite, equipped to purchase and read an ever-expanding folio *Faerie Queene* about a magnific Arthurian-romance hero who can fulfill the dreams of both Essex and Elizabeth, Shakespeare enacts on stage a 'mirror of all Christian kings' who playfully imagines himself 'of all humours' and seriously debates his militarism.[40] This self-conscious messianic hero could displace even the Christian dimension of Spenser's epic and, as in *A Midsummer Night's Dream*, assert magisterial male dominion over a subjugated royal consort.

If, however, the éclat of *A Midsummer Night's Dream* and the *Henriad* helped Shakespeare to surpass the reigning laureate in the hearts of English folk, the triumph was also Spenser's, for the greatness of *A Midsummer Night's Dream* has less to do with parodic mockery than with brilliant confiscation of the noblest features of Spenser's art: mythic allegory of a grand range of beings who quest for loving fulfillment under a fairy queen's mesmerizing aura, all in musical, richly imaged verse (Shakespeare, at this point, only omitting Spenser's carefully prudent morality). These elements distinctly elevate *A Midsummer Night's Dream* over the earlier comedies. Though lovemaking is still farcical (as in *Comedy of Errors*, *Two Gentlemen*, *The Taming of the Shrew*, *Love's Labours*), it widens to mythic dimensions. Desire conquers all, *omnia vincit amor*, from base commoners to lofty aristocrats, despite quasi-deification as legendary heroes and fairy immortals. But whereas Spenser enforces divinely-ordained social hierarchy, as in Belphoebe's curt disposal of Braggadocchio, Shakespeare allows metamorphic desire to make momentary hash of social distinctions, *pace* Titania and Bottom. Their astonishing union is Shakespeare's most daring use of 'allegory', which Judith Anderson shows to be the major artistic element he appropriates from Spenser,[41] but this richly thematic and mythic allusiveness is transformed by Shakespeare into allegory of a different sort, celebrating the sensory particularity and commonness of experience, in contrast to Spenser's celebration of the elite, universal, Godlike ideal.

Spenser's influence on Shakespeare does not end with a grandly comic fairy queen, nor with paralleling Henry V and Essex to appropriate Spenser's best candidate for Prince Arthur. Shakespeare's 'abso-

---

[40] See Robert L. Reid, 'Humoral Psychology in Shakespeare's *Henriad*', *Comparative Drama*, 30 (1996–97), 471–502.

[41] Anderson, 'The Conspiracy of Realism: Impasse and Vision in *King Lear*', *Studies in Philology*, 84 (1987), 1–23.

lute absorption of the precursor' (as Bloom calls it)[42] continues to operate, for in the year after the second installment of *The Faerie Queene* Shakespeare even more radically alters and extends his comic vision by designing *The Merchant of Venice* with a serious dimension of moral, even religious, allegory.[43] Portia, whose restrained self-mastery gradually takes over the play,[44] inverts Titania, as if Gloriana's mythic power is now seriously felt (though partly by male disguise). Portia's mockery of many princely suitors cleverly reflects Elizabeth's celebrated evasions of marriage. The English audience could relish her privately-sharp, publicly-tactful condescensions. They could likewise relish the concluding fantasy of a perfect English match, a gentleman without title but handsome, witty, and morally capable of the casket-test. An important subtext of this wish-fulfilment is its implicit resolution of succession anxiety. Portia initiates a series of great female leads, several with marked resemblance to Elizabeth I: Beatrice, Rosalind,[45] Viola/Olivia,[46] Helena, Cleopatra.[47] The love quests of *The Merchant of Venice* are re-

---

[42] Harold Bloom, *The Anxiety of Influence* (New York: Oxford University Press, 1973), 11: 'Shakespeare is the largest instance in the language of ... the absolute absorption of the precursor'.

[43] Spenser's moral-religious allegory is rivaled by that in *The Merchant of Venice*: Shylock's vengeful legalism is displaced by a merciful New Law fitfully unfolding in Portia, Antonio, Bassanio, and the Venetians to redeem Shylock from hatred, Bassanio from prodigality, Antonio from melancholy, Portia from a shaky marriage. The allegorical dimension is, however, deeply qualified by Antonio's homoerotic bond with Bassanio and by Portia's use of male transvestism. The biblical subtext provides a smokescreen and justification for the same-sex bond (i.e., the forbidden true love) at the embattled heart of the play. Judith Rosenheim, 'Allegorical Commentary in *The Merchant of Venice*', *Shakespeare Studies*, 24 (1996), 156–210, explains how the allegory is further qualified by the subplots of Launcelot/Old Gobbo and Jessica/Shylock.

[44] Ultimately the play is dominated by Shylock's unleashed, unresolved passion. But Portia's masterful self-possession surpasses Shakespeare's previous comic females and has no basis in the source-material for *The Merchant of Venice*. Portia demonstrates Elizabeth's masterful sovereignty but also the male fantasy of her marital acessibility. On Shakespeare's subtextual allusions to Elizabeth I, see Leah S. Marcus, *Puzzling Shakespeare: Local Reading and Its Discontents* (Berkeley: University of California Press, 1988), chap. 2: 'Elizabeth', 51–105; esp. 96–105.

[45] The name 'Rosalind', possibly alluding to Queen Elizabeth, is traceable through Lodge to *The Shepheardes Calendar*. See Richard Mallette, 'Rosalind' in *SpEncy*. Again Shakespeare appropriates a favorite Spenserian trope for Elizabeth—and inverts it: from the pastoral name springs his fantasy of a sovereign mind that is wittily and personally accessible.

[46] For Leslie Hotson, *The First Night of Twelfth Night* (London: Hart-Davis, 1954), chaps 2 and 6, Countess Olivia is intended as a flattering portrait of Elizabeth I when she was visited by the Italian duke, Orsino. If so, Shakespeare again provides a wishful resolution of succession anxiety, as well as of Elizabeth's increasing moody detachment.

[47] See Helen Morris, 'Queen Elizabeth I "Shadowed" in Cleopatra', *Huntingdon Library Quarterly*, 32 (1969), 271–8; Keith Rinehart, 'Shakespeare's Cleopatra and England's Elizabeth', *Shakespeare Quarterly*, 23 (1972), 81–6; Eggert, *Showing like a Queen*, 133–54, 157–61.

solved not by the providential power of a whimsical male (Petruchio, Oberon) but by the decorous rational craft of a female magus, one who is capable of attending to serious social and economic realities and whose wisdom is repeatedly given gospel allusiveness: 'How far that little candle throws his beams!' (*MV* 5.1.90)

The gleam of moral-religious allegory evolves more deeply and darkly in the tragedies and romances—not only, as Judith Anderson shows, in *King Lear*[48] but also in *Othello*, *Measure for Measure*, *Macbeth*, *Pericles*, *The Winter's Tale*, and especially *The Tempest*, which recasts *A Midsummer Night's Dream* with elevated mythic ambience and, at last, with allegorical names and identities for central characters. Puck (a projector of Oberon's daemonic urges) splits into 'Ariel' and 'Caliban', a division that gives 'Prospero' a responsible and linguistically-powerful magic far beyond his prototype. If Titania evoked laughter at the fairy queen's vanity, as well as awe at her erotic majesty and oratorical power, 'Miranda' exemplifies Gloriana's innocent essence: the compelling authority of her chastity, her frank intelligence, her command of universal admiration. Spenser's influence on *The Tempest* is especially evident in the play's Vergilian[49] and Christian[50] subtexts, but also in Shakespeare's

---

[48] Anderson, 'Conspiracy of Realism'.

[49] See Jim Nosworthy, 'The Narrative Sources of *The Tempest*', *Review of English Studies*, ns 24 (1948), 281–94; Jan Kott, '*The Aeneid* and *The Tempest*', *Arion*, ns 3:4 (1976), 424–51; Kott, '*The Tempest*, or Repetition', *Mosaic*, 10 (1977), 9–36; Gary Schmidgall, *Shakespeare and the Courtly Aesthetic* (Berkeley: University of California Press, 1981), 74–5, 165–73; John Pitcher, 'A Theatre of the Future: *The Aeneid* and *The Tempest*', *Essays in Criticism*, 34 (1984), 193–215; Barbara J. Bono, *Literary Transvaluation: From Vergilian Epic to Shakespearean Tragicomedy* (Berkeley: University of California Press, 1984); Robert Miola, 'Vergil in Shakespeare: From Allusion to Imitation', *Vergil at 2000*, ed. John D. Bernard (New York: AMS Press, 1986), 254–6; Robert Wiltenberg, 'The Aeneid in *The Tempest*', *Shakespeare Survey*, 39 (1987), 159–68; Donna B. Hamilton, *Virgil and 'The Tempest': The Politics of Imitation* (Columbus: Ohio State University Press, 1990); James, *Shakespeare's Troy*, 189–221; Margaret Tudeau-Clayton, *Jonson, Shakespeare, and Early Modern Virgil* (Cambridge: Cambridge University Press, 1998); Robin Headlam Wells, 'Blessing Europe: Virgil, Ovid, and Seneca in *The Tempest*', in *Shakespeare and Intertextuality: The Transition of Cultures Between Italy and England in the Early Modern Period*, ed. Michele Marrapodi (Rome: Bulzoni, 2000), 69–84.

[50] See, Robert L. Reid, 'Sacerdotal Vestiges in The Tempest', *Comparative Drama*, 41 (Winter 2007-8), 493–513. On Isaiah as source for Ariel and providential themes in *The Tempest*, see Ann P. Slater, *Shakespeare Survey*, 25 (1972), 125–35; Karol Berger, *Shakespeare Studies*, 10 (1977), 211–39; Anthony Esolen, *Studies in Philology*, 94 (1997), 221–48. On sacramental symbols in *The Tempest*, Robert G. Hunter, *Shakespeare and the Comedy of Forgiveness* (New York: Columbia University Press, 1965); E. J. Devereux, *Bulletin de l'Association Canadienne des Humanités*, 19 (1968), 50–62. On spirituality in Prospero's 'Art', David Woodman, *White Magic and English Renaissance Drama* (Rutherford: Fairleigh Dickinson Press, 1973); Barbara Traister, *Heavenly Necromancers: The Magician in English Renaissance Drama* (Columbia: University of Missouri Press, 1984); John S. Mebane, *Renaissance Magic and the Return of the Golden Age: The Occult Tradition and Marlowe, Jonson, and Shakespeare* (Lincoln, NE: University of Nebraska Press, 1989); George Slover, 'Magic, Mystery, and Make-Believe: An Analogical Reading of *The Tempest*', *Shakespeare Studies*, 11 (1978), 180–205; Roy Battenhouse, *Shakespeare's Christian Dimension: An Anthology of*

recasting of Colin Clout's breaking of pipes (*FQ* VI.x.18; *SC*, 'Jan' 72). Prospero's 'I'll break my staff' and 'drown my book' (*Temp* 5.1.54–7) is a more comprehensive disavowal of artistic prowess, and his eloquent comment on his own anger at Caliban's interruption of the masque is far more self-possessed than Colin's loss of temper. Shakespeare thus internalizes and transforms the moral and mythic dimensions of Spenser's art, a signal example of what Greenblatt calls his 'limitless talent for entering into the consciousness of another, perceiving its deepest structures as a manipulable fiction, reinscribing it into his own narrative form'.[51]

As Shakespeare absorbed Spenser's art and thereby expanded his own, widening its intellectual and spiritual scope, was Spenser similarly aware of Shakespeare's work? Missing the final half of Spenser's epic, we have no record of his reaction to a revamped fairy queen, provocatively and physically actualized; nor do we know if the *Henriad* influenced Spenser's view of the militant quest for honor. But the dark elements at the end of *The Faerie Queene*'s second installment clearly presage Shakespeare's increased questioning of the militaristic quest for glory in the *Henriad*, *Julius Caesar*, *Hamlet*, *Troilus and Cressida*, *Othello*, *Macbeth*, and *Coriolanus*. Most centrally, each poet shows deepening concern for the problem of self-love in the English court—both in the complex fictive heroines who reflect Elizabeth's powerful presence and in the frustrated aspirants for honor through her recognition—notably Essex, whose patronage both poets sought during the 1590s, especially after the much-bruited enterprises at Rouen and Cadiz (1591, 1596) and before the disastrous campaigns in the Azores (1597) and Ireland (1598–99).

It is instructive to trace during the English Renaissance, from *The Shepheardes Calendar* (1579) to *Samson Agonistes* (1674), an increasing use of 'self-love' by poets, preachers, politicians, and philosophers, with growing awareness of its centrality and complexity, and in literature a growing interest in attaining *proper* self-love. The phrase alerts us to changing concepts of both 'self' (subjectivity, self-fashioning) and 'love' (desire, relationship, bonding) during the early modern period. In their romance-epics, Sidney and Spenser stress the destructive self-love of *philautia*, a vainglorious pride that obstructs the fashioning of virtuous ladies and gentlemen.[52] Self-love also challenges Spenser's fash-

---

Commentary (Bloomington and Indianapolis: Indiana University Press, 1994), 250–79.

[51] Greenblatt, *Renaissance Self-fashioning* (Chicago, IL: University of Chicago Press, 1980), 252.

[52] On *philautia* in Sidney, see Robert E. Stillman, 'The Perils of Fancy: Poetry and Self-Love in *The Old Arcadia*', *Texas Studies in Language and Literature*, 26 (1984), 1–17; 'The Truths of a Slippery World: Poetry and Tyranny in Sidney's "Defense"', *Renaissance Quarterly*, 55 (2002), 1287–1319. On Sidney's advocacy of selfless and self-sacrificial love, see William Craft, 'Remaking the Heroic Self in the *New Arcadia*', *Studies in English Literature*,

ioning of a laureate image since he seeks true moral authority more than celebrity and patronage. A more alluring portrayal of self-love occurs in the popular theater, where Marlowe and Jonson exploit the primal appeal of ambitious self-interest, while Shakespeare, though at first imitating Marlovian self-assertion (in early histories, in *Titus Andronicus*, and in comedies through *A Midsummer Night's Dream*), eventually portrays self-love as complexly life-affirming. During the first half of the seventeenth century, Stuart rule brings an exploding obsession with self-love. As James Bednarz observes, it is a key feature in the 'Poets' War' of 1599–1601,[53] and building on *Cynthia's Revels or The Fountain of Self-Love* it figures prominently in Jonson's court masques.[54] It is a catchword in Puritan sermons and political tracts as England moves to civil war, and Milton portrays it as the central problem for both humans and angels in his final works, especially *Paradise Lost*, though he shifts the main burden of self-love to Eve, while giving her one special power for dealing with it.[55] Here I focus simply on the polar contrast of Spenser's and Shakespeare's portrayal of self-love during the 1590s when their remarkable poetic achievements suggest rival laureateships.

III. Spenser's Repudiation of Self-Love

Spenser subsumes self-love within the deadly sin of pride (and the subordinate support-sins of presumption, ambition, and vanity).[56] He rarely mentions 'self-love' (two adjectival uses, compared with 344 uses of 'pride/proud' and its cognates), and with pious zeal he presents self-love only negatively as *philautia*, a passive preening vanity that paralyzes virtuous action. In 252 lines on Lucifera and her 'progress' with seven vices (FQ I.iv.7–12, 16–37), four lines deal with self-love:

---

25 (1985), 45–67; Craft, *Labyrinth of Desire: Invention and Culture in the Work of Sir Philip Sidney* (Newark, NJ: University of Delaware Press, 1994), 26–39, 56–67, 87–99.

[53] See James P. Bednarz, *Shakespeare and the Poets' War* (New York: Columbia University Press, 2001), 155–202.

[54] See Robert Wiltenburg, *Ben Jonson and Self-Love* (Columbia: University of Missouri Press, 1990), x–xi, 7, 19, 30, 44, 64, 89, 92, 124, 127–8.

[55] For a fine analysis of self-love in Milton and seventeenth century England, see David Robertson, 'My self / Before me': *Self-Love in the Works of John Milton* (Tampere: University of Tampere, Dept. of Philology, 1992). That Milton gives Adam, but not Eve, the intellect and will to transform self-love into 'self-esteem' is argued by John Guillory, 'Milton, Narcissism, Gender: On the Genealogy of Male Self-Esteem' in *Critical Essays on John Milton*, ed. Christopher Kendrick (New York: G. K. Hale, 1995), 194–233.

[56] Donald V. Stump, 'pride', *SpEncy*; Stump and John M. Crossett, 'Spenser's Inferno: The Order of the Seven Deadly Sins at the Palace of Pride', *Journal of Medieval and Renaissance Studies*, 14 (1984), 203–18; Joan Heiges Blythe, 'Spenser and the Seven Deadly Sins: Book 1, Cantos 4 and 5', *ELH*, 39 (1972), 342–52; Tuve, *Allegorical Imagery*, 36, 38, 59, 106, 108n, 120–30, 175–6, 182–4, 188n, 192, 195, 206, 229; Morton W. Bloomfield, *The Seven Deadly Sins* (East Lansing: University of Michigan Press, 1952), 74–8, 87–8, 145, 181–3, 188, 201, 223, 241, 349. See also Ronald Horton's paper in the present volume.

> in her hand she held a mirrhour bright,
> Wherein her face she often vewed fayne,
> And in her selfe-lou'd semblance tooke delight;
> For she was wondrous faire, as any liuing wight.

Her self-admiration, inspiring ruthless competition among courtiers, culminates in a 'progress' of deadly sins to exhibit herself more widely.[57] Consummating her vanity by putting it on wheels (thus demonizing Ezekiel's mobilized, enwheeled ark of the covenant), she undercuts her self-glorying by craving others' admiration. Like Phaëthon, who similarly abuses the gift of light, Lucifera is 'Proud of such glory and aduancement vaine' (9). Her 'Husher' (marvelous pun) is Vanitie (13); and 'vain', a favorite Spenserian adjective (an easy rhyme), punctuates much of his moral terrain. The primary meaning of 'vain' (self-admiring) is deflated by subsidiary meanings, implying that its cause and effect are 'in vain' (unmerited and self-deluding; ineffective and self-destructive): 'loose loues ... are vaine, and vanish into nought' (I.x.62). Thus self-love, when viewed as *philautia*, disfigures genuine selfhood by distracting from the quest for true glory. Moreover, it is utterly subordinate to pride, the 'radical ur-sin' (as Tuve calls it)[58] which led Satan to rebel against God and to infect Adam and Eve with the same urge. Pride is the main obstacle in Spenser's Legend of Holiness, where he traces its assault on each level of human nature. As pride is both instigator (the whipster Satan) and substance (the monarch Lucifera) of the vices' progress in Book 1, it likewise motivates and informs foes of subsequent legends—Mammon, Maleager, and Acrasia; Malecasta, Argante, and Busyrane; Lust and Proteus; Radigund, Souldan, and Grantorto; Sanglier, Turpine, and Disdain; Mutability. Defeating pride is the quintessential struggle in each quest, and to overcome it each virtue must achieve self-mortification, which then allows charitable service to others. Primary attention, especially in the legends of holiness, temperance, and chastity, is given to self-mortification, and the mirroring act of overthrowing the self-indulgent, before performing charitable service.

---

[57] As usurper (I.iv.12) Lucifera has been identified with the vainglorious Mary Queen of Scots, a lover of progresses. But the analogy with Elizabeth I is inescapable, as is the allusion to Accession Day tourneys and 'prodigy houses', especially Burghley's many-turreted palace. See Introduction, *Books I and II of 'The Faerie Queene'*, ed. Robert Kellogg & Oliver Steele (New York: Odyssey Press, 1969), 25–7; Mark Eccles, 'Burghley, William Cecil, Lord', *SpEncy*.

[58] Aquinas cites Gregory: pride, 'queen and mother of all the vices', 'when it has vanquished and captured the heart, forthwith delivers it into the hands of [...] the seven principal vices, that they may despoil it and produce vices of all kinds', *The Summa Theologica of Saint Thomas Aquinas* [hereafter *ST*], trans. by Fathers of the Dominican Province (Chicago, IL: Encyclopedia Britannica, 1952), II-II.162.8. On Spenser's persistent depiction of pride's hegemony in all sinfulness, see n56 above.

'Self-love' appears explicitly only once more in *The Faerie Queene*. In Book 2, a temporal parallel to Book I's eternal perspective, we find the clownish underside of self-love when Braggadoccio steals Guyon's horse and spear, exults in intimidating the peacock Trompart, and deceives even Archimago into promising to steal for him Prince Arthur's sword, before Belphoebe exposes the base boastful commoner:

>   a losell wandring by the way,
> One that to bountie neuer cast his mynd,
> Ne thought of honour euer did assay
> His baser brest, but in his kestrell kind
> A pleasing vaine of glory he did find,
> To which his flowing toung and troublous spright
> Gaue him great ayd, and made him more inclind:
> He, that braue steed there finding ready dight,
> Purloyned both steed and speare, and ran away full light.
>
> Now gan his hart all swell in jollitie,
> And of him selfe great hope and helpe conceiu'd,
> That puffed vp with smoke of vanitie,
> And with selfe-loued personage deceiu'd,
> He gan to hope of men to be receiu'd
> For such, as he him thought, or faine would bee:
> But for in court gay portaunce he perceiu'd
> And gallant shew to be in greatest gree,
> Eftsoones to court he cast t'aduaunce his first degree.
>   (II.iii.4–5)

Lucifera and Braggadocchio exemplify the upper and lower reaches of vainglorious self-love. Both are perversions of the quest for honor, derived from Classical, Medieval, and Italian Renaissance praise for magnanimity, the high-minded noble virtue which merits leadership roles, public acclaim, and self-approval.[59] Maurice McNamee, S. J., in *Honor and the Epic Hero* (1960), traces the evolution of a Christian form of magnanimity from the self-interested Homeric hero (an *arête* defended by Aristotle's *Nicomachean Ethics*) to the nationally-dutiful Vergilian hero (a

---

[59] Maurice B. McNamee, S. J., *Honor and the Epic Hero: A Study of the Shifting Concept of Magnanimity in Philosophy and Epic Poetry* (New York: Holt, Rinehart & Winston, 1960); Curtis Brown Watson, *Shakespeare and the Renaissance Concept of Honor* (Princeton, NJ: Princeton University Press, 1960). For more recent studies of Shakespeare's treatment of honor, see Mervyn James, *Society, Politics and Culture: Studies in Early Modern England* (Cambridge: Cambridge University Press, 1986), 308–465; John Alvis, *Shakespeare's Understanding of Honor* (Durham: Carolina Academic Press, 1990); Reta A. Terry, '"Vows to the Blackest Devil": Hamlet and the Evolving Code of Honor in Early Modern England', *Renaissance Quarterly*, 52 (1999), 1070–86. Cf. Charles Barber, *The Idea of Honour in the English Drama 1591–1700* (Stockholm: Almqvist & Wiksell, 1957); Norman Council, *When Honour's at the Stake: Ideas of Honour in Shakespeare's Plays* (London: George Allen & Unwin, 1973).

pietas promoted by Cicero's *De Officiis*) to the self-denying, charitable chivalry of Spenser's heroes (a humble charity taught by Augustine's *City of God* and Aquinas's *Summa Theologica*—but combined with the quest for honor extolled by Italian handbooks on the perfect courtier's service to an idealized earthly prince). In contrast, Curtis Watson in *Shakespeare and the Renaissance Concept of Honor* (1960), to explain Shakespeare's ethos, stresses the resurgence of ancient self-assertion, transmitted by Renaissance Italians like Castiglione and Machiavelli and only mildly qualified by Medieval and humanist Christianity.[60] Each of these critiques leans only one way. Watson focuses on Shakespeare's secularism and does not acknowledge the playwright's change, the growing appearance of 'epiphanal' revelation in the mature comedies, tragedies, and romances.[61] McNamee acknowledges Spenser's partial approval of the quest for earthly glory (despite Augustine's disdain for it, which is only slightly moderated by Aquinas), but McNamee is unsure how much Spenser affirms the self-approval, the self-love, implicit in the quest for fame, honor, and glory.

For Linda Gregerson and James Broaddus, Britomart is centrally motivated by self-love, or as Broaddus helpfully qualifies, 'subordinated self-love'.[62] But despite my admiration for these studies, I do not find in Spenser's works a consciously positive view of self-love. Britomart's viewing her ideal mate in Merlin's mirror (a 'world of glas' showing whatever 'to the looker appertaynd', III.ii.19) *inverts* Narcissus' self-mirroring; she laments the possible analogy between herself and 'Cephisus foolish child' (III.ii.44). She desires neither her own physical image nor Artegall's but rather his moral discipline, his justice based on self-restraint (the controlled Bacchus of V.i.2). Such an image reflects her own chaste power to control (indeed to mortify) her self-love, to replace her own image with a male other who exemplifies Justice—a foreshadowing of Milton's angel teaching Eve to replace her beauteous external image with the sexual other as an *imago Dei*. In contrast to Milton's untested and unfallen Eve, Britomart is provided with symbolic arms—the lance of Will, the sword-word of Intellect, the armor of restraint—in order to shape her identity and her relationships

---

[60] Watson, *Shakespeare and the Renaissance Concept of Honor*, 279–366.

[61] See Reid, *Shakespeare's Tragic Form*, chap. 3.

[62] Linda Gregerson, *The Reformation of the Subject: Spenser, Milton, and the English Protestant Epic* (Cambridge: Cambridge University Press, 1995), 6–147; James W. Broaddus, *Spenser's Allegory of Love* (Newark, NJ: University of Delaware Press, 1999), 23–4, 45, 60, 109, 124–5, 156–8, 163n12. For a more skeptical view, see Elizabeth J. Bellamy, *Translations of Power: Narcissism and the Unconscious in Epic History* (Ithaca, NY: Cornell University Press, 1992), 189–211: 'If epic history is dependent on the ideological position of the absent phallus, if the lesson of Ryence's mirror is that anatomy is (epic) destiny, then the woman within epic history must be made to stand in for (anatomical) difference and loss'. Despite Britomart's 'combative androgyny', little in her 'internal violence' shows Spenser 'exploring a new kind of female subjectivity'.

in a fallen world.⁶³ Thus, though Britomart actively affirms her chaste virtue, for Spenser this approval of self-abnegation is not 'self-love'.⁶⁴

Only once, at the beginning of *Amoretti*, does Spenser suggest that proper pride motivates virtuous gentlefolk, but he does not call it 'self-love' and he quickly reforms it. The narrator (representing, as Dunlop says, a naïve initial stage of the poet-wooer)⁶⁵ proudly defends his beloved's 'portly pride' since it indicates her 'scorn of base things':

> Such pride is praise, such portlinesse is honor,
> that boldned innocence beares in hir eies ... .
> Was never in this world ought worthy tride,
> without some spark of such self-pleasing pride.
> (Sonnet 5)⁶⁶

The remainder of the *Amoretti*, however, studiously reforms that pride, both in his beloved and in himself. (His courtship of Elizabeth Boyle apparently coincides with Mirabella's struggle with Disdain, *FQ* VI.vii.28–viii.30.) Thus Spenser and his beloved, like Britomart, reverse Narcissus' mirroring, struggling up the Platonic ladder of admiration: from body, to soul, to an Idea drawing the soul to God (see *Amoretti* 35, 45, 78, 87). Moreover, instead of viewing Narcissus' obsession with his *likeness* as a crucial initiating inspiration, Spenser like Petrarch emphasizes the beloved's sexual *unlikeness*, her otherness, since it reinforces the body-spirit distinction and thus—like Gloriana, Una, and Sapience—reflects the Godlikeness that fosters virtue. The same principle informs Britomart's apprehension of heroic virtue via male otherness in Merlin's mirror.

For Spenser, one can be proud only of serving a higher glory and, with regard to oneself, proud only of self-abnegation, implicit in the shamefast desire, chaste integrity, and self-sacrifice achieved by his heroes. They exemplify a Reformation mode of magnanimity which admits only a severely qualified victory over oneself while serving a worthy prince. Redcrosse's defeat by Orgoglio (Italian 'pride') in I.vii makes us question Guyon's integrity at the corresponding episode in

---

⁶³ See Michael Leslie, *Spenser's 'Fierce Warres and Faithfull Loves': Martial and Chivalric Symbolism in 'The Faerie Queene'* (Cambridge: D. S. Brewer, 1983), 68–84.

⁶⁴ See David Lee Miller, *The Poem's Two Bodies: The Poetics of the 1590 'Faerie Queene'* (Princeton, NJ: Princeton University Press, 1988), 71, 81; Harry Berger, Jr., 'Narrative as Rhetoric in *The Faerie Queene*', *ELR* 21 (1991), 3–48, esp. 36 ff; Donald V. Stump, 'pride', *SpEncy*.

⁶⁵ Alexander Dunlop, 'Drama of *Amoretti*', 109 ff. Arthur F. Marotti is harsher: 'the speaker teasingly criticizes his mistress' personal vanity and egotism (Sonnets 27, 45), her coquettishness (Sonnet 47), her hubristic self-assurance (Sonnet 58), and [...] her fear of commitment (Sonnet 65)': '"Love Is Not Love": Elizabethan Sonnet Sequences and the Social Order', *ELH*, 49 (1982), 396–428; 413–17.

⁶⁶ *The Yale Edition of the Shorter Poems of Edmund Spenser*, ed. William Oram et al. (New Haven, CT: Yale University Press, 1989), 603–4.

Book 2. Before meeting Mammon and without the Palmer, Guyon 'euermore himselfe with comfort feedes / Of his owne virtues, and prayse-worthy deedes' (II.vii.2). In Aristotle's ethics and Cicero's *Offices*, cornerstone texts in Renaissance education, self-interest and desire of praise are essential motives, though (as refined by Aquinas and others) subordinated to humility and obedience. The heart-parlor of Alma's Castle, where Guyon and Arthur see their complementary motives, clarifies the nature of Guyon's comfort in 'prays-worthy deedes'. One imagines Shamefastnesse and Prays-desire to be contraries, yet Prays-desire does not make Arthur swell with pride: like Guyon he blushes with embarrassment, following Augustine's advice in *The City of God*:

> let the love of human praise blush and give place to the love of truth. For this is a great enemy of our faith, if the desire for glory have more room in our hearts than the fear of God; and therefore [says Christ, *John*, 5:22]: 'How can you believe that expect honour one from another and seek not the honour that cometh of God?'[67]

Like the 'too solemn sad' Redcrosse Knight, Arthur's Prays-desire calls herself 'pensiue' and 'sad in mind, / Through great desire of glory and of fame': Arthur responds by 'change of colour', 'Now seeming flaming whot, now stony cold'. The drama of self-abasement peaks in Guyon's demur courtship of Shamefastnesse, who 'answerd nought, but more abasht for shame, / Held downe her head, the whiles her louely face / The flashing bloud with blushing did inflame, / And the strong passion mard her modest grace'. On hearing that she mirrors his own heart, Guyon 'did blush in priuitee, / And turnd his face away; but she the same / Dissembled faire, and faynd to ouersee' (II.ix.36–44). Michael Schoenfeldt stresses the pleasurable goals of Spenser's temperate knight and the need for 'construction' to achieve those pleasures.[68] But one must contextualize those rare, brief moments of pleasure within the far more insistent focus on a self-discipline which is less concerned with self-construction than with annihilating the prolific spawn of false selves: Spenser's emphasis in the belly is on endless sweating labors to achieve the 'goodly order' of digestion, concluding with the humbling evacuation from Port Esquiline. Moving to heart and head brings the deeper 'sadness' of containing the higher energies of passion and will: complementary modes of embarrassed courtship in the heart, errant

---

[67] Augustine, *The City of God*, trans. John Healey (London: J. M. Dent & Sons, 1950), I.162.

[68] 'The Construction of Inwardness in *The Faerie Queene*, Book 2', in *Worldmaking Spenser*, ed. Patrick Cheney and Lauren Silberman (Lexington: University of Kentucky Press, 2000), 234–43.

imagination and tragic chronicles in the brain.[69] Thus Guyon's comforting 'deedes' do not focus on enjoying Medina's moderate pleasures but on heroic feats of self-restraint and self-mortification: Guyon must avoid Occasion and Furor, avoid Cymochles and Pyrochles's extremes, resist Phaedria's seductions, repudiate Mammon's offers, and utterly eradicate the Bower of Bliss.

Holiness, Temperance, and Chastity share this central principle of self-control that finds 'comfort' (but not pride) in *self-abnegation* rather than self-love. That heroes of odd-numbered legends (Redcrosse, Britomart, Artegall) surpass the heroes of even-numbered legends in every combat shows their superiority in exercising this self-denying principle. William Nelson saw the moral paradox governing Redcrosse's quest: the 'bloudie Crosse' recalls 'his dying Lord', and *'dead as liuing* euer him ador'd' (I.I.2).[70] By dying-living in faith and loving service, one can glimpse the glory of eternal life, for though self-abnegation does not *merit* glory, it allows intense acknowledgment of gifts of grace. The rigor of Holiness brings appreciation of the view of heavenly bliss and of the momentary 'sea of blisfull ioy' on seeing Una unveiled. Likewise, Chastity's self-restrained and charitable rigor affords a glimpse (later withdrawn) of joyous marital union. After Book 1 each virtue is shadowed by the daunting paradox of its moral achievement (sainthood = consummate self-defeat) and of its plot (the utterly comprehensive quest for holiness is utterly unfinished): no subsequent hero attains a comparable sense of unworthiness and dependence on divine grace. We can only imagine that Arthur (perhaps in league with all the knights) will like Redcrosse finally envision the 'chosen' saints of 'new Hierusalem', 'purg'd from sinfull guilt' not by their own deeds but by the 'pretious bloud [...] of that unspotted lam'. Such a vision, when 'this bright Angels towre quite dims that towre of glas' (I.x.57-8), will reorient Arthur's blushing desire for praise in Cleopolis. Simultaneously Elizabeth-as-Gloriana can complete her own quest, her exemplification of full power and wisdom, by acknowledging glory's true source. Such, I believe, was the goal of Spenser's epic.

Thus the alternating virtues of *The Faerie Queene* are not simply complementary; nor are they easily compatible. A deep and at times violent tension must be negotiated between them—between the rigorous spiritual restraint of Holiness, Chastity, and Justice, and the softer but deeply entrammeling engagement in natural virtue (and, as Schoenfeldt says, in natural pleasure) by the fairy heroes of Temperance, Friendship, and Courtesy. Nor are they equal: as Aquinas notes, the virtues form a

---

[69] See Douglas Trevor, 'Sadness in *The Faerie Queene*', in *Reading the Early Modern Passions*, ed. Gail Kern Paster, Katherine Rowe, Mary Floyd-Wilson (Philadelphia: University of Pennsylvania Press, 2004), 240–52.

[70] Nelson, *The Poetry of Edmund Spenser* (New York: Columbia University Press, 1963), 147 ff.

hierarchy matching the powers in human nature.[71] Of the six completed legends, Holiness is most exalted precisely because it is paradoxically based on humility, the conquest of pride. In its victory over self, Holiness sets the pattern and precepts for all the virtues. Though Temperance usefully seeks comfort and public approval for its self-restrained deeds, its touchstone is still self-abasement, avoiding arrogant pride with its resulting self-indulgence in power-hunger, covetousness, and cruelty. Likewise, the other 'soft', 'fairy' virtues of Friendship and Courtesy, despite their idealized access to the gifts of a natural world, are ultimately achieved by self-sacrifice, using those gifts restrainedly and eradicating self-indulgent excess in order to serve the good of others.

Book 1 establishes the basis for shunning self-love as Spenser, aligning himself with the Reformation stringency of Calvin and Luther,[72] stresses the rooted sinfulness of human nature: 'If any strength we have, it is to ill, / But all the good is God's, both power and eke will' (I.x.1). Spenser never seriously promotes an attraction to self-love, and he never explores its allure and complexity within himself.[73] He disapproves of any self-mirroring that brings obsessive regard for one's own physical beauty and possessions, prowess, and even honor. For Redcrosse there is no proper pride or self-love. The Legend of Holiness enforces the ultimate moral scruple of the glory-quest: though service to Gloriana in Cleopolis mirrors service to God in New Jerusalem, all the glory is God's, and Gloriana simply reflects it. This crucial revela-

---

[71] On the hierarchy of virtues in relation to the hierarchy of human faculties, see Aquinas, *ST* I-II.61.2; I.77.2 and 4; Disputations, *de Virtutibus Cardinalibus*, 1. On this structure as a component of the *imago Dei* principle, see *ST* I.60.5: 'Every creature is entirely of God'; and *ST* I.13.5: 'creatures are shaped to God as to their principle; their perfections surpassingly preexist in him'. Aquinas's emphasis of Prudence's dominant role in virtuous action supports the placement of 'Sophy' as a culminating virtue of *The Faerie Queene*, perhaps Book 11. But Aquinas acknowledges the mystical supremacy of the soul's affective power: 'Our will can reach higher than can our intelligence when we are confronted by things that are above us. Whereas our notions about moral matters, which are below man, are enlightened by a cognitive habit (for prudence informs the other moral virtues), when it comes to the divine virtues about God, a will-virtue, namely charity, informs the mind-virtue, namely faith' (Disputations, *de Caritate* 3, ad 13). The Disputations are cited from *Saint Thomas Aquinas: Philosophical Texts*, selected and trans. by Thomas Gilby (New York: Oxford University Press, 1960), 94, 213–14.

[72] See Calvin, *Institutes of the Christian Religion*, trans. Henry Beveridge (Grand Rapids: Wm. B. Eerdmans, 1845, repr. 1972), I.xv.8; II.i.5, 8; *Commentary on Genesis*, trans. John King (Edinburgh, 1847), III.6; *Commentary on Romans*, trans. John King (Edinburgh, 1847), VII.15; William Perkins, *A Golden Chaine: Or, The Description of Theologie* (London, 1600), 911–12.

[73] Spenser's self-love has been viewed in relation to his laureate aspirations (Helgerson), his *Amoretti* courtship (Dunlop), and his Irish governance (Hadfield). But Spenser, like Sidney, never approves of self-love in any form. His ideal of self-abnegation is quite distinct from Shakespeare's 'negative capability', which is resolved in imaginative identification with the central psychological principle of self-love, from which self-sacrifice may surprisingly spring.

tion at the peak of Redcrosse's training becomes increasingly less overt in Spenser's epic. Far more coherently and emphatically than in subsequent legends (with their diverse protagonists and interlaced quests), Redcrosse's foes mirror himself: each setting (Error's forest and den, Lucifera's envious court, Duessa's lascivious fountain, Despair's cave) mirrors his presumption, changing honor to arrogance. Thus Redcrosse must resist militant self-assertion until Una guides him to training in three stages of Holiness: humble faith in God (rather than personal pride), charitable works (rather than warfare), and contemplation of a spiritual goal (rather than glory in earthly conquest).

In the final six cantos of Book 1 the Sansboys (and other perverse triplets) are displaced by three definitive forms of pride, which sequentially assault the soul's three hierarchic levels: the giant Orgoglio mirrors Redcrosse's pride in his fleshly powers; withered Despair mirrors his heart's proud rebellion over the body's limitations; and the Dragon mirrors a culminating pride in collective worldly power.[74] For Spenser the 'cure' of pride (with its three lusts) requires three progressive hierarchic stages of training in the House of Holiness. To prevent Orgoglio's assault requires purgative faith in God's atoning self-sacrifice, rather than one's own fleshly power. To prevent Despair's rebellious heart requires illuminative charity, sharing God's love with the needy rather than resorting to proud suicidal vengeance. To prevent the Dragon's consummate, politically-magnified pride requires unitive contemplation of joining an all-loving God and a communion of saints and angels in New Jerusalem, rather than pomp and fame in earthly cities.

Defeating the three psychic levels of pride also requires a supernaturally-gifted supporting cast. First, Arthur, blessed with Magnificence (veiled in pre-Christian symbolism), saves Redcrosse from Orgoglio's self-assertive carnal pride. Next Una, a figural type of the Church, rescues Redcrosse from Despair's inverse pride of self-destruction and leads him to the House of Holiness's *imitatio Christi*, a lesson Arthur has not yet consciously experienced. Finally, counteracting the proud political tyranny of the Dragon that hovers over the 'city' of Eden requires revival by a 'springing well' and 'tree of life'. Thomas Dughi convincingly explains this mysterious symbolism as Redcrosse's internalizing (even in a half-conscious state) the 'springing well' of gospel promises (John 4.1–14; Rev. 22.1): this spiritual nourishment which renews the scriptural teaching in the House of Holiness is received without a priest and only *figuratively* affirms the sacraments

---

[74] On the dragon, well of life, and tree of life in *FQ* I.xi, see Carol V. Kaske, 'The Dragon's Spark and Sting and the Structure of Red Cross's Dragon-Fight: *The Faerie Queene*, I.xi-xii', *Studies in Philology*, 66 (1969), 609–38; Nohrnberg, *Analogy*, 135–47, 159, 181–7, 195–7, 203–4, 241n, 286, 335–6n, 341n, 485–6, 643, 666, 692n; Belinda Humfrey, 'dragons', *SpEncy*; Gless, *Interpretation and Theology*, 163–71; Harold Weatherby, *Mirrors of Celestial Grace* (Toronto: University of Toronto Press, 1994), chap. 1.

of baptism and communion.[75] These prototypes of Christ, Church, and Word, all implying a free gift of divine love, bring deliverance from pride.

In each book of *The Faerie Queene* (definitively in the first) the protagonist achieves the titular virtue, first, by self-mortification, overcoming personal projections of his own monstrous pride on each level of his being, assisted by heroic/providential rescue, religious training, and internalizing of gospel promises; and second, by seeing him/herself as an other, especially in a purified sexual other who mirrors divine beauty and glory by encouraging loving service to all. Subsequent virtues, descending ever more deeply into materiality, may seem increasingly tolerant of self-approval in the quest for glory, but this constricting perspective on virtue simply 'dilates' the holy goal and thereby incurs a special danger.[76] In the subtle combat with pride, a major problem for Spenser—as part of Leicester, Sidney, and Essex's Protestant party—lay in the conflict between their militancy (sometimes with Talus's savage aid) and the harder quest for a Christlike 'gentleness' that extends the beadsmen's charity to all: Irish as well as English, commoners as well as gentlefolk. In arousing the highest power of scripturally-fed Intellect as a basis for faith, the Legend of Holiness uses troubling metaphors: the Pauline 'armor of God' (Ephesians 6) and Revelation's apocalyptic 'warfare'. If these militant tropes are taken literally (as increasingly

---

[75] See Thomas A. Dughi, 'Redcrosse's "Springing Well" of Scriptural Faith', *Studies in English Literature*, 37 (1997), 21–38. On Spenser's Reformation focus on the power of the Word, see John N. Wall, *Transformations of the Word: Spenser, Herbert, Vaughan* (Athens: University of Georgia Press, 1988), 83–8; John N. King, *Spenser's Poetry and the Reformation Tradition* (Princeton, NJ: Princeton University Press, 1990), 58–65, 212–16; Richard Mallette, *Spenser and the Discourses of Reformation England* (Lincoln: University of Nebraska Press, 1997), 1–49.

[76] The descent into material-historical-personal reality ('dilation') would perhaps reach crisis level in the Legend of Constancy (like Redcrosse's captivity by carnal pride in I.vii). Constancy's hero must cope with Christian-Platonic anxiety over Mutability, the impact of change on the body and natural world, on the soul and human history. To lay the ontological basis for that crisis, the Legends of Justice and Courtesy depict allegory in a sensory realm (a descent from the intellectual realm of Books 1–2 and passional realm of Books 3–4). In Books 5 and 6 the antagonists are objectified, completely 'other': heroes do not face villains who are projections of their own flaws—in striking contrast to Book 1 where the mirror principle is most insistent. Artegall's enslavement by Radigund and Calidore's truancy with Pastorella do not suggest absolute falls from Justice and Courtesy (not like Redcrosse's imprisonment by Orgoglio-Duessa-beast). Errancy in Books 5 and 6 is depicted as subservience to woman, as reduction to commonness, and as ceding the arms that enable full power. In contrast to Artegall's shaming by aggressive Radigund, Calidore seems justified in disarming, becoming a shepherd, and serving demure Pastorella to learn Courtesy: he 'thought it best / To change the manner of his loftie looke; / And doffing his bright armes himselfe addrest / In shepheards weed' (VI.ix.36). Yet these complementary modes of bondage to woman (resembling Colin's homage to graces and muses on Acidale) diverge from the heroic quest, showing the humble nadir (the fullest 'dilation') of the quest for Gloriana.

occurs in Books 1–6 of *The Faerie Queene*),[77] the tandem evils of Errour and Hypocrisie may be endlessly reborn. Can Spenser's hero truly defeat self-loving pride unless like Erasmus in *Enchiridion* he/she fully perceives that 'one crysten man hath not warre with an other: but with himself'?[78]

IV. Shakespeare's Affirmation of Self-Love: 'Grounded Inward'

Shakespeare portrays self-love as morally ambivalent but deeply attractive. This radical difference from Spenser points to an alternate tradition, more Roman Catholic than Protestant, which views self-love positively.[79] Aquinas, like Aristotle, applauds self-interest as the basis of magnanimity and friendship, though he sharply questions the desire for fame. Of the commandment to love one's neighbor as oneself, Aquinas notes that 'the model always exceeds the copy'.[80] Even angelic love, says Aquinas, is centered in self-love, which in turn is centered in God.[81] Pierre de la Primaudaye, Shakespeare's favorite analyst of human nature, treats self-love as the 'wel-spring' of all passions and virtues:

> We love ourselves naturally . . . . For it is an affection which is as it were a beame of the love that God beareth towards all his creatures, . . . so that it is not possible, that they which are capable of any affection of love, should not love their owne bloud and their like . . . . Wherefore if this love and this affection were well ruled and ordered, it is so farre from being vicious, that contrariwise the spirit of God condemneth as monsters those . . . that want it. And

---

[77] Though the noble knights of Book 6 (Calepine, Arthur, Calidore) eschew weapons to learn and manifest courtesy and grace, the results of disarming in a fallen world are disastrous. Increasingly Books 1–6 fail to fulfill Book 1's militant, apocalyptic pattern as the allegory engages with increasingly materialist dimensions of human life.

[78] Erasmus, *Enchiridion Militis Christiani, An English Version*, ed. Anne M. O'Donnell, S. N. D. for E.E.T.S. (Oxford: Oxford University Press, 1981), 59: 'so it is that one christen man hath not warre with an other but with hymselfe/ & verily a great hoost of aduersaryes spryng out of our owne fleshe/ out of the very bowels & inwarde parte of vs. Lykewyse as it is redde in certeyn poetes tales of the bretherne gendred of the erth. And there is so lytell difference bytwene our enemy & our frende/and so harde to knowe the one fro the other'. Calvin too abandons the popular military analogy of God and Christ leading a war against the devil (*Inst*. 1.17.8). Cf. Aristotle, *Metaphysics* 12.10 (1075a); Augustine, *Confessions* 7.21.27; Aquinas, *Summa Contra Gentiles* 3.64; Gregory of Nyssa, *The Great Catechism*, 35. Christian militancy has been justified by the presumed oneness of the church's body politic: non-believers must be plucked out. See n38 above.

[79] See Robert L. Reid, 'The Problem of Self-Love in Shakespeare's Tragedies and in Renaissance and Reformation Theology', in *Shakespeare's Christianity: The Protestant and Catholic Poetics of 'Julius Caesar', 'Macbeth', and 'Hamlet'*, ed. Beatrice Batson (Waco: Baylor University Press, 2006), 35–56, 136–43.

[80] Aristotle, *Nicomachean Ethics*, Bk 8, chap. 5; Bk 9, chaps 4 & 8; Aquinas, *ST*, I.6.1, I-II.25.2–3, I-II.28.1–3, II-II.26.4.

[81] *ST* I.60.1–5.

therefore God ... appointeth it to be the rule of our love towards our neighbour.

Primaudaye acknowledges the potential 'unrulinesse' of self-love:

> when this love and affection is disordered in us, it is not only vicious, but also as it were the original and fountaine of all other vices and sins, whereas if it were wel-ordered & ruled according to the will and law of God, it would be ... the originall and welspring of all vertues.[82]

Augustine too considered good self-love as central to human nature, its norm, yet he emphasizes that original sin has distorted this primal impulse into an ambitious lust to build worldly cities of destruction. Nevertheless, Augustine maintains a belief in the possibility of true self-love, which can draw one to the City of God—if only it allies with communal well-being and with the sense of oneself as *imago Dei*. In *On the Trinity* Augustine describes self-love as the memory of the Holy Spirit implanted in the soul at Creation, a memory mediated by Christ.[83] Likewise for Aquinas, 'proper self-love consists in love for the self in God' (I.6.1 ad 2; see I.20.1–4), as well as reciprocal 'bond[s] of affection' and 'mutual indwelling' with other souls (I-II.28.1–2).

In two decades of playwriting Shakespeare evolves characters increasingly sophisticated in self-love, matching the growing complexity of their self-identity: 'I am not what I am' (*Twelfth Night* 2.5; *Othello* 1.1). A crucial question is gender. How does Shakespeare designate the most confident, privileged, and efflorescent self: masculine, feminine, an androgynous combination, or an unlimited protean power of impersonation and improvisation? A similar question involves self and otherness regardless of gender. Self-love seems to imply the radical, exclusive singularity of Narcissus, but if 'the marriage of true minds' in deepest friendship can unite souls (as is increasingly implied in the *Sonnets*), does 'self-love' (and self-identity) then include the bonded other? In the still broader context of social class identity, is the self-love of aristocrats (the main interest for Sidney and Spenser) matched by the self-love of commoners, as in the compelling characters of Bottom, Juliet's nurse, Dogberry, Mistress Quickly, Caliban? And finally if, as Aquinas says, 'Every creature is entirely of God' (*ST* 1a.60.5), then self-identity is inextricably bound to the vision of God, and 'proper self-love consists of love for the self in God' (1.6.1 ad 2).

In Shakespeare's earliest plays, which imitate Marlowe far more than Spenser, self-love is sinister but universally alluring as a drive for

---

[82] Pierre de la Primaudaye, *The Second Part of The French Academie* (London, 1618; orig. Paris, 1586), 458–61.

[83] See Oliver O'Donovan, *The Problem of Self-Love in St. Augustine* (New Haven, CT: Yale University Press, 1980), 75–111, 127–36.

empowerment, aggrandizement, and self-display. Noting the powerful theatrical impact of amoral self-love in Marlowe's protagonists, he spun this mesmerizing toy extravagantly and recklessly in the host of electrifying but morally shallow figures in *Titus Andronicus, Henry VI, Richard III,* and *Two Gentlemen of Verona*. This lustful, ruthless power-hunger still glimmers on the edges of *The Taming of the Shrew, Romeo and Juliet,* and *A Midsummer Night's Dream*. Like Sidney and Spenser, however, Shakespeare increasingly aspired to the status, mannerly behavior, limitless privilege and honor exemplified in Southampton and Essex's circle, the elitist ideal of gentility that Spenser praised and emulated in *The Faerie Queene*.

Beginning in 1596–97, just after the publication of the second installment of *The Faerie Queene*, Shakespeare largely abandons farcical comedy, and he moves away from the simplistic blood-revenge principle that governed his early histories and tragedies. He treats self-love more comprehensively and seriously, disclosing its tragic potential if mismanaged, yet emphasizing its basic goodness and natural attraction. Why? One cause of radical maturing could be the death of Hamnet, but one senses other influences. Why does *The Merchant of Venice* introduce a new form of romantic comedy with a much more complex exploration of self-love? We observe Shakespeare's gradual weaning from Marlowe's influence, notably between 1597 and 1600. Though still attentive to primal narcissistic drives, he now shapes characters with a more complex form of self-love, conscience-driven figures who struggle specifically with self-love, developing a restrained awareness that sometimes allows loving mutuality. Grotesque Barabas becomes the nuanced figure of Shylock, whose wounded self-love overshadows the play's other narcissists (Bassanio, Antonio and Portia)[84] and becomes a moral touchstone in this first great drama of social difference. Tamburlaine the conqueror becomes Henry V, who questions and debates his militarism with his soldiers, giving them 'a little touch of Harry in the night' and rousing them on Crispin's Day with a dream of social equality. Tamburlaine as self-appointed scourge of corruption is further reformed in Hamlet, whose scourging is long delayed and deeply reflective. A Marlovian willfulness haunts the core of Shakespeare's vision, but his final recensions of Tamburlaine's power-hunger in Macbeth and Coriolanus stress its self-destructive evisceration of life's meaning and joy. Dido is displaced by Cleopatra, and Faustus by Prospero, who

---

[84] With arrogant Aragon Portia refers to *'my worthless self'* and, encouraging Bassanio to be a Herculean savior, *'I stand for sacrifice'* (2.9.18, 3.2.57, my italics). Such phrases epitomize Portia's bent for self-derogation: her initial melancholy (1.2.1–34), tact with Morocco and submissive modesty with Bassanio, masterful restraint in the trial and the ruse of rings. Each episode, however, also shows ever-stronger self-love: snippy gibes at the self-indulgent suitors, dismissive farewells to Morocco and Aragon, self-gratulation at Bassanio's half-assisted success and in artfully managing the trial and ring-trickery.

uses theatrical word-magic not to trivialize earthly authorities but to reform and reunite wayward kings, lovers, and clowns into a harmonious ship of state. Shakespeare's protagonists still indulge in the mirrorings of self-love, but, having learned the dangers of exclusivist narcissism, they increasingly use the mirror of others' souls to build self-love into loving mutuality. In the ending of *Hamlet* (5.22.10, 157–61), *King Lear* (5.3.16–17, 160–1), and *The Tempest* (5.1.189, 201–13; Epilogue 16–18) each protagonist even begins to adapt self-love to the workings of divine providence.

Spenser's anxious endings of Books 5 and 6 of *The Faerie Queene* and Shakespeare's descent into tragedy indicate growing concern with perversions of self-love and declining ability to control its outcome, but their approach to this problem is strikingly different. For Spenser self-love is pride, an apparitional 'monster' projected from within and assuming enough reality to imprison and disable the soul on all levels. In Book 1 (and with growing opacity in Books 3 and 5) the protagonist is aided by religious 'arms', by scripture, and by mirrorings of heavenly light to overthrow pride's monstrous apparitions and make them shrivel into nothing—that is, to reveal the basic unreality of self-loving pride and keep it 'outside the self'.[85] For Shakespeare, on the other hand, self-love forms one's double or shadow-self, which must be acknowledged and integrated. This growing awareness of the profound problems and intricacies of self-love partly results from both poets' courtship of Southampton and Essex, leading literary patrons of the 1590s—a decade that developed into Southampton's near-bankruptcy and near-beheading, and the more traumatizing drama of Essex, whose marvelous gifts drew extravagant praise from Elizabeth and her court, and from Spenser and Shakespeare, but aroused in him an arrogant self-love which could not patiently bear military failure and the resulting public correction, house arrest, and withdrawal of his main income by Elizabeth—all leading to his abortive effort to usurp power in early 1601.

When in 1591 Southampton neared the end of his wardship but refused to marry Lord Burghley's granddaughter, Lady Elizabeth Vere, he was assessed an enormous fine and lost favor at court. In response to this crisis, Burghley's clerk, John Clapham, wrote the young earl a cautionary but flattering poem entitled 'Narcissus'.[86] In 1593 Shakespeare appropriates the Narcissus theme to court Southampton's patronage in *Venus and Adonis*, which (along with the success of chauvinistic *Henry*

---

[85] Though Books 2, 4, and 6 acknowledge the natural world's pleasure-principle, the heroes avoid exploiting it; victories are achieved only by abstinence and self-restraint, and in the natural realm weapons are less effective, cast aside especially in Book 6.

[86] See Charles Martindale and Colin Burrow, 'Clapham's *Narcissus*: A Pretext for Shakespeare's *Venus and Adonis*? (text, translation, commentary)', *ELR*, 22 (1992), 147–76.

VI) ingratiated Shakespeare in Southampton's circle. At the same time and perhaps for the same patron, Shakespeare again uses the Narcissus theme in his opening seventeen sonnets, which urge a lovely lad to marry in order to duplicate his beauty in children. Thus Sonnet 1:

> From fairest creatures we desire increase,
> That thereby beauties *Rose* [Wriothesley's name and emblem][87] might neuer die, [...]
> But thou contracted to thine owne bright eyes,
> Feed'st thy lights flame with selfe substantiall fewell,
> Making a famine where aboundance lies. [Narcissus's *'inopem me copia fecit,'* my plenty makes me poor].

In Sonnet 3 Shakespeare tries to resolve Narcissus' dilemma by recommending a more expansive 'mirroring'. Learn to admire your face not just in itself but in the imitative beauty of others (literally offspring, but perhaps figuratively any 'other' you influence):

> Looke in thy glasse and tell the face thou vewest,
> Now is the time that face should forme an other
> ...
> For who is he so fond will be the tombe
> Of his selfe loue to stop posterity?

As in *Venus and Adonis*, Shakespeare in the *Sonnets*' marriage-sequence (which shifts from urging marriage to stressing the power of his verse to immortalize) treats the Narcissus impulse not as an alluring deadly sin but as both natural and admirable.

Even in Sonnet 62 (following sonnets of jealousy and despair), instead of lamenting the 'Sinne of selfe-loue' that utterly possesses his eye/I, the poet imitates the beloved youth's narcissism by admiring (perhaps feignedly) his own imagined perfection.

> Sinne of selfe-love possesseth al mine eie,
> And all my soule, and al my every part;
> And for this sinne there is no remedie,
> It is so grounded inward in my heart.
> Me thinkes no face so gratious is as mine,

---

[87] On the insistent, capitalized 'Rose' of Shakespeare's sonnets (notably nos. 1, 54, 67, 95, 99, 109) as a reference to Henry Wriothesley ('rosely'), his ancestral home at Titchfield adorned with stone roses (ancient heraldic emblem of the town of Southampton), see Green, *Wriothesley's Roses* (n38 above). Also see Martha Hale Shackford, '*Rose* in Shakespeare's Sonnets', *Modern Language Notes*, 33 (1918), 122; *A New Variorum Edition of Shakespeare's Sonnets*, 2 vols. Ed. Hyder Edward Rollins (Philadelphia: J. B. Lippincott, 1944); G. P. V. Akrigg, *Shakespeare and the Earl of Southampton* (London: Hamish Hamilton, 1968), 3, 231–4; Lisa Freinkel, 'The Name of the Rose: Christian Figurality and Shakespeare's Sonnets', in *Shakespeare's Sonnets: Critical Essays*, ed. James Schiffer (New York: Garland, 1999), 241–61.

> No shape so true, no truth of such account,
> And for my selfe mine owne worth do define,
> As I all other in all worths surmount.

The sestet reverses this narcissism in a completely opposite way from Spenser. Instead of deemphasizing bodily and worldly pride by turning inward to reflect on soul and mind, Shakespeare uses the mirror to acknowledge his own physical and social shortcomings, while lauding these features in the youth, which the poet can enjoy by identification:

> But when my glasse shewes me my selfe indeed
> Beated and chopt with tand antiquitie,
> Mine owne selfe love quite contrary I read
> Selfe, so selfe loving were iniquity,
> T'is thee (my selfe) that for my selfe I praise,
> Painting my age with beauty of thy daies.

Thus self-love is not *sinful* per se; it is only *inappropriate for himself* ('iniquity' punning on inequity). The jarring line 'beated and chopt with tand antiquity' recalls his father's glove-making business. Did the poet work there, abusing and tanning his own flesh along with animal skins, a striking contrast to the leisured lifestyle and lily-white skin of the youth he idolizes? Modern readers cannot fully grasp the social-class dimension of the enchanting *'beauty of thy daies'*—not just a comely face but days, years, of highest privilege: luxurious clothing, food, servants, horses and carriages, a London mansion and palatial country estates like Titchfield, where favored plays like *Love's Labour's Lost* were performed. Add to this dazzling environ the youth's well-trained mind, learned in the classics and languages, sophisticated with travel and refined acquaintance, smoothly articulate. The crowning touch is the youth's confidence of his worth, reinforced by constant rituals of social obeisance and the assumed destiny of high political office.

The Narcissus motif that colors the devotion to a beauteous youth in the *Sonnets* and *Venus and Adonis* also attaches to the meteoric courtly and military career of the Earl of Essex. Seizing Occasion at every chance, he groomed himself for highest governance. In 1586 when Essex at age 20 distinguished himself for bravery at Zutphen, the dying Sidney gave him his sword. Essex then married Sidney's widow, and for the rest of his life tried to match Sidney's name in courteous chivalric honor. In the decade from 1586 until the celebrated victory at Cadiz in 1596, Essex confirmed his position as the queen's favorite, pushing himself to extremes in Accession Day tourneys and in wars against Spanish imperialism, maintaining a magnificent public image with hundreds of liveried men at extravagant cost (which Elizabeth underwrote with lavish concessions like the sweet wine monopoly), ardently attending to the Queen, and attributing his virile exploits to her godlike sponsorship. No wonder his patronage was so widely sought.

In a prefatory sonnet for the 1590 *Faerie Queene* Spenser vows to commemorate Essex's 'Heroicke parts', and in the 1596 installment he delivers. In Book 5 Artegall's rescue of Burbon (V.xi) celebrates Essex's defense of Henri IV of France against the Holy Catholic League (1593–94).[88] Book 6 greatly extends the flattery: in 'Essex, the Ideal Courtier' Ray Heffner cites abundant evidence that, during 1590–1596 when Book 6 was composed, Essex rather than Sidney was widely acknowledged as the main exemplar of Calidore's traits: politeness even in crises, chivalry in tourneys and in warfare, skill in athletic sports (running, leaping, wrestling), promotion of poetry and scholarship, eloquence which (as precautions for his execution make clear) could 'steal men's hearts away', intense love of pastoral retreat and dislike of courtly pretensions.[89] The historical allegory fits Essex equally well: marriage to a social inferior (Walsingham's daughter, Sidney's widow), courtship just before the death of her father (Walsingham-Meliboe), counsel with her insightful father about dangers of court and joys of retirement, and defense of courtly friends (Southampton and Elizabeth Vernon) from scandal. For further appeal to Essex's rising star, Spenser in *Prothalamion* (1596) praises Essex's victory at Cadiz over a new Armada threat— despite efforts of Burghley, Ralegh, and others to redirect credit for the victory and to blame Essex for not giving more plunder to her majesty. Finally, in *A Vewe of the Present State of Ireland* (1596) Spenser urges that Essex be given the Lord Lieutenancy in order to establish the high authority needed both to resolve the Irish troubles and make him impregnable to the detractions showered on Lord Grey.

While considerable evidence exists for Essex's patronage of Shakespeare's plays, especially *Richard II* and the *Henriad*, almost none indicates that Spenser won Essex's support, despite his arduous three-fold celebration of Essex in 1596. Jonson wryly notes that Spenser declined an offer that came too late, and John Lane testifies that Essex paid for the poet's burial only under pressure. Charles Mounts suggests reasons for Essex's disaffection, including unflattering allusions in Spenser's poems to Essex's mother, Lettice Knollys, as well as awkward references to Essex's sister Penelope Rich and to Essex's wife Frances Walsingham Devereux.[90] To this list one might add that Spenser's attempt to restore

---

[88] Ray Heffner, 'Essex and Book Five of *The Faerie Queene*', *ELH*, 3 (1936), 67–82.

[89] Ray Heffner, 'Essex, the Ideal Courtier', *ELH*, 1 (1934), 7–36; John Pitcher, 'Essex, Robert Devereux, second Earl of', *SpEncy*; Rudolph B. Gottfried, 'Spenser's *View* and Essex', *PMLA*, 52 (1937), 645–51; Alastair Fowler, *Conceitful Thought: The Interpretation of English Renaissance Poems* (Edinburgh: University of Edinburgh Press, 1975), chap. 4.

[90] Charles E. Mounts, 'Spenser and the Countess of Leicester,' in *That Soueraine Light: Essays in Honor of Edmund Spenser, 1552–1952*, ed. W. R. Mueller & D. C. Allen (Baltimore: Johns Hopkins University Press, 1952), 11–22; Mounts, 'Spenser and the Earl of Essex', *Renaissance Papers*, (1958–1960), 12–19; David Lee Miller, 'Spenser's Vocation, Spenser's Career', *ELH*, 50 (1983), 197–231; H. R. Woudhuysen, 'Leicester, Robert Dudley, Earl

Ralegh's standing with Elizabeth in the tales of Timias and Belphoebe (*FQ*, 3, 4, 6) cannot have pleased Essex; and if Spenser tried to flatter Essex in Calidore's defense of Calepine and Serena, that shameful tale cannot have been well-received by Southampton and Elizabeth Vernon. Finally, Spenser's *Prothalamion* complains about lack of patronage and implicitly cautions the great lord against hubris.[91]

During the 1590's Essex groomed himself for the queen's favor and for literary glory, presenting himself as a hero of chivalric romance in Accession Day tourneys and in war, and commissioning scholars to search the chronicles for appropriate scripts for his advancement. In 1595 Essex made a special appeal for the Queen's favor with the aid of Francis Bacon, whose device 'Love and Self-Love' implied that Elizabeth must adequately love and honor Essex to prevent his turning to forms of self-love. That Bacon would compose such a piece, and Essex so ardently approve it, is deeply telling.[92] In the troubled closing years of the century Southampton and Essex distanced themselves from Shakespeare, and infuriated the Queen, in three ways: in 1595–1597 Southampton's affair with Elizabeth Vernon, volatile maid-in-waiting to the queen, ended in pregnancy and secret marriage; in the Irish campaign of 1598–1599, with Southampton serving as Master of Horse, Essex's lavish expenditure for pomp and knighting of many followers did not avert administrative and military failure; and 1599–1600 brought Essex's house arrest, financial paralysis, and near-madness as he, Southampton, and other lords brewed conspiratorial fury and the ill-fated rebellion. Centrally motivating these lords was an ardent self-love, eager to attain honor, and so accustomed to privilege and praise that they assumed a dotage in the heart of all England.

Shakespeare seems to have felt deeply implicated in Essex's fall, for after the *Henriad*, which applauded Essex's popularity and implied his royal deserving (while warning against Hotspur's rashness), Shakespeare's great tragedies view with deepening complexity the problem of

---

of', *SpEncy*; Gordon Braden, '*Complaints: Virgil's Gnat*', *SpEncy*.

[91] *Prothalamion*, 5–10, 135–42, laments the proud who neglect poets. Cf. Fowler, 'Spenser's *Prothalamion*', in *Conceitful Thought*, 79–85; Patrick Cheney, 'The Old Poet Presents Himself: *Prothalamion* as a Defense of Spenser's Career', *Spenser Studies*, 8 (1990) 211–38; Anne Lake Prescott, 'Spenser's Shorter Poems', in *Cambridge Companion to Spenser* (n7 above), 143–61.

[92] See Linda Gregerson's probing account of Essex's 1595 Accession Day device, in *Reformation of the Subject*, 80–110. On Essex's career as courtier, general, scholar, politician, see Paul J. Hammer, 'Devereux, Robert, second earl of Essex', *Oxford Dictionary of National Biography* (London: Oxford University Press, 2004), 15:945–60; *Polarization*, n34 above; G. B. Harrison, *The Life and Death of Robert Devereux, Earl of Essex* (New York: Henry Holt, 1937), chaps 6–11; Robert Lacey, *Robert, Earl of Essex: An Elizabethan Icarus* (London: Weidenfeld and Nicolson, 1971); Richard C. McCoy, '"A Dangerous Image": the Earl of Essex and Elizabethan chivalry', *Journal of Medieval and Renaissance Studies*, 13 (1983), 313–29.

self-love in magnanimous, great-souled leaders.[93] *Julius Caesar* implies Shakespeare's knowledge of the conspiracy against Elizabeth, cautioning the noblest conspirators by the tragedy of Brutus.[94] *Hamlet*, a disturbing analogue for Essex's philosophic quagmire during the planned and failed coup, is Shakespeare's most compellingly unresolved brooding on self-love.[95] *Troilus and Cressida*, showing the utter breakdown of chivalry, is Shakespeare's darkest critique of the hypocrisies of envious emulation and selfish pride.[96] In *Othello* Iago dismantles magnanimity more thoroughly than in Cassius' seduction of Brutus, though despite T. S. Eliot's skepticism, we know Othello's self-love is grounded in goodness. From his elaborate opening ritual Lear is impelled by royal self-love ('Which of you shall we say doth love us most?' 1.1.51), which results in personal and political chaos but finally in recovery of true self-love and sovereign identity. Cleopatra's similar but playful vanity ('If it be love indeed, tell me how much', 1.1.14), along with Antony's battlefield bravado and their gamy flytings, gains immeasurably with Elizabeth and Essex as subtext, a poignant reunion of the phoenix and turtle.[97] And Coriolanus's insistent self-exaltation offers a final trenchant commentary on Essex's tragedy.

Shakespeare's mature tragedies do not, however, support Roy Battenhouse's indictment of self-love as these heroes' fatal flaw—a hubris severely compounded by Original Sin. In *Shakespearean Tragedy: Its Art and Christian Premises*, he explains Hamlet's problem as 'inordinate

---

[93] On the complexity of Shakespeare's fictional allusions to Essex, see Evelyn May Albright, 'The Folio Version of *Henry V* in Relation to Shakespeare's Times', *PMLA*, 43 (1928), 722–56; *Troilus and Cressida, A New Variorum*, ed. Harold N. Hillebrand (Philadelphia: Lippincott, 1953), 375–82; Anthony Esler, *The Aspiring Mind of the Elizabethan Younger Generation* (Durham: Duke University Press, 1966), 87–99; Richard S. Ide, *Possessed with Greatness: The Heroic Tragedies of Chapman and Shakespeare* (Chapel Hill: University of North Carolina Press, 1980), xiv, 3–4, 6, 16–18, 31–3, 46–9, 71–5, 98–9, 129, 132, 161, 198–201; Peter Erickson, *Rewriting Shakespeare, Rewriting Ourselves* (Berkeley: University of California Press, 1991), 26–8, 74–91; Gregerson, *Reformation of the Subject*, 80–110; Patterson, *Shakespeare and the Popular Voice*, 11, 27–31, 71–92. Also, see nn90–92 above.

[94] Rebhorn, 'The Crisis of the Aristocracy in *Julius Caesar*'; Jeffrey Kahan, 'Shakespeare's *Julius Caesar* and the Anticipation of 1603', *Cithara*, 44 (2004), 3–21.

[95] J. Dover Wilson, *The Essential Shakespeare* (Cambridge: Cambridge University Press, 1932), 79–87, 92–107; Edward S. Le Comte, 'The Ending of *Hamlet* as a Farewell to Essex', *ELH*, 17 (1950), 87–114; Karin S. Coddin, '"Such Strange Desygns": Madness, Subjectivity, and Treason in *Hamlet* and Elizabethan Culture', *Renaissance Drama*, ns 20 (1989), 51–75; Eric S. Mallin, *Inscribing the Time: Shakespeare and the End of Elizabethan England* (Berkeley: University of California Press, 1995), 106–66; James Shapiro, *A Year in the Life of William Shakespeare 1599* (New York: HarperCollins, 2005), 43–57, 85–106, 173–87, 253–333.

[96] See n38 above.

[97] See Anthea Hume, 'Love's Martyr, "The Phoenix and the Turtle", and the Aftermath of the Essex Rebellion', *Review of English Studies*, ns 40 (1989), 48–71; Alzada Tipton, 'The Transformation of the Earl of Essex: Post-Execution Ballads and "The Phoenix and the Turtle"', *Studies in Philology*, 99 (2002), 57–80.

love of self' or 'inordinate love of glory for the self'.[98] Although self-love is indeed the heart of the problem, Battenhouse's Augustinian-Reformation rigor does not match Shakespeare's view of human nature. Each Shakespearean tragedy (except satiric *Troilus and Cressida*) conveys genuine admiration for the Grandiose Self cultivated by all—male and female, aristocrat and commoner—and especially sought by the magnanimous protagonist who is thereby so vulnerable to perversion. Each tragedy ends with a tribute to the tragic hero, notably to Romeo and Juliet, Brutus, Hamlet, Lear, Antony and Cleopatra, and Coriolanus. As Ernest Schanzer notes, Othello and Timon provide their own epitaphs;[99] and even ruthless Macbeth evokes admiration for his sustained self-indictment and final courageous assertion of will.

Deepest tribute is bestowed on the self-love that finds consummation in relationship. Hamlet's fear for his 'wounded name' echoes Essex's dying appeal for auditors to restore his reputation, and Horatio's eulogy also echoes that magnanimous lord's call to angels to carry him to God: 'Now cracks a noble heart. Good night, sweet prince, / And flights of angels sing thee to thy rest!' (5.2.341–6).[100] *Julius Caesar* ends by admiring 'the noblest Roman', who acted 'only in a general honest thought / And common good to all' (5.5.68–70). In each ending Shakespeare affirms human goodness not despite self-love but because of it, especially when, as with Lear, the self-approval so fully identifies with the goodness of another. Though both *King Lear* and *Antony and Cleopatra* begin with a public ritual of self-love (if you love me, tell me how much), they end with an intensely mutual love (Aquinas's reciprocal 'bond[s] of affection' and 'mutual indwelling') that builds on *persistent self-love*. Even when Shakespeare escalates the waywardness of self-love, as in *The Winter's Tale* (his most extreme version of the slandered innocent), he still affirms the bold self-assertion of Perdita and Hermione that restores proper self-love in Leontes. Shakespeare's characters are most compelling when they display the truest self-love. We identify with Cleopatra's arranging an easy and beautiful death, with her desire to reunite with generous-spirited Antony. We identify with Desdemona's desire to be 'great of heart' like Othello, wishing 'That heaven had made her such a man' (1.3.164–5), yet also with her resistance to being slain. We identify with the eloquent *voicing* of self-love—the marvelous sparrings of Katherina and Petruchio, Titania and Oberon, Hal and Falstaff, Beatrice and Benedick, Antony and Cleopatra, and the captivating self-affirmation of soliloquies, whether of Hamlet or Parolles.

---

[98] *Shakespearean Tragedy: Its Art and Christian Premises* (Bloomington and London: Indiana University Press, 1969), 204–66, esp. 220–7.

[99] 'The Tragedy of Shakespeare's Brutus', *ELH*, 22 (1955), 1–15, esp. 15.

[100] Le Comte, 'The Ending of *Hamlet* as a Farewell to Essex'; Beach Langston, 'Essex and the Art of Dying', *Huntingdon Library Quarterly*, 2 (1950), 109–29.

The centrality of self-love emerges most clearly in the response of wronged characters to evil: Hero's silent faint and Beatrice's outraged vow; Ophelia's torrential release chiding those who have silenced her; Cordelia's rebuke of sisters who pretend to love a powerful sire more than themselves, and him for eliciting that falseness; Hermione's consistently healthy self-love (which evoked Leontes' fear of lost power) and her magnificent self-defense.

For the Spenserian hero such assertive self-love is never an option for either sex, their glory verified only in downcast eyes and blushing. Even when the hero is most fully celebrated, as in Redcrosse's apocalyptic defeat of the Dragon and union with Una in Eden, the victory is decisively undercut by eleventh-hour slanders by Archimago and Duessa—slanders based on his real abandonment of Truth, his dalliance with Duplicity. Their libels underscore the knight's vulnerability to *inordinate, impure self-love*, which Spenser translates as Pride: the senses' swollen carnal pride (Orgoglio), the heart's inverse pride of self-abuse (Despair), and arising from both, the mind's obsessive pride in worldly power, the Dragon eternally hovering over fallen Eden. Archimago and Duessa's slander drives home to Redcrosse, to denizens of Eden and all subsequent admirers, that he cannot boast of this remarkable victory, which was emphatically the work of divine providence: Arthur's heaven-assisted grace, Una's holy house of training in humility, and the 'springing well' and 'goodly tree' of gospel hope and healing. For Spenser, 'all the good is God's'. Instead of evoking our admiration for a heroic individual like Hamlet, Lear, or Cleopatra, the definitive first legend of *The Faerie Queene* persistently elides the hero's name (george, earth-spirit) figuring humankind. The first double-mention of his name is filled with irony, implying an unworthiness to be sanctified, as Archimago displaces him:

> *Saint George* himself ye would haue deemed him to be.
>
> But he the knight, whose semblaunt he did beare,
> The true *Saint George* was wandred far away,
> Still flying from his thoughts and gealous feare;
> Will was his guide, and grief led him astray.
> (I.ii.11.9 - 12.4)

His name's final double-mention is Contemplation's glorious enlightenment: 'thou Saint *George* shalt called bee, / Saint *George* of mery England, the signe of victoree' (I.x.61). Yet the knight, after crying out that he is 'Vnworthy wretch [...] of so great grace, [...] such glory' (I.x.62), continues in the final cantos to be identified, named, simply by the central iconic red cross he bears (I.xi.15, I.xii.31): his own identity is abnegated, or merged, in the definitively glorious self-sacrifice of the divine redeemer. At the ends of Books 5 and 6 moral vulnerability is compounded by the insecurity of Artegall's and Calidore's achievements, by literalization of demonic slander in the historical realities of Envy, Detraction, and the Blatant Beast. While Shakespeare's epiphanic vision of human goodness is finally affirmed in the Spenserian Elizabeth-type of Miranda, Spenser's elusive Gloriana disappears in the majestic unfinished ruin of his epic. With a longing like that of Redcrosse Knight in viewing the New Jerusalem, Spenser, tragically cut off in the midst of his race, turns from mutable, self-loving humanity toward the 'sabbaoth sight'.

Perdita, Pastorella, and the Romance of Literary Form: Shakespeare's Counter-Spenserian Authorship

Patrick Cheney

We have long known that Shakespeare models the Perdita story in *The Winter's Tale* partly on the story of Pastorella in Book 6 of Spenser's *Faerie Queene*. As Richard Neuse writes in *The Spenser Encyclopedia*, 'Both are exposed as infants by aristocratic or royal parents, both grow up ignorant of their origins in a society of shepherds, both are wooed by aristocratic or royal suitor disguised as a shepherd, and both are eventually reunited with their true parents'.[1] Even so, we have not examined this moment of intertextuality in any detail in order to re-think the character of Shakespearean authorship.

We need to re-think Shakespearean authorship because today most critics continue to see Shakespeare as the consummate 'man of the theatre'.[2] or 'working dramatist'[3] According to this *theatrical* model, the jobbing playwright eschews individuated literary authorship for commercial collaboration; he rejects printed publication for public performance; he recoils from self-presentation for self-concealment; and he sidesteps the goal of a literary career, artistic fame, for enigmatic anonymity:

> Shakespeare has become virtually the iconic name for authorship itself, but he wrote in circumstances in which his individual achievement was inevitably dispersed into—if not compromised by—the collaboration necessary for both play and book production. Nonetheless, Shakespeare's apparent indifference to the publication of his plays, his manifest lack of interest in reasserting his authority over them, suggest how little he had invested in the notion of individuated authorship that, ironically, his name has come so triumphantly to represent. Literally his investment was elsewhere: in the lucrative partnership of the acting company.[4]

According to this reading, Shakespeare did not suffer from 'the fantasy of literary autonomy', and thus he 'never demonstrated anything like

---

[1] 'Pastorella', *The Spenser Encyclopedia*, ed. A. C. Hamilton (Toronto: University of Toronto Press, 1990), 533

[2] *The Oxford Shakespeare: William Shakespeare: The Complete Works: Compact Edition*, ed. Stanley Wells and Gary Taylor (Oxford: Clarendon Press, 1988), xxxvi.

[3] *Norton Shakespeare: Based on the Oxford Edition*, ed., Stephen Greenblatt, et al. (New York: Norton, 1997), 1.

[4] David Scott Kastan, *Shakespeare and the Book* (Cambridge: Cambridge University Press, 2001), 16.

the extraordinary literary ambitions of Ben Jonson'.[5] Indeed, for many in the profession today, Shakespeare was not an author with a literary career but became constructed as such in the 1623 First Folio and then by subsequent generations.[6] Methodologically, such an approach relies on recent textual theories regarding the materiality of the text to respond to a performance model of Shakespeare as a theatrical man. Yet, as the quotations above indicate, the textual approach joins performance criticism in seeing the theatrical Shakespeare turned into a literary author only after his death.

Both the textual and the performance models have a long pedigree in Shakespeare studies. From Jonson and Milton, to Coleridge and Keats, to Greenblatt and Garber, a fundamental claim holds: Shakespeare is not a learned author with a literary career; he is a theatrical man who disappears into his theatrical medium, addressing audiences, but not his own literariness. In such models, the theatrical and the literary remain deep binary opposites.[7]

During the past few years, however, critics have been forming 'a concerted back-lash against the long-standing certainty that Shakespeare is primarily defined by his role in the theatre'.[8] The most important book has been by Lukas Erne, who in 2003 classified Shakespeare as a 'literary dramatist', arguing that this author shows 'a fair amount of artistic ambition and self-consciousness', and that he was committed to 'the theme of poetry as immortalization':[9] 'Shakespeare ... could afford to write plays for the stage *and* the page.... The assumption of Shakespeare's indifference to the publication of his plays is a myth'.[10] While Erne sees Shakespeare as a literary dramatist, he does not concern himself much with the literariness that makes up the authorial texts that he

---

[5] Kastan, *Shakespeare and the Book*, 5, 52; see 135.

[6] Michael Dobson, *The Making of the National Poet: Shakespeare, Adaptation, and Authorship, 1660–1769* (Oxford: Clarendon Press, 1992); Margreta de Grazia, *Shakespeare Verbatim: The Reproduction of Authenticity and the 1790 Apparatus* (Oxford: Clarendon Press, 1991).

[7] For a short history of such 'Negative Capability', mentioning the commentators cited, as well as discussion of textual and performance criticism, see Patrick Cheney, *Shakespeare's Literary Authorship* (Cambridge: Cambridge University Press, 2007), Introduction. All quotations from Shakespeare will be from the Riverside edition, while all quotations from Spenser will be from the Oxford edition of Smith and de Selincourt. The i-j and u-v have been modernized in all relevant early modern texts, as have other early modern typographical conventions, such as the italicizing of names and places.

[8] Richard Dutton, Review of Patrick Cheney, *Shakespeare, National Poet-Playwright*, *Shakespeare Quarterly*, 56 (2005), 371–4, here 374.

[9] Lukas Erne, *Shakespeare as Literary Dramatist* (Cambridge: Cambridge University Press, 2003), 5.

[10] Erne *Shakespeare*, 20, 23, 25–6. As progenitors of his project, Erne cites Harry Berger, Jr., *Imaginary Audition: Shakespeare on Stage and Page* (Berkeley: University of California Press, 1989); Julie Stone Peters, *The Theatre of the Book, 1480–1880: Print, Text, and Performance in Europe* (Oxford: Oxford University Press, 2000).

examines in large part bibliographically. Nor does he free Shakespeare from a 'dramatic' template. Thus, we need to extend Erne's classification, especially if we wish to account for the presence in Shakespeare's corpus of some of the most important freestanding poems in English: not simply the Sonnets and 'The Phoenix and Turtle', but also the three narrative poems, *Venus and Adonis, The Rape of Lucrece*, and *A Lover's Complaint*. Building on Erne, we might re-classify Shakespeare as a *literary poet-playwright*, an author who produces an important corpus of English poems and plays, both on page and on stage, before a national audience.[11] In this authorial role, Shakespeare invents his famed naturalist poetics (Jonson and Milton)—his 'negative capability' (Keats and Coleridge), which 'conceals' authorship[12] with 'undecidability'[13]—not out of personal reticence, a love of endless linguistic play, or a primal scene, but rather in professional response to the most famous model of authorship available in Elizabethan England: the laureate self-fashioning of Edmund Spenser, national poet, successor to Virgil and Chaucer.[14] By recognizing the self-consciousness of Shakespeare's enigmatic strategy of authorship, we may more satisfactorily account for why subsequent generations chose Shakespeare, not Spenser, to play the part of 'National Poet'.[15]

Shakespeare became the National Poet, and remains so today, but overwhelming evidence suggests that he participated in his own historical making. During the past few decades, invaluable studies of Shakespeare's literary relationship with such authors as Homer, Virgil, Ovid;[16] Chaucer, Petrarch, Sidney, Marlowe and Jonson,[17] as well as of the prin-

---

[11] Cheney, *Poet-Playwright*.

[12] Stephen Greenblatt, *Will in the World: How Shakespeare Became Shakespeare* (New York: Norton, 2004), 155.

[13] Marjorie Garber, *Shakespeare's Ghost Writers: Literature as Uncanny Causality* (New York: Routledge, 1987), 26.

[14] For the idea of Spenser as an English Renaissance laureate poet, I am indebted to Richard Helgerson, *Self-Crowned Laureates: Spenser, Jonson, Milton, and the Literary System* (Berkeley: University of California Press, 1983).

[15] For details on Shakespeare's counter-laureate response to Spenser, see Cheney, *Shakespeare's Literary Authorship*, esp. ch. 1.

[16] On Homer: Reuben A Brower, *Hero and Saint: Shakespeare and the Graeco-Roman Tradition* (Oxford: Oxford University Press, 1971); Richard S. Ide, *Possessed with Greatness: The Heroic Tragedies of Chapman and Shakespeare* (Chapel Hill: University of North Carolina Press, 1980); on Virgil: Barbara J. Bono, *Literary Transvaluation: From Vergilian Epic to Shakespearean Tragicomedy* (Berkeley: University of California Press, 1984); Donna Hamilton, *Virgil and 'The Tempest': The Politics of Imitation* (Columbus: Ohio State University Press, 1990); Margaret Tudeau-Clayton, *Jonson, Shakespeare and Early Modern Virgil* (Cambridge: Cambridge University Press, 1998), and on Ovid: Jonathan Bate, *Shakespeare and Ovid* (Oxford: Clarendon Press, 1993); Heather James, *Shakespeare's Troy: Drama, Politics, and the Translation of Empire* (Cambridge: Cambridge University Press, 1997).

[17] On Chaucer: Ann Thompson, *Shakespeare's Chaucer: A Study in Literary Origins* (Liverpool: Liverpool University Press, 1978); E. Talbot Donaldson, *The Swan at the Well:*

ciple of intertextuality underwriting these relationships,[18] and even of the author's acute literary language[19] join to form a composite challenge to the performance and textual idea that Shakespeare is simply a man of the theater. He *is* a man of the theater, but he is much more. He is an arch-theatrical man who, in plays and poems alike, engages fully the major canonical authors of Western literature. In intertextual studies, however, Spenser receives only intermittent attention; we still lack a comprehensive study—and on the very relationship that can clarify, arguably more than any other, the historic invention of Shakespeare's authorship. For, during Shakespeare's career, Spenser is the premier national author, the touchstone for achievement in English.[20]

In the remainder of this essay, I propose to look at just one example of what we might call Shakespeare's *counter-Spenserian authorship*. The goal will be, not to sever the literary from the theatrical, but to recover Shakespeare's Spenserian concern for literary authorship precisely within the anonymity of the theatrical medium. In *The Winter's Tale*, Shakespeare presents Perdita not simply as a graceful young woman of matchless beauty and character, but also, simultaneously, as a profound screen for masculine invention and authorship. During Jacobean performances, the boy actor playing the part of Perdita would formally rehearse this cross-dressing principle.[21] Since Shakespeare models Perdita on Spenser's Pastorella, we may begin by classifying Shakespeare's authorship in *The Winter's Tale* as in some sense *Spenserian*. I call it *counter-Spenserian*, because Shakespeare both *pays*

Shakespeare Reading Chaucer (New Haven: Yale University Press, 1985); on Petrarch: Lynn Enterline, *The Rhetoric of the Body: From Ovid to Shakespeare* (Cambridge: Cambridge University Press, 2000); on Sidney: Katherine Duncan-Jones, *Ungentle Shakespeare: Scenes from His Life*, Arden Shakespeare, 3rd Series (London: Thomson Learning, 2001); on Marlowe: James Shapiro, *Rival Playwrights: Marlowe, Jonson, Shakespeare* (New York: Columbia University Press, 1991); Thomas Cartelli, *Marlowe, Shakespeare, and the Economy of Theatrical Experience* (Philadelphia: University of Pennsylvania Press, 1991), and on Jonson: Russ McDonald, *Shakespeare and Jonson/Jonson and Shakespeare* (Lincoln: University of Nebraska Press, 1988); James. P. Bednarz, 'Imitations of Spenser in *A Midsummer Night's Dream'*, *Renaissance Drama*, 14 (1983), 79–102, and *Shakespeare & the Poets' War* (New York: Columbia University Press, 2001).

[18] Douglas Bruster, *Quoting Shakespeare: Form and Culture in Early Modern Drama* (Lincoln: University of Nebraska Press, 2000).

[19] Frank Kermode *Shakespeare's Language* (London: Allen Lane-Penguin, 2000); Lisa Freinkel, *Reading Shakespeare's Will: The Theology of Figure from Augustine to the Sonnets* (New York: Columbia University Press, 2002).

[20] For a review of commentary linking Shakespeare and Spenser from the late sixteenth through the nineteenth centuries, see Patrick Cheney, 'Shakespeare's Sonnet 106, Spenser's National Epic, and Counter-Petrarchism', *English Literary Renaissance*, 31 (2001), 331–64.

[21] For resonant commentary on the presence of authorship in Shakespearean 'theatre, in which there is a boy actor inside every represented woman', see Jonathan Crewe, *Trials of Authorship: Anterior Forms and Poetic Reconstruction from Wyatt to Shakespeare* (Berkeley: University of California Press, 1990), 160.

homage to Spenser as England's national poet and *critiques* Spenser's laureate self-presentation.[22] Most importantly for the developing history of modern English authorship, Shakespeare replaces Spenserian self-presentation with a principle of self-concealment—and changes that history forever.[23]

As the evidence of recent scholarship listed in this volume's bibliography demonstrates piecemeal, Shakespeare does counter Spenser, and he does so throughout his career. In particular, he responds to Spenser in the late romances.[24] Accordingly, most critics writing on *The Winter's Tale* mention Shakespeare's debt to Spenser—yet almost always in passing.[25] In his 2005 Cambridge edition of *Cymbeline*, Martin Butler identifies the historical occasion that likely prompts Shakespeare's engagement with Spenser at this time: the 1609 publication of the First Folio

---

[22] On this meaning to the term 'counter', see W. R. Johnson, who labels Spenser and Virgil 'classical' poets and Ovid a 'counter-classical' one; 'The Problem of the Counter-Classical Sensibility and Its Critics', *California Studies in Classical Antiquity*, 3 (1970), 123–51. For Shakespeare's simultaneous homage and critique of Spenser in *A Midsummer Night's Dream*, see Bednarz, 'Imitations'. In 1994, Gary Taylor showed how the 'blank' or negative capability that is 'Shakespeare' is an 'illusion'—a 'self-erasure': 'Forms of Opposition: Shakespeare and Middleton', *English Literary Renaissance*, 24 (1994), 283–314, here 313–14.

[23] For a rare word on the historic shift from Spenserian laureateship to Shakespearean negative capability, see Helgerson *Self-Crowned Laureates*, 4.

[24] See, e.g., A. Kent Hieatt;, 'Shakespeare, William', in *Spenser Encyclopedia*, 641–3; Neuse, 'Pastorella'; Paul Alpers, *What is Pastoral?* (Chicago: University of Chicago Press, 1996), 204–5; Simon Palfrey, *Late Shakespeare: A New World of Words* (Oxford: Clarendon Press, 1997), 14, 36–7, 109, 113–14; Michael O'Connell, 'The Experiment of Romance', in *The Cambridge Companion to Shakespearean Comedy*, ed. Alexander Leggatt (Cambridge: Cambridge University Press, 2002), 215–29, here 221; Cheney, *Shakespeare's Literary Authorship*, ch. 8 (on *Cymbeline*).

[25] For editions, see, e.g., John Dover Wilson ed., *The Winter's Tale*, Cambridge Shakespeare (Cambridge: Cambridge University Press, 1931), 167–8; J. H. P. Pafford, ed., *The Winter's Tale*. Arden Shakespeare. 2nd Series (London: Methuen, 1963), 96–7; Stephen Orgel, ed., *The Winter's Tale* (Oxford: Oxford University Press, 1996), 10, 35, 43, 45, 173, 175; *New Variorum Edition of Shakespeare: 'The Winter's Tale'*, ed. Robert Kean Turner and Virginia Westling Haas (New York: MLA, 2005), 353, 359, 366. For critics, see, e.g., Humphrey Tonkin, *Spenser's Courteous Pastoral: Book Six of the 'Faerie Queene'* (Oxford: Clarendon Press, 1972), 304; B. J. Sokol, 'Perdita's Tale: Dubious Piedness', in *Art and Illusion in 'The Winter's Tale'* (Manchester: Manchester University Press, 1994), 116–41, here 131; James H. Sims, 'Perdita's "Flowers o' th' spring" and "vernal flowers" in *Lycidas*', *Shakespeare Quarterly*, 22 (1971), 87–90, here 87, 89; Barbara Estrin, 'The Foundling Plot: Stories in *The Winter's Tale*', *Modern Language Studies*, 7 (1977), 27–38, here 178; John Pitcher, 'Some Call Him Autolycus', in *In Arden: Editing Shakespeare: Essays in Honour of Richard Proudfoot*, ed. Ann Thompson and Gordon McMullan (London: Arden Shakespeare, 2003), 252–68, here 263; Stephen Guy-Bray, '*The Winter's Tale*', in, *Homoerotic Space: The Poetics of Loss in Renaissance Literature* (Toronto: University of Toronto Press, 2002), 198–215, here 199, 202, 204, 210; James Ellison, '*The Winter's Tale* and the Religious Politics of Europe', in *Shakespeare's Romances*, ed., Alison Thorne, (Basingstoke: Palgrave Macmillan, 2003), 171–204, here 177, 179, 183–4. Critics have also seen Perdita and *The Winter's Tale* inflected with the romance world of Sidney's *Arcadia*, among other works, including the main source-text, Robert Greene's *Pandosto*.

edition of *The Faerie Queene*. According to Butler, 'traces of Spenser in *The Winter's Tale* suggest that [the] ... reissue [of the 1609 *Faerie Queene*] affected Shakespeare profoundly'.[26] Observing that Spenser became attractive to disaffected intellectuals of James I's court, Butler reminds us that the great Elizabethan poet of 'epic romance'[27] relies on a politics that locates courtly critique within an affirmative visionary poetics. The 'skepticism about courtly civility' that Butler finds particularly in *Cymbeline* becomes 'a sign that its debt to ... Spenser was political as well as literary'.[28]

If Jacobean contemporaries found Spenser's Elizabethan politics compatible with their critique of James' monarchy, it follows that Shakespeare's 'literary' dynamics in the romances might also cohere with that in Spenser's literary project. Shakespeare, I suggest, takes cues for his self-concealing authorship from Spenser but overgoes England's Virgil by *displacing* individuated authorship.[29] It is the Shakespearean authorial principle of displacement that makes discussion of it so difficult. Yet by looking in on Shakespeare's counter-Spenserian methodology, we may witness the poet-playwright competing with Spenser in the national arena of literary authorship. The arena is *national* in the sense that the King's Men performed *The Winter's Tale* in 1611 both in the popular Globe Theatre and in the royal Banqueting House, as well as 'sometime between December and February 1612–13 ... during the festivities preceding the wedding of King James's daughter Elizabeth to Prince Frederick the Elector Palatine'.[30]

In *The Winter's Tale*, Shakespeare's competition with Spenser before a national audience depends on four primary representations of literary authorship. Two of them are more obvious, so we may mention them only briefly; they present characters in the fiction, Autolycus and Paulina, as artist figures who have long been understand as such. The third is even more obvious, but, paradoxically, the anonymous poet at the court of Leontes who makes a cameo appearance in Act 5 is rarely remembered. The last (and perhaps most surprising) author figure is Perdita, who requires more attention, because critics continue to view her largely as an endearing representation of female beauty and grace—in other words, as a purely 'dramatic character' on the stage.

---

[26] *Cymbeline*, New Cambridge Shakespeare (Cambridge: Cambridge University Press, 2005), 11.

[27] Colin Burrow, *Epic Romance: Homer to Milton* (Oxford: Clarendon Press, 1993).

[28] Butler, ed., *Cymbeline*, 13.

[29] According to Spenser's glossarist, E. K. (who likely represents Spenser, perhaps in collusion with Gabriel Harvey), the New Poet relies on the figure of Colin Clout who 'secretly shadoweth himself, as sometime did Virgil under the name of Tityrus' (*Januarye* 85–6).

[30] Orgel, ed., *The Winter's Tale*, 80.

'Autolican wit': 'termed not laureat but poet . . . loreat'

In the first representation, Shakespeare uses the trickster Autolycus as a mock poet-playwright[31] in part to counter Spenser's persona, Colin Clout. Spenser's self-presentation emphasizes a distinct icon of authorial agency: in Book 6 of *The Faerie Queene*, Colin sits on Mount Acidale, serenely set apart from civilized society. Piping to the Three Graces in celebration of his beloved, the rose-crowned Fourth Grace, Colin creates a poetic vision that becomes vulnerable only to intrusion by the Knight of Courtesy, Sir Calidore, who causes it to 'vanish' when stepping forth 'to know' it (VI.x.17–18). In 'displeasure', Colin breaks his 'bag-pipe quight' (18), even though he goes on to befriend the knight. The contours of the narrative allow Spenser to present himself as a socially detached, visionary poet: a Neoplatonic mystagogue, able to commune serenely, if ephemerally, with the highest spiritual order of artistic 'grace'.[32] Here no reader could fail to see Spenser's laureate self-presentation; this learned leader of the nation produces his wondrous poetry outside the pale.[33]

Correspondingly, many critics recognize Colin's photographic negative, Autolycus, as an author-figure. According to John Pitcher, however, we need to 'be careful when advancing the proposition that we can see Shakespeare in Autolycus or even . . . Autolycus in Shakespeare'.[34] Pitcher proceeds to do so because he has turned up 'some new evidence' (252): Autolycus 'is an objectification of the thief that Shakespeare was accused of being in [Robert Greene's] *Groatsworth [of Wit]*' (255). By looking into Autolycus' literary pedigree, which traces to Homer's *Odyssey* and migrates to Shakespeare's favorite author, Ovid in the *Metamorphoses*, Pitcher comes to Thomas Walkington's 1607 *The Optic Glass of Humours*, which defines 'An *Autolican* wit' in terms relevant to Shakespeare's trickster:

> An *Autolican* wit is in our thread-bare humourous cavialeroes, who like chap-fallen hackneies feed at others rack and manger: never once glutting their mindes with the heavenlie Ambrosia of speculation whose braines are the very broakers shoppes of al ragged inventions: or rather their heads bee the block houses of all cast and outcast peeces of poetrie: . . . *they bee tearmed not laureat*

---

[31] Orgel, ed., *The Winter's Tale*, 52.

[32] Elizabeth Jane Bellamy, 'Colin and Orphic Interpretation: Reading Neoplatonically on Spenser's Acidale', *Comparative Literature Studies*, 27 (1990), 172–92.

[33] In 'Colin Clouts Come Home Againe' (1595), Spenser presents his persona as a Neoplatonic mystagogue inside the pale, surrounded by a community of admiring shepherds; see Patrick Cheney, 'Spenser's Pastorals: *The Shepheardes Calender* and *Colin Clouts Come Home Againe*', in *The Cambridge Companion to Spenser*, ed., Andrew Hadfield (Cambridge: Cambridge University Press, 2001), 79–105, here 97–101.

[34] 'Some Call Him Autolycus', 252.

> but poets loreat that are worthy to bee jirkt at with the lashes of the wittiest Epigrammatists.³⁵

Pitcher believes that this passage, which calls Shakespeare 'a poet of good note' (cit. 265), gave Shakespeare 'the opportunity' to present Autolycus as an author-figure: 'a parody of the control freaks Leontes and Polixenes' (265). Pitcher is not sure 'why Shakespeare did all this', but he suggests that it is 'possible that he felt that at least part of him *was* a thief—the Autolycus in Shakespeare—and maybe this was a way of owning up': 'the upstart persona may have continued to serve him well, as a stimulus in private. He was an actor too, ... so perhaps the slippery thief ... was just another of the roles ... that made up his personality' (265).

Another possibility is that Shakespeare used 'the upstart persona'— Autolycus as arch-'poet loreat', 'not laureate'—to *steal* from the 1609 printing of Book 6 of Elizabethan England's 'first laureate poet', Edmund Spenser.³⁶ In contrast to Colin Clout piping alone in serenity on Mount Acidale, Autolycus fully embeds himself in the noisy society of Bohemia, entering the pastoral world of sheep-shearing in Act 4, scene 4 simply to make his living (rather than sing consoling songs while tending his sheep, as is a shepherd's wont). Yet Autolycus is more than an 'actor'; he also sings songs and puts on plays, in a professional practice that resembles that of his creator.³⁷ Not simply does Shakespeare *conceal* his authorship in Autolycus (requiring Pitcher to argue for its *presence* as late as 2003), but Shakespeare offers a mockingly endearing self-image of an author who *lacks agency*. As Autolycus is forced to admit, he is swept along by events he cannot control: 'I have done good ... against my will' (5.2.124). If Spenser presents Colin Clout as a sage and serious Neoplatonic poet detached from society, engaged in a poetic art that celebrates the inward authority of the author over and against the Elizabethan monarchy, Shakespeare presents Autolycus as a witty trickster, both poet and playwright, wryly performing an art caught up in larger social and political events.³⁸

'A wave o' th' sea': Perdita and Pastorella

In the second representation, Shakespeare reworks Spenser's Pastorella story to recapitulate a career-long model of counter-Spenserian author-

---

³⁵ Walkington, *The Optic Glass of Humour*, cit, Pitcher, 'Some Call Him Autolycus', 263; emphasis added.

³⁶ Helgerson, *Self-Crowned Laureates*, 100.

³⁷ Cheney, *Poet-Playwright*, 273–4.

³⁸ This view of Autolycus coheres with Bednarz's view of Shakespeare himself; see *Poets' War*, 257–64. On Spenser's darkening attitude toward the Elizabethan monarchy, see Richard A. McCabe, *Spenser's Monstrous Regiment: Elizabethan Ireland and the Poetics of Difference* (Oxford: Oxford University Press, 2002), 101–20, 213–31.

ship. Rather than *secret* himself in a male author figure like Autolycus, he projects his authorship onto the screen of a romance heroine who *lacks a literary career*. Unlike Autolycus, that is, Perdita has no 'profession' (4.4.683) or literary vocation that maps directly onto that of her creator. Yet Shakespeare's enigmatic strategy helps explain what otherwise seems so curious: that Perdita, a lovely young woman of royal birth yet humble rearing, becomes an eloquent interlocutor in one of Shakespeare's most famous conversations about 'art'. Indeed, Perdita turns out to possess a *theory of art*, even *giving voice* to 'an unfallen nature that would be its own art',[39] and her character goes so far as to *personalize* Spenser's philosophical representation of the Gardens of Adonis, with its 'continuall Spring, and harvest' (*FQ* III.vi.42).[40] Moreover, others, especially Florizel, recurrently imagine her in literary terms. Without trying to diminish her beauty of character, we may wish to account for the literary features that compose her characterization. If we do so, we find ourselves in something like the author's literary workshop, in ways perhaps we have not often been. In Shakespeare's dramatic hands, intertextuality forms an especially rich site for exploring his model of self-concealing, counter-Spenserian authorship.

For this strategy of characterization, Shakespeare could have taken the lead of Spenser in the Pastorella episode. Critics remind us that the name *Pastorella* is multi-resonant, meaning, 1) 'in Italian "a shepheardesse, a young prettie countrie wench keeping sheep"'; 2) 'pastoral artifice'; and, most importantly here, 3) 'the pastourella, a poetic genre of OF origin'.[41] In other words, Spenser uses a pretty young shepherdess in part to dress up the pastoral domain in the masculine genre of epic romance that he himself pens.[42]

While we can view Pastorella as a romance heroine with her own character and action, or, as many now do, as a 'historical allegory' for Queen Elizabeth I, '[m]ore plausibly' we can see in Pastorella 'the poet ... weighing his own (not necessarily past) ideals and aspirations. She harks back to the pseudo-naive ceremonial world of *The Shepheardes Calender*', especially the *Aprill* eclogue, with 'Colin's song honoring Eliza, "Queene of shepheardes all" (*Aprill* 34)'.[43] Yet in the figure of Eliza, Spenser precisely fuses historical allegory with an allegory of his own authorship, as we have learned from Louis Montrose. In 'The Elizabethan Subject and the Spenserian Text', Montrose sees Colin's Song

---

[39] Harold Bloom, *Shakespeare: The Invention of the Human* (New York: Riverhead-Penguin Putnam, 1998), 657.

[40] See Orgel, ed., *The Winter's Tale*, 45.

[41] Neuse, 'Pastorella', 533.

[42] On pastoral as traditionally a self-reflexive genre, see Helen Cooper, 'Pastoral', in *Spenser Encyclopedia*, 529–32.

[43] Neuse, 'Pastorella', 532–3.

of Eliza in *Aprill* exemplifying an ideological process of 'Laureate' authorship that Spenser 'invents' as a 'new Elizabethan author-function': 'by gesturing toward the controlling power of the writing subject over the representation he has made, the *Aprill* eclogue works to suggest that in fact the ruler and the ruled [the queen and the poet] are mutually defining, reciprocally constituted'.[44] To support this argument, Montrose notices that Spenser's representation of Queen Elizabeth in the *Aprill* eclogue relies on an intricate authorial apparatus: 'The first stanza is an invocation of the Muses; the second stanza expresses the conception of an image through a genealogical procreation myth', that of Pan and Syrinx, the ur-myth of pastoral; 'in the third stanza, the unfolding of the image commences with the imperative, "See, where she sits upon the grasssie greene" (55); in the final stanza, Colin bids his perfected image to go forth into the world, to be received by the queen: "Now ryse up Elisa, decked as thou art, / In royall array" (145–6)'.[45] To this apparatus, we could add stanzas 8–12, in which Colin sees the muse of epic, Calliope, 'speede her to the place', to be joined by the other muses, who collectively crown Eliza with 'Bay braunches' (100–4) and celebrate her as 'a fourth grace' (113), joined as well by 'Ladyes of the lake', especially Chloris (Flora) (120–2), and finally by the 'shepheards daughters' (127). During the ensuing floral ceremony, these female pastoral figures adorn Eliza with 'Pincke and purple Cullambine', 'Gelliflowres', 'Coronations, and Sops in wine', 'Daffadowndillies, / And Cowslips, and Kingcups, and loved Lillies, / The pretie Pawnce, / And the Chevisaunce', matched by 'the fayre flowre Delice' (136–44). In this innovative representational strategy, Colin 'sees' Eliza in the terms of his own national poetry: 'Elisa becomes a personification of pastoral poetry; she embodies the literary mode of the poem in which she exists'.[46]

Because critics connect Eliza in *Aprill* with Pastorella in Book 6 of *The Faerie Queene*, we might wish to see Spenser using the royal pastoral female to construct an authorial typology, which proceeds along the Virgilian path of pastoral and epic, linking the early and late parts of his career. Set within a pastoral landscape in his epic romance, Pastorella typologically fulfills the poet's national ambitions promised in his inaugural pastoral through Eliza. For Spenser, the royal romance heroine dressed in pastoral attire becomes a representation of generic form within the pattern of a literary career. The heroine's biographical

---

[44] 'The Elizabethan Subject and the Spenserian Text', in *Literary Theory/Renaissance Texts*, ed., Patricia Parker and David Quint (Baltimore: Johns Hopkins University Press, 1986), 303–40, here 319–20.

[45] Montrose, 'Elizabethan Subject', 321–2.

[46] Montrose, 'Elizabethan Subject', 321. While Montrose carefully fuses the literary with the ideological, his primary interest remains political: 'royal representations may be construed as privileged instances of Elizabethan ideology at work' (*ibid.*, 303).

pattern—moving from pastoral fields to the world of the epic court—models the career pattern of the poet himself, as introduced famously in the Proem to Book 1: 'Lo I the man, whose Muse whilome did maske, / As time her taught, in lowly Shepheards weeds, / Am now enforst a far unfitter taske, / For trumpets sterne to chaunge mine Oaten reeds' (1). As her name intimates, Pastorella embodies the feminine-based inspiration for Spenser's 'pastoral of progression', which organizes his laureate self-presentation.[47] While it is now a commonplace for critics to *trouble* Spenser's Virgilian career presentation, we might see the Pastorella episode as an anxious attempt late in his career to re-assert his Virgilian standing.

To my knowledge, no one has traced either the origins or the afterlife of Spenser's striking technique of representing a beautiful female in the terms of masculine authorship, as Montrose influentially describes Eliza in *Aprill*.[48] No doubt, origins lie in both Ovid's Corinna and Petrarch's Laura, two famed masculine representations of the female written through with the discourse of their authors' art and career.[49] I am trying to suggest that we place Shakespeare's Perdita in this Ovidian and Petrarchan tradition, and in particular to see in this lovely young woman a Shakespearean *counter* to the Spenserian technique.

First, just as Eliza joins Pastorella in figuring Elizabeth Tudor, so may the chaste virgin Perdita 'recall ... Queen Elizabeth's steadfast maintenance of her virginity'.[50] If so, Shakespeare's play forms 'part of a national effort to recuperate Elizabeth Tudor as a new, less threatening Elizabeth, one who safeguards her chastity so that she may eventually

---

[47] Alpers, *What is Pastoral?*, rightly recalls that during the Renaissance the 'most common schematic placing of pastoral was by means of the genera dicendi—the high, middle, and low styles to which, by a coincidence which had a great deal of weight for critics since late antiquity, Virgil's three major works seemed to correspond. Thinking of pastoral as the humble member of this stylistic triad clearly affected writers' sense of it, perhaps mainly through giving pastoral poems a place in Renaissance schooling'. But then Alpers adds, mistakenly, 'But nothing very sustained came out of all this—nothing that can serve as a critical starting point, much less a model' (9). For a rebuttal, in argument of Spenser's 'pastoral of progression', a typological relation between pastoral and epic, see Cheney, 'Spenser's Pastorals', 82–5.

[48] In a personal communication, Professor Montrose says he does not know of anyone who has followed up on this particular feature of his work.

[49] The name Corinna evokes that of the sixth-century Greek lyricist; on Ovid's Corinna as a 'poem', see Alison Sharrock, 'Ovid and the Discourses of Love: The Amatory Works', in *The Cambridge Companion to Ovid*, ed. Philip Hardie (Cambridge: Cambridge University Press, 2002), 151–2. On Petrarch's Laura as both a real woman and an icon of poetic fame, see Robert M. Durling, ed. and trans., *Petrarch's Lyric Poems: The 'Rime sparse' and Other Lyrics* (Cambridge, MA: Harvard University Press, 1976), 4–7, 27. In glosses on Rosalinde in *The Shepheardes Calender*, E. K. mentions both Corinna (*Januarye* 120–2) and Laura (*Aprill* 190–1).

[50] M. Lindsay Kaplan and Katherine Eggert, '"Good queen, my lord, good queen": Sexual Slander and the Trials of Female Authority in *The Winter's Tale*', *Renaissance Drama*, 25 (1994), 89–118, here 101.

deliver it into her husband's keeping' (103). Second, also reminiscent of Pastorella, Perdita's biographical pattern may 'signal ... the end of ... pastoral' in a national romance drama about the formation of an epic 'dynasty'.[51] In these terms, in *The Winter's Tale*, as in Book 6 of *The Faerie Queene*, Shakespeare delivers a career-closing farewell to a genre that has preoccupied him from *Two Gentlemen of Vernona* to *As You Like It* to *Cymbeline*. Late in his career, Shakespeare relies on Perdita to transact a Spenserian career move, transposed from print-poetry to stage-drama.[52]

In her important 1997 monograph, *Shakespeare's Monarchies: Ruler and Subject in the Romances*, Constance Jordan is on the verge of this argument, when she concludes her chapter on *The Winter's Tale* with two invaluable sentences:

> Renaissance poets saw pastoral as the genre in which filiation or the right of a poetic son to his father's place was most directly acknowledged. Shakespeare made use of pastoral convention to remind his audience both of generation and the passing on of political authority, and of the conditions in which a monarch and his people might best cohere in one body politic.[53]

Jordan distinguishes between Shakespeare, who uses pastoral *politically* to shore up James's monarchy, and 'Renaissance poets', who use pastoral *professionally* to advertise their filiation in the literary canon. For her, poets like Spenser use pastoral to process a generic progression in their literary career, yet Shakespeare differs, using pastoral to process his government's ideology.

By locating Spenserian intertextuality within Shakespearean pastoral, however, we can see Shakespeare joining England's Virgil in using the royal pastoral heroine to wed the literary to the political—indeed, to see the literary as an anima of the political.[54] In *The Winter's Tale*, I suggest, Shakespeare establishes himself as a 'poetic son' who uses the stage to acknowledge his 'filiation or right ... to his father's place'. That father, I am further trying to suggest, is almost certainly Edmund Spenser. Not simply in Autolycus but in Perdita, Shakespeare invents ways to represent and counter the *Spenserian literary* on the Jacobean stage.

---

[51] Guy-Bray, *Homoerotic Space*, 210, 212, 214.

[52] See Orgel, ed. *The Winter's Tale*: 'For Shakespeare's age, the restoration of Perdita is the crucial element' (78).

[53] Ithaca: Cornell University Press, 1997, 146.

[54] See Harry Berger, Jr., 'The Origins of Bucolic Representation: Disenchantment and Revision in Theocritus's Seventh Idyll', in *Situated Utterances: Texts, Bodies, and Cultural Representations* (New York: Fordham University Press, 2005), 131–72. Pastoral is 'the process of revisionary filiation, that is, the establishment of identity by the creative misreading of one's sources'. Berger goes on to see the 'practice' of 'Shakespeare' joining that of 'Spenser' in illustrating a 'strong pastoral or meta-pastoral', by which he means 'pastoral that presents itself in the act of (mis)representing the pastoral that fathered it' (132; Berger's emphasis).

Shakespeare's counter-Spenserian representation of Perdita as a literary character functions as a crown to a career-long method. From early in his career till late, he frequently presents a male character who describes the body or person of a female with reference to the terms and classical myths of print-authorship. An early comedic version appears in *Love's Labor's Lost*, when the courtier Berowne delivers a nearly hundred-line speech celebrating 'the beauty of a woman's face', referring to the learned textualizing myth of Prometheus, yet without describing a particular woman: 'From women's eyes this doctrine I derive: / They are the ground, the books, the academes / From whence doth spring the true Promethean fire' (4.3.298–300). While this representation looks conventional—as simply a blazoning instance of male inspiration originating in female beauty—in reality it is doing something more. For Berowne, the male gazes at the body of a female through the lens of masculine authorship, compelling the audience to see the feminine origin not just of male sexual thought but also of male erotic art.[55]

The most notorious moment comes earlier, in *Titus Andronicus*, when Marcus describes the ravished body of Lavinia by comparing her, rather surprisingly, with Orpheus, and with Philomela: 'Fair Philomela, why, she but lost her tongue ... . / O, had the monster [who raped you] seen those lily hands ... / He would have dropp'd his knife and fell asleep, / As Cerberus at the Thracian poet's feet' (2.4.38–51).[56] Critics have long had difficulty comprehending the oddity of Marcus' speech, primarily because it seems to violate psychological realism. Even though recent productions demonstrate the stage worthiness of this speech, Shakespeare seems concerned in it to lay bare his own literariness, his intertextual authorship, especially with Ovid.[57] Marcus voices horror at the tragedy he sees, yet Shakespeare reveals how he makes such tragedy.

---

[55] On Prometheus as a figure for the poet, see Cheney, *Shakespeare's Literary Authorship*, ch. 2 (including the textual crux in the repetition of the two 'Prometheus' passages), citing George Chapman's 1594 'Shadow of Night': 'Therefore Promethean poets with the coals Of their most genial, more than human souls, In living verse created men like these' (cit. Richard David, ed., *Love's Labour's Lost*. Arden Shakespeare, 2nd series (London: Methuen, 1968), 111.

[56] Here we encounter what has proved an insolvable conundrum, for which Kristevan intertextuality (devoid of an interest in influence) seems the only remedy. In his Arden text (2nd edition), J. C. Maxwell (*Titus Andronicus* [London: Methuen, 1968]) glosses this part of Marcus' speech with Spenser's Amoretti 1.1–4: 'Happy ye leaves when as those lilly hands, / which hold my life in their dead doing might, / shall handle you and hold in loves soft bands, / lyke captives trembling at the victors sight'. But, he adds, 'It is probably a coincidence; if not, Spenser must presumably have seen the printed text of *Titus*. Amoretti was entered on the Stationers' Register on 19 November 1594, and published in 1594' (57).

[57] On Ovid in *Titus Andronicus*, see esp. Bate, *Shakespeare and Ovid*, 101–17.

A curiously allied moment recurs at the mid-point of Shakespeare's career, in *Much Ado about Nothing*, when Leonato describes the unconscious body of his daughter Hero, her cheek bearing the stamp of a blush, after she has fainted in recoilment from Claudio's public accusation of her infidelity: 'The story ... is printed in her blood' (4.1.122). Yet Friar Francis responds with an apocalyptic 'noting of the lady' (158): 'Trust not my reading, ... / Which with experimental seal doth warrant / The tenure of my book ... / If this sweet lady lie not guiltless here' (165–9). In Leonato's remark, Shakespeare uses the blush of the female to evoke the so-called stigma of print;[58] but in the Friar's rejoinder the poet-playwright deploys the discourse of the book to locate the truth of the unconscious young woman in the physiognomy of her inner character.

Similarly, in *Othello* the tragic hero is about to kill his wife, Desdemona, while she sleeps, but he does so with reference to Berowne's myth of masculine authorial invention, compelling us to re-visit one of the most breathtaking moments in the Shakespeare canon: 'but once put out thy light / Thou cunning'st pattern of excelling nature, / I know not where is that Promethean heat / That can thy light relume' (5.2.10–13). Such dramaturgy invites us to see in Othello's portrait of his beautiful wife an originary moment of masculine artistic creation—one that makes less sense with regard to the military hero in the fiction than to the author inventing him.

Finally, at about the time Shakespeare wrote *The Winter's Tale*, *Cymbeline* returns the book of Ovid's *Metamorphoses* to the stage, when Iachimo penetrates Imogen's bedchamber, to discover that she 'hath been reading late / The tale of Tereus; here the leaf's turn'd down / Where Philomel gave up' (2.2.44–6). As critics have long recognized, *Cymbeline* is 'Shakespeare's most recapitulatory play',[59] and many view Imogen's Ovidian bedchamber as a recapitulation of Lavinia's Ovidian scene back in *Titus*.[60] This masculine perception of the female, like the others, is intricate and complex, but in all of them Shakespeare presents a male figure expressing the vulnerability of female consciousness and identity in the terms of masculine authorship.[61] The examples are notable for the way in which they conceal Shakespearean authorship beneath the cover of lost or compromised feminine agency. By reading

---

[58] J. W. Saunders, 'The Stigma of Print: A Note on the Social Bases of Tudor Poetry', *Essays in Criticism*, (1951), 139–64; see also Wendy Wall, *The Imprint of Gender: Authorship and Publication in the English Renaissance* (Ithaca: Cornell University Press, 1993).

[59] Harold C. Goddard, *The Meaning of Shakespeare*, 2 vols (1951; Chicago: University of Chicago Press-Phoenix, 1960), 2:245.

[60] Ann Thompson, 'Philomel in *Titus Andronicus* and *Cymbeline*', *Shakespeare Survey*, 31 (1978), 23–32.

[61] For supporting details, see Cheney, *Shakespeare's Literary Authorship*, esp. chaps 1 (on Lavinia), 2 (on Desdemona), 6 (on Hero), and 8 (on Imogen).

the terms of authorship intertextually, we can glean not just a stunning fiction of male consciousness but also an intriguing window into male authorship.

In *The Winter's Tale*, Perdita forms an unusual variation on this pattern, so much so that we might miss the connection. For instance, critics notice how often male characters record their perceptions of this young woman—as if Shakespeare were trying to illuminate Perdita as the play's nonpareil.[62] Appropriately, the most famous description comes from Florizel, who reads into the humble shepherdess not merely the genealogy of royalty but an exquisite voice and the feminine motion of literary form itself:

> What you do
> Still betters what is done. When you speak, sweet,
> I'ld have you do it ever; when you sing,
> I'd have you buy and sell so; so give alms;
> Pray so; and for the ord'ring your affairs,
> To sing them too. When you do dance, I wish you
> A wave o' th' sea, that you might ever do
> Nothing but that; move still, still so,
> And own no other function. Each your doing
> (So singular in each particular)
> Crowns what you are doing in the present deeds,
> That all your acts are queens.
>   (4.4.135–46)

In this 'eleven-line lyric',[63] which is 'among the finest instances of the Renaissance lyric mode',[64] Florizel sees in Perdita 'a Sidneyan view of a golden reality': 'The deeds to which Florizel refers are primarily acts of expression. More precisely, he describes his beloved ascending from less to more perfect kinds of self-expression'.[65] First, Perdita speaks; then she sings; and finally she dances, while the 'wave provides Shakespeare's context for the dance in which motion and stillness mystically merge into something beyond nature and art and their union'—a 'permanence beyond flux'.[66] Exquisitely, Perdita enacts an immortalizing fusion of lyric poetry with dramatic theater. In Montrose's terms, Perdita embodies the literary mode of the play in which she exists.

---

[62] Goddard remarks, 'The best thing we can say about Perdita is that she lives up to all this adulation' (*Meaning of Shakespeare*, 2: 268). For eloquent admiration of Perdita's 'passionate naturalism', see Bloom, *Invention of the Human*, 656.

[63] Maurice Hunt, ' "Standing in Rich Place": The Importance of Context in *The Winter's Tale*', *Rocky Mountain Review of Language and Literature*, 38 (1984), 13–33, here 29.

[64] Lynne Magnusson, 'Finding Place for a Faultless Lyric: Verbal Virtuosity in *The Winter's Tale*', *Upstart Crow*, 9 (1989), 96–106, here 96.

[65] Hunt, 'Rich Place', 27, 28.

[66] *Ibid.*, 29.

Moreover, we have some intriguing support for reading into Perdita a kind of Shakespearean signature. For, as John Lee reminds us, Hazlitt found in the Perditean image of the sea wave an apt expression for the famed interiority of Hamlet: ' "The character of Hamlet is made up of undulating lines; it has the yielding flexibility of "a wave 'o the sea" '.[67] More recently, in a stunning comparison of Shakespeare with Spenser appropriate to quote at length here, Camille Paglia deploys the Perditaean image (yet without mentioning the royal shepherdess herself):

> Spenser is an iconicist, Shakespeare a dramaturge. Spenser is ruled by the eye, Shakespeare by the ear. Spenser is an Apollonian, presenting his personae in a linear series of epiphanies, carved out by the Botticellian hard edge .... Shakespeare is a metamorphosist and therefore closer to Dionysus than to Apollo. He shows *process*, not objects. Everything is in flux—thought, language, identity, action. He enormously expands the inner life of his personae and sets them into the huge fateful rhythm which is his plot, an overwhelming force entering the play from beyond society. Shakespeare's elemental energy comes from nature itself. I think this remark by G. Wilson Knight the most brilliant thing ever said about Shakespeare's plays: 'In such poetry we are aware less of any surface than of a turbulent power, a heave and swell, from deeps beyond verbal definition; and, as the thing progresses, a gathering of power, a ninth wave of passion, an increase in tempo and intensity' [from *Byron's Dramatic Prose*]. The sea, Dionysian liquid nature, is the master image in Shakespeare's plays. It is the wave-motion within Shakespearean speech which transfixes the audience even when we don't understand a word of it'.[68]

Like Hazlitt, Paglia sees the 'master image' of the Dionysian Shakespeare in the 'ninth wave of passion' that is Perdita's motional achievement, yet she does so in order to offset Spenser's Apollonian brittleness.

Perhaps accordingly, Perdita overgoes both Spenser's Eliza and his Pastorella, because she herself actively precipitates Florizel's literary representation, giving her lover his prompt:

> Methinks I play as I have seem them do
> In Whitsun pastorals. Sure this robe of mine
> Does change my disposition.
> (4.4.133–5)

Here Perdita expresses the very fusion of pastoral drama with dynastic epic.[69] While referring to a May-day ritual, the princess also evokes

---

[67] John Lee, *Shakespeare's 'Hamlet' and the Controversies of Self* (Oxford: Oxford University Press, 2000), 142.

[68] *Sexual Personae: Art and Decadence from Nefertiti to Emily Dickinson* (New Haven: Yale University Press, 1990), 195, Paglia's emphasis.

[69] For details on the pan-European politics of *The Winter's Tale*, see Ellison '*The Winter's Tale* and Religious Politics'.

the medium the audience watches, through the author's self-reflexive phrase 'Methinks I play', and in the idea of costume 'change'. Similarly, Perdita evokes the formal genre of pastoral in 'Whitsun pastorals'.[70] Unlike Spenser, Shakespeare makes explicit the female's active role in the formation of the author function. Proceeding along a dramatic Virgilian path, he turns the romance heroine—the heroine wearing the costume of romance—into a full character. She commands a striking theatrical voice; she performs a dramatic action; and thus she exhibits a literary consciousness. By contrast, in Spenser's Book 6 'we never once hear [Pastorella] ... speak ... and rarely do we get a sense of what she thinks or feels'.[71] In Perdita, the romance heroine acquires identity and agency. She becomes an international wonder, the subject of everyone's admiration, all the way from the pastoral world of Bohemia to the epic court of Sicilia. As Polixenes concedes, 'This is the prettiest low-born lass that ever / Ran on the green-sord. Nothing she does, or seems, / But smacks of something greater than herself' (4.4.156–8). 'Good sooth', adds Camillo, 'she is / The queen of curds and cream' (160–1).

During the sheep-shearing scene, Perdita's floral ceremony more specifically evokes a counter-Spenserian authorship.[72] Recurrently, critics find Perdita's flower-giving action recapitulating an earlier scene in the Shakespeare canon, that of Ophelia during her lyric madness,[73] without registering a fuller significance. If Shakespeare stages Perdita in part to remind the audience of Ophelia, he draws attention to his own art-form, his own authorship. In particular, the moment of recapitulation announces the author's generic transformation of feminine madness at the heart of his patriarchal tragedy into feminine lucidity in his dynastic romance.

The *intratextual* dynamics of Perdita's flower-giving ceremony find literary reinforcement in the scene's *Spenserian intertextuality*. While Shakespeare has been seen to imitate both Eliza and Pastorella in characterizing Perdita, we may also wish to recall the final floral ceremony of Spenser's career: in *Prothalamion*.[74] In this 1596 'Spousall Verse', the poet presents himself turning from 'Prince's Court' (7) to the River Thames, where he 'chance[s] to espy' a group of 'Nymphs' who collect 'flowers' in 'wicker basket[s]' (20–4). Spenser re-writes Ovid's myth

---

[70] On the Pentecostal significance of 'Whitsun', see Marjorie Garber, *Shakespeare After All* (New York: Pantheon, 2004), 847.

[71] Neuse, 'Pastorella', 533.

[72] On the link between Perdita'a flower-giving and lyricism, see esp. Charles R. Forker, 'Perdita's Distribution of Flowers and the Function of Lyricism in *The Winter's Tale*', in *Fancy's Images: Contexts, Settings, and Perspectives in Shakespeare and His Contemporaries* (Carbondale: Southern Illinois University Press, 1990), 113–26.

[73] E.g., Garber, *Shakespeare After All*, 845

[74] On Shakespeare's well-established response to 'Prothalamion' in 'A Lover's Complaint', see Cheney, *Poet-Playwright*, 246–56.

of Proserpina, who, while gathering flowers with her maids at Henna, is tragically abducted for eternal life by Pluto, god of the underworld. Through her mother, Ceres, Proserpina is allowed to spend part of the year on earth, and the rest in Hades, becoming a figure for the natural cycle and its fertility.[75] Yet, taking a cue from Ovid, Spenser turns Proserpina's flower-collecting at Henna into an allegory of masculine poetic invention.[76] For Spenser, the Proserpina story is not simply the 'classic model for the destructive intrusion of royalty into pastoral';[77] it is also the classic model for the regenerative pattern of pastoral and epic within a literary career.

In keeping with his counter-Spenserian authorship, Shakespeare presents Perdita voicing an apostrophe to Proserpina herself:

> O Proserpina,
> For the flow'rs now, that, frighted, thou let'st fall
> From Dis's waggon! daffadils,
> That come before the swallow dares, and take
> The winds of March with beauty; violets, dim,
> . . .
> The crown imperial; lilies of all kinds
> (The flow'r-de-luce being one). O, these I lack,
> To make you garlands of, and my sweet friend,
> To strew him o'er and o'er!
> (4.4.116–29)

While the mythic parallel between Perdita and Proserpina encourages us to follow Northrop Frye (and others such as Harold S. Wilson and Janet Wolf) in seeing Shakespeare modeling his narrative on the seasonal cycle and its ritual patterns of fertility,[78] we can also discover in the parallel a generic pattern of romance form within a literary career. Unlike Pastorella, Perdita shows *consciousness* of the tragic *raptus* that

---

[75] William Elford Rogers, 'Proserpina in *Prothalamion*', *American Notes and Queries*, 15 (1977), 131–5. See William A. Oram, et al., ed., *The Yale Edition of the Shorter Poems of Edmund Spenser* (New Haven: Yale University Press, 1989), 762; Richard McCabe, ed., *Edmund Spenser: The Shorter Poems* (Harmondsworth: Penguin, 1999), 730.

[76] On 'Prothalamion', see Patrick Cheney, *Spenser's Famous Flight: A Renaissance Idea of a Literary Career* (Toronto: University of Toronto Press, 1993), 225–45. On the metapoetic origins of the Proserpina myth in Ovid, see Stephen Hinds, *The Metamorphosis of Persephone: Ovid and the Self-Conscious Muse* (Cambridge: Cambridge University Press, 1997). On Pastorella and Proserpina, see Neuse, 'Pastorella', 533.

[77] Orgel, ed., *The Winter's Tale*, 43.

[78] Northrop Frye, 'Recognition in *The Winter's Tale*', in *Fables of Identity: Studies in Poetic Mythology* (New York: Harcourt-Harbinger, 1963), 107–18; Harold S. Wilson, ' "Nature and Art" in *The Winter's Tale*', *Shakespeare Association Bulletin*, 18 (1943), 114–20; Janet S. Wolf, ' "Like an old tale still": Paulina, "triple Hecate", and the Persephone Myth in *The Winter's Tale*', in *Images of Persephone: Feminist Readings in Western Literature*, ed., Elizabeth T. Hayes (Gainesville: University of Florida Press, 1994), 32–44.

the male author makes of the feminine when forming his literary career. Hence, Perdita underscores her lack of agency: she can only wish she had a 'garland' to crown Florizel. Yet, as the reference to 'crown imperial' indicates, Perdita evokes laureate self-crowning in the age of Spenser. In Shakespeare's hands, the garland crowns not the self but the beloved other.

Poetry and Theatre at the Court of Leontes: Paulina and the King's Servant-Poet

At the end of *The Winter's Tale*, during the statue scene, Shakespeare assimilates Perdita's feminine art to a third representation, when Paulina transforms Spenser's 'pictorial' poetry into the feminine motion of living theater. If Paulina 'speaks ... at times in an almost Spenserian fashion',[79] she also joins both Perdita and Autolycus in using literary invention to fulfill the Spenserian maxim made famous by Polixenes: 'The art itself is Nature' (4.4.97).[80] In context, Polixenes defends the gardening practice of grafting, in which a gardener weds the stock of one plant to another, preserving its status as 'nature', yet doing so through 'art'. In Polixenes' blank verse line, generations of Shakespeareans have found a memorable *poetics of theatre*, the very one that Sir Philip Sidney outlines in *The Defence of Poesy* and that Spenser articulates in *The Letter to Ralegh* prefacing the 1590 *Faerie Queene*: 'The generall end ... of all the booke is to fashion a gentleman or noble person in vertuous and gentle discipline' (Hamilton, ed., 714). Perdita, the principal auditor of Polixenes' remark, is the theatrical icon of that poetics.[81]

In particular, Paulina performs the resurrection of Hermione before the newly found lost one, who is happily joined by her father, her beloved, his father, and the counselor Camillo, among others.[82] While detailed discussion of this apocalyptic scene is beyond the scope of the present essay, we may note that Shakespeare's staging of a counter-Spenserian authorship does not suddenly appear, but has been carefully prepared for by the preceding action we have outlined. Paulina's resurrection of Hermione is *counter-Spenserian*, first because it appears to gesture to arguably the most magical scene in Spenser, Colin's creation of the Graces on Mount Acidale; and second because it reverses the

---

[79] Orgel, ed., *The Winter's Tale*, 35

[80] On the Spenserian underpinnings of this utterance, see Millar MacLure, 'Nature and Art in *The Faerie Queene*', *Critical Essays on Spenser from ELH* (Baltimore: Johns Hopkins Press, 1970), 138–57, here 155, 157 (with reference to *The Winter's Tale*, see 143, 153); Tonkin *Spenser's Courteous Pastoral*, 212–13, 219.

[81] On how 'each of the two debaters [Polixenes and Perdita] winds up arguing against his or her own interest' here, with Perdita the 'distrust[er] of art' supporting faith in art, see Garber, *Shakespeare After All*, 846–7, 851.

[82] On the liturgical underpinnings of Shakespeare's resurrected heroines in the romances, see an unpublished paper by Sarah Beckwith, 'Shakespeare's Resurrections'. Thanks to Professor Beckwith for sharing her manuscript with me.

metaphysical direction of Colin's dance. Whereas Colin produces the motion of the feminine dance only to witness its evaporation, Paulina brings the Apollonian statue of Hermione to Dionysian life. 'O she's warm', an astounded Leontes exclaims (5.3.109), only to witness his once-deceased wife blessing their newly found daughter, in terms appropriate to Shakespeare's liquid art: 'You gods look down / And from your sacred vial pour your graces / Upon my daughter's head!' (121–3).[83]

Often neglected in this conversation is the play's only formal portrait of a poet. Given what we have seen, perhaps it is no surprise that in this anonymous figure at the court of Leontes we glimpse a Shakespearean photograph if not of Edmund Spenser at least of his laureate poetics. In Act 5, scene 1, a 'servant' enters to announce to Leontes and Paulina the arrival of a mysterious beauty the audience knows as Perdita. When the servant relies on blank verse to describe the princess of Bohemia—'the most peerless piece of earth, I think, / That e'er the sun shone bright on' (94–5)—Paulina rebukes him for betraying his career-long celebration of Sicilia's deceased queen:

> Sir, you yourself
> Have said and writ so, but your writing now
> Is colder than that theme, 'She had not been,
> Nor was not to be equall'd'—thus your verse
> Flow'd with her beauty once. 'Tis shrewdly ebb'd,
> To say you have seen a better.
> (5.1.98–103)

Courteously, the servant-poet asks for pardon, but remains true to what he voices as a new poetic form of religious faith: 'This is a creature, / Would she begin a sect, might quench the zeal / Of all professors else, make proselytes / Of who she but did follow' (106–9). Neither torn to pieces like Cinna in *Julius Caesar*, nor mocked like the poet in Theseus' famous speech on imagination in *A Midsummer Night's Dream*, this gentle poet, intimate with king and counselor, emerges suddenly to announce the play's momentous event: the return of Perdita to her home and parents, in a stunning prophesy of the apocalyptic resurrection of Hermione.[84]

Yet this is not all. Leontes' poet resembles the 'laureate' poet as described by Richard Helgerson: the poet 'belongs at the court' and cre-

---

[83] See Garber, *Shakespeare After All*: 'Generations of scholars, directors, actors, and audiences have recognized that the astonishing phenomenon with which this play closes, the statue that comes to life, is a strong and apt figure for the transformative power of drama in general and of Shakespearean drama in particular . . . . The art itself is nature' (850–1).

[84] Hunter discusses Leontes' court poet as one of only two 'Persons who Draw Favorable Comment for Poetizing' in Shakespeare, the other being the Second Citizen in the opening act of *Coriolanus*: Edwin R. Hunter, *Shakespeare and the Common Sense* (Boston: Christopher Publishing, 1954), 126–31.

ates 'an ideal community' at 'the side of the monarch'.[85] In particular, Leontes' laureate poet has devoted his career to praising the unequalled beauty of a queen who no longer lives. While we can speculate that Paulina has secretly patronized this poet to keep Hermione *evergreen* in Leontes' memory, in preparation for the apocalyptic ending she will bring about, this poet-figure rather perfectly evokes the laureate art of Spenser at the court of Queen Elizabeth—not simply Spenser's career-long use of poetry to celebrate a royal feminine beauty, but also the principal metaphor by which he became known to contemporaries, that of the water-trope: 'your verse / Flow'd with her beauty once: 'Tis shrewdly ebb'd'.

Spenser may be our arch-Apollonian poet, but he himself is careful to locate the origin of his 'Botticellian hard edge' right at the water's font. Thus, around the turn of the seventeenth century, those alert Cambridge authors of *The Return from Parnassus* register Spenser's use of the water-fall as his signature trope for a poetics of Elizabethan glory: 'the waters fall he tun'd for fame, / And in each barke engrav'd Elizaes name' (7: 279–80). No doubt the origin of the signature traces to *The Shepheardes Calender*, where Spenser habitually presents Colin creating his art beside a waterfall (*Aprill* 33–6, *June* 7–8, *August* 153–6, *December* 1–4)—a portrait engraved in the woodcuts to both *Aprill* and *December*.[86] Moreover, in the middle of his career, in *Amoretti* 75, Spenser presents himself walking on the beach with his fiancé, another Elizabeth (as he says in Sonnet 74), and writing 'her name upon the strand' (1), in a representation that Shakespeare likely imitates in his own Sonnet 60, 'Like as the waves make towards the pibbled shore' (1).[87] Finally, at the very end of his career, as we have seen in *Prothalamion*, Spenser presents himself beside a body of water, the most famous on English soil: 'Sweete Themmes runne softly, till I end my Song' (18).

While commonplace, Paulina's reference to the court poet's verse, which 'Flow'd once' with Hermione's 'beauty', but now has 'ebb'd' in light of 'the rarest of all women' (112), supports the evidence we have reviewed, to suggest that late in his career Shakespeare rehearses the laureate career of Spenser before a national audience.

---

[85] *Self-Crowned Laureates*, 239.

[86] For Marlowe's response to Spenser's water-trope in 'The Passionate Shepherd to His Love', and Sir Hugh Evans' obsessive voicing of its shallowness in *Merry Wives of Windsor*, see Patrick Cheney, *Marlowe's Counterfeit Profession: Ovid, Spenser, Counter-Nationhood* (Toronto: University of Toronto Press, 1997), 78–87.

[87] On the likelihood of a borrowing here, see William J. Kennedy, 'Shakespeare and the Development of English Poetry', in *The Cambridge Companion to Shakespeare's Poetry*, ed., Patrick Cheney (Cambridge: Cambridge University Press, 2007), 14–32, here 27.

Conclusion

The preceding analysis helps us call into question two popular and interrelated views of Shakespeare's career: first, that he came to London to be a print-poet but then 'abandoned' this literary career to become a man of the theatre;[88] and second, that 'Shakespeare had to throw off Spenser in order to get on with his own creative mission'.[89] As we have seen, in 1611 he still confronts Spenser to pursue his creative mission, and he makes this confrontation a central feature of both his plays and his poems, from early to late. Thus, we may wish to resist a view of Shakespeare that depends on the binary opposition between the literary and the theatrical. Throughout his career, on page and on stage, his art refuses that binary.

Through intertextuality in *The Winter's Tale*, Shakespeare intricately fuses the literary to the theatrical in order to revise Spenser's laureate authorship. He creates a *counter-authorship*, which subtly displays a national literary imaginary concealing authorship, superimposing Ovidian myths of invention onto the dramatic character of a young romance heroine. Thereby, Shakespeare illuminates rather than asserts a feminine origin to his creativity as England's post-Spenserian National Poet. The politics of Shakespeare's engagement with Spenser remains elusive, as politics often does in Shakespeare, but perhaps in this play we see Shakespeare not just critiquing James' monarchy but revising it, when in the last line of the play a king chooses to locate authority in a feminine-directed form: 'Hastily lead away', Leontes tells Paulina (5.3.155).[90] For Shakespeare, Spenserian intertextuality becomes a dramatic site of a nationally ambitious authorship, and Perdita becomes the icon not simply of a royal romance heroine, but of a cross-gender, cross-genre authorship: a theatre of Spenserian epic romance form exquisitely wed to lyric poetry.

---

[88] Gary Schmidgall, *Shakespeare and the Poet's Life* (Lexington: University Press of Kentucky, 1990), 1; and Kermode, *Shakespeare's Language*, 3, 17.

[89] Paglia, *Sexual Personae*, 194.

[90] For the idea that Spenser centralizes the major genres of his career—pastoral, epic, love lyric, and hymn—around the masculine perception of the feminine, see Cheney, *Spenser's Famous Flight*, 76.

Pastoral Forms and Religious Reform in Spenser and Shakespeare

Karen Nelson

What does an examination of the pastoral literature written by Edmund Spenser and William Shakespeare in the 1590s contribute to current efforts to understand both authors' relationships to religious controversies of the decade?[1] English authors of pastoral literature, along with their continental counterparts, were often engaged in 'figuring forth' debates about reform and counter-reform with their shepherds and shepherdesses.[2] While Spenser's *Shepheardes Calender* and the Books of Holinesse and Justice of the *Faerie Queene* have been considered extensively in light of these controversies, the Book of Courtesie, Book Six of the *Faerie Queene*, with its numerous pastoral sequences, has garnered less attention.[3] Similarly, while many of Shakespeare's plays have been

---

[1] Scholarship on this topic is vast. As Samuel Schoenbaum noted in *Shakespeare's Lives* (1970; Oxford: Clarendon Press, 1991), biographers and literary historians have advanced a multiplicity of arguments surrounding Shakespeare's religion, and the same is true for Spenser. Representative recent monographs include Arthur Marotti, *Religious Ideology and Cultural Fantasy: Catholic and anti-Catholic Discourses in Early Modern England* (Notre Dame: University of Notre Dame Press, 2005); Daniel W. Doerksen and Christopher Hodgkins, *Centered on the Word: Literature, Scripture, and the Tudor-Stuart Middle Way* (Newark: University of Delaware Press, 2004); Richard Wilson, *Secret Shakespeare: Studies in Theatre, Religion, and Resistance* (Manchester: Manchester University Press, 2004); Richard Dutton, Alison Findlay, and Richard Wilson, eds., *Region, Religion, and Patronage: Lancastrian Shakespeare* (Manchester: Manchester University Press, 2003); and Andrew Hadfield, *Shakespeare, Spenser, and the Matter of Britain* (New York: Palgrave Macmillan, 2004).

[2] For a persuasive assessment of the romance tradition in light of these debates, along with a most useful outline of some issues of central concern to the 1590s, see Donna Hamilton, *Anthony Munday and the Catholics* (Aldershot: Ashgate, 2005), especially 'The Translation of Iberian Chivalric Romances, 1581–1619', 73–112.

[3] See especially Harry Berger, Jr., 'Archimago: Between Text and Countertext', *Studies in English Literature*, 43:1 (2003), 19–64; Todd Butler, 'That "Saluage Nation": Contextualizing the Multitudes in Edmund Spenser's *The Faerie Queene*', *Spenser Studies*, 19 (2004), 93–124; Gerald Morgan, ' "Add faith vnto your force": The Perfecting of Spenser's Knight of Holiness in Faith and Humility', *Renaissance Studies*, 18:3 (2004), 449–74; and Lauren Silberman, '*The Faerie Queene*, Book V, and the Politics of Text', *Spenser Studies*, 19 (2004), 1–16. Anne Lake Prescott, in 'Complicating the Allegory: Spenser and Religion in Recent Scholarship', *Renaissance and Reformation*, 25:4 (2001), 9–23, notes 'an increased sense of Spenser's own slipperiness' and 'a sharper awareness of the Reformation's dynamic instability' (11) and also observes tendencies to read the last books of the epic as, 'if not less religious, at least more secular' (14). She asserts, 'Hence the Book of Courtesy, for example, is also the smooth-tongued Book of Kindly Lying, the Book of Flattery, the Book of Evasion (narrative and rhetorical)' (14) and concludes her lightening-quick reading of Book Six by stating that Spenser's 'awareness that protecting or serving the Gospel and the Church of England in the 1590s required problematic compromises and entailed some painful defeats or postponements' (15).

examined against the backdrop of the politics of religion, *As You Like It* is less often studied within this context.[4] Both, though, emerged during the period that followed the defeat of the Spanish Armada and preceded the Gunpowder Plot, and both refract a range of responses to what was called the 'Catholic threat' by those anxious to shore up and consolidate reforms within the English church. These responses are especially available from the ways that Spenser and Shakespeare characterize hermits, wild men, and ritualistic sacrifices, and also in the ways that both authors explore the dynamics of communities in exile in the wildernesses of Faeryland and Arden. These literary elements carry with them specific referents to Catholic and anti-Catholic debates of the 1590s, especially controversies surrounding the Eucharist, the priests and Jesuits of the Roman Catholic missions to England, and issues that emerged for English communities of religious exile on the Continent.[5] Set beside one another, they illuminate the complexity of representing religious debates as poesy and reveal the ways that both authors play with the 'bodies' available to them from the rhetorical figures of their counterparts writing more dogmatic tracts.[6]

In order to show some of the ways Shakespeare and Spenser manipulate these debates in two works that are more traditionally appreciated for their playfulness with poetic form and for their ability to entertain, I will first outline quickly some of the reasons that pastoral poetics were available to reflect controversies concerning religion. Throughout the discussion I will identify and describe, briefly, some of the more central religious debates and concerns in England in the 1590s. From there,

---

[4] Carol Enos's recent work is most illuminating. See 'Catholic Exiles in Flanders and *As You Like It*; or, What If You Don't Like It At All?' in *Theatre and Religion: Lancasterian Shakespeare*, ed. Richard Dutton, Alison Findlay, and Richard Wilson (Manchester: Manchester University Press, 2003), 130–42.

[5] For a most useful study of exile communities in the Irish context, see Christopher Highley, *Shakespeare, Spenser, and Ireland* (Cambridge: Cambridge University Press, 1997). Highley also discusses English Catholics in '"Lost British lamb": English Catholic Exiles and the Problem of Britain', *British Identities and English Renaissance Literature*, ed. David J. Baker and Willy Maley (Cambridge: Cambridge University Press, 2002) 37–50. See also Dorothy Latz, 'Introduction', *Neglected English Literature: Recusant Writings of the 16th–17th Centuries*, Salzburg Studies in English Literature 92 (Salzburg: Institut für Anglistik und Amerikanistik, Universität Salzburg, 1997); Margaret Mary Littlehales, *Mary Ward: Pilgrim and Mystic 1585–1645* (1998; London: Burns & Oates, 2001); Claire Walker, *Gender and Politics in Early Modern Europe: English Convents in France and the Low Countries* (Basingstoke: Palgrave Macmillan, 2003). For additional information about Protestants in exile, see David Shorney, *Protestant Nonconformity and Roman Catholicism: A Guide to the Sources in the Public Record Office* (London: PRO Publications, 1996); see also the essays included in *Tolerance and Intolerance in the European Reformation*, ed. Ole Peter Grell and Bob Scribner (Cambridge: Cambridge University Press, 1996), especially 'Exile and Tolerance' by Ole Peter Grell, 182–98.

[6] Annabel Patterson, *Pastoral Ideology: Virgil to Valery* (Berkeley: University of California Press, 1987), reminds readers to ask what pastoral can do, rather than attempting yet another definition of pastoral conventions. Her call is most instructive.

I will examine some of the ways that the hermits and savage men of Spenser's Book of Courtesie reflect conversations about the roles of religious leaders and the ceremonies surrounding communion. I will then place these figures alongside the hermits in the wildernesses of *As You Like It*, and consider the ways in which Shakespeare's hermits diverge in key ways from similar figures in Thomas Lodge's *Rosalind*.[7] Finally, I will consider briefly the situations in which Spenser and Shakespeare leave their shepherdesses and complete their narratives; these endings provide perspective upon the sorts of resolution each author offered as closure.

When set against one another, these texts reveal subtleties about the debates surrounding Catholicism in England. As Richard Strier has pointed out, 'the early modern period ... was bursting with manifold and contradictory views and positions, old and new, orthodox and heterodox—and all in print'.[8] An examination of exile, sacrifice, the hermits, and the beloved in Spenser's Book Six of *The Faerie Queene* and Shakespeare's *As You Like It* emphasizes that Spenser and Shakespeare, as authors of literature rather than polemic, shared the luxury that literary production provided. Poets and dramatists of the 1590s could 'figure forth' multiple positions in single works. All within one play or book, authors could play with the implications of characters as extremists, of positions explored to their most hyperbolic, of contradictory perspectives alongside one another or in battle, of literary conventions and their boundaries.[9]

One convention in the sixteenth century was to write and read pastoral poetics as commentary upon matters surrounding the church.[10] One visual link between the two comes from a woodcut (see figure one) that was used to embellish various early print documents that provided structural support to the Church of the early sixteenth century, including missals and *Constitutiones legitime seu legatine regionis anglicane cu[m] subtilissima interpretatione d[omi]ni Johannis de Athon*.[11] Virgil's *Eclogues*, es-

---

[7] I am indebted in many ways to Clare R. Kinney, especially her methods in 'Feigning Female Faining: Spenser, Lodge, Shakespeare, and Rosalind', *Modern Philology*, 95:3 (1998), 291–315.

[8] Richard Strier, *Resistant Structures: Particularity, Radicalism, and Renaissance Texts* (Berkeley: University of California Press, 1995), 120.

[9] Lisa Freinkel, in *Reading Shakespeare's Will: The Theology of Figure from Augustine to the Sonnets* (New York: Columbia University Press, 2002), offers a most helpful methodological model. She locates her effort not in identifying Shakespeare's religious affiliation but instead in considering *figura*, or rhetoric writ large, within many varied traditions. I oversimplify here a very elegant project.

[10] Francesco Petrarca, *Bucolicum Carmen*, trans. Thomas G. Bergin (New Haven: Yale University Press, 1974).

[11] Missals include those printed in 1500, 1501, 1502, and 1508 in Rouen and Paris; *Constitutiones* is dated to 1504.

pecially the fourth and fifth, were most frequently read as Christian or as pre-figuring Christian themes by medieval and Renaissance commentators.[12] Francesco Petrarch, in the *Bucolicum Carmen*, made this sort of allegorical reading more immediately available, especially as a model of church critique, with inquiries into the role of the pastor in the world and instructions for culling a sick flock and returning shepherds to a pure vocation.[13] Early sixteenth-century practitioners in England and on the continent, including Baptista Mantuan, Barnabe Googe, Alexander Barclay, George Tuberville, and Giles Fletcher the Elder, also used pastoral literature that they wrote and translated for religious education and polemic.[14] Edmund Spenser's *Shepheardes Calendar* is the most familiar rendering of shepherds for the purposes of placing various kinds of pastors in conversation with one another, in part to comment upon their successes and failures in meeting their obligations to their flocks, but the practice was widespread.[15]

The debate between a hermit figure and a shepherd figure about the relative merits of contemplative life and active engagement with the Christian flock also wends its way into pastoral poetics from Petrarch's *Bucolicum Carmen*. Petrarch opens his eclogue sequence with an exchange between two speakers he identifies as brothers and names Monicus and Silvius; Monicus is a monk leading the contemplative life, while Silvius is the poet and the shepherd. Sixteenth-century practi-

---

[12] Virgil, *The Eclogues*, trans. Guy Lee (1980; London: Penguin Books, 1984), esp. 55. In *Renaissance Pastoral and Its English Development* (Oxford: Oxford University Press, 1989), Sukanta Chaudhuri points to Juan Luis Vives' reading of *The Eclogues* in *Bucolica ... in eadem allegorical* (Milan, 1539) as it describes 'the whole history of the Church' (16).

[13] Also instructive is Francesco Petrarca, *The Life of Solitude*, trans. Jacob Zeitlin (1924; Westport, CT: Hyperion Press, 1978), especially the Fourth Tractate, 'Digressive, complaining, and lamenting for the loss of the Holy Land, and the negligence, sloth, and cowardice of our princes and popes', 237–53. See also *The anatomie of the Romane clergie, or a discoverie of the abuses thereof* (London, 1623), including 'certaine verses taken out of the Epistles of Francis Petrarch', and an anthology gathered by Francois Perrot, *Auiso piaceuole dato alla bella Italia, da vn nobile giouane francese, sopra la mentita data dal serenissimo Re di Nauarra a Papa Sisto V* ([London,] 1586), which consists of anti-clerical verse quotations from Dante Alighieri, Giovanni Boccaccio, and Francesco Petrarca.

[14] Baptista (Spagnoli) Mantuanus, *Adulescentia: The Eclogues of Mantuan*, ed. and trans. Lee Piepho (New York: Garland, 1989); Baptista Spagnuoli, *The Eclogues of Mantuan*, trans. George Tuberville (1567), ed. Douglas Bush (New York: Scholars' Facsimiles and Reprints, 1937); Barbara White, ed., *The Eclogues of Alexander Barclay from the Original Edition by John Cawood* (1928; London: Oxford University Press for Early English Text Society, 1960); Barnabe Googe, *Eclogues, Epitaphs, and Sonnets*, ed. Judith M. Kennedy (Toronto: University of Toronto Press, 1989). See Lee Piepho, 'Mantuan's Eclogues in the English Reformation', *Sixteenth Century Journal*, 25:3 (1994), 623–32, for a discussion of Mantuan's centrality in English education.

[15] Louis Adrian Montrose has inspired numerous scholarly readings with his articles 'Of Gentlemen and Shepherds: The Politics of Elizabethan Pastoral Form', *English Literary History*, 50:3 (1983), 415–59 and ' "Eliza, Queene of the Shepherdes", and the Pastoral of Power', *English Literary Renaissance*, 10 (1980), 153–82.

tioners of the form added hermit figures and wild men with increasing regularity, and again, they followed Petrarch's model but deployed it for uses of their own. These hermit figures, savage men, and ritualistic sacrifices remained a part of pastoral literature into the seventeenth century.

In religious polemics, Roman Catholic authors associated hermits with the Church Fathers, and categorized the fasting, study, and contemplation as virtuous behavior that indicated extraordinary striving for perfection.[16] This tradition is prevalent; William Caxton prints an early example in English with St. Jerome's *Vitas Patrum* in 1495, a volume which was reprinted again in a 1633 St. Omer translation as a decidedly Catholic project.[17] Critics of Catholics took up the figure of the hermit and surrounded him with wild men and savages, those engaged in the 'cannibalism' of eating human sacrifice, a literal interpretation of debates about the Christian Eucharist. Creeds of the churches are one of the most succinct sources of these debates; the Second Helvetic Confession of 1566, for example, declared unequivocally that, 'For as the flesh of Christ could not be eaten bodily, without great wickedness and cruelty, so is it not food for the body, as all men do confess ... . For neither did godly antiquity believe, neither yet do we believe, that the body of Christ can be eaten corporeally and essentially, with a bodily mouth'.[18] Catholic practices and beliefs surrounding the Eucharist re-emerged as an issue in the polemics of the 1590s.[19] One effort to promulgate and preserve the Roman Catholic faith in England from

---

[16] One example is Miguel de Comalada, *Desiderius, a Most Godly, Religious, and Delectabel Dialogue, Teaching the True and Ready Way, by which we may Attayne to the Perfect Loue of God* (1604), ed. D. M. Rogers, English Recusant Literature 1558–1640, vol. 77 (Menston: Scolar Press, 1971).

[17] Saint Jerome, *Vitas Patrum* (Westmynstre, 1495), The English Experience no. 874 (Amsterdam: Theatrum Orbis Terrarum, 1977); Saint Jerome, *Certain selected epistles of S. Hierome as also the liues of Saint Paul the first hermite, of Saint Hilarian the first monke of Syria ...*, trans. Henry Hawkins [Saint Omer: English College Press, 1630]. See also Alexandra Walsham, *Church Papists*, Royal Historical Society Studies in History (Woodbridge: Boydel Press, 1993), especially 24–49. See figures two, three, and four below for some examples of the illustrations that accompanied Caxton's text.

[18] John H. Leith, ed., *Creeds of the Churches: A Reader in Christian Doctrine from the Bible to the Present*, 3rd ed. (Louisville: John Knox Press, 1982), has compiled and reprinted translations of most church creeds. For the codification of positions within religious debates, the following documents are most useful: 'The Second Helvetic Confession: Confession and Simple Exposition of the True Faith and Catholic Articles of the Pure Christian Religion', (1566) trans. Philip Schaff, 131–192; 'The Augsburg Confession', (1530) trans. Theodore G. Tappert, 64–106; 'The Thirty-Nine Articles of the English Church', (1563) 266–281; 'The Canons and Decrees of the Council of Trent', (1563) trans. H. J. Schroeder, 400–439; and 'The Creed of the Council of Trent', (1564), trans. H. J. Schroeder, 439–442. For specific discussion of the eucharist within these various creeds, see especially 84–5, 276, 440–2. This quotation is from 'The Second Helvetic Confession', 71.

[19] Peter Milward provides an overview of five tracts printed between 1590 and 1602

the late 1590s includes a hymn that is especially filled with images glorifying the feast and sacrifice of communion: 'At supper of the lamb prepar'd / And with white vestures pure and chaste, / To Christe our prince let vs sing praise, / The red seas being ouerpast'. The hymn continues with an emphasis on the sacred body of Christ, the Lamb of God, sacrificed for the feast of believers: 'By tasting of his blood so red, / Our lyf alone in God doth rest'.[20]

The imagery of this hymn—the white lamb, pure, tortured, and bound for sacrifice—serves as a useful context for the treatment of Serena, the almost-victim of savages in Book Six of the *Faerie Queene*. In this Book of Courtesie, Spenser thrusts Serena into a situation that he describes with terms that link it, in many ways, with the Roman Catholic mass, especially the Easter mass at which communion was served.[21] The 'saluage men' find Serena 'like a sheepe astray', and they decide,

> That since by grace of God she there was sent,
> Vnto their God they wold her sacrifize,
> Whose share, her guiltlesse bloud they would present,
> But of her dainty flesh they did deuize
> To make a common feast, and feed with gurmandize.[22]

Spenser emphasizes their belief that God's grace is inherent in the sacrifice and indeed provides it. He notes the wild men's willingness to repay God's blessing with a ritual killing and a communal feast upon her flesh. Serena becomes the Paschal lamb, a pure white vestal figure that the savages prepare to sacrifice.

As they make their preparations, they strip her and bind her, and she assumes additional characteristics of Christ prepared for the crucifixion. Spenser revels in the blazon of her purity and pallor:

> Her heart does quake, and deadly pallid hew
> Benumbes her cheekes: Then out aloud she cries,
> Where none is nigh to heare, that will her rew,
> And rends her golden locks, and snowy brests embrew ... .

---

that specifically debate the Eucharist in *Religious Controversies of the Elizabethan Age* (Lincoln: University of Nebraska Press, 1977), 133.

[20] *The Primer, or, the Office of the Blessed Virgin, in Latin and English, according to the reformed Latin, and vvith lyke graces priuileged.* (Antwerp, 1599; Menston: The Scolar Press, 1975), sig. Cc12.

[21] The Council of Trent decreed that Roman Catholics should receive communion at least once a year, at Easter. See Leith, *Creeds of the Church*, 437.

[22] Edmund Spenser, *The Faerie Queene*, ed. Thomas P. Roche, Jr., and C. Patrick O'Donnell, Jr. (1978; London: Penguin Books, 1987), 972, VI.viii.38.5–9. Subsequent references are to this edition.

> Her yuorie necke, her alabaster brest,
> Her paps, which like white silken pillowes were,
> For loue in soft delight thereon to rest;
> Her tender sides, her bellie white and clere,
> Which like an Altar did it selfe vprere,
> To offer sacrifice diuine thereon;
> Her goodly thighes, whose glorie did appeare
> Like a triumphal Arch, and thereupon
> The spoiles of Princes hang'd, which were in battel won.
> (VI.viii.40.6–9; 42.1–9)

As is true for many subjects described in terms of Petrarchan conventions, Serena's skin is pale: ivory neck, snowy and alabaster breast, white and clear belly. Her fear removes the roses from her cheeks and turns them into a 'deadly pallid hew'. Thomas Roche connects the blazon with the Song of Songs,[23] and Spenser's use of the words 'Altar' and 'sacrifice diuine' indicate additional biblical links to the Paschal lamb, the image appropriated by Christians for Christ. Spenser completes the allusion to Christ with the remark that she cries aloud 'where none is nigh to heare', just as Christ on the cross asks why God has forsaken him. Spenser links this cannibal feast with the Christian traditions surrounding Easter, particularly the Roman Catholic interpretation of ritual ceremonies.

Indeed, the passages surrounding this blazon reveal additional connections with the Catholic Eucharist. The savages are led by a priest, who vests himself and prepares the chalice: 'The Priest him selfe a garland doth compose / Of finest flowres, and with full busie care / His bloudy vessels wash; and holy fire prepares' (VI.viii.39). These preliminaries resemble a Catholic priest's actions before serving the Mass, and Spenser continues to describe the ceremonial sacrifice in similar terms. When the savages, at the Priest's insistence, agree not to rape Serena but instead to preserve her purity for the ceremony, the preparations begin in earnest:

> the Priest with naked arms full net
> Approaching nigh, and murdrous knife well whet,
> Gan mutter close a certain secret charmee,
> With other diuelish ceremonies met:
> Which doen he gan aloft t'aduance his arme,
> Whereat they shouted all, and made a loud alarme.
> (VI.viii.45)

The magical charm muttered secretly, the cleansed, 'full net' arms raised aloft, and the noise at the moment of the sacrifice all reflect characterizations of the Roman Catholic service, with its Latin liturgy, its conver-

---

[23] *Faerie Queene*, ed., 1223n43.

sion of wine to blood, and its bell rung at the moment of the mystical transformation.

Spenser places this ceremony in the hands of savages, men who are marauders and cannibals, who prey upon the weak and lost and who pose an internal as well as an external threat. They especially covet those 'which on their border / Were brought by errour, or by wreckfull wynde' (VI.viii.36). In Book One, the Book of Holinesse, Spenser embodies Errour and gives it qualities attributed to Roman Catholics, and here he uses similar tactics.[24] English knights such as Redcrosse Knight face the seduction of error, as do the confused victims brought before the cannibals. Spenser also links the cannibals to Roman Catholic nations threatening England; he tells the reader they are 'a saluage nation, which did liue / Of stealth and spoile, and making nightly rode / Into their neighbors borders' (VI.viii.35). They are also men who 'happily serue their owne necessities with others need'. They participate in slaughters of innocents, and rob and steal from their neighbors. This 'nation' assumes attributes of Spain, Ireland, and other Catholic countries viewed as threats in England.[25]

Spenser constructs his villains in terms common to religious debates and uses images of men out of control that were employed by propagandists in all parties. Peter Brueghel draws upon this sort of imagery in his portrayal of Spanish Catholic soldiers slaughtering Belgian Protestant women and children in *Massacre of the Innocents* (ca. 1566). In England, John Foxe represents Marian martyrs as victims of crazed mobs. Richard Versteegan publicizes the torture of Edmund Campion and other English Roman Catholics killed by Protestant wild men.[26] Spenser marks his savages as Roman Catholics by emphasizing their fondness for human flesh, but the trope itself is a standard one in representations of religious violence in art as well as in literature.

Indeed, as Richard Mallette reminds readers of Spenser, 'we cannot stop there. *The Faerie Queene* invites, indeed it requires, that we interpret cognate episodes correspondingly'.[27] In this case, to re-read this episode

---

[24] For one of many tracts outlining the dangers wrought by Catholic priests, see *To the seminarye priests lately come ouer some like gentlemen, some like marchants, some like seruingmen, and some like maymed soldiours: who in wordes speake like angelles of light, but are angelles of darkenes, and so proued in this small pamphlet*, by an anonymous author (London, 1592).

[25] For a discussion of the ways in which English Protestants used this fear to unify their forces, see Anthony Milton, *Catholic and Reformed: The Roman and Protestant Churches in English Protestant Thought, 1600–1640* (Cambridge: Cambridge University Press, 2002), 31–46. Many critics explore Spenser's relationship with Ireland; see Highley, *Crisis in Ireland;* and Andrew Hadfield, *Shakespeare, Spenser and the Matter of Britain*. See also Donna /xhamid Hamilton, *Anthony Munday*, 76–7.

[26] Richard Versteegan, *Théâtre des Cruatés des hérétiques de notre temps*, ed. Frank Lestringant (Paris: Editions Chandeigne, 1995), especially 129–39.

[27] Richard Mallette, *Spenser and the Discourses of Reformation England* (Lincoln: University of Nebraska Press, 1997), 3.

of the bound victim awaiting sacrifice in the context of historical events of the early 1590s does not lead one solely to anti-Catholic invective. Rather, Serena, caught while sleeping, is bound by zealots whose rituals emphasize their discourtesy. These zealots and their rituals call to mind the Catholic priests being imprisoned, tortured, and executed in England as treasonous terrorists threatening Elizabeth's safety. These prosecutions were at their height from 1590; the 1595 execution of Robert Southwell was met with especially strong criticism both within and outside England.[28] Brad Gregory defines martyrs as those who die for their faith. Spenser does not include markers of her faith in his construction of Serena, but her availability as the figure of the Bride of the Song of Songs conflates her at once with Una and with Catholic martyrs, all the potential victims of those wild men willing to destroy people in the name of 'God's grace'.

Serena falls victim to these predators in part because she has just been healed by a hermit. Serena, like Redcrosse Knight in Book One, is exposed to the attractive aspects of Roman Catholicism and is led astray, into the arms of savages, because she relaxes her guard. The hermit and the savage nation do not work in concert here, but the structure of this series of events repeats many that Redcrosse Knight encounters in Book One. He thinks he is secure, or is seduced by someone like Duessa who appears attractive, only to be captured or attacked or caught sleeping. The hermit figure offers different sorts of attractions at different moments in *The Faerie Queene;* Serena suffers from false confidence that differs from that of Redcrosse Knight. The hermit offers her spiritual health and respite from the wounds of the Blatant Beast. He, like Archimago and Duessa in Book One, has characteristics that mark him as Catholic. He lives in a little ivy-covered chapel, '[In] which his life here led / In straight obseruance of his religious vow / Was wont his howres and holy things to bed' (VI.v.35). He says the hours of the Blessed Virgin, lives the vows, and observes a life similar to that of an anchorite. This lifestyle's simplicity is part of its attraction, especially for someone suffering from wounds from the Blatant Beast:

> Small was his house, and like a little cage,
> For his owne turne, yet inly neate and cleane,

---

[28] See Arthur F. Marotti, 'Manuscript Transmission and the Catholic Martyrdom Account in Early Modern England', in *Print, Manuscript, and Performance: The Changing Relations of the Media in Early Modern England*, ed. Arthur F. Marotti and Michael D. Bristol (Columbus: Ohio State University Press, 2000), 172–99, and 'Alienating Catholics in Early Modern England: Recusant Women, Jesuits and Ideological Fantasies', in *Catholicism and Anti-Catholicism in Early Modern English Texts*, ed. Arthur F. Marotti (New York: Macmillan, 1999), 1–34. See also Brad S. Gregory, *Salvation at Stake: Christian Martyrdom in Early Modern Europe* (Cambridge, MA: Harvard University Press, 1999); Susannah Brietz Monta, *Martyrdom and Literature in Early Modern England* (Cambridge: Cambridge University Press, 2005); Sarah Covington, *The Trail of Martyrdom: Persecution and Resistance in Sixteenth-Century England* (Notre Dame: University of Notre Dame Press, 2003).

> Deckt with green boughes, and flowers gay beseene.
> Therein he them full faired did entertaine
> Not with forged showes, as fitter beene
> For courting fooles, that curtesies would faine,
> But with entire affection and appearaunce plaine
> (VI.v.38)

The hermit lives a remote, simple life, one oozing with the romantic appeal of remove from court life and steeped in the ancient simplicity of the fathers. In this book of courtesy, the hermit exemplifies the courteous host in part because he gives his guests solace when they particularly need it, and in part because he does not use false ceremonies but instead bases his hospitality upon 'entire affection'. Retreat is seductive for those seeking relief from gossip and pretentious, competitive entertaining, and the hermit embodies those seductions as completely as Duessa figures the physical attractions of Roman ritual for those seeking holiness.

Polemicists recognized these physical attractions; invectives in the 1590s included calls to preserve English citizens from popery, with tracts categorizing the dangers. One especially illustrative title is: *A Toile for Two-Legged Foxes: Wherein their noisome properties, their hunting and unkenelling, with the duties of principall hunters and guardians of the spiritual vineyard is livelie discovered, for the comfort of all her Highnes trustie and true-hearted subiects, and their encouragement against all Popish practices.*[29] The decade also held an increasing perception of priestly invasion, in part since Catholics were themselves heavily engaged in print debates about the relative merits of seminary priests and Jesuits, and this proliferation in print, along with the continued persecution of priests in England, contributed to a sense of priestly invasion for non-Catholics and an increase in opportunities for encounters leading to conversion.[30]

William Shakespeare 'figures forth' the issues surrounding communion a bit differently in *As You Like It*, a play usually dated to 1598–1600 and first published in the First Folio of 1623.[31] In *As You Like It*, Shakespeare

---

[29] The title of this text, printed in 1600, continues with information that makes the author's position even more clear: 'by I. B. Preacher of the Word of God'. Milward describes the debates about preserving English protestants from popery and the Watchward controversy in *Religious Controversies*, 134–9.

[30] Milward summarizes the issues and polemics in the Appellant controversy, *Religious Controversies*, 116–24. James Shapiro assesses a general sense of impending threat from Spanish Catholics in 1599 that has roots in earlier efforts, in 'The Invisible Armada', *A Year in the Life of William Shakespeare* (New York: Harper Collins, 2005), 173–87. See also Brad Gregory, who suggests that in the 1580s and 1590s, 'the social impact of martyrdom paralleled the glory it conferred on the martyrs themselves' and 'made martyrdom "the seed of the Church"', *Salvation at Stake*, 284, 285.

[31] *As You Like It*, ed. Agnes Latham (London: Methuen, 1975), Arden ed. Subsequent references are to this edition.

takes a story from Thomas Lodge's *Rosalind* and removes from it many of the elements that carry the loudest resonances regarding church–state debates.[32] He replaces many of these scenes with exchanges that explore loyalty and usurpation, issues that concerned Catholics but that did not carry the decidedly pro-Catholic advocacy that Lodge offers. The most telling, especially with Spenser's representation of the savage nation and its cannibalistic communion practices in the background, is Shakespeare's treatment of the young hero and his aged retainer Adam.

Lodge's character Adam Spencer loyally supports the young protagonist Rosader in conflicts with his tyrannous brother Saladyne, in much the same way Shakespeare's Adam succors Orlando. The situation in Lodge is much more extreme and protracted, however. Shakespeare's Orlando returns victorious from the wrestling match to the rumor that his brother will destroy him in the night with a fire, and Adam offers money to support his flight to safety. Lodge's Rosader is wronged to a much greater extent by his brother, and the resulting violence includes Saladyne binding Rosader in chains and proclaiming his madness to relatives. Rosader rebels; he and Adam attack the company with poleaxes and injure many. Saladyn returns with the sheriff and twenty-five men. Rosader and Adam flee the house, wounding and killing more people as they depart. Lodge's Adam must do more than offer a warning; he must act against his master Saladyne in order to honor the brothers' father's wishes, he must choose the brother he views as more deserving and honorable, and he must fight on the behalf of that brother and his cause. The two wander the forest without food for 'five or six days'; after Adam Spencer recovers from a faint, he spies Rosader, 'as feeble and as ill perplexed'.[33] Adam decides to sacrifice himself for Rosader, and 'let the death of one preserve the life of the other'. Rosader should sustain his own life with Adam's: 'I will presently cut my veins, and, master, with the warm blood relieve your fainting spirits. Suck on that till I end and you be comforted'.[34] The old man's willingness to sacrifice himself moves Rosader to action on their behalf; Lodge then introduces

---

[32] Donald Beecher, in his introduction to *Rosalind: Euphues' Golden Legacy Found After His Death in his Cell in Silexedra* by Thomas Lodge (1590, Barnabe Riche Society Publications no. 7, Ottawa: Dovehouse Editions, 1997), surveys Shakespeare-Lodge criticism and notes that the many comparisons between Shakespeare's text and Lodge's slight Lodge's, 11–13. My comparison here is by necessity abridged, since to juggle Spenser and Shakespeare and the religious controversies of the 1590s is already an unrealistically large project for an essay. Spenser's and Shakespeare's literary variations are more evident, though, when their works are placed within the context offered by the poesy of the period. Lodge's *Rosalind*, originally published in 1590, provides one point of reference; the anonymous drama of the 1590s is also especially useful and in many cases offers scenes, characters, situations, and speeches that are more easily identified as pro- or anti-Catholic.

[33] See especially 138–41.

[34] Lodge, *Rosalind*, 143.

the feasting nobles, and Rosader's encounter with them is quite providential.

The dangers of the forest offer opportunity—for Lodge's Adam Spencer, martyrdom is the ultimate sacrifice and show of loyalty to a higher cause. In terms that echo Jesus' words to his disciples at the last supper, Adam promises to sustain another with his blood.[35] The hymn from the *Primer*, cited earlier in reference to Serena, continues with this language: 'Our Paschal Christe is now become / The Lamb he was and sacrifiz'd: His flesh the bread both sweet and pure / That for the offering hath suffiz'd'. At issue, in the days following Easter, is Christ's sacrifice, and the participation of the communicant, in the feast that includes Christ's blood. The sacrifice he would willingly make is as honorable as Serena's almost-death is fearsome.

This model behavior, an endorsement of the Roman Catholic position on the Eucharist, is one that Shakespeare removes from *As You Like It*. The structure of Shakespeare's play underscores the contrast between the romanticized version of 'exile in the desert' and its more fearsome realities. Shakespeare brings Orlando, seeking sustenance for the starving Adam, to the Duke's table and thereby echoes the situation, earlier in the scene, when Celia and Rosalind have the opportunity to act as patrons for the bereft shepherd Corin. Celia and Rosalind play at being shepherdesses, and the mirror that Corin holds up to their playacting is one that others have recognized in *As You Like It* and in other texts, among them *Don Quixote*, that juxtapose real sheep herders with their literary counterparts. In *As You Like It*, Celia and Rosalind also prepare the way for this second patronage situation, the patronage of the Duke for an old man and his companion wandering alone in the desert.

Throughout the play, Shakespeare mocks the conventions of the pastoral world by contrasting the reality of the shepherd Corin's life with the romanticized version embraced by Celia, Rosalind, and Touchstone.[36] He offers a similar mockery of the idealized version of the life of the hermit as he contrasts Duke Senior's luxury-laden forays into academic retreat with the dangerous exile which Adam and Orlando face. The lines along which he constructs his hermits echo, in many ways, the debates that Catholics, conformists, and non-conformists were having about the value of 'eremetic' life. In addition, all of the characters that populate the forest of Arden allow Shakespeare to explore communities of exile, those disenfranchised from their properties and places, in ways that resemble tellingly the issues facing English Catholic exile communities on the continent. While Shakespeare's portrayal is

---

[35] *Primer*, sig. Cc12.

[36] See Latham, 'Introduction' to *As You Like It*; Walter Davis, 'Sidney's *Arcadia*. A Map of Arcadia: Sidney's Romance in its Tradition', in *Sidney's Arcadia* (New Haven: Yale University Press, 1965), 34, 35.

more sympathetic to Catholic concerns than some of the conformist and non-conformist polemicists, it is more moderate than the positions staged in some of the anonymous drama of the period.[37]

Duke Senior and his co-mates in exile are, 'in these woods / More free from peril than the envious court' (II.i.3–4) and have the opportunity to 'Find tongues in trees, books in running brooks / Sermons in stones, and good in everything' (II.i.16–17). Exile offers the opportunity, free from care, for study and fellowship. The situation Duke Senior describes in the opening of Act Two resembles the attractions of monastic retreat, but the scenes that follow show that the emphasis is on the fellowship rather than contemplation, as the Duke commands hunts, feasts, and song. 'Come, shall we go and kill us a venison?' he asks almost immediately after praising life in exile (II.i.21). In the next appearance of his company, Amiens and Jacques exchange banter and song ('Under the greenwood tree', etc.), and the men prepare the area so that the Duke may 'drink under this tree' (II.v.29). While this life in exile may very well represent a courtier's hunting party, or a noble's attempts at recreating Robin Hood's merry band, it also shares some of the milder characteristics of monastic life. John Calvin, for example, remarks that, 'Our monks place the principal part of their holiness in idleness [and in living on others' means]',[38] in much the same way that Jacques criticizes the brotherhood of 'fat and greasy citizens' who live upon the 'poor and broken' as 'usurpers, tyrants, and what's worse, / To fright the animals and to kill them up / In their assigned and native dwelling place' (II.i.55, 57, 61–3). Certainly, Jacques' comments are the subject of ridicule by his fellows, and point to other sorts of social commentary, as countless critics have noted.[39] They also reflect, though, the indignation at the exploitation of local citizens that Calvin aims at monastic residents.

Here is the life of the hermit as it is described countless times in romance and in religious tracts,[40] but with a more realistic version of

---

[37] Some of the most interesting, and most overtly pro- or anti-Catholic, appear in the anonymous drama of the period: *Mucedorus*, printed in 1598 and reprinted sixteen times by 1700, and *A Knack to Know an Honest Man*, printed in 1596 and performed throughout the decade.

[38] Calvin, *Institutes of the Christian Religion*, trans. Henry Beveridge (1989; Grand Rapids, MI: Wm B. Eerdmans Press, 1993), 3.481.

[39] Among them, Claus Uhlig, ' "The sobbing deer": *As You Like It* and the Historical Context', *Renaissance Drama*, 3 (1970), 79–109; G. F. Bradby, 'Jacques', in *Short Studies in Shakespeare* (London: J. Murray, 1929), 87–97; *As You Like It*, ed. G. S. Gordon (Oxford: Oxford University Press, 1912), xlii.

[40] For examples from romance, see Laura A. Hibbard Loomis, *Medieval Romance in England* (1924; New York: Burt Franklin, 1960); Ludovico Ariosto, *Orlando Furioso*, especially the hermit in cantos 41–4 who baptizes Ruggiero and Sobrino. Foxe mentions the 'ancient hermits' in *Acts and Monuments*, 2.54–7; see also Calvin, *Institutes*, 3.481–5. For a Roman Catholic portrayal, the model hermit striving for perfection is described in commentaries

events than ever appears in these glorified accounts. Instead of having epiphanies or meeting the devil and his temptations, Orlando and Adam almost die. Adam says, 'Dear master, I can go no further. O I die for food. Here lie I down, and measure out my grave. Farewell kind master'. (II.vi.1–3). His distress offers Orlando the opportunity to offer heroism and humor; Orlando responds, 'No greater heart in thee? Live a little, comfort a little, cheer thyself a little. If this uncouth forest yield anything savage, I will either be food for it, or bring it for food to thee .... I will be herewith thee presently, and if I bring thee not something to eat, I will give thee leave to die; but if thou diest before I come, thou art a mocker of my labour' (II.vi.4–7, 10–13). Adam, in particular, faces the difficulties one would expect for an old man accustomed to household servitude rather than outdoor life, exposed to the cold conditions of the 'uncouth' forest of Arden, but Orlando remains ready to conquer the forest.

In this scene, Shakespeare deviates tellingly from his source, Thomas Lodge's *Rosalind*. In the source, Adam behaves in a way that is especially relevant in terms of cannibalism and Roman Catholic sacraments. Lodge's character, Adam Spencer, offers to allow the hero Rosader to take sustenance from his own body. The sacrifice that Shakespeare's Adam makes of his life's savings is, in comparison, a modest contribution to the hero's survival when compared to Adam Spencer's behest. Rosader springs to action once he hears the old man's suggestion and finds the Duke's banquet, just as Orlando does in *As You Like It*, so he does not need to resort to the extremes that Adam proposes. Clearly, though, in both the source and in Shakespeare's version, the desert is a dangerous place for men alone in exile; in Shakespeare's retelling, romanticized notions of the hermit are as insidious, or are more potent, than idealized versions of shepherds, since shepherds, at least, earn a livelihood of sorts.

While Shakespeare tempers the representation of martyrdom in his version for the stage, the overall narrative retains a sympathy with Roman Catholic issues and concerns, especially in more general terms concerning representations of exile. Shakespeare repeatedly sounds notes of tyrannous usurpation as the root of that move to the forest. By relating representations of retreat and exile specifically with issues of property, inheritance, and education, he connects them with Catholic concerns. Recently, religious historians, especially Michael Questier, have observed that Catholics relied heavily on two strategies to preserve Catholic culture and practices during the sixteenth and seventeenth centuries: retreat from active engagement in English civic life, and, in

---

to the Rheims New Testament. See *The Nevv Testament of Iesus Christ faithfully translated into English ... by the English College then resident in Rhemes* (Antwerp, 1600), STC 875:01, sigs A4v, Ccccc2.

more extreme cases, relocation to continental settlements, where they could ensure Catholic communion and education. They further bolstered the community of Catholics by emphasizing marriage alliances that preserved Catholicism within families.[41]

Questier could, quite easily, be describing the world of *As You Like It* and the strategies of its protagonists. The ending of *As You Like It* offers the consolation of a peaceful return to court for Duke Senior, Rosalind, Celia, and Orlando, precipitated by Duke Frederick's decision to enter a monastery. Here, too, Shakespeare engages with religious debates of the day; here, again, Shakespeare moderates the message of *Rosalind*. Catholic polemicists and policy-makers advocated England's return to Rome, explored alliances with Ireland and Scotland to circumvent England's efforts at reform, continued to send both Jesuits and seminary priests to provide the communion required by covert Catholic communities, and hoped for England's next monarch's Catholicity.[42] Lodge's text is quite overt in the ways that its protagonists reach this solution; once the lovers are paired and married, the scholar-brother tells his brothers to 'change your loves into lances and now this day show yourselves as valiant as hitherto you have been passionate'. This brother has brought along 'twelve peers of France ... up in arms to recover [the Duke's] right ... . The armies are ready to join'. All they require is the Duke; he should 'show [himself] in the field to encourage [his] subjects'. The brothers, too, should join in the battle: 'show yourselves as hardy soldiers as you have been hearty lovers. So shall you for the benefit of your country discover the idea of your father's virtues to be stamped in your thoughts, and prove children worthy of an honorable parent'.[43] Since both Protestants and Catholics were by this time advancing their own claims as to the universality and antiquity of their versions of worship, these calls to 'prove children worthy of an honorable parent' link Lodge's text neither to one nor the other with any certainty.

The readiness to battle for the cause, though, suggests the French and Spanish plan of action already at work with invasion efforts in the 1580s and 1590s—overt efforts to retake England for the Pope.[44] Sir

---

[41] Michael C. Questier, *Catholicism and Community in Early Modern England: Politics, Aristocratic Patronage and Religion, c. 1550–1640* (Cambridge: Cambridge University Press, 2006).

[42] Questier focuses on the 'context of a particular Catholic "entourage"' but notes that these themes are at the heart of his study; because his discussion considers networks rather than themes, it is difficult to point to particular places where he outlines specific support for these points, but he offers an overview of these themes in his introduction, especially 6, and these strands run through his work.

[43] Lodge, *Rosalind*, 226.

[44] For Catholic arguments regarding a Catholic succession, see G. Guilielmo Rossaeo [William Rainolds], *De Iusta Reipub ...* (Douai, 1590); [Robert Parsons], *Newes from*

George Cary offers a view of these concerted Catholic attempts from 1593: 'The Spaniard already hath sent seven thousand Pistolets of Gold into Scotland to corrupt the Nobility, and to the King twenty thousand crowns now lately were dispatched out of France into Scotland for the levying of three thousand, which the Scottish Lords have promised; and the King of Spain will levy thirty thousand more and give them all Pay'.[45] Lodge's narrative closes with the proper ruler, restored through the combined efforts of soldiers and the nobiltity: 'When the peers perceived that their lawful king was there, they grew more eager .... To be short, the peers were conquerors, Torismond's army put to flight and himself slain in battle. The peers then gathered themselves together and, saluting their king, conducted him royally into Paris, where he was received with great joy of all the citizens'.[46] Lodge's happy end rests not upon the multiple marriages of his lovers, but instead upon armed insurrection that replaces a usurper with the rightful heir to the throne and relies upon the support of the peers and the citizens, all awaiting the opportunity to cast off the false king.

Shakespeare expunges this resolution from *As You Like It*. As in Lodge's *Rosalind*, the middle brother fortuitously appears to bring news. The aggressor, however, in this instance is not the assemblage in the woods, but instead the usurping ruler, Duke Frederick. Jaques du Boys tells the company: 'Duke Frederick hearing how that every day / Men of great worth resorted to this forest, / Address'd a mighty power, which were on foot / In his own conduct, purposely to take / His brother here, and put him to the sword' (V.iv.153–7). Shakespeare's peers continue to support the cause of the exiles, since every day these men of great worth join Duke Senior, and the threat is one that Duke Frederick recognizes, a threat against which he must raise arms and must himself lead the assault. However, in this staged comedy, providence intervenes in the form of a hermit. Jacques du Boys continues:

> And to the skirts of this wide wood he came,
> Where, meeting with an old religious man,

Spayne and Holland conteyning An Information of Inglish Affairs in Spayne (Antwerp, 1593), and William Allen, *A Conference about the Next Succession to the Crowne of Ingland* (Antwerp, 1595). Milward offers a brief overview of the issues in these tracts in *Religious Controversies*, (114–16). In addition to the defeat of the Armada in 1588, Marotti notes that the Spanish landed in Cornwall in 1595 and made other attempts both in 1595 and 1597: *Religious Ideology & Cultural Fantasy*, 233n76. Internal seditious plots were discovered at the rate of one a year in the five years preceding the Essex Rebellion in 1601. See also Harry Kelsey, *Sir Francis Drake: The Queen's Pirate* (1998; New Haven: Yale University Press, 2000), for descriptions of England's privateering response to French and Spanish efforts, especially 367–91 for the late 1580s and the early 1590s.

[45] Simonds D'Ewes, ed., *The Journals of all the Parliaments, during the Reign of Queen Elizabeth, Both of the House of Lords and House of Commons* (London, 1682), Wing D1250, volume 1, 484. Cited in Kelsey, *Sir Francis Drake*, 512n37.

[46] Lodge, *Rosalind*, 227.

> After some question with him, was converted
> Both from his enterprise and from the world,
> His crown bequeathing to his banish'd brother,
> And all their lands restor'd to them again
> That were with him exil'd.
>
> (V.iv.158–64)

No rebellion is required to restore order in this pastoral landscape. A right-thinking holy man wandering on the edge of this forest persuades Duke Frederick to save himself by converting, return the kingdom to his brother's rule, and restore the lands appropriated from those in exile. While the message in *As You Like It* is not as incendiary as that in Lodge, it retains pro-Catholic reverberations and leaves one with the sense that a few among the nobility might welcome a return to the Catholic fold. In the happy world of the play, such a reconciliation would occur without violence, and words would lead to conversion and resolution.

The end of Book Six of *The Faerie Queene* arrives without this tidy sense of closure. Spenser leaves the reader of the scenes surrounding Serena quite unsettled; the sun rises to reveal to Calipone that the stripped and shamed woman he has rescued is his beloved (VI.viii.50–1). The patterning of the narrative suggests that Serena's woes are in part a result of her own unwillingness to recognize her own errors. The hermit has provided the methods for spiritual and bodily discipline (VI.vi.5, VI.vi.13–15), but reminds her 'For in your selfe your onely helpe doth lie, / To heale your selues, and must proceed alone / From your own will, to cure your maladie' (VI.vi.7). Bodily discipline provides part of Serena's cure; soon after she has continued on her way, though, Spenser interpolates the story of Mirabella. Even when Arthur offers to free Mirabella from Scorne and Disdaine, she refuses the opportunity. She recognizes her error and acknowledges the need for contrition in ways that Serena does not; 'euermore she blamed Calepine ... the onely author of her wofull tine' (VI.viii.33) Nevertheless, her encounter with the wild men is an alarming penalty for her pridefulness.

The Book of Courtesie does not end on this note; it continues with the story of Pastorella, Calidore's beloved. Richard Helgerson is among those who read Calidore's abandonment of Pastorella and the pastoral landscape, and Colin's destruction of his pipe, as an indication that 'the pastoral world is meant to be left behind', in part because 'in both Book VI and [in Philip Sidney's] *Arcadia*, private affection opposes public obligation'.[47] Helgerson's analysis provides useful information for read-

---

[47] Richard Helgerson, *Self-Crowned Laureates: Spenser, Jonson, and Milton and the Literary System* (Berkeley: University of California Press, 1983), 95, 94. See also Paul E. McLane, *Spenser's 'Shepheardes Calender': A Study in Elizabethan Allegory* (Notre Dame: University of Notre Dame Press, 1961); Michael O'Connell, *Mirror and Veil: The Historical Dimension of Spenser's 'Faerie Queene'* (Chapel Hill: University of North Carolina Press, 1977).

ing genre. However, it occludes the events of the last canto. This canto provides the history of Pastorella in terms that link her firmly to the tradition of debates about the church; here, rather than focusing upon the figure of the hermit, Spenser makes use of the figure of the beloved to characterize the church itself.[48]

Pastorella has at this point survived kidnapping, the destruction of home and flocks, lengthy captivity, and the almost-complete destruction of her adopted people. Her brigand captors, ready to profit by selling the shepherds into slavery to rich merchants, begin to fight amongst themselves when the Brigand Captain refuses to include Pastorella in the sale. Coridon, 'escaping craftily ... flyes away as fast as he can hye / Ne stayeth leaue to take, before his friends do dye' (VI.xi.18). He alone among the shepherds escapes the carnage, but his escape is not admirable; he does not defend his friends or confront the attackers, and the scope of his active response is limited to self-protection. Nonetheless, he survives to lead Calidore back to Pastorella, a Pastorella who has been left for dead, covered in brigands' corpses, recovered only to be left in the hands of 'one the best / Of many worst, who with vnkind disdaine / And cruell rigour her did much molest' (VI.xi.24).[49] Calidore releases a weakened Pastorella from this thralldom, gives to her the best of the spoils from the thieves' den, and restores Coridon to his flocks. Here, as in *As You Like It*, the usurping hordes are vanquished, and the proper ruler is restored, but in this case, as is repeatedly so within Protestant poetics, the ruler is the shepherd. Spenser, though, by constructing Coridon as such as coward and a sneak, and as so completely unwilling to defend Pastorella from the dangers the brigands bring, does not unilaterally defend Protestant leaders. Coridon is much more reminiscent of Sidney's 'dumb dog' Dametas, or other foppish

---

[48] Patrick Cheney, in his essay in the present volume, offers an excellent assessment of Pastorella as a figure within the framework of the pastoral literary genre. He builds on Montrose's reading of Pastorella figuring Elizabeth and makes a persuasive argument about the links between Pastorella and Eliza-figures throughout *The Faerie Queene* and also considers both Pastorella and Perdita in terms of Petrarchan and Ovidian conventions.

[49] Thomas Herron and Vincent Carey noted connections between the atrocities committed against the Irish by English settlers and this passage in the *Faerie Queene* in lectures associated with *Inquisitions and Persecutions in Early Modern Europe and the Americas* (an institute for university and college teachers funded by the National Endowment for the Humanities and organized by the Center for Renaissance & Baroque Studies at the University of Maryland, summer 2005). Vincent Carey's published work on the subject includes 'John Derricke's Image of Irelande, Sir Henry, and the Massacre at Mullaghmast, 1578', *IHS*, 31:123 (1999), 319–22; Vincent Carey and Clare Carroll, 'Factions and Fictions: Spenser's Reflections of and on Elizabethan Politics', in *Spenser's Life and the Subject of Biography*, ed. Judith H. Anderson, Donald Cheney, and David A. Richardson (Amherst: University of Massachusetts Press, 1996), 31–44. See also Thomas Herron, 'The Spanish Armada, Ireland, and Spenser's *The Faerie Queene*', *The New Hibernia Review* 6:2 (2002), 82–105. For additional information about the Irish historical context, see Alan Ford and John McCafferty, eds., *The Origins of Sectarianism in Early Modern Ireland* (Cambridge: Cambridge University Press, 2005).

failures that thread pastoral narratives and drama. He is restored to his flock by the largesse of the courteous knight rather than by his own right thinking or leadership.

In contrast, Calidore invests enormous energy into aiding Pastorella; after single-handedly defeating the wild men and restoring order to the pastoral world, Calidorre carries Pastorella to a castle where she can be cared for and restored. The hermit was able to help Serena. Here, something larger is required, and the king and queen must intervene. Happily, the king and queen are also Pastorella's parents; her illness reveals her true identity to the loyal maidservant Melissa in a vignette worthy of any romance.

This vignette, and the subsequent binding of the Blatant Beast, closes the circle of the dance through which Spenser has led his reader for the last six cantos, but the variation he offers in Book Six contrasts the closing scenes of Book One in ways that are quite telling. Here, again, the daughter is reunited with her regal parents; here, again, the knight triumphs in his quest. As many critics have noted, the Beast is merely bound, though, and Spenser makes sure the audience knows that it will ultimately triumph. It is the situation of the daughter, though, that carries the most relevance for church politics. Pastorella is wounded and beaten, so traumatized that she cannot travel alone and must be nursed to return to her former strength: 'Als Claribell / No lesse did tender the faire Pastorell, / Seeing her weake and wan, through durance long. / There they a while together thus did dwell / In much delight, and many ioyes among, / Vntill the damzell gan to wex more sound and strong' (VI.xii.11). Once Pastorella's strength begins to return, Calidore remembers his quest, 'now perrill being past' (VI.xii.13). Pastorella continues to require aid: 'During his absence left in heauy care, / Through daily mourning, and nightly misfare: / Yet did that auncient matrone all she might, / To cherish her with all things choice and rare; / And her owne handmayd, that Melissa hight, / Appointed to attend her dewly day and night' (VI.xii.14). Claribel is an 'auncient matrone', and here Spenser links her, as Shakespeare has done with Duke Senior, to the old traditions, the ancient heritage of the church, the argument that both Catholics and Protestants were by this time making for their church polities.

That Spenser invokes this debate is even more clear as Melissa, the handmaid, helps the queen identify Pastorella as her own daughter. The maid bears a birthmark shaped like a rose, and it is this mark that Melissa recognizes. The conversation between Melissa and Claribell could come directly from the religious tracts of the 1590s. Melissa tells the queen, 'The same is yonder Lady, whom high God did saue' (VI.xii.17). The queen requires proof: 'Much was the Lady troubled at that speach, / And gan to question streight how she it knew' (VI.xii.18). The proof is directly upon Pastorella's body:

> Most certaine markes, (sayd [Melissa]), do me it teach,
> For on her brest I with these eyes did vew
> The little purple rose, which thereon did grew,
> Whereof her name ye then to her did giue.
> Beside her countenaunce, and her likely hew,
> Matched with equall yeares, do surely prieue
> That yond same is your daughter sure, which yet doth liue.
> (VI.xii.18)

Melissa's proof is based on evidence that Protestant polemicists valued: evidence from the text, witnessed by the individual believer, bolstered with verification from the knowledge of an educated interpreter.

Milward enumerates the notes of the controversies: 'The main theme of the sporadic controversies during this period was the question of the true Catholic church and its four marks—unity, sanctity, universality (or catholicity), and apostolicity. These had notably been claimed by Bristow and others for the Church of Rome; but the Protestants now became increasingly loud in their counter-claim: that they alone were truly Catholic, and that the papists were heretics'.[50] Included in the wrangling was precisely the sort of language that Spenser employs to describe Pastorella and her mother's recognition of her lineage. Milward counts fifteen or more efforts to describe the Protestant signs during the 1580s and 1590s. One title, in particular, offers a useful summary of these arguments:

> *The knowledge or appearance of the Church, gathered out of the holy Scriptures, declaring and plainly shewing, both the Church that cannot but erre, and also the Church that cannot erre. With so evident notes and manifest signes of eaither them, that no man reading it, needeth be in doubt which he should believe. Written by R. Phinch, and now published in this yeare 1590. for the benefite of all such as desire the truth concerning the church.*

Phinch's main points dovetail neatly with Spenser's recognition scene; Spenser translates the rhetoric into plot and character in the figure of Pastorella and Claribel. The Queen cannot be in doubt which she should believe; she should nurture this daughter and restore her to health, to position, to strength and acknowledge her right inheritance. This directive is clear and quite strong; England, especially its ruler, needs to recognize and restore the Protestant church to her proper position and nurture her accordingly, rather than casting her out to wander in the wilderness and face the enormous dangers and damage such an experience holds for her.

That Spenser cannot leave his story to end here sounds a note of uncertainty, of non-resolution, that, alongside Shakespeare's *As You Like It* and Lodge's *Rosalind*, reveals a general sense of unrest and ambiguity.

---

[50] Milward, *Religious Controversies*, 127.

It carries the reverberations of the civil unrest surrounding controversies concerned with religion all through the 1590s. Lodge's happy outcome includes insurrection, armed warfare and the peers rising up to defend their rights and regain their property. Shakespeare's end is not as violent; providential conversion of the usurper, persuaded by a right-thinking cleric to turn to a truly religious life, restores his protagonists to their rightful place. Spenser would enlist the help of the monarch to restore the true beloved to her proper position, but her restoration would only solve part of the problems at work in the land of Faerie. The Blatant Beast will continue to sow destruction and disorder, no matter what course of action the knights and ladies of Faerie follow. Ultimately, Book Six of the *Faerie Queene* is the work of a man who has come to terms with the limits of humanity's ability to make changes in the world. He refuses to offer a utopian vision enacted by any one knight or any one lady, by any group working in concert, by any institution of Faerieland.

Figure One: *Constitutiones legitime seu legatine regionis anglicane...*, 1504. Title page. STC 17108. By permission of the Folger Shakespeare Library.

Pastoral Forms and Religious Reform 165

Figure Two: Saint John of Egypt. In St. Jerome, *Vitae patrum*, English, *Vitas patrum*, 1495. Sig. aii[r] (or page ii[r]), image only. STC 14507. By permission of the Folger Shakespeare Library.

Figure Three: Saint Anthony. In St. Jerome, *Vitae patrum*, English, *Vitas patrum*, 1495. Sig. dviii[r] (or page xxxii[r]), image only. STC 14507. By permission of the Folger Shakespeare Library.

Pastoral Forms and Religious Reform 167

Figure Four: Saint Paphnutius. In St. Jerome, *Vitae patrum*, English, *Vitas patrum*, 1495. Sig. ciii[r] (or page xix [r]), image only. STC 14507. By permission of the Folger Shakespeare Library.

The Equinoctial Boar: Venus and Adonis in Spenser's Garden, Shakespeare's Epyllion, and *Richard III*'s England

Anne Lake Prescott

Juxtaposing Spenser's movingly fertile Garden of Adonis (*Faerie Queene* III.vi) and Shakespeare's seriocomic *Venus and Adonis* is an old exercise, and to note that both texts evoke, revise, or reject traditional mythographical readings of the Venus and Adonis story is likewise hardly new. In this essay I do, however, have two suggestions for further thought on these texts, Shakespeare's *Richard III*, and the boar of winter.

I am assuming for the moment that nobody in the 1590s writing for an educated reader—or for an audience that included the educated—could use the names 'Venus' and 'Adonis' without evoking memories of one widespread view, found in any number of commentaries, dictionaries, and mythographies, of what their story might mean. True, what 'means' means can be puzzling. To mention the mythographers' reading of the myth is only responsible; to take extended account of it can seem to move poems such as *Venus and Adonis* into a Spenserian world of allegory where many scholars, even those who would assume that he was roughly familiar in one way or another with mythographical traditions, do not want their Shakespeare to go slumming. A recent study by Anthony Mortimer, for example, refers with distaste to 'the solemnities of allegory', and he has plenty of company.[1] Another modern critic, R. W. Maslen, who reads Shakespeare's 'cheeky' poem as a rejection of Spenserian allegory (which could be true in some regards, although Judith Anderson thinks it a 'revelling' in Spenserian eros), calls such 'myth ... a falsification of history, a consoling lie designed to conceal the 'black Chaos' that underlies the veneer of historical order'.[2] Such

---

[1] Anthony Mortimer, *Variable Passions: A Reading of Shakespeare's 'Venus and Adonis'* (New York: AMS Press, 2000), 13, in an introduction impatient with moralizing allegory and Platonic idealization. On criticism up to the mid-1990s, see Philip C. Kolin's Introduction to his invaluable *'Venus and Adonis': Critical Essays* (New York: Garland, 1997) and its full bibliography. Ellen A. Harwood, 'Venus and Adonis: Shakespeare's Critique of Spenser', *Rutgers University ... Journal* 39 (1977), 44–60, notes, 49, that Spenser 'acknowledges Ovid's moral neutrality', but tends to read Shakespeare as complex and Spenser as simple. For more on the matter, see Judith H. Anderson's paper in the present volume.

[2] R. W. Maslen, 'Venus and Adonis and the death of Orpheus', *The Glasgow Review*, 1 (1993), 67–78 (www.arts.gla.ac.uk/sesll/stella/comet/glasrev/issue1; accessed 1/12/07) and Judith H. Anderson, 'Venus and Adonis: Spenser, Shakespeare, and the Forms of Desire', in *Grief and Gender: 700–1700* ed Jennifer C. Vaught, with Lynne D. Bruckner (New York: Palgrave, 2003), 149–60. Maslen remarks that 'Commentators have repeatedly tried to read the boar as an allegory, whether of winter, of war, or of homosexual desire, but it resists moral or generic classifications'. True, but so may Spenser's. He also associates Shakespeare's Venus with Elizabeth when claiming that the poem 'charts that disintegra-

impatience with moralizing allegory might, however, make recalling cosmological allegory more helpful, even if Shakespeare's treatment of it is ironic, playful, or tragic, for if the mythographers moralized they also described processes beyond the reach of human preferences.

Much myth, on the other hand, seems to express resignation or a recurrent pattern of chaotic eruption. Allegory in the right hands can, moreover, be witty as well as morally astute, just as can an anti-allegory that evokes its conventional other. In readings of Renaissance texts, in sum, the equation of allegoresis with moralism or political acquiescence may be a modern prejudice. As Sayre Greenfield remarks sensibly (in an essay making the clever suggestion that Spenser stresses 'the eternal in the mutable, and Shakespeare, the mutable in the eternal'), 'some allegories are themselves unsettling'.[3] This is entirely true of Spenser's allegories, and indeed it seems wrong to read them, therefore, in binary good/bad terms or as unambiguous. For example, his Garden of Adonis (*FQ* III.vi) looks like, and in large part presumably is, a reply to and correction of his artifice-laden and oddly barren Bower of Bliss (II.vii). Yet in a hollow under the Garden's pubic, myrtle-covered *mons veneris* where Venus and her lover lie in their disorientingly anamorphic landscape there lurks a boar that makes that hollow (as it was said of the newborn Richard) 'not untoothed', and not untoothed just where most lovers would not want their beloveds to have teeth. Did Shakespeare ponder that boar in these terms? His own Venus says of the creature that killed her beloved, 'Had I been tooth'd like him, I must confess, / With kissing him I should have kill'd him first' (1117–18). In Spenser's Bower, however, and thanks to its very artificiality, are fine verses taken from Tasso and (Spenser can be self-mocking) laurel. There are, admittedly, some transformed pigs—but no tusked boars.

In view of our time's frequently expressed anti-allegorical bias, though, we may need a new vocabulary for poems such as Shakespeare's—and, I will argue, his *Richard III*—that without imposing allegory or alien discourse on them can nevertheless be enriching. 'Vibes' might do, if a bit colloquial. *Venus and Adonis* is not Spenserian allegory. But it has vibes, and even if Mortimer and others are right that the poem rejects the ambiguous consolations offered by mythographers and Spenser, then that rejection depends for its full force on our

---

tion' of the political myth advanced by the *Shepheardes Calender* (although I would argue that the April and November eclogues may be as much monitory as laudatory). One early reader took Venus as Elizabeth and Adonis as himself, writing to the queen to explain this and calling her a 'merie wench'; see Katherine Duncan-Jones, 'Much Ado with Red and White: The Earliest Readers of Shakespeare's *Venus and Adonis* (1593)', *Review of English Studies*, 44 (1993), 479–501. Did the 'red and white' that he noted recall for him the Tudor rose?

[3] Sayre Greenfield, 'Allegorical Impulses and Critical Ends: Shakespeare's and Spenser's Venus and Adonis', *Criticism*, 36 (1994), 475–98. For Greenfield, refreshingly, allegory need not be 'conservative' (which usually, in our culture, means moralistic).

memory of those consolations. The poem, that is, may have anti-vibes, whether comic ones (there *is* something funny about a sweating goddess in pursuit of a reluctant *ephebe*, not unlike Spenser's lustful giantess Argante chasing down young squires in the 1590 *Faerie Queene*), serious ones (brightness falls from the air and beauty is but a flower), or the admonitory (your death is inevitable, but if you want to grow again, if only as a plant, then do your sexual duty and if you don't believe me, read my sonnets).

Before making my two suggestions, let me recall the major mythographical tradition concerning the story's figures, not least the boar that tusked Adonis in what some delicately called his thigh and others his genitalia. In the Third Part of his *Countesse of Pembrokes Yvychurch* (1592) Abraham Fraunce summarizes the basics: 'by *Adonis*, is meant the sunne, by *Venus*, the upper hemisphere of the earth (as by *Proserpina* the lower) by the boare, winter: by the death of *Adonis*, the absence of the sunne for the sixe wintrie moneths; all which time, the earth lamenteth: *Adonis* is wounded in those parts, which are the instruments of propagation: for, in winter the son seemeth impotent, and the earth barren'.[4] To be sure, a cosmological reading did not, for such commentators, preclude a moral one, whatever the logical contradictions produced: Adonis' fate, says Fraunce, shows what happens to the lustful, although one might reply that as a solar figure in a fallen cosmos Adonis, chaste or promiscuous, is in any case doomed to die, over and over. As A. C. Hamilton put it some years ago, writing of Shakespeare's character, 'His dilemma is simply that he is Adonis. If he yields to Venus he will not grow to himself, but be plucked. If he does not yield, he will be plucked by the enemies of Beauty', by mortality and time, 'by the imperfections in nature'.[5] Whether cosmological or moral, however, the mythographical readings often evoke the story's sexual implications,

---

[4] Sig. M3v. I believe that this essay gives the fullest description so far of this tradition as it applies to Spenser and Shakespeare; for a crisper outline see Christopher Butler and Alastair Fowler, 'Time-Beguiling Sport: Number Symbolism in Shakespeare's *Venus and Adonis*', in *Shakespeare 1564–1964*, ed. Edward A. Bloom (Providence: Brown University Press, 1964). Noting (125) that the usual reading of the myth concerned a 'contrast of summer fulfillment and winter deprivation' and 'the transition from one to the other at the equinox', they find some complex if not always convincing numerological patterns. See also Robert P. Miller, 'The Myth of Mars's Hot Minion in *Venus and Adonis*', *ELH*, 26 (1959), 470–81 and Clark Hulse, 'Shakespeare's Myth of Venus and Adonis', *PMLA*, 93 (1978), 95–105. Robert P. Merrix, 'Lo, in This Hollow Cradle Take Thy Rest', in Kolin, ed. *Venus and Adonis*, 341–58, says that 'we cannot escape some kind of allegorical or mythic meaning in the metamorphosis of Adonis' but need not let that dominate our reading of the whole work; he cites Leonard Barkan on the loose way older writers treated myth, (343).

[5] A. C. Hamilton, 'Venus and Adonis', *Studies in English Literature*, 1 (1961), 1–15, a subtle essay that takes some account of mythography. As Nancy Lindheim says in 'The Shakespearean Venus and Adonis', *Shakespeare Quarterly*, 37 (1986), 190–203, 'Adonis is not killed for what he does but for what he is' (197).

and modern critics have likewise tended to read Shakespeare's figures, and Spenser's as well, in terms of a sexuality involving the misused, wrongly unused, or transgendered phallus.[6]

For the cosmology, many mythographers send the reader back to the *Saturnalia* of Macrobius (perhaps some reflecting that Saturnalia is a feast welcoming the first hints of the sun's arousal from its equinoctial burial). He is worth quoting at some length:

> Adonis too is the sun .... Physicists have given to the earth's upper hemisphere (part of which we inhabit) the revered name of Venus, and they have called the earth's lower hemisphere Proserpine. Now six of the twelve signs of the zodiac are regarded as the upper signs and six as the lower, and so the Assyrians, or Phoenicians, represent the goddess Venus as going into mourning when the sun, in the course of its yearly progress through the series of the twelve signs, proceeds to enter the sector of the lower hemisphere. For when the sun is among the lower signs, and therefore makes the days shorter, it is as if it had been carried off for a time by death and had been lost and had passed into the power of Proserpine ... just as Adonis is believed to have been restored to her when the sun, after passing completely through the six signs of the lower series, begins again to traverse the circle of our hemisphere, with brighter light and longer days. In the story which they tell of Adonis killed by the boar the animal is intended to represent winter, for the boar is an unkempt and rude creature delighting in damp, muddy, and frost-covered places and feeding on the acorn, which is especially a winter fruit. And so winter, as it were, inflicts a wound on the sun, for in winter we find the sun's light and heat ebbing, and it is an ebbing of light and heat that befalls all living creatures at death.[7]

---

[6] Sometimes the boar itself is a phallus: Harry Berger, Jr., takes it as a Venereal phallus that further masculinizes a dominant female; see 'Acteon at the Hinder Gate: The Stag Party in Spenser's Gardens of Adonis', in *Desire in the Renaissance: Psychoanalysis and Literature*, ed. Valeria Finucci (Princeton, NJ: Princeton University Press, 1994), 91–117. Others have found gender subversion in Shakespeare's poem thanks to its epicene Adonis and sexually interested boar; see Madhavi Menon, 'Spurning Teleology in *Venus and Adonis*', *GLQ: A Journal of Lesbian and Gay Studies*, 11 (2005), 491–519. In *Richard III*, for that matter, Richard will coyly 'play the maid's part' (III.vii.50) while thrusting his way to the throne with an energy that most rapists would envy. For a humoral explanation of Richard's fiercely sterile sexuality, see Ian Frederick Moulton, '"A Monster Great Deformed": The Unruly Masculinity of Richard III', *Shakespeare Quarterly*, 47 (1996), 251–68, who also notes the similarity in this regard between the play's and the poem's boar. (Perhaps, in Galenic terms, high uterine heat might also explain the king's prenatal eruption of teeth—his tusks.) William E. Sheidley, '"Unless it be a Boar": Love and Wisdom in Shakespeare's *Venus and Adonis*', *Modern Language Quarterly*, 35 (1974), 3–15, reads the boar as Adonis' repressed phallicism and says that its hypervirility recalls Richard III (a merely virile boar, presumably, would find a sow and make piglets).

[7] Macrobius, *The Saturnalia*, trans. and ed. Percival Vaughan Davies (New York: Columbia University Press, 1969), 141–2.

In the late Middle Ages and early Renaissance such a reading became common. Boccaccio's *Genealogia deorum*, which paraphrases Macrobius, and Thomas Walsingham's early fifteenth-century *De archana deorum* say more or less the same: Adonis is the sun and Venus, the earth, weeps for his absence after he is killed by the foul and wintry rigor of the boar's teeth; Walsingham adds that Adonis is the sweet gum of the myrrh tree and that autumn storms are the earth's lament.[8] Every year, he reports (for his age was not ignorant of ancient near-eastern ritual), during the rites in honor of Adonis a chorus of women would weep for his bloody death.

Ambrose Calepine likewise cites Macrobius, as does Charles Estienne's widely used *Dictionarum historicum, geographicum, poeticum* (1553). Estienne also notes that the Orphic hymns consider Adonis the sun— 'Solem esse'. So too did other ancients, he says, and adds that the fierce hairy boar represents the hairy fierceness of winter and the sun's feebleness ('ab Apro, hirsuta et aspera fera, ictum, quia aspera sit et hirsuta hiems, sub qua solis vires paulatim deficiunt'). The boar, after all, opposes everything to do with Venus.[9] Natalis Comes' *Mythologia*, most important of the mythographies, describes Adonis' life as well as the rites associated with his cult and says that classical authors took Adonis as the sun slain by winter as it moves south at the equinox. So too thinks Vincenzo Cartari's *Imagines Deorum* (the illustrations showing Time eating the Nature's babes and the babes tumbling out of a place guarded by Genius are strikingly relevant to Spenser's Garden). It is at least possible, moreover, that Spenser knew the *Hieroglyphica* of Valerianus (1477–1558), less often (if ever) cited in the scholarship on these two poets. It is pleasant to think that he took a look, for there he would have found a whole chapter on boars that associates them not only with ruin, brutality, and a taste for trampling crops, but also with bad scholarship: the boar is a sophist, explains Valerianus, for his cloven trotter represents *recherché* distinctions of a sophistical sort. That boars do not ruminate, moreover, symbolizes a refusal to meditate upon the Law. Sows are like the summer, fertile, but boars are wintry, and Valerianus gives Venus and Adonis the usual cosmological reading.[10] His boar sounds not un-

---

[8] *Genealogiae Joannis Boccatii* (Venice, 1494), a facsimile ed. Stephen Orgel (New York: Garland, 1976), Book II, ch. 53; to call Adonis myrrh makes sense, for he is the son of Myrrha, born from her incestuous body after it became a tree. Thomas Walsingham, *De archana deorum*, ed. Robert A. van Kluyve (Durham, NC: Duke University Press, 1968), 155–6, also quotes Jerome, whose similar mythological reading presumably derives from Macrobius; Jerome notes that wintry raindrops are the earth's tears for the death of Adonis the sun.

[9] Ambrosius Calepinus, *Dictionarium ... additamenta Pauli Manutii* (Venice: Aldus, 1571), under 'Adonis'; Charles Estienne, *Dictionarium historicum, geographicum, poeticum* (1553; Paris, 1596), a facsimile ed. Stephen Orgel (New York: Garland: 1976), under 'Adonis'.

[10] G. P. Valeriano Bolzani, *Hieroglyphica* (1556). I cite the French translation by Jean

like Spenser's Grill, the pig—not a wild boar, to be sure, but at least a stubborn male porker—who will not shape up after Sir Guyon reforms the Bower of Bliss (*FQ* II.xii) and whose similarly recalcitrant ancestor in Plutarch's *Moralia* had been, the creature reports, a sophist philosopher before Circe changed him.[11]

Commentaries on Ovid also offered such information, although also evidence of disagreement over just when Adonis dies. Georgio Sabino's 1584 *Fabulum Ovidii*, itself indebted to the mythography of Natalis Comes, calls Adonis' death a moral warning against softness and part of a cosmological allegory in which Venus is the earth and Adonis the sun, than which nothing is more beautiful, and its 'virilia' that generate whatever grows from the earth. For him, the boar is Capricorn (a goat: astrology makes strange signfellows), for it 'amputates the sun's rays' ('radios solares amputat', sig. Cc8v) in what sounds like a solar castration. Agreement that the boar is winter need not mean consensus as to the date—and to what Sabino says it could be objected that Capricorn starts the sun's recovery into vigor, its renewed and extended beams, not its decline.

Those who wanted images along with their mythography could look, for example, at emblem 77 in Andrea Alciato's *Emblemata* with its surprisingly feeble-looking boar; the one in Henry Peacham's 1612 *Minerva Britannia*, shown on top of a dead or swooning Adonis in a disconcertingly sexual position, is much fiercer and suits current responses to Shakespeare's poem that—rightly—sexualize the youth's relation to his killer (see figure 1). To be sure, the story did not always inspire pathos: in 1586, William Charke reported in an anti-papist tract that at one time in Orleans an image of Venus lamenting the death of Adonis was venerated by the superstitious in the belief that it showed the Virgin Mary with her dead son, and George Buchanan's life of Mary Stuart recounts the death of Darnley but then scoffingly, if not altogether logically, calls Bothwell the murderous queen's 'faire Adonis'. Shakespeare was not alone in seeing the story's comic or ironic possibilities.[12]

---

de Montlyart (Lyon, 1615; facsimile ed. Stephen Orgel, 1976), Book IX. In this essay I omit George Sandys' notes to his sumptuous translation of Ovid's *Metamorphoses* because it appeared well after the texts I am exploring.

[11] See 'Gryllus', a dialogue on the rationality of brutes, in *Plutarch's Moralia*, trans. Harold Cherniss (Cambridge, MA: Harvard University Press, 1984), XII:493–533. Both Spenser's and Plutarch's Grills seem mere pigs, but as male ones, are, technically, boars.

[12] See William Fulke, the second part of *A Treatise Against the Defense of the Censure* ... (Cambridge: Thomas, 1586), sig. Mm6v (the Fulke volume prints Charke); George Buchanan, *Ane Detectioun of the Duinges of Marie Quene of Scottes* (London: Day, 1571), sig. K2v. For Thomas Watson, however, the dead Walsingham is an Adonis over whom the planet Venus weeps; see his *Eclogue upon the Death of the Right Honorable Sir Francis Walsingham* (London: Robinson, 1590), sig. B4v. In 'Beyond Binarism', but with more worldly sophistication than those deluded faithful whom Fulke scorns, Anderson notes the visual resemblances between Spenser's and Shakespeare's female figures who bend over a

My first suggestion, then, is that when considering how Spenser and Shakespeare exploit this material (whether through adoption, refusal, or revision) we remember how the story was usually read not just as the vegetation myth or seasonal myth that many scholars call it even if sometimes after a passing mention of cosmology, but also as explicitly calendrical and astronomical or astrological. In other words, what the mythographers have in mind is not only the coming of the cold down here as the days shorten, flowers wither, and sunlight makes but winter arches, but also, even primarily, what is happening up there in the circling zodiac and along the horizon. The myth is as much matter for almanacs as for moralists. It looks downward to the intermittently chilly earth but also upward and outward to the signs and to the sun— not to the sun as divine Apollo but as a vulnerable star, one not, before Galileo, subject to change in his person but horribly subject to change in motions that were tracked by human beings worried not only about winter but also about eclipses and the precession of the equinox. Our attention, that is, is directed not only at vegetation and weather but also upwards to the rotating sky, to the kinetic, even problematic heavens. I would add that both Spenser and Shakespeare would have been well aware that the moment of Adonis' death was now a matter of international and intellectual dispute. In England, and until 1752, Adonis died around September 11 or 12, whereas on much of the Continent ever since 1582 the boar had obeyed Pope Gregory XIII and done his equinoctial dirty work around September 21 or 22.[13] Of course, one could object that the sun starts to dim at the summer solstice (which Spenser's *Epithalamion*, in good English and Julian style, identifies with June 11, his marriage day) and to recover at the winter one, right after having passed what Donne calls the year's midnight, even if he too follows the old Julian system by putting Adonis' nadir on St. Lucy's day. It is hard to worry much about the sun in July and August, however, which is why it is the equinox that figures in most mythographical commentaries, whatever the actual cultic practices in the ancient Near East and whatever the familiarity of educated Renaissance readers with those practices as described by, for example, Plutarch.[14]

To be sure, the seasons also 'circle' by, at least imaginatively and in one view of time, but in the Renaissance imagination they parallel,

younger male and the traditional pietà.

[13] On the relevance to English poets, see my 'Refusing Translation: The Gregorian Calendar and Early Modern English Writers', *YWES*, 36 (2006), 1–11.

[14] Lodowick Lloyd's *First Part of the Diall of Daies* (London: Ward, 1590), sig. N1, sets the date for the feast of Adonis on March 18, when women mourn for the boar's victim, which seems backwards. See Plutarch's *The Lives of the Noble Grecians and Romanes*, trans. Thomas North from the French of J. Amyot (London: Vautrollier, 1579), sig. T2v, on Alcibiades, and sig. 3C5v, on Nicias. For another allusion, see Vincenzo Cartari, *Les Images des dieux des anciens* (Lyon, 1581), sigs. 4I4–4K1, on how women would grieve for the death of Adonis (the usual interpretation follows).

indeed are caused by, visible celestial rotations. This fact can involve, I think, a question of tone—what for us is the come-and-go of the months and the weather was in the past, and much more consciously than for us, a matter of skies, stars, constellations, and signs. (New Yorkers, for example, tend to experience the year's cycles as the absence or presence of snow and heat and the length of the day; their sun moves from over Gracie Mansion to over New Jersey, not around the ecliptic with its twice a year rendezvous with a celestial equator hardly visible from the sidewalks.) That may be why many Renaissance scholars who note the mythographers' explication of Ovid's story mention cosmology then rapidly return to earth with a vocabulary that is still with us and that seems less uncomfortably occult in its astrological overtones: 'vegetation', 'season', and so forth. In the myth, Adonis does become a flower, but in that he is also solar, he is not only vegetable but also starry.[15] Whatever her celestial nature and status as both planet and goddess, Venus—born on this earth, after all, if from the water and spilled semen—is his Astrophil.

That Adonis is, mythologically, a star (or planet, in the pre-Copernican world), and that his story became a fertility cult—unless it is the other way around—likewise makes it an image of *recurrent* loss and recovery; thus Erasmus tells how in the spring women would plant little 'gardens of Adonis', often potted and sacred to Venus, that would soon fade (only, presumably, to be planted again the next year; Erasmus' modern editor's note explains that the faded gardens would be tossed out in the fall).[16] Such evanescence, adds Erasmus, explains why a 'garden of Adonis' became a byword among the ancients for frivolity and triviality, something that should give readers of Spenser pause for various sorts of reflection. That same circularity, to cite another relevant text, explains the stunning end of Bion's great lament for Adonis, a poem from which Spenser seems to have borrowed for his elegy on the thigh-wounded Philip Sidney, 'Astrophel' (1595), if possibly by way of Ronsard's 1563 'Adonis'. Bion's speaker, it will be recalled, has been repeating some version of 'Weep, weep for Adonis, Cythera's beloved is dead', but then changes the refrain to say, 'Cease thy laments today, Cythera; stay thy dirges. Again must thou lament, again must thou weep another year'.[17]

---

[15] True, in the Renaissance these could be connected. See the marvelous passage on stars and flowers as parallels, and on the flowers as the stars' creations, from *Traité des signatures* (Lyons, 1624), 18, by Osvaldus Crollius, a Paracelsian and alchemist (c. 1560–1609), in Michel Foucault *The Order of Things: An Archaeology of the Human Sciences* (New York: Random House, Vintage Books, 1973), 19–20.

[16] *Adagia*, I.i.4 ('Adonidis horti'), in *The Adages of Erasmus*, selected and ed. William Barker (Toronto: Toronto University Press, 2001), 31–2.

[17] *The Greek Bucolic Poets*, trans. A. S. Gow (Cambridge: Cambridge University Press, 1953), 147. Much in this elegy seems relevant to Spenser (its elements appear scattered here and there, which is how Spenser seems to have worked when interested in some

Spenser's Adonis, then, is the father of all forms, but only because the forms he begets (or experiences) must die that others may be born; as Ronsard puts it in an elegy lamenting the destruction of a forest he had loved, matter remains and form is lost ('La matière demeure, et la forme se perd').[18] Unless for Spenser it is the reverse, for his views of matter's relation to form in the Garden of Adonis are notoriously difficult to identify. In either case, even if Adonis is, as Spenser puts it, 'eterne in mutabilitie', his eternity rotates, whether as recipient or donor. We know that Spenser read the poetry of Guillaume du Bartas, who describes matter's relation to form in ways that seem to anticipate at least one possible significance of a less-than-chaste Venus and a form-bearing Adonis. In the 'Second Day' of the *First Weeke* the narrator observes that 'Heere's nothing constant: nothing still doth stay: / For Birth and Death have still successive sway'. Matter, the 'Body of this All', is immortal, being 'Change-less in Essence; changeable in face', and in this is 'like a Lais, whose inconstant Love / Doth every day a thousand times remove; / Who's scarce unfolded from one Youthes embraces / Yet in her thought another she embraces'. Thus matter 'Forme after Forme receaves: so that, one face / Another face features doth deface'.[19] However we relate these ideas to Spenser's own (or to the contemptuous remark by Shakespeare's Adonis that under the excuse of promoting 'increase' Venus 'lends imbracements unto every stranger', 790–1), clearly profusion has its price—for fathers of forms as well as for mothers. Is Venus the mother of all forms? If so, as Theresa Krier says in a recent essay on Spenser's Garden, then she too has mourning to perform, at least periodically; birth, too, entails loss.[20]

Is any of this relevant to Shakespeare's *Richard III*? There are lexical traces of Spenser in this play; Judith Anderson cites Richard's adoption of some imagery from the Garden of Adonis when he is trying to talk

---

other text). For example, Bion says that Cythera's 'love-girdle' is now 'perished' (compare the loss of a girdle by Florimell, who likewise loves a male figure who must disappear for a time). Bion's mourning goddess, like Shakespeare's Venus, has a striking resemblance to the female figures, good and bad, who hover over young men in *The Faerie Queene* like secular pietàs, see also n12 above. The goddess puts Adonis' body in her own bed, embraces him, and says 'Kiss me so long as life is in the kiss, until thy spirit has passed into my lips, thy breath flowed into my heart, and I have drained thy sweet love-philtre and drunk up thy love ... '. Compare Acrasia sucking Verdant's sprite in II.xii.

[18] Ronsard's Elegie XXIV, in *Oeuvres Complètes*, ed. Jean Céard et al. (Paris: Gallimard, 1994) II, 409. The forest was real, but woods are an ancient metaphor for the multiple created world.

[19] Guillaume de Saluste, Sieur du Bartas, *The Divine Weeks and Works*, tr. Josuah Sylvester, ed. Susan Snyder (Oxford: Clarendon Press, 1979) I, 141–2; Spenser praises du Bartas in his 'Ruines of Rome'.

[20] Theresa M. Krier, 'Mother's Sorrow, Mother's Joy: Mourning Birth in Edmund Spenser's Garden of Adonis', in Vaught, *Grief and Gender*, 133–47, with some resonant comments on the boar's presence.

Queen Elizabeth into letting him marry her daughter.[21] There are yet other echoes, resonant ones, that suggest a thoughtful engagement with Spenser's imagery, particularly that of a ripe fertility threatened by a hollow darkness underneath and yet also, in some fashion sustained by or further defined by that hollow darkness. Shakespeare's Richard is a barren tyrant, and yet the underlying myth in which he plays a part hints not only at tragedy but at a sort of necessity. Perpetual spring, in a fallen world, would preclude harvest. It seems right, then, that Spenser's Venus should 'reape sweet pleasure' (VI.vi.46) from a recovered Adonis for he is no longer exclusively vernal, no longer an *ephebe*, but the 'father of all formes', just as Richmond hopes to 'reap the harvest of perpetual peace'(V.ii.15). And just as the mount under which Spenser's boar lies is 'right in the middest of that Paradise' (III.vi.43), so in the passage calling Richard a 'foul swine' we hear that he 'Lies now even in the centry of this isle' (V.ii.11; Spenser's boar is imprisoned 'In a strong rocky Caue ... Hewen vnderneath that Mount', [III.vi.48]; compare the phrase 'the blind cave of eternal night'). The terror of course is that the darkness is in the middle, like a modern astronomer's black hole, not at the periphery. A Garden of Adonis without that cave, though, would be a lie, as would history without its Richards or a year without a dimmed sun. This does not justify boars and tyrants, of course, and the contrast can risk edging into a sort of dualism that both poets might think heretical, but it does suggest in some sense that *lux perpetua*, while desirable someday, is bad for the crops. Venus and Adonis lie, after all, in the shade as they make love on their rich mount. Richmond, whatever his virtues, is delusional if he thinks he can 'reap' perpetual peace: in this world perpetuity and reaping do not go together, and the new king's very metaphor thus suggests, in its slight dissonance, the ultimately fruitful tensions of the century that will follow.

Shakespeare seems, if this is right, to have listened to Spenser's overtones, and so although some commentators have noted the importance of Richard's boar-like nature in the play (paralleling his hypermasculinity, or his problematic replacement of moisture by the choleric), there is more to be said about the cosmological myth's role, minor though it might be, in this play's resonance and ironies.[22] Although

---

[21] See Judith H. Anderson, 'Venus and Adonis', who cites IV.iv.423; Richard responds to the queen's complaint that he has killed her children by promising their rebirth in her daughter's womb, that 'nest of spicery'. I am less comfortable with Anderson's suggestion that a 'garden of Adonis' was commonly thought a 'forcing bed' or even a paradise (151); see my note 16 above.

[22] Moulton, '"A Monster Great"' explicitly connects Richard with the boar of Adonis, as does, with a useful list of the play's boar-allusions, Romuald Ian Lakowski, 'From History to Myth: The Misogyny of Richard III in More's History and Shakespeare's Play', *Q/W/E/R/T/Y*, 9 (1999), 15–23. A. T. Hatto, '"Venus and Adonis"—and the Boar', *Modern Language Review*, 41 (1946), 353–61, notes that in the Middle Ages the boar was 'a symbol of overmastering virility'. Maybe boars lost their noble reputation, he suggests, as

no sane critic would argue that calendrical or seasonal allegory is the secret key with which to unlock the work's mysteries, the mythographers have a little to contribute to its understanding. Shakespeare, moreover, seems to have exploited this material deliberately, for it appears hardly at all in the *Henry VI* plays that precede it, although some of the play's sources and analogues hint at it, if haphazardly.

Richard, of course, carried as his cognizance the white boar (white for the Yorkist faction in the Wars of the Roses), a noble beast in older opinion but also allowing insult, for a boar is both irascible and, if domesticated, a mere pig. Not that epithets for Richard were limited to swine; a number of historians and writers had reached for their bestiaries in describing Richard. For example, John Rous, who had praised Richard during his lifetime, calls the dead tyrant a scorpion, while Bernard André says he was a tiger. Thomas More's study of the king thinks him a serpent, a 'cur dogge', a wolf. And in Polydore Vergil's history he is a pestilence, which at least suggests bad air if not, at that time, microorganisms.[23] Not all historians treated Richard so vividly, of course, but his reputation (or the historian's agenda) was apt to prompt such snarls of animal metaphors.[24]

Inevitably such imagery included comparisons of the king to the boar that was his sign, although one did need to be careful: the poet Collingbourne notoriously won what Edward Hall's history calls Richard's 'bloudy furye' by making a couplet on the king and his advisors Ratcliffe, Catesby, and Lovell: 'The Rat, the Catte and Lovell our dogge / Rule all Englande under the hogge'.[25] And Hall himself describes Richard's end as he is bound on a horse and trussed 'lyke a hogge or calfe'. When the people heard of his death, adds Hall, 'the proude braggyng white bore (which was his badge) was violently rased and plucked doune from every signe and place where it myght be espied ... .'[26] Such allusions enliven More's biography, but they had al-

---

pigs replaced the wild ones.

[23] See John Rous's account of Richard's reign (composed before 1492), in Alison Hanham's *Richard the Third and His Early Historians* (Oxford: Oxford University Press, 1975), 118–24; Bernard André, *Historia Regis Henrici Septimi* (c. 1502), ed. James Gairdner (Rolls ser., London, 1858), 31; Thomas More, *The History of King Richard III*, ed. Richard Sylvester (New Haven, CT: Yale University Press, 1963), 12, 24, 87; and Polydore Vergil, *Historie of England*, ed. Sir Henry Ellis (Camden Society reprint 29, London, 1844), 186.

[24] See Greta Olson, 'Richard III's Animalistic Criminal Body', *Philological Quarterly*, 82 (2003), 301–24; I do not share her puzzlement, perhaps due to confusing boars with farm pigs, at finding a boar with 'bloodthirstiness' (315).

[25] Edward Hall, *The Union of the Two Noble and Illustre Famelies of Lancastre and Yorke* (1548), ed. H. Ellis (1809; repr. New York: AMS Press, 1965), 398.

[26] Hall, *Union*, 421. The house of York was also associated with the sun, and Richard's banner included some roses *en soleil*, but for good symbolic reasons it was the boar that won comment and solar splendor shifted to Henry Richmond. On such arms and badges, see C. W. Scott-Giles, *Shakespeare's Heraldry* (London: AMS Press, 1950), who suggests

ready appeared elsewhere in less famous contexts. Bernard André's 'Douze Triomphes de Henry VII', for instance, makes Henry VII a Herculean monster-slayer, killing such irascible energies afflicting England as the 'senglyer Archadique' who, says André, represents Richard III (Spenser's readers, as Julian Lethbridge reminds me, might think of the violent Sir Sanglier defeated by Sir Artegall, solar knight of Justice, in *Faerie Queene* V.i).[27] If Richard is the boar, moreover, Richmond is the sun and his victory a return of the light, a scattering of the clouds, the coming of Apollo.[28] So too, Pietro Carmeliano, in a birthday poem for the newborn Tudor prince Arthur, includes an account of how the baby's father won the kingdom: Richmond lands and assures his followers that soon the white boar will relinquish his rule and lie bloody on the thirsty earth. As for the victor, 'Apollo freed from the clouds does not flash with so many golden rays'.[29]

Similar imagery ironically or tragically connecting Richard to his symbol inevitably intensifies the rhetoric of the monologues in the *Mirror for Magistrates*, not least that of the poet Collingbourne when explaining his imprudent lines on Richard as England's hog—and defending a poet's right to free speech. The most vivid, if hardly the most poetically adroit, description of Richard explicitly links him to the seasons, if not precisely to the equinoxes. Richard enters the council chamber, hot for Lord Hastings' blood:

> Frownyng he enters, with so chaunged cheare,
> As for myld May had chopped fowle Januere.
> And lowrying on me with the goggle ye,
> The whetted tuske, and furrowed forhead hye,
> His Crooked shoulder bristllyke set up,
> With frothy Jawes, whose foame he chawed and suppd,
> With angry lookes that flamed as the fyer:
> Thus gan at last to grunt the grymest syre.[30]

---

that the white boar was in part a pun on the Latin Eboricum, York.

[27] Published with *Historia Regis*, 138: 'Or avoit il retins pour sa devise / Le grant pourceau qui est trèsorde beste; / Et ne sçait on pour quoy il avoit prise'.

[28] André, *Historia Regis*, 35–6, in a poem associating Richmond's victory with roses and zephyrs, and 'Aureus ... Apollo / Nubis obscurae tenebras quadrigis / Vectus exsolvat referatque lucem ... Sic dies atras religat querelas / Quo suos princeps repetit Penates, / Et nitent soles melius potenti / Rege sub isto'.

[29] See Henry A. Kelley, *Divine Providence in the England of Shakespeare's Histories* (Cambridge, MA: Harvard University Press), Appendix C, 322.

[30] William Baldwin et al., *The Mirror for Magistrates*, ed. Lily B. Campbell (1938; repr. New York: Barnes and Noble, 1960); I quote the complaint by Lord Hastings, 289, but see also Clarence on his brother as a boar, 230. Jonson's poem is on sigs. D1-D3v; see also, on the relevance to Shakespeare of a ballad on the murdered princes, sigs. E3-E5, David Carlson, 'The Princes' Embrace in Richard III', *Shakespeare Quarterly*, 41 (1990), 344–7.

Such language is largely missing from the anonymous *True Tragedie of Richard the Third* (1594, although written earlier), but the pattern at which Shakespeare will hint or allude is dimly adumbrated in Thomas Legge's Latin trilogy *Richardus Tertius*, performed at Cambridge in 1579.[31] Here Richard is several times called a destructive boar, a lacerating *aper frendens*, and according to Lord Strange at the end, Richmond's victory shows that storms cannot last forever and that soon Titan shows his radiant head.[32] Like Shakespeare, and perhaps with the same irony, Legge gives his protagonist an initial allusion to the sun and only later shows him as the shadow: in Shakespeare's play, Richard says that, 'the winter of our discontent' is made 'glorious summer' by the sun/son of York; in the first play of Legge's trilogy he first looks forward to the dawn (1II.i) and London's mayor tells him to shine like the sun (1III.iii). Legge's irony, if such it really is, seems not incompatible with a sense of political as well as seasonal circularity.

Denigration of Richard as a boar, together with reading the murdered princes as pretty vegetation (roses and the like, and the genealogically appropriate 'branches'), was versified in popular texts, too: in the early and anonymous 'Rose of England', for instance, we read that there was once a pretty garden but 'came in a beast men call a bore, / And he rooted this garden upp and downe .... He tooke the branches of this rose away, / And all in sunder did them teare; / And he buryed them under a clodd of clay, / Swore they should never bloome nor beare'. But an eagle rescues a rose branch and now 'this garden fflourishes ffreshly and gay'.[33] Presumably the garden is England, now recovering from its own winter of discontent and tyranny. Several generations later in 1620, but perhaps written earlier, Richard Johnson's *Golden Garland* offered several poems on Richard III's life; in one, Johnson says of the king on his way to battle that he 'frets, he fumes, and ragingly, / A madding fury showes'; a little later he is explicitly called 'this bloody Boare of Yorke'. So long as Tudors and even the early Stuarts were on the throne such imagery was unlikely to fade from popular memory; it survives yet.

---

[31] *The True Tragedie of Richard the Third* (London: Creede, 1594). True, there are hints of a wintry Richard destroying England's vegetation. Richard roars that 'Ile burne you up like chaffe, / Ile rend your stock up by the rootes, that yet in triumphs laffe' (sig. C3v), which sounds boarlike, while Richmond calls England a 'grove, / Where brambles, briars, and thornes over-grow those sprigs' that might 'prove such members of the Commonweale, / That England should in them be honoured, / As much as ever was the Romane state, / When it was governd by the Councels rule' (sigs. G2v-G3; a quasi-Republican touch?).

[32] Thomas Legge, *Ricardus Tertius*, in *The Complete Plays*, ed. and trans. Dana F. Sutton (New York: Peter Lang, 1993), I. For boar references see, e.g., 1II.i; 3I.liii, and 3II.i; Richmond's solar victory is in 3V.v.

[33] Geoffrey Bullough, ed., *Narrative and Dramatic Sources of Shakespeare* (London and New York: Routledge, 1960), III, 346–9.

I would not attempt to prove that Shakespeare (or for that matter Spenser) read any particular one of these texts, with the obvious exception of the *Mirror* and More, whose truncated biography was incorporated into the histories on which the play is based. But collectively they add to the Tudor mythology that was part of the atmosphere in the 1590s, that his play obviously follows, and that it may also, if less obviously, interrogate. They do so, I believe, because the imagery suggests not just a battle down here between the forces of light and dark but also analogues in the skies and the year with which we are now, as I have said, less familiar and less comfortable. Richard the boar is dark, isolated, and wintry; Richmond is solar, harmonious, and warm. After all, even aside from this set of images, themselves cosmological, one could not call Richard a wretched and bloody boar without, in the days of school-room readings of Ovid and the proliferation of mythographical dictionaries, recalling the story about a boar's most famous victim. To repeat: if boars had acquired a dark reputation in the later Middle Ages as representing lust and violence, they were also cosmological, rooting about not just in human vineyards (see Psalm 79) and forests but in the skies, not just in wintry weather but in the whirling zodiac.

Shakespeare seems to go out of his way to incorporate such imagery. Even his tiresomely repetitive chorus of grieving women, one might argue, distantly echoes the specifically female lamentation over the dead Adonis in the old rites noted by many mythographers, and not least because Shakespeare wastes no time in establishing Richard as a boar or, as Queen Margaret puts it, an 'elvish-marked, abortive, rooting hog' and 'son of Hell' (I.iii.228–30; Queen Anne had scornfully called him a 'hedgehog' [I.ii.104]). Male victims can also fear the boar's predations, of course. Lord Stanley, who had earlier had his famous prophetic dream of a boar killing Lord Hastings, reports that his son is held hostage 'in the sty of the most deadly boar', (IV.v.2). Or they can vow to defeat it, as when Richmond, before a night in which Richard's victims pray that 'Good angels' will guard him 'from the boar's annoy' (V.iii.157), promises to expel

> The wretched, bloody, and usurping boar,
> That spoiled your summer fields and fruitful vines,
> Swills your warm blood like wash, and makes his trough
> In your embowled bosoms, this foul swine ... .
>   (V.ii.7–10)

A 'swine' is a boar that has lost its charisma.

Boars, if we believe the mythographers, are also creatures ill at ease in the light, all too likely, as Richard says of himself, to prefer their 'shadow in the sun' (I.i.26; cf. 262–3). Indeed, Richard casts a long shadow in this play, for Shakespeare takes pains to stress his darkness. As Queen Margaret says, grieving for her own dead offspring, he has turned 'the sun to shade ... Witness my son, now in the shade of death, / Whose bright out-shining beams thy cloudy wrath / Hath in eternal darkness folded up' (I.iii.266–9)—a destruction of specifically solar beams, a sort of helioectomy, that vividly recalls the old mythological tradition, particularly Sabino and his image of 'amputated' sunbeams. Shakespeare carefully ties these references to others in which Richard, not unlike his cousin in *Venus and Adonis* that kills as it kisses Adonis' thigh, is counter-intuitively (granted his looks and misogyny) yet compellingly sexual even while being also sterile and a destroyer of fertility.[34] Richard seduces both a queen and a crowd, even as the play quietly ignores his fathering of a son, and yet he orders the deaths of young princes whose lips are like 'four red roses on a stalk' in their 'summer beauty' (IV.iii.12–13). No wonder such a paradoxical figure is said by one of Clarence's murderers to be as 'kind' as 'snow in harvest' (I.iv.230–1)—this last a pun on 'kind' meaning 'natural', I assume, for it is in the nature of boars to be coldly raging killers.

The play has other passages in which Richard is cold and dark and the victims and victors are warm and shiny. The end of the play is particularly rich with them, and indeed before the battle of Bosworth Field Richard cannot even *see* the sun that is quite visible to Richmond. Such imagery is not in itself surprising: on the whole, and leaving racism aside, villains are darker than heroes, the dragon darker than St. Michael, and Python certainly darker than Apollo. But Shakespeare stresses this pattern well beyond what he needed to do in order to establish Richard's hellish loathsomeness and Richmond's salvific light—the latter's victory can be seen as a sort of Harrowing of England. Unlike *Venus and Adonis*, this is a text in which it is the gnashing boar who dies and the exiled Adonis, the sun/son of Lancaster, who recovers, for even if not quite an Adonis, young Henry Tudor is what one might, if rashly, call Adonoid. As one recent critic has succinctly said, when Shakespeare wrote this play 'he had already learned how to integrate the realistic and the symbolic'.[35]

At least Adonis recovers in this play, even if we know he will turn into the somewhat sour Henry VII, the king whose own son was at first welcomed as the young, radiant, and hopeful prince before he darkened into despotism and what we would call paranoia. One could, in these terms, read the play as calendrical allegory. I hasten to add that I am not doing so, for so simple an allegory would be both criminally thin and chronologically incoherent—Richmond's victory has vernal 'vibes', but history puts it in late August, closer to the fall equinox. Remembering

---

[34] On Richard's sexual magnetism see Donna J. Oestreich-Hart, '"Therefore, Since I Cannot Prove a Lover"', *Studies in English Literature*, 40:2 (2000), 241–60, who cites Ovidian and Medieval parallels between the martial and amatory arts.

[35] E. Pearlman, 'The Invention of Richard of Gloucester', *Shakespeare Quarterly*, 43 (1992), 410–29, here 424.

the cosmological and *cyclic* myth that Spenser and Shakespeare adopted and adapted, though, adds resonance and irony to that victory, for even among those Renaissance writers who officially and with varying degrees of genuine feeling admired the Tudors there can be hints of a more cyclic than triumphalist understanding of history. Thus, for example, Spenser's *Mutabilitie Cantos* never really do answer the claim of the Titaness Mutabilitie that history, including English history, is a long story of usurpation. Time confers legitimacy but only while waiting for the next conqueror who wins the throne by force. Boars come and boars go.[36] So does Adonis: as Shakespeare's Buckingham says to the 'cloudy' mourners of Edward IV (if, in the event, inaccurately), although they have 'spent the harvest' of one king England will now 'reap the harvest of his son' (II.ii.115–16). The reign of Henry VII is no assurance, despite the sunlight and fertility of the last few lines in the play, that winter will not return—or that spring will not follow the next winter, of which England's future will have no small supply.

Such views, even when modified by a more biblical view of history as linear, explain in part why Spenser must keep the boar alive: to the extent that the Garden of Adonis is, as Humphrey Tonkin has argued, both in and out of time, to that extent its boar is a present absence, explicitly captured yet implicitly dangerous.[37] On the other hand, Shakespeare can kill off Adonis without *necessarily* thinking that all is now winter, forever and ever. It is not to insist on giving Shakespeare's mischievous poem a happy ending, let alone a moral, to suggest that the calendrical meaning of the myth as recounted by so many mythographers lurks in the background of his story and can, despite his teasing revisions and deviations, limit any dismay that might mix with our amusement at the tragedy befalling his Adonis. Even if Adonis becomes merely a *plucked* flower (plucked flowers do not last long, whatever love poets like to tell their mistresses or Venus tell Adonis, 131–2), Shakespeare is still evoking the myth's recognition of cyclic time. To deny or to revise is still to notice, just as to say your mistress' 'eyes are nothing like the sun' is to say 'look at me being (not)Petrarch'. To what others have said about Shakespeare's post-Spenserian poem, moreover, one that both turns cosmology to comedy and (as the husband in the *Epithalamion* might say) cuts off through hasty hunting accidents what

---

[36] Compare, in the next century, the frontispiece of Michael Drayton's *Poly-Olbion*, with its somewhat smirking map-draped Britain surrounded by four successive mates: Brutus, Caesar, Hengist, and William. As Chaucer's Wife of Bath might put it, 'Welcome the fift'?

[37] Humphrey Tonkin, 'Spenser's Garden of Adonis and Britomart's Quest', *PMLA*, 88 (1973), 408–17. For Tonkin, Book III has two great metaphors: the quest and generation, the latter being 'cyclical, kinetic, expressed principally through the myth of Venus and Adonis'. Adonis is matter, the father not of Platonic forms but of shapes. In either case the boar is his enemy.

in the *Faerie Queene* is a tale of a partial escape from due time, I would add the possibility of finding yet one more witty touch. If it is true that Adonis must be killed once a year by the boar, what happens if we imagine Adonis at the very lowest point of his life cycle? Should not Venus have better chosen her time of year? If so, I would second those critics who deemphasize the poem's *moral* meaning. It may be imprudent as well as priggish (or otherwise oriented) to reject the Goddess of Love and go hunt, but Adonis must, willy-nilly, meet the boar once a year. What happens to him is not chance, not just one of those things, a moment of 'shit happens'. The process may lack meaning, but only if the cosmos lacks meaning and the fall into temporality is a fable. For what happens to Adonis, when read cosmologically and without, for the moment, concern for the poem's mixed tone or rhetorical expansiveness, is no accident, let alone the result of evil energies in the cosmos; time and winter, whatever Shakespeare's and our taste for personification, have no agency. Adonis *must* be killed or the sun will forsake the lower hemisphere and the seasons will come to a halt, which cannot happen until, as Spenser says at the end of his epic, the world rests on the pillars of eternity. What will happen to the Adonis-flower, though, we do not in fact learn. Whether Shakespeare envisions the youth as permanently dead or about-to-be-dead flower or whether the boy's Adonis-ness survives in the root to bloom again half a year later, the poem does not say.[38] To remember the myth or cult is inevitably to remember the vernal (or solstitial) resurrection when he meets not a boar but a ram (or crab), but within the text the flower's story is left untold. The rest, so to speak, is silence.

There is silence at the end of *Richard III*, too, after the applause, but here the astrological, calendrical, or cosmological meaning of boars can modify what seems a happy ending. Modern scholarship has recently perceived in Shakespeare's history plays less support of a self-contented Tudor myth and more doubt about political power, including the power that ruled England. If there is a touch of the Adonis myth to the play (not allegory, just vibes) that would give the end more bite. After all, if Richard is a boar vanquished by a solar Richmond, he himself had come along only after the death of a brother—the 'son of York'—whose cognizance was the sun. That is yet one more reason why Robert Ornstein was right to say some years ago that the mood at the end is one 'of somber reflection, not one of joyous celebration'.[39] Like kings, the

---

[38] Catherine Belsey, 'Love as Trompe-L'Oeil: Taxonomies of Desire in *Venus and Adonis*', *Shakespeare Quarterly*, 46 (1995), 257–76, calls the poem a 'myth of origins', just as the myth itself explains the origins of the cult of Adonis (259–60). Compare Marlowe's seriocomic explanatory myth in *Hero and Leander* that purports to account for poets' poverty.

[39] Robert Ornstein, *A Kingdom for a Stage* (Cambridge, MA: Harvard University Press, 1972), 81. Richard served (and serves) many a political agenda; Michelle O'Callaghan shows in '"Talking Politics": Tyranny, Politics, and Christopher Brooke's *The Ghost of*

play's boar has two bodies: one is bound bloodily on his horse and no threat; the other will never die until division, darkness, cold, and death are gone. Audiences would have known, in the 1590s, that even the Tudor rose could not be England's final flower.

Richard the Third (1614)', *The Historical Journal*, 41 (1998), 97–120, that Brooke's poem emerged from a group opposed to Jacobean royal absolutism; there is some animal imagery: Richard grins like a wolf, lies like a fox, and notes that others are as corrupt as Circe's swine (sig. D4v, cit 117). Richard is all darkness, the murdered princes are floral, and Richmond is 'Brittaine Phoebus' who reorders 'Englands chaos' (L3; cit 119).

Figure 1: *Henry Peacham, Haud conveniunt, Minerva Britanna, 169.* Used with permission from Special Collections at Middlebury College, courtesy of Prof. Timothy Billings.

Hamlet's Debt to Spenser's *Mother Hubberds Tale*: A Satire on Robert Cecil?

Rachel E. Hile

> Though he endeavour all he can,
> An Ape, will never be a Man.
> —George Wither,
> *A Collection of Emblems*, 1635

> And as the body of an Ape is Ridiculous, by reason of an indecent likenesse and imitation of Man, so is his soule or spirit.
> —Edward Topsell,
> *The Historie of Foure-Footed Beasts*, 1607

In *Hamlet*, in addition to something rotten, the court of Denmark houses a strange menagerie of beasts: images of frog, cat, bat, camel, weasel, fox, ape, mouse, rat, and ostrich, among others, appear in the play, creating meaning through reference to extratextual traditions of animal symbolism, but also signaling an affiliation with the tradition of satirical beast fables.[1] Although numerous scholars have catalogued Shakespeare's repeated use of animal imagery in this play,[2] analyses of these images have tended to focus on symbolic and iconographic meanings rather than looking at this image pattern as connecting the play to the beast fable genre, with the political and satirical implications such an association implies. At the time of *Hamlet*'s composition, Edmund Spenser's *Prosopopoia: or Mother Hubberds Tale* was a well-known model of a beast fable with a clearly discernible satiric intent. The animal imagery in *Hamlet*, in conjunction with plot parallels with *Mother Hubberds Tale*, suggest that a consideration of Shakespeare's debt to Spenser's

---

[1] An earlier version of this paper was presented in the Spenser and Shakespeare seminar at the 34th Annual Meeting of the Shakespeare Association of America, Philadelphia, PA, April 13–15, 2006. I appreciate the careful readings of earlier drafts by seminar members as well as by J. B. Lethbridge, Troy J. Bassett, Michael Stapleton, Paul Hecht, and anonymous reviewers.

[2] See, for example, Caroline Spurgeon, *Shakespeare's Imagery and What It Tells Us* (1935; Cambridge: Cambridge University Press, 1999), 368; Audrey Yoder, *Animal Analogy in Shakespeare's Character Portrayal* (New York: King's Crown Press at Columbia University, 1947), 72; Maurice Charney, *Style in Hamlet* (Princeton, NJ: Princeton University Press, 1969), 63–74; and Karl P. Wentersdorf, 'Animal Symbolism in Shakespeare's *Hamlet*', *Comparative Drama*, 17 (1983), 348–82.

poem might yield insights into the ways in which Shakespeare uses the play to criticize or satirize those in political power.

Mother Hubberds Tale appears to be an analogue[3] for *Hamlet*, raising the question of Shakespeare's satirical intention. I argue that, given *Mother Hubberds Tale*'s reputation as a satire directed against William Cecil, Lord Burghley, and his son Robert Cecil, allusions to it would cue a contemporary audience to consider the ways in which *Hamlet* may satirize the Cecils, specifically Robert Cecil, given that Lord Burghley died before the composition of *Hamlet*. In particular, a composition date of 1601 would suggest the value of examining the ways in which the play may criticize Cecil's role in the downfall of Robert Devereux, Earl of Essex.

Did Shakespeare Read Mother Hubberds Tale?

Awareness of Spenser's satirical work as part of his poetic achievements remained strong following his death; in particular, Spenser's contemporaries knew of *Mother Hubberds Tale,* best known for having angered Lord Burghley sufficiently that government authorities recalled the work following its publication in 1591. In *Mother Hubberds Tale,* an ape and a fox, tired of their poverty, manage through deceit to infiltrate each of the three estates. Predictably, their greed and dishonesty lead to disasters for those around them. Whereas the villains' exploits as laborers and churchmen appear to be generalized estates satire, without any particular targets, the satire becomes sharper when the ape and fox infiltrate the court, and especially when they usurp the royal power of the lion.

Spenser's use of the ape and fox characters gave offense to Lord Burghley and to Robert Cecil because these characters drew upon animal imagery that was already widely used for the two men, making the attack seem thinly veiled indeed.[4] Additionally, the satire, by targeting the fox's greed and the physical disability of the fox's children—Robert Cecil's humpback was partly responsible for the ape imagery attached

---

[3] I borrow the term from Richard Dutton, '*Volpone* and Beast Fable: Early Modern Analogic Reading', *Huntington Library Quarterly*, 67 (2004), 347–70, at 367, who argues that *Mother Hubberds Tale*, though not strictly speaking a source for *Volpone*, serves as an analogue for the play.

[4] Anthony G. Petti, 'Beasts and Politics in Elizabethan Literature', *Essays and Studies*, 16 (1963), 68–90. Whereas scholars have agreed in connecting the Fox to William Cecil, there has been debate regarding the identity of the Ape; A. C. Judson, in 'Mother Hubberd's Ape', *Modern Language Notes*, 63 (1948), 145–9, provides an overview of the possible identifications put forth in the early Twentieth Century, with Edwin Greenlaw arguing for Jehan de Simier (the agent of the duke of Alençon in the marriage negotiations of 1579), Harold Stein proposing James VI of Scotland, and Brice Harris connecting the Ape with Robert Cecil. More recent critics have tended to align themselves with the reading that associates the Ape with Robert Cecil. See, for example, Richard S. Peterson, 'Laurel Crown and Ape's Tail: New Light on Spenser's Career from Sir Thomas Tresham', *Spenser Studies*, 12 (1998), 1–35, here 14; Dutton, '*Volpone* and Beast Fable', 354.

to him—was perceived as focusing attention in specifically unflattering ways on the father and son. The following lines were perceived by contemporaries as offering the most pointed criticism of Lord Burghley and his son:[5]

> [The fox] fed his cubs with fat of all the soyle,
> And with the sweete of others sweating toyle,
> He crammed them with crumbs of Benefices,
> And fild their mouthes with meeds of malefices,
> He cloathed them with all colours save white,
> And loded them with lordships and with might,
> So much as they were able well to beare,
> That with the weight their backs nigh broken were.[6]

According to a letter by Thomas Tresham written shortly after the publication of *Mother Hubberds Tale*, the recall of the poem succeeded in raising the price of the book from sixpence to a crown (five shillings), but not in silencing the poem altogether.[7] The recall presumably contributed as well to the wide popularity of the poem in manuscript in the two decades between printings of the poem.[8] Because of its satire of Lord Burghley, the poem was still considered too politically incendiary to be included in the 1611 edition of Spenser's complete works. The inclusion of the poem in the second edition of the works in 1612/13, following the death of Robert Cecil, inspired a new generation of political satirists.[9] Gabriel Harvey had already foreseen in 1592 the influence *Mother Hubberds Tale* would have; but he did not approve, because 'if mother Hubbard in the vaine of Chawcer, happen to tel one Canicular Tale', lesser poets 'will counterfeit an hundred dogged Fables, Libles, Calumnies, Slaunders, [and] Lies'.[10]

---

[5] See Brice Harris, 'The Ape in Mother Hubberds Tale', *Huntington Library Quarterly*, 4 (1941), 191–203, for contemporary commentary connecting these lines with Lord Burghley and Robert Cecil.

[6] Lines 1151–58. Quotations from *Prosopopoia; or, Mother Hubberds Tale*, are from William A. Oram, et al., eds., *The Yale Edition of the Shorter Poems of Edmund Spenser* (New Haven, CT: Yale University Press, 1989), 327–79.

[7] Peterson, 'Laurel Crown', 7.

[8] Peter Beal, *Index of English Literary Manuscripts*, 4 vols (London: Mansell; New York: Bowker, 1980), vol. I, part 2, 527–8.

[9] See William Wells, ed., *Spenser Allusions in the Sixteenth and Seventeenth Centuries* (Chapel Hill: University of North Carolina Press, 1972) for numerous examples of poetry influenced by *Mother Hubberds Tale*. See also Michelle O'Callaghan, *The 'Shepheards Nation': Jacobean Spenserians and Early Stuart Political Culture, 1612–25* (Oxford: Clarendon Press, 2000), 14; and Andrew McRae, *Literature, Satire, and the Early Stuart State* (Cambridge: Cambridge University Press, 2004), 91, for discussions of the significance of the popularity of Spenserian satiric imitations.

[10] Gabriel Harvey, from *Foure Letters and Certaine Sonnets* (1592), reprinted in R. M. Cummings, ed., *Spenser: The Critical Heritage* (London: Routledge & Kegan Paul, 1971), 53.

Although *Mother Hubberds Tale* may not have led to fully one hundred derivative 'Canicular Tales', it certainly had an influence on satires written in the following decades. Satirical works that drew upon *Mother Hubberds Tale* for inspiration imitated the beast fable in their use of ape and fox characters and Spenser's estates satire in their anti-court orientation. For example, a pointed reference to *Mother Hubberds Tale* occurs in Richard Brathwaite's *A Strappado for the Diuell* (1615), where, to close out his satirical portrait of the 'complete Courtier', he quotes directly two lines from *Mother Hubberds Tale*: 'Save what is common, and is knowne to all / "That Courtiers as the tide doe rise and fall"'.[11]

Another allusion to Spenser's poem, especially significant in terms of how early seventeenth-century readers interpreted the political satire of *Mother Hubberds Tale*, appears in Richard Niccols's *The Beggers Ape*. Niccols closely imitates the opening lines of *Mother Hubberds Tale* to set up his own tale. More broadly, he imitates Spenser's poem by using ape and fox characters for an anti-court satire, but with an enhancement of the theme of disability, presumably to strengthen the association of the ape with Robert Cecil.[12] Niccols emphasizes the deformity of the ape, calling to mind Robert Cecil's humpback. The narrator, describing the Ape's creation—transformed by Jove from a man into a beast because of his deceitfulness—notes that 'His limbes in lesser space then mans are knit', and the fox comments to the ape that 'scarce your legs your limbs vpholden can'.[13] By emphasizing details that support a reading of the Ape as Robert Cecil, Niccols works to close off the ambiguity of the Ape identification present in Spenser's poem, suggesting that by the first decade of the seventeenth century, the identification of the Ape with Cecil had solidified in readers' minds.

Richard Dutton develops the implications of this identification in his analysis of the influence of *Mother Hubberds Tale* on Jonson's *Volpone*, arguing that Spenser's poem's notorious reputation as an anti-Cecil satire allowed Jonson to imply a wealth of anti-Cecil criticism simply by alluding to *Mother Hubberds Tale*. Dutton argues that Jonson's animosity toward Robert Cecil at the time of *Volpone*'s composition in 1607 stemmed specifically from the anti-Catholic policies pursued by Cecil following the Gunpowder Plot,[14] though of course other Cecil critics had different reasons for disliking him. In particular, in 1601, Cecil's role in the downfall of the Earl of Essex opened him to criticism from the pro-Essex faction.

---

[11] Quoted in Wells, *Spenser Allusions*, 140–1.

[12] Dutton, '*Volpone* and Beast Fable', 357.

[13] Richard Niccols, *The Beggers Ape*, written c. 1607 (London, 1627); (Eugene, OR: Renascence Editions, 2000), www.uoregon.edu/~rbear/ape.html, accessed December 7, 2006.

[14] Dutton, '*Volpone* and Beast Fable', 349.

Thus, at the time of *Hamlet*'s composition at the beginning of the seventeenth century, *Mother Hubberds Tale*, though overshadowed by Spenser's achievements in *The Shepheardes Calender* and *The Faerie Queene*, remained a well-known and still relevant example of Spenser's satirical work, and other poets imitated it by making reference to ape and fox characters. Although we cannot with absolute certainty declare that Shakespeare read *Mother Hubberds Tale*, A. Kent Hieatt has demonstrated Shakespeare's debt in the *Sonnets* to Spenser's *Ruines of Rome: by Bellay*, which appeared along with *Mother Hubberds Tale* in the *Complaints* volume of 1591.[15] Hieatt notes the possibility that Shakespeare also read *Mother Hubberds Tale* by calling attention to a verbal parallel in the second quarto of *Titus Andronicus* (1600); the closing lines of the play, 'Then afterwards, to order well the state, / That like events may ne'er it ruinate' (V.iii.203–4) echo the rhyme and sense of lines 1039–1040 of *Mother Hubberds Tale* ('for gouvernment of state / Will without wisedome soone be ruinate').[16] In addition to this work connecting Shakespeare's work with the *Complaints* volume, studies of Shakespeare's debts to *The Faerie Queene*,[17] including Abbie Findlay Potts's comment on the greater number of 'Spenserian images, phrases, and situations' in the second quarto of *Hamlet* than in the first quarto,[18] suggest Shakespeare's continuing and perhaps even deepening debt to Spenser at the time of *Hamlet*'s composition.

Additionally, Shakespeare himself provides clues to connect *Hamlet* with the beast fable tradition in general and *Mother Hubberds Tale* in particular. Numerous comparisons of humans to animals illustrate the preoccupation with distinctions between man and beast, and Shakespeare's playful references to animals in beast fable and proverb traditions provide a rationale for considering the influence of the beast fable tradition on *Hamlet*. Additionally, plot parallels suggest connections between characters in the play and the animal figures in *Mother Hubberds Tale*.

Hamlet's repeated comparisons of humanity to beasts suggest the same preoccupations and anxieties to which satiric beast fables respond: What makes us human? And can we devolve into mere beasts? Fredric V. Bogel argues that the 'originating moment' of satire occurs not when the satirist recognizes something different and attacks it; 'rather it is at least as likely that we attack figures, distance ourselves from them, be-

---

[15] A. Kent Hieatt, 'The Genesis of Shakespeare's Sonnets: Spenser's "Ruines of Rome: by Bellay"', *PMLA*, 98 (1983), 800–4; see also the correspondence related to the article: *PMLA*, 99 (1984), 244–5 and *PMLA*, 100 (1985), 820–2.

[16] Hieatt, 'Genesis', 805.

[17] For example, W. B. C. Watkins, *Shakespeare & Spenser* (Princeton, NJ: Princeton University Press, 1950); Abbie Findlay Potts, *Shakespeare and 'The Faerie Queene'* (Ithaca, NY: Cornell University Press, 1958).

[18] Potts, *Shakespeare and 'The Faerie Queene'*, 129.

cause we sense their threatening proximity to us'. From this perspective, we can see satire as connected to ritual acts of 'casting-out and exclusion'.[19] Beast fables, by meditating on the boundaries between man and beast, suggest a desire to contain or cast out humanity's beastly qualities.

Both Hamlet and Claudius pay close attention to the similarities between humans and animals, though Hamlet seems more troubled by the connections than Claudius does. According to Hamlet, Gertrude's speed in posting to incestuous sheets is made worse by the fact that 'a beast that wants discourse of Reason / Would have mourn'd longer' (I.ii.150–1).[20] Hamlet laments the animal part of human nature when he asks, 'What is a man / If his chiefe good and market of his time / Be but to sleepe and feede, a beast, no more' (Q2 IV.iv.34–6). Shortly afterward, he considers the possibility that his delay in exacting his father's revenge may result from his own 'Bestiall obliuion' (Q2 IV.iv.41). Hamlet thus participates here in the psychological project of satiric beast fables, using comparisons with animals to render as 'other' the distressing and objectionable behavior of humans.

Hamlet's musings evince an anxiety that humans may not differ as much from animals as they might wish, and Claudius implies how easy the transformation from human to beast can be. Claudius reiterates the common philosophical understanding of the differences between humans and animals when he refers to Ophelia's separation from her 'faire Iudgement, / Without the which we are Pictures, or mere Beasts' (IV.v.85–6). The fluid boundaries between human and animal become laudable in his description of the horseman, who 'grew into his Seat, / And to such wondrous doing brought his Horse, / As had he beene encorps't and demy-Natur'd / With the braue Beast' (IV.vii.85–8).

In their attention to the similarities between humans and animals, these lines suggest an anxiety related to the fears expressed in the scene with the Gravedigger over the similarities between living and dead bodies. Shakespeare knew of the philosophical tradition exploring the differences (and potential similarities) between humans and beasts, including Cicero's and Sallust's emphasis on the importance of humans' exerting themselves to avoid living a merely animal life.[21] Certainly he knew as well of the satirical tradition that explores human qualities and failings with reference to the animal kingdom. Shakespeare displays

---

[19] Fredric V. Bogel, *The Difference Satire Makes: Rhetoric and Reading from Jonson to Byron* (Ithaca, NY: Cornell University Press, 2001), 12.

[20] Quotations from *Hamlet* are from *The Three-Text Hamlet: Parallel Texts of the First and Second Quartos and First Folio*, ed. Paul Bertram and Bernice W. Kliman (New York: AMS Press, 1991). Except where noted otherwise, all quotations are from the folio.

[21] Harold Jenkins, in his Arden edition of *Hamlet* (London: Methuen, 1982), at 438–9, 528, argues for Hamlet's indebtedness to Ciceronian ideas. Clifford J. Ronan, in 'Sallust, Beasts That "Sleep and Feed", and *Hamlet*, 5.2', *Hamlet Studies*, 7 (1985), 72–80, connects Hamlet's ideas to specific beast imagery in Sallust.

his debts to the beast fable tradition by referencing the folk tradition of proverbs and animal fables, presenting material that he actually invented as though it were proverbial or fabled.

Hamlet explains Osric's standing at court with reference to his wealth in land by offering a proverb about beasts: 'Let a Beast be Lord of Beasts, and his Crib shall stand at the Kings Messe' (V.ii.86–8). The repetition of *beast* cues the audience to consider the beast fable as one of the generic traditions informing Osric's character. The use of language reminiscent of proverbs, although we have no record of any contemporary proverbs similar to this,[22] provides another clue of the genre shift, suggesting the 'old wives' tale' frame story of *Mother Hubberds Tale*. Additionally, the proximity of *beast* to *king* calls to mind the lines from *Mother Hubberds Tale* in which the Fox tells the Ape that 'we may our selves .../ Make Kings of Beasts, and Lords of forests all, / Subiect unto that powre imperiall' (970–2). Certainly the sense of arbitrary and dangerous connections between beastliness and royal power appears in both statements.

Similarly, the fabricated beast fable in the closet scene with Gertrude highlights the importance of the beast fable genre to the play. In this scene, Hamlet's lesson on what not to do includes advice not to

> Vnpegge the Basket on the houses top:
> Let the Birds flye, and like the famous Ape
> To try Conclusions in the Basket, creepe
> And breake your owne necke downe.
>   (III.iv.193–6)

Numerous commentators have sought unsuccessfully to identify this fable and have concluded that the story has been 'lost' over time.[23] It seems equally possible that Shakespeare simply made the story up, providing connections with both the beast fable tradition as a whole and with *Mother Hubberds Tale* in particular by means of the ape character who represents an overreaching fool.

Beast Satire in Hamlet

Critics have tended to examine Shakespeare's satiric voice as influenced primarily by the Juvenalian satiric tradition, particularly as exemplified by the works of John Marston.[24] The shift of this vein of satire

---

[22] Morris Palmer Tilley, *A Dictionary of the Proverbs in England in the Sixteenth and Seventeenth Centuries* (Ann Arbor: University of Michigan Press, 1950).

[23] See commentary notes on lines 2569–2570 at hamletworks.org www.leoyan.com/global-language.com/ENFOLDED/index.html. Accessed October 3, 2006.

[24] Oscar James Campbell, in *Shakespeare's Satire* (New York: Oxford University Press, 1943; rpt. New York: Gordian Press, 1971), 149–59, connects both Hamlet and Marston's Malevole to the older Juvenalian tradition.

from printed poetry to the stage following the so-called Bishops' Ban of 1599, which outlawed the Juvenalian type of formal verse satire, makes it natural to seek the Marstonian first-person satiric speaker in dramatic works of the period, including Shakespeare's. For this reason, many critics have explored Shakespeare's indebtedness to the Juvenalian tradition and the formal verse satires of the 1590s in creating the character of Hamlet.[25] Nevertheless, some other satirical moments in *Hamlet* do not show affinities with the embittered, ranting Juvenalian speaker. Rather than approaching these differing satirical impulses taxonomically—looking, for example, to classify individual satirical moments with reference to a prescriptive taxonomy of satiric types (Menippean satire as opposed to Juvenalian satire,[26] for instance, or beast fable as a genre with specific requirements[27])—it seems more useful to examine their social functions. As already mentioned, as a genre, satiric beast fables function in part to react to the perceived permeability of the boundary between human and animal. Another well-known social function of beast fables is to satirize and instruct powerful people. In *The Defence of Poesy*, Philip Sidney explains this purpose with reference to Aesop:

> the Poet is indeed, the right populer Philosopher. Whereof Esops Tales give good proofe, whose prettie Allegories stealing under the formall Tales of beastes, makes many more beastly than beasts: begin to hear the sound of vertue from those dumbe speakers.[28]

Looking at the connections between *Mother Hubberds Tale* and *Hamlet* suggests interesting possibilities regarding Shakespeare's satire of royal power. These oblique references to *Mother Hubberds Tale* include plot parallels as well as animal imagery that connects Claudius to the ape and Polonius to the fox. Finally, in an interesting departure from the ape/fox dyad, following Polonius's death, Shakespeare creates in Osric a young counterpart to the self-interested royal adviser, ensuring that the death of Polonius does not mean the death of corruption at the court of

---

[25] For example, Alvin Kernan, *The Cankered Muse: Satire of the English Renaissance* (New Haven, CT: Yale University Press, 1959), 220–1; James Taylor, '*Hamlet*'s Debt to Sixteenth-Century Satire', *Modern Language Studies*, 22 (1986), 374–84. See also Shanti Padhi, 'Hamlet's Satirical Rogue', *Hamlet Studies*, 6 (1984), 68–71, which connects Hamlet to Mateo Aleman's *The Rogue*, a Spanish satire published in 1599.

[26] For example, Juanita Sullivan Williams, *Towards a Definition of Menippean Satire* (Ann Arbor, MI: University Microfilms, 1969).

[27] Ellen Douglas Leyburn, *Satiric Allegory: Mirror of Man* (New Haven, CT: Yale University Press, 1969); Rama Rani Lall, *Satiric Fable in English: A Critical Study of the Animal Tales of Chaucer, Spenser, Dryden, and Orwell* (New Delhi: New Statesman Publishing, 1979).

[28] Philip Sidney, *The Defence of Poesie* (London, 1595); Eugene, OR: Renascence Editions, 1992, http://darkwing.uoregon.edu/˜rbear/defence.html, accessed December 12, 2006.

Denmark. Osric, too, is described with metaphors of beasts, specifically bird images.

The satire of royal power in *Mother Hubberds Tale* involves an Ape who, with help from his adviser the Fox, usurps royal power from the true king, the Lion, whom the Fox has drugged. Order is restored by means of divine intervention when Mercury descends to awaken the Lion. In *Hamlet*, Claudius—an 'adulterate beast', a 'satyr', an 'ape'—usurps the throne by killing his brother with drugs. He maintains his power with help from his beastly advisers Polonius and, later, Osric. Claudius' reign ends when young Hamlet, spurred to revenge by the otherworldly intervention of his father's ghost, succeeds, at great cost, in setting things right.

The wide variety of animal images attached to both Claudius and Polonius serves to outnumber the ape and fox images, and yet this may well be intentional: the overwhelming association of fox imagery with William Cecil and ape imagery with Robert Cecil[29] would make an obvious association of Claudius with apes and Polonius with foxes unwise. Whereas Karl P. Wentersdorf examines the iconographic and literary meanings associated with the many animal images attached to Claudius and Polonius (generally finding patterns of animal imagery signaling lust), the political meanings associated with the ape and the fox suggest that they may have more topical significance than the other animal images connected with these characters.

Shakespeare uses imagery to connect Claudius with numerous animals, generally animals with negative connotations. For Hamlet, Claudius is 'a Paddocke, . . . a Bat, a Gibbe' (III.iv.190). His drunken revels cause other nations to clepe the Danes 'drunkards, and with Swinish phrase / Soyle our addition' (Q2 I.iv.19–20); and Hamlet intensifies his comparison of Claudius with swine by imagining him 'honying and making loue / Ouer the nasty Stye' (III.iv.93–4). Hamlet criticizes Claudius' intemperate, undiscriminating lust by referring to him as a satyr; and the Ghost seconds this interpretation by calling Claudius 'that incestuous, that adulterate Beast' (I.v.42).

In among this wealth of negative animal imagery, the reference to Claudius as an ape might pass unnoticed, except for its close proximity to the image connecting Polonius to a fox (only twelve lines separate the two images) and the absence of both images from both the first and the second quartos. The ape and fox images thus did not appear at all in printed versions of *Hamlet* until the folio edition, by which time both William Cecil and Robert Cecil were dead. The second quarto gives, 'he keepes them like an apple in the corner of his iaw', whereas the folio reads, 'He keepes them like an Ape in the corner of his iaw' (Q2 IV.ii.18–19); editors have tended to collate the two versions to create

---

[29] Petti, 'Beasts and Politics', 79.

'like an ape an apple'. Linkages between apes and apples in iconographic and literary traditions would presumably have enabled early modern readers of the second quarto to make the connection.[30]

Shakespeare connects Polonius to *Mother Hubberds Tale* both by linking him to William Cecil, Lord Burghley, and by using the image of a fox to describe him. Numerous Oxfordian Shakespeare scholars have argued for links between Polonius and Lord Burghley, on the assumption that an identification of Polonius with Burghley would also serve to connect Shakespeare to Edward de Vere—Burghley's son-in-law—since (by their logic) the commoner William Shakespeare, being unacquainted with Burghley, therefore would be unlikely to satirize him. Although the overall argument is unconvincing—after all, no one argues that Spenser's satire of Burghley in *Mother Hubberds Tale* arises from a personal acquaintanceship—the industry of these scholars has uncovered a number of similarities based upon parallel family circumstances and verbal sententiousness. One observation that supports a reading of Polonius as specifically anti-Burghley satire stems from the first quarto's use of the name 'Corambis' for Polonius; Corambis, roughly translated as 'double-hearted' or duplicitous, serves as a satirical contradiction to Burghley's Latin motto, *Cor unum, via una* ('One heart, one way').[31] Bernice W. Kliman cautiously endorses this interpretation by mentioning the possibility that Shakespeare changed the name from Corambis in the first quarto to Polonius in the second quarto 'to make clear that he intended no parody' of Lord Burghley.[32]

My interest here lies not in what Polonius-Burghley parallels may tell us about the authorship of *Hamlet*, but in what they tell us about the links between this play and the anti-court and anti-Burghley satire of *Mother Hubberds Tale*. An image connecting Polonius to Burghley and to Spenser's satire of Burghley appears in the folio, when Hamlet leads the search for Polonius' body with the phrase 'Hide Fox, and all after' (IV.ii.31). The phrase is of course idiomatic, being the opening call for the game of hide-and-seek; yet Polonius' status as the sought-after person clearly attaches the image of the fox to him. The second quarto does not include these lines, perhaps because of a perception of danger in using fox imagery for a courtier so similar in many ways to William Cecil, especially in conjunction with the ape image that appears twelve lines earlier.

---

[30] Wentersdorf, 'Animal Symbolism', 374–5, illustrates the ape-apple connection by reference to continental pictorial tradition. This connection occurs in a specifically English context in Niccols's *The Beggers Ape*, where the Ape is said to love apples 'wondrous well'.

[31] Gordon C. Cyr, 'Polonius as Lord Burleigh: Oxford's Revenge on His Father-in-Law?' *The Shakespeare Newsletter*, 30:6 (1980), 48.

[32] Bernice W. Kliman, 'Three Notes on Polonius: Position, Residence, and Name', *Shakespeare Bulletin*, 20 (2002), 5–7, here 6.

Images connecting Claudius with an ape and Polonius with a fox provide a neat parallel with the main characters in *Mother Hubberds Tale*, but the bird imagery of Osric does not correspond to an animal character in *Mother Hubberds Tale*. Speaking of Edmund Spenser's references to birds, Thomas P. Harrison points out that Spenser draws upon symbolism to the exclusion of an interest in birds as actual creatures.[33] This symbolic emphasis is especially pronounced in the beast fable of *Mother Hubberds Tale*. With reference to birds, we see the interest in symbolism in the warning that whoever goes to Court in hopes of preferment 'will a daw trie' (913).[34] Here, the image draws upon the traditional symbolic meaning of daw as 'fool or simpleton'.[35] Thus, Spenser does include birds in *Mother Hubberds Tale,* but he emphasizes their symbolic meanings rather than personifying them. Of course, *Mother Hubberds Tale* does not represent Spenser's only efforts at satire involving anthropomorphized animals. The bird imagery used for Osric may represent the influence not of the Chaucerian estates satire of *Mother Hubberds Tale,* but rather of the Ovidian metamorphic satire of Spenser's insect tales, *Virgil's Gnat* and *Muiopotmos*.

Although he is unconnected to characters in *Mother Hubberds Tale,* Osric's character—bearing the name of an animal and clear parallels to the anti-court satire that Spenser was known for—seems to function to direct attention to the beast fable as an analogue for the play. In the chain of influence connecting these two works, Hotspur's popinjay (i.e., parrot; *1 Henry IV,* I.iii) may represent an intermediate iteration of the character type. Whereas most of the details Hotspur uses to describe the unnamed messenger emphasize his effeminacy (he is 'perfumèd like a milliner', uses 'holiday and lady terms', and speaks 'like a waiting gentlewoman', I.iii.35, 45, 54[36]), the use of the epithet 'popinjay' connects the effeminate courtier type with a bird image. Later, in Osric, Shakespeare causes the bird imagery to take precedence over his feminine qualities.

Osric's beginnings as a 'Bragart Gentleman' in the first quarto may point to a Spenserian origin in *The Faerie Queene*'s Braggadochio, as Potts observes;[37] the second quarto name Ostricke (Osric in the folio) cues the audience to approach the character from the interpretative per-

---

[33] Thomas P. Harrison, *They Tell of Birds: Chaucer, Spenser, Milton, Drayton* (Austin: University of Texas Press, 1956), 109.

[34] Thomas Herron, in 'Exotic Beasts: The Earl of Ormond and Nicholas Dawtry in "Mother Hubberds Tale"?', *Spenser Studies*, 19 (2004), 245–51, provides a topical explanation for the awkwardness of the syntax in this line.

[35] Beryl Rowland, *Birds with Human Souls: A Guide to Bird Symbolism* (Knoxville: University of Tennessee Press, 1978), 86.

[36] Quotations from *1 Henry IV* are from *The Norton Shakespeare*, ed. Stephen Greenblatt et al. (New York: W. W. Norton, 1997), 1147–224.

[37] Potts, *Shakespeare and 'The Faerie Queene'*, 133.

spective of the beast fable. Alone of characters in the play, Osric actually bears the name of an animal, and in his character we see the most obvious connections to the beast fable tradition.

Critics have responded to the apparent anomaly of the comic tone of the Osric scene by emphasizing that Osric should not be played or read as merely a fool[38]—the most compelling reason not to underestimate Osric, either in performance or criticism, is his clear importance to the plot. As the judge of the fencing match between Hamlet and Laertes, Osric must know about the plot against Hamlet.[39] Additionally, being one of the very few characters to survive the last scene in a sense means that Osric prevails. Unharmed and unchanged by the tragedy that has unfolded around him, Osric heralds the approach of Fortinbras. He stands at the ready, prepared to transfer his sycophancy, flattery, and treachery to a new sovereign.

These reasons to take Osric seriously, however, are difficult to reconcile with the language of the scene, which clearly invites actors to play and readers to imagine him as a fool. Considering the scene as a species of satire rather than comedy helps to reconcile these two opposing readings. Specifically, we can view Osric from the perspective of the beast fable satirical tradition by examining the pervasive animal imagery in the scene. Looking at the symbolism ascribed to particular animals and birds helps to illuminate the meanings of a beast fable.

In the Osric scene, other than Hamlet's reference to Osric as a 'water-fly', all of the animal metaphors for Osric connect him to birds. Osric's very name connects him not only to ostriches but to the cowardice and slothfulness symbolically associated with them because of ostriches' supposed habits of burying their heads to avoid being seen and abandoning their nests.[40] Hamlet and Horatio specifically describe Osric as a 'chuff' (i.e., jackdaw), a 'lapwing', and one of a 'bevy' of similar creatures. 'Chough', as a synonym for jackdaw, includes as well the symbolic reference to foolishness. Specific to the courtly context, the chough is 'the bird which decked itself out in fine feathers but deceived no one'; more significant for Hamlet's own situation, symbolism associates the chough with detection of guilt and with portents of bad events.[41] The lapwing has similarly negative symbolism associated

---

[38] See, e.g., Marvin Rosenberg, *The Masks of Hamlet* (Newark: University of Delaware Press, 1992), 868, for a catalogue of numerous 'extravagances' to which theatrical interpreters of the character have been tempted, sacrificing a more complex presentation of the character for easy laughs.

[39] For more on Osric's collusion with Claudius in the plot against Hamlet, see J. Anthony Burton, 'Hamlet, Osric, and the Duel', *Shakespeare Bulletin*, 2:10 (1984), 5–7, 22–5; William G. Wall, 'The Importance of Being Osric: Death, Fate, and Foppery in Shakespeare's *Hamlet*', *Shakespeare Newsletter*, 42 (1992), 62.

[40] Rowland, *Birds with Human Souls*, 114.

[41] Ibid., 19–20.

with it; the tricks the lapwing uses to protect its young gave it a reputation for deceit and treachery,[42] and Osric illustrates this quality: 'he draws Hamlet away [from attention to danger] with a verbal fluttering of wings into a distracting exchange of repartee and quibbles'.[43] This 'verbal fluttering', the most noted and noticeable of Osric's qualities,[44] as well as the beast fable symbolism, provide the audience with cues for how to interpret the character.

Interpreting Hamlet's Analogies to Mother Hubberds Tale

The difficulty in dating *Hamlet* complicates the project of finding topical interpretations for the connections between *Hamlet* and *Mother Hubberds Tale*. Additionally, the sheer volume of animal imagery in *Hamlet* serves to obscure specific satiric targets. As Anthony Petti remarks about Elizabethan beast satire in general, authors had to disguise personalities to such a degree by an arbitrary selection of animals, that the point of the attack must have been lost on all but the highly initiated—the author's patron, an intimate circle of friends, and those with sufficient shrewdness to read accurately between the lines.[45]

Nevertheless, assuming the play to have been composed in the first year or two of the seventeenth century allows speculation regarding possible historical events that might have inspired Shakespeare to include veiled anti-Cecil satire in *Hamlet*. As the Earl of Essex's fortunes declined between 1599 and 1601, pro-Essex poetry utilized beast imagery and the fable genre to express criticism of Essex's enemy Robert Cecil.[46] Shakespeare's admiration of Essex, illustrated in *Henry V* in the chorus to Act 5 and suggested as well by the willingness of Shakespeare's company to stage a performance of *Richard II* in advance of Essex's rebellion, would give him motivation not only to elegize Essex, as many critics have suggested,[47] but also to criticize Cecil.

Hamlet, likely written following Essex's rebellion and his execution for treason on February 25, 1601, presumably alludes to Spenser's

---

[42] *Ibid.*, 96.

[43] Burton, 'Hamlet, Osric, and the Duel', 24.

[44] For specific interpretations of Osric's use of language, see Potts, *Shakespeare and 'The Faerie Queene'*, at 133; Burton, 'Hamlet, Osric, and the Duel', 23; Donald K. Hedrick, '"It Is No Novelty for a Prince to Be a Prince": An Enantiomorphous Hamlet', *Shakespeare Quarterly*, 35 (1984), 72–6, here 74; and Wall, 'Importance of Being Osric', 62.

[45] Petti, 'Beasts and Politics', 85.

[46] *Ibid.*, 81–4.

[47] Edward S. LeComte, in 'The Ending of *Hamlet* as a Farewell to Essex', *ELH*, 17 (1959), 87–114, summarizes the extensive previous work connecting the character Hamlet to Essex. A more recent treatment of the topic occurs in Karin S. Coddon's '"Suche Strange Desygns": Madness, Subjectivity, and Treason in *Hamlet* and Elizabethan Culture', *Renaissance Drama*, n.s. 20 (1989), 51–75, which reads Hamlet's 'madness' against contemporary discourses regarding madness, especially in Essex. See also Robert L. Reid's paper in the present volume, pp. 93ff.

Mother Hubberds Tale and the beast fable genre in order to cue audience members to interpret the play as a satire of Robert Cecil. The fox and ape images for Polonius and Claudius (which may have been included in stage productions, despite their absence from the first and second quartos) suggest identifications with William Cecil and Robert Cecil. Claudius' murder of Old Hamlet in order to woo his queen is reminiscent of Robert Cecil's role in the trial and execution of Essex and his concomitant increase in political power under Elizabeth. Cecil's post as Secretary, his dramatic intervention into the trial (described below), and the belief of Essex's supporters that Cecil bore the responsibility for Essex's decline in Elizabeth's favor led to contemporary suggestions that Cecil was the villain in the story of Essex's fall.

A tantalizing detail that connects the play specifically with the theatricality of the trial of Essex involves Polonius' concealing himself behind the arras in the closet scene. During the trial of Essex, Robert Cecil hid himself behind a tapestry to listen to the proceedings, eventually revealing himself dramatically in order to refute one of Essex's statements.[48] The bizarre theatricality of the moment in the play may thus allude to a historical moment of even more melodramatic theatricality, and Hamlet neatly conflates the identities of Polonius and Claudius with the comment 'I tooke thee for thy better' (II.iv.32).

Finally, Hamlet's repeated attention to the disparity in physical attractiveness between Old Hamlet and Claudius recalls the rivalry between Essex and Robert Cecil, who were in a sense 'brothers' in that Essex spent part of his childhood in Lord Burghley's household. Essex's attractiveness was of course legendary, and Cecil's unattractiveness—caused in part by the humpback that contributed to the ape symbolism applied to him—was equally well-known. Shakespeare's choice to refer to Old Hamlet twice as Hyperion seems unusually pointed, suggesting the sun imagery applied to Essex in works such as Robert Pricket's *Honors Fame in Triumph Riding; or, the Life and Death of the Late Honorable Earle of Essex* (1604).

These topical speculations cannot be proven definitively, and I certainly am not arguing for the sort of *roman-à-clef* correspondences that would rule out, for example, both Hamlet *and* Old Hamlet serving as compliments to Essex. Rather, I argue for the intriguing possibility that, in response to Old Hamlet's injunction 'Remember me!' Shakespeare labors not only to re-member Essex, but also to criticize, however obliquely, one of the principal actors in the tragedy of Essex's downfall.

---

[48] Alan Haynes, *Robert Cecil, Earl of Salisbury, 1563–1612: Servant of Two Sovereigns* (London: Peter Owen, 1989), 64.

Fusion: Spenserian Metaphor and Sidnean Example in Shakespeare's *King Lear*

Susan Oldrieve

Judith Anderson has said of *King Lear* that 'to keep insisting that the play *King Lear* ... is not really, vitally allegorical at its core is effectually to cut it off both from its richest contemporary analogue, *The Faerie Queene*, and from the insight of the best recent work on the nature of allegory itself'.[1] In his introduction to *King Lear* in *The Norton Shakespeare*, Greenblatt acknowledges that 'It is possible to detect in *King Lear* one of the great structural rhythms of Christianity: a passage through suffering, humiliation, and pain to a transcendent wisdom and love'[2] suggesting not so much Christian allegory in the play as analogues that suggest allegory. Greenblatt, Anderson, and others have shown that *The Faerie Queene* and allegory play a significant role in the structure of Shakespeare's play, but some questions remain. How are we to define the allegory that we find in Shakespeare, and how can we explain the relationship of that allegory to the sense that we have as readers, actors, and viewers of the plays that they go beyond allegory to involve us in the realities of human experience?

Allegory in Spenser is difficult enough to define, but consensus has been reached, at least, that Spenser is in some way allegorical. Whether it is the double moral and spiritual allegorical imagery described by Rosemund Tuve,[3] or the personification allegory described by Maureen Quilligan,[4] or more recently, the affective allegory defined by Judith Anderson,[5] Spenser seems to have it. Shakespeare, however, is another matter. To suggest that Shakespeare is allegorical drama makes readers think of *Everyman*—flatly representational and alien to their experience of the complexity and beauty of Shakespeare's genius. Judith Anderson successfully resists a reductive definition of Shakespeare's allegory by highlighting the expansiveness of Shakespeare's allegorical mode, showing it to be an emotional, even a spiritual element of the plays. Her

---

[1] Judith Anderson, 'The Conspiracy of Realism: Impasse and Vision in *King Lear*', *Studies in Philology* 54 (1987), 1–23; here 14.

[2] *King Lear*, in *The Norton Shakespeare*, ed. Stephen Greenblatt (New York: W. W. Norton, 1997), 2307–2553; here 2313. Further quotations from Shakespeare are from this edition.

[3] Rosemund Tuve, *Allegorical Imagery: Some Medieval Books and Their Posterity*, (Princeton: Princeton University Press, 1966). See especially chapters 1 and 2.

[4] Maureen Quilligan, *The Language of Allegory: Defining the Genre*, (Ithaca: Cornell University Press, 1979), esp. 101–21.

[5] 'Conspiracy of Realism', *passim*.

reading of *King Lear* captures the complexity of Shakespeare's allegory, the play's treatment of Spenserian themes, and the power with which in this play the 'human character emerges explosively', something that does not happen, she claims, in Spenser's works.[6] Putting this explosive quality of Shakespeare's work into its historical context, I hope to show, both corroborates Anderson's view and explains in more detail what the relationship between allegory and the sense of real human character in Shakespeare might be.

Two historical influences upon Shakespeare that have not yet been brought to bear upon the question of his allegorical method are the poetic theory of the fifteenth- and sixteenth-century commentators upon Aristotle's *Rhetoric* and *Poetics*, and the influence of Sidney's *New Arcadia*. A study of the poetic theory circulating in Shakespeare's own day can help to explain the particular nature of the allegory Shakespeare is using in *King Lear*, and a closer analysis of Sidney's influence upon the play reveals how Shakespeare was able to move through the allegorical mode into the 'wonder' that Aristotle and others identify as a key to tragedy,[7] and to achieve that wonder through his characteristic focus upon particular human experiences.

Both Shakespeare and Spenser would have known of at least some of the theories of the fifteenth- and sixteenth-century Italian commentaries about Aristotle's works, if not directly, then by means of Sir Philip Sidney's 'Defence of Poesy'. About one hundred and fifty works of various such commentators were recorded as being included in the library of John Dee,[8] Elizabeth's court 'magus', who at one time tutored Philip Sidney in chemistry.[9] So they clearly made their way to England, although it is unclear how widely they were read and known.[10] We can

---

[6] Ibid., 12.

[7] For discussions of 'wonder' in Shakespeare's work, see J. V. Cunningham, *Woe or Wonder: The Emotional Effect of Shakespearean Tragedy* (Denver: University of Denver Press, 1951), particularly 62–105; T. G. Bishop, *Shakespeare and the Theatre of Wonder* (Cambridge: Cambridge University Press, 1996); Peter G. Platt, *Reason Diminished: Shakespeare and the Marvellous* (Lincoln: University of Nebraska Press, 1997); and David Richman, *Laughter, Pain, and Wonder: Shakespeare's Comedies and the Audience in the Theater* (Newark: University of Delaware Press, 1990).

[8] My listing comes from *The Private Diary of Dr. John Dee, and the catalogue of his library of manuscripts, from the original manuscripts in the Ashmolean museum at Oxford and Trinity College Library, Cambridge*, ed. James Orchard Halliwell (London: John Bowyer Nichols and Son, 1842), but see also R. J. Roberts and A. G. Watson, *John Dee's Library Catalogue* (London: Bibliographical Society, 1990).

[9] For the relationship between Sidney and Dee, see Roger Howell, *Sir Philip Sidney: The Shepherd Knight* (Toronto: Little, Brown and Company, 1968), 112, 137, and 224–5; and Katherine Duncan-Jones, *Sir Philip Sidney: Courtier Poet* (New Haven: Yale University Press, 1991), 115–17.

[10] For a discussion of how John Dee's library might have been read, see William Sherman, 'The Place of Reading in the Renaissance: John Dee Revisited', in *The Practice and Representation of Reading in England*, ed. James Raven, Helen Small, and Naomi Tadmor

assume, I think, that poets then, as now, would have some interest in the poetic theories of their day, although the level of influence upon their practice would, of course, vary from individual to individual. The work of these theorists can provide a vocabulary that makes it easier to define how Spenser and Shakespeare construct allegory and to identify the palpably different allegorical tendencies in their works.

The Renaissance literary theorists defined poetry as the art of imitation, and the subject of that imitation was to be human actions and human *mores,* or in the Italian, *costumi.*[11] In practice, the imitation of action translated into the development of the plot, while the imitation of *mores* resulted in what today we consider characterization—the development of fictional personae and the examination of human nature.

Mores as defined by Renaissance theorists were passions, dispositions, or habits of mind. Antonio Minturno's explanation is typical:

> De' costumi non hò à diriui qui punto de quel, che i Philosophi ne scriuono. Ma per quelli intendo tutte le dispositioni dell'animo, e della mente. Percioche, come ciascuno alla vertû, ò pur al vitio s'inchina, ò per natura ò per costumanza; così egli ben, ò mal costumato, è tenuto: e qual'e il suo costume, tal'è riputato, e si dice esser buono ò tristo. Laonde in queste luogo pigliamo per li costumi gli appetiti, & i proponimenti, e le dispositioni dell'animo, che sorgano dal fonte della natura, e da qualche nostro studio prendon forma, & aumento dall'usanza.[12]
>
> [Of *costumi* I have no direction, because the philosophers do not write of them. But by these I mean all the dispositions of the spirit

---

(Cambridge: Cambridge University Press, 1996), 62–75.

[11] The discussion of characterization upon which this essay is based comes from readings of about seventy-five of the works listed as being in John Dee's library. Some of the sources for the argument made here are: Vincentii Madii Brixiani et Bartholomaei Lombardi Veronensis, *In Aristotelis Librum De Poetica Communes Explanationes* (1550) (rpt. Munich: Wilhelm Fink, 1969); Alessandro Cariero, *Breve et Ingenioso Discorso Contra L'Opera di Dante (Parte Teorica)* (1582), in *Trattati di Poetica e Retorica del Cinquecento*, vol. III, ed. Bernard Weinberg, *Scrittoria d'Italia* #253 (Bari: Laterza, 1972); Giovanni Georgio Trissino, *La Quinta e la Sesta Divisione della Poetica*, (1562), in Weinberg, *Trattati di Poetica*, vol. III; Antonio Sebastiano Minturno, *L'Arte Poetica Del Sig. Antonio Minturno* (Venice, 1563); Lodovico Castelvetro, *Poetica D'Aristotele Vulgarizzata et Sposta per Lodovico Castelvetro* (Basle, 1576); Giason Denores, *Discorso Intorno a Que Principii, Cause et Accrescimenti che la Comedia, la Tragedia, et il Poema Heroico: Ricevono dalla Filosofia Morale e Civile e Da Governatori delle Republiche ...* (1587), in Weinberg, *Trattati di Poetica*, vol. III; Girolamo Fracastoro Naugerius, *Sive De Poetica Dialogus*, trans. Ruth Kelso (Chicago: University of Illinois Press, 1924); Francesco Bonciani, 'Lezione Della Prosopopea' (1578), in Weinberg, *Trattati di Poetica*, vol. III; Torquato Tasso, *Scritti Sull'Arte Poetica*, ed. Ettore Mazzali, (Milan/Naples: Ricciardi, 1959), vol. II; Jacob Mantino Hispano Haebreo, *Aristotelis De Rhetorica, Et Poetica Libri cum Averrois in Eosdem Paraphrasibus, Venetiis apud Junctas*, 1562, vol. 2, facsimile edition (Frankfurt am Main: Minerva, 1962); Scipio Gentili, *La Gerusalemme Liberata di Torquato Tasso con le annotationi di Scipion Gentili, e di Giulio Guastavini, e li argomenti Di Orazio Ariosti*, (Geneva, 1617). All translations are my own.

[12] Antonio Sebastiano Minturno, *L'Arte Poetica*, 45.

and of the mind. And since everyone is inclined either to virtue or to vice, either by nature or by habit, so he is reputed to be of good or evil *costumi* and is said to be either good or villainous. Whence in this place we interpret the *costumi* to be the appetites and intentions and the dispositions of the spirit, which arise from the fountain of nature and take form according to our particular care and are augmented by use.]

According to this definition, the *costumi* were not the virtues and vices themselves, but attitudes and passions that resulted from virtue or vice; they were the bent of mind that translated virtue or vice into action. Renaissance discussions of the imitation of *mores* portrayed the character as a vehicle that on the one hand propelled the action, and on the other manifested virtuous or vicious modes of behavior.

This manner of constructing literary characters grew out of the rhetorical *paradigma* or example, of which Peacham's definition is just one typical example:

> Paradigma, is the rehearsal of a deede, or saying past, and applying it to our purpose ... and it is of great force to perswade, move, and enflame men with the loue of virtue, and also to deterre them from vyce, and not used only to confirm matters but also to augment, inrich, and garnish them with much comeliness.[13]

Any educated person in the Renaissance would have been familiar with this rhetorical trope and with its special efficacy, for the example was much touted by the rhetoricians as being of great value in persuasion and clarification. In a typical passage, William Webbe demonstrates the application of *paradigma* to the interpretation of character in his discussion of *The Iliad* and *The Odyssey*:

> For so did that worthy Poet frame those his two workes, that in reading the first, that is his *Iliads*, by declaring and setting forth so liuely the Grecians assembly against Troy, together with their prowess and fortitude against their foes, a Prince shall learne not onely courage and valiantnesse, but discretions also and policie to encounter with his enemies, yea a perfect forme of wyse consultations with his captaines and exhortations to the people, with other infinite commodities.[14]

Here we see how actions could lead the readers to a recognition of various *costumi*—fortitude, courage, and discretion—and could offer practical suggestions for imitating the character in their own actions. Sidney's

---

[13] Henry Peacham, *The Garden of Eloquence* (London: H. Jackson, 1577), Facsimile, ed. R. C. Alson (Menston: Scholar Press, 1971), quarto O. ii-iii.

[14] William Webbe, 'A Discourse of English Poetrie', in *Elizabethan Critical Essays*, ed. Gregory Smith (Oxford: Oxford University Press, 1971), 234–5.

version of this idea occurs in the context of his comparison between the philosopher and the poet. He begins by stating that:

> for whatsoever the philosopher saith should be done, he giveth a perfect picture of it in someone by whom he presupposeth it was done, so as he coupleth the general notion with the particular example.[15]

He follows this passage with a list that clearly reflects the commentators' views that literary characters are examples of virtues or vices in action:

> Anger, the Stoics said, was a short madness: let but Sophocles bring you Ajax on a stage, killing or whipping sheep and oxen, thinking them the army of Greeks, with their chieftains Agamemnon and Menelaus, and tell me if you have not a more familiar insight into anger than finding in the schoolmen his *genus* and difference. See whether wisdome and temperance in Ulysses and Diomedes, valour in Achilles, friendship in Nisus and Euryalus, even to an ignorant man carry not an apparent shining; and contrarily, the remorse of conscience in Oedipus, the soon repenting pride in Agamemnon, the self-devouring cruelty in his father Atreus, the violence of ambition in the two Theban brothers, the sour-sweetness of revenge in Medea; and, to fall lower, the Terentian Gnato and our Chaucer's Pandar so expressed that we now use their names to signify their trades: and finally, all virtues, vices, and passions so in their own natural seats laid to the view, that we seem not to hear of them, but clearly to see through them. (222)

Sidney's exposition clearly derives from the Renaissance commentators and would have provided Shakespeare and Spenser with Renaissance theories of character even if they were unable directly to access rhetorical textbooks, such as those in Dee's library, themselves.

In both Italian and English Renaissance poetic theory, then, the imitation of *mores* by example boiled down to the demonstration, through a character's actions, of a specific attitude or mode of behavior that translated virtue or vice into action. The exemplary character was a dynamic one, always doing something to illustrate his or her *costume*. The character represented a virtue or vice, a human characteristic or tendency in action, providing an allegory dressed to varying degrees in the likeness of what today we would consider to be a 'realistic' character.

The range of possibilities for such characters in drama might best be illustrated by comparing Marlowe's example of ambition, Tamburlaine, to those characters whom Shakespeare developed in response—Richard III and Macbeth. All three characters demonstrate the vice of ambition

---

[15] Sir Philip Sidney, *The Defence of Poesy*, ed. Katherine Duncan-Jones (New York: Oxford University Press, 1989), 221.

in action, but their three-dimensionality varies greatly. Tamburlaine is probably the 'flattest' of the three, closest in type to the representational allegory we find in the medieval morality plays. Macbeth is a more three-dimensional character because Shakespeare has him not only represent the actions of ambition, but also the motivations, doubts, and psychological damage that come to the human soul that allows ambition to consume it. Richard III is yet more complex; his character explores the causes, manipulations, and unmotivated dark spots in the soul of ambition and the relationship of ambition to other human passions—anger, loss, revenge, desire, and filial love. We experience these characters quite differently, but they are all examples of ambition put into action, and they all point us towards an understanding of the role that ambition plays in our lives and the lives of those around us.

This description of character as example is by far the most prevalent definition of characterization in the commentaries upon Aristotle. However, it does not account for all of the analysis of character in Renaissance poetics. Throughout the body of Renaissance critical theory, there are references to character and to the composition of character that seem to have little to do with its exemplary function. Representational allegory with its corresponding significances, imitations of characters from other authors, iconographical descriptions, and the discussions of praising and blaming contemporary figures or customs through imitation, indicated that characters could function in other than exemplary ways.[16] The poetic practice of Spenser contains many samples of this second style of characterization. To a lesser degree, we can find the same technique in the works of Sidney and Shakespeare: the Fool in *King Lear* and Philisides in Sidney's *Arcadia* are just two examples that come to mind. This is the style that we most frequently think of today as 'allegory'.

The Renaissance theorists would have referred to this style rhetorically as a form of metaphor. Rhetorical treatises defined allegory as an extended metaphor, and metaphor as the 'transporting' of one word out of its natural (i.e., familiar) context into another unnatural but appropriate context, as in Puttenham's example, 'I cannot *digest* your unkinde words' for 'I cannot take them in good part'.[17] Or, as Wilson says, 'An Allegorie is none other thing, but a Metaphore, used throughout a whole sentence, or Oration' (176).

---

[16] See, for example, Francesco Bonciani, 'Lezione Della Prosopopea' (1578), *Trattati di Poetica e Retorica del Cinquecento*, vol. III, ed. Bernard Weinberg, (Bari: Laterza, 1972): 'In molte maniere appresso i buoni autori si è costumato di fare questa finzione di persone: avvenga che alcuni hanno le cose incorporee finte in figura umana, come l'invidia in forma di donna pallida e magia ... ' (237). (In the many ways to follow good authors are accustomed to make some imitation of a person: it happens that some have an immaterial thing made into a human figure, like envy in the form of a pale and thin lady.)

[17] George Puttenham, *The Arte of English Poesie* (1589), ed. Edward Arber (London, 1869), 189.

In creating characters according to the metaphorical concept of allegory, poets created figures that served as metaphorical vehicles for ideas, as do Spenser's titular knights. However, they also often transported attributes belonging to one character—usually a persona from pagan myth, history, contemporary poetry or politics—into the new context of their own work. Into Belphoebe, for example, Spenser has transported Diana and Elizabeth. Hobbinol is a transported Harvey, Colin Clout a transported Spenser, and Shakespeare's Iago a vice figure transported from medieval drama.

In transporting characters from other writers into their own work, they are able to take with those characters all the significances that go with them. So, for example, when Artegall appears wearing Achilles's armor in *The Faerie Queene*, III.ii. 25, the allusion brings into his character the strength and heroism of Achilles, and suggests as well the dangers of passion and inaction that Achilles's story also evokes.

Renaissance poets, then, had in their rhetorical toolboxes a variety of metaphorical techniques for transporting characters, images, events, or philosophical ideas from one work into their own for the purpose of pointing their stories towards universal ideas. Forming characters as metaphors is a method that engages the mind first, before the emotions, and is inherently intertextual in nature, as evidenced by Castelvetro's description of the kind of delightful instruction that poetry can provide:

> Rende Aristotele la ragione, perche gli huomini tutti prendano diletto del mirare l'opere fatte per rassomiglianza, la quale è questa, che lo 'mparare è cosa diletteuolissima ad ogni maniera di gente, u'habbiano tanta parte di diletto. Ma perche non si puo riconoscere alcuna rassomiglianza, che non s'impari, seguita, che ogni rassomiglianza, in quanto è rassomiglianza & è riconosciuta per tale, diletti tutti i riconoscitori, uolendo secondo me dire Aristotele, che il comporre con lo'ntelleto insieme le similitudini, & le dissimilitudini, che sono in diuerse cose, è il mezzo da imparare, o lo'mparare che sia ciascuna cosa.[18]

> [Aristotle gives the reason why all men take delight in looking at works created through imitation, which is this: that to learn is the most delightful thing to all types of people, delighting in so far as they are learning. But because one cannot recognize any imitation which is unfamiliar, it follows that all imitation which is recognized as such delights all those recognizing it: following what Aristotle says, that to arrange with the mind the similarities and differences together which are in diverse things is the way to learn or the acquiring of the knowledge of what everything might be.]

---

[18] Ludovico Castelvetro, *Poetica D'Aristotele*, 70. Cf. also Andrew Bongiorno's edition and translation, *Castelvetro on the Art of Poetry* (Binghamton, NY: Medieval and Renaissance Texts and Studies, 1984), 45.

The metaphorical character works by inviting us to recognize imitations of already familiar ideas, images, or characters, giving pleasure through recognition of the familiar in the new. The reader's knowledge base grows by comparing the similarities and differences between the use of this image or character element in the original and the new context.

We can recognize metaphorical characterization throughout Spenser's work, and particularly, of course, in *The Faerie Queene*. Spenser imitates *mores* primarily through the wide and varied uses of metaphor, and when we read *The Faerie Queene*, we are immediately struck by the wealth of philosophical, classical, Christian, and political material transported into the creation of Spenser's knights.

Granted, the 'Letter to Raleigh' stresses the exemplary character of Spenser's characters, at least in their foundational premise. In this letter, Spenser calls *The Faerie Queene* a 'continued Allegory', but also claims that his Arthur is an example of 'a good governour and a vertuous man'. He says that, because 'so much more profitable and gratious is doctrine by ensample, then by rule', he follows Xenophon in creating in Arthur and in the subsidiary knights examples of what 'might best be'.[19]

Yet, when discussing his characters specifically, he does not call them examples, but instead uses terms like 'image' ('I labour to pourtraict in Arthure, before he was king, the image of a brave knight' [15]), 'shadow', and 'picture' (16), and apologizes for expressing his 'good discipline' 'thus clowdily enwrapped in Allegorical devises' (16). In addition, when he briefly describes the process by which he makes Arthur an example of 'magnificence in particular', Spenser tells us that his method is to 'mention the deedes of Arthure applyable to that vertue, which I write of in that booke' (16). At the center of Spenser's exemplary technique is, therefore, the inextricable relationship between action and *mores* in which action embodies *mores* in concrete behavior. The characters' deeds are illuminations of the virtues they illustrate, and the nature of their particular virtues determines their actions. For Spenser, allegory (or metaphor) and example become one process in achieving his 'generall end ... to fashion a gentleman or noble person in vertuous and gentle discipline' (15).

To look at this process in the text itself, let us examine the instigating episodes of Book II of *The Faerie Queene*. As *The Book of Temperance* opens, Archimago is seeking still to entrap Redcrosse, the Knight of Holiness, with his 'craftie stales' and 'cunning traines' (II.i.4). Coming upon Guyon, he 'changed his minde from one to other ill: / For to all good he enimy was still' (II.i.5). At this moment, Archimago shifts from the image of deceitful, false faith and hypocrisy that he figured forth in

---

[19] All references to *The Faerie Queene* and the 'Letter', are from *The Faerie Queene*, ed. Thomas P. Roche, Jr. and C. Patrick O'Donnell, Jr. (New York: Penguin Books, 1978); here 15 and 16.

Book I to an image of the occasion to wrath. His ploy with Guyon is to use false wiles and Duessa's lying claims of rape to enrage Guyon against Redcrosse. He very nearly succeeds in pushing them into potentially deadly battle, leaving Guyon 'inflam'd with wrathfulness' (II.i.25) as he prepares to joust with Redcrosse. Only respect for the sign of the cross on Redcrosse's shield stops Guyon. He restrains his wrath and cries mercy

> For mine offense and heedless hardiment
> That had almost committed crime abhord
> Whiles cursed steele against the badge I bent
> The sacred badge of my Redeemer's death.
> (II.1.27)

Here the images of deceit, occasion to wrath, and the restraining power of Christian love as symbolized by the cross all point clearly towards the allegorical meaning of Guyon's exemplary actions. Guyon shows us how Christian faith can help to restrain an intemperate, if righteous, wrath, but we know the meaning of those actions only if we are able to read the metaphorical images of Archimago's, Guyon's, and Redcrosse's words and accoutrements.[20]

The next episode treats of the other major passion that threatens to undo temperance. While Guyon's encounter with Archimago, Duessa, and Redcrosse exemplifies temperance's ability to restrain wrath, his encounter with Amavia and her babe initiates the more complex challenge of facing down and restraining the concupiscent passions.

Amavia and Sir Mordant's deaths exemplify the effects of intemperate concupiscence. Mortdant succumbs to the Acrasian wiles, and Amavia's subsequent grief at this loss leads to her suicide.[21] However, Guyon's response is not simply to head immediately for Acrasia's Bower of Bliss. That exemplary response of temperance to unbridled, deceptive concupiscence is first complicated by the metaphorical figure of Amavia's bloody-handed baby who in his mother's 'streaming blood ... did embay / His little hands, and tender ioynts embrew; /

---

[20] Cf. William Nelson, *The Poetry of Edmund Spenser* (New York: Columbia University Press, 1965), 130. Nelson, too sees Renaissance allegory as made up of metaphor and example, both subsumed under his broader definition of allegory as the 'investigation of the inward as well as the outward motions of man'. He concludes that 'Spenser himself makes no sharp division between allegory and fictional example' (127–30). His analysis is very close to my own, but I believe that the distinctions between the exemplary and metaphorical techniques are greater than he allows, and that the ways in which specific authors emphasized and mingled these two techniques reflect in their works different critical assumptions.

[21] For discussion of the role of concupiscence in intemperance see J. Carscallen, 'Temperance', *The Spenser Encyclopedia*, ed. A. C. Hamilton et al. (Toronto: University of Toronto Press, 1990), esp. 681, col. 2.

Pitiful spectacle, as euer eye did view' (II.ii.40). Ruddymane, as an infant, is incapable as yet of exemplary action. He can function only as a metaphorical image—but of what?

Ruddymane and his bloody hands have most frequently been interpreted as an image of original sin,[22] as Guyon himself suggests to us at II.ii.4. Guyon at first thinks 'that high God, in lieu of innocence, / Imprinted had that token of his wrath / To show how sore bloud guiltinesse he ha'th' (II.ii.4). But, as Lewis H. Miller pointed out, the Palmer contradicts this reading of Ruddymane's problem, explaining instead that the well of chastity in which Guyon is washing the baby's hands refuses to be stained 'with any filthe' (II.ii.9–10).[23] Sexual purity cannot wash away the effects of intemperance, for one extreme does not cancel out the other.[24] Only Medina's tutoring Ruddymane to achieve the Aristotelian mean can undo the effects of the babe's bloody hands and avenge his parents' deaths. To accomplish that end, Guyon asks Medina

---

[22] Cf. Lilian Winstanley, ed. *The Faerie Queene: Book II* (Cambridge: Cambridge University Press, 1914), cit. *The Works of Edmund Spenser: A Variorum Edition*, vol. 2, ed. Edwin Greenlaw, Charles Grosvenor Osgood, and Frederick Morgan Padelford (Baltimore: Johns Hopkins Press, 1933), 195; A. C. Hamilton, 'A Theological Reading of *The Faerie Queene*, Book II', *ELH*, 25:3 (1958), 155–62; James Nohrnberg, *The Analogy of 'The Faerie Queene'* (Princeton: Princeton University Press, 1976), 298–89 and 292n; and Carol V. Kaske, ' Amavia, Mortdant, Ruddymane', *The Spenser Encyclopedia*, 27.

[23] Lewis H. Miller, Jr., 'A Secular Reading of *The Faerie Queene*, Book II', *ELH*, 33:2 (1966). 154–69; here 156–9. Cf. Harry Berger, Jr., *The Allegorical Temper: Vision and Reality in Book II of Spenser's 'Faerie Queene'* (New Haven: Yale University Press, 1957), 46. However, Berger reads the Palmer's explanation to mean that Ruddymane's blood-stained hands are 'symbolic of innocence—the innocence not only of Amavia but of the stream's nymph and all "chast Dames"' (46). Cf. Arnold A. Sanders, 'Ruddymane and Canace, Lost and Found: Spenser's Reception of Gower's *Confessio Amantis* 3 and Chaucer's *Squire's Tale*', in *The Work of Dissimilitude: Essays from the Sixth Citadel Conference on Medieval and Renaissance Literature*, ed. David G. Allen and Robert A. White (Newark: University of Delaware Press, 1992), 196–215. Sanders argues that the image of Ruddymane is taken from Ovid and Gower, where the image of the baby bathed in its mother's blood creates empathy for Canace that mitigates for the reader the impact of her incest. However, what the Palmer says is that the blood on the baby's hands should be a 'sacred Symbole' in his flesh, 'to mind reuengement / And be for all chast Dames an endlesse moniment' (II.ii.10). That is, the blood should remain to remind Ruddymane of his responsibility to avenge his mother's death, as Medina is charged with preparing him to do (II.iii.2), and as an endless 'moniment' or a warning reminder for all chaste women of the tragedy that self-indulgent love can lead to (see OED, 'monument', definition 5b). 'Sacred' here seems to me to refer to a 'sacred trust' that Ruddymane owes his mother rather than meaning 'sacred' in a Christian sense.

[24] Cf. Miller, 'Secular Reading': 'Under the secular scheme presented to us in Medina's castle (ii.13–38)—the Aristotelian ethic in which moral virtue is described as a mean between two vicious extremes—the fountain itself comes to represent an extreme'. He goes on to show that 'Desperately fleeing the advances of Faunus, the Nymphe of the fountain, like Daphne of the myth and unlike the virgin Belphoebe of canto iii, displays an extreme sense of fear and shame', and that 'Spenser employs stone, ice and snow [both here and in describing Florimell in Books III and IV] to denote extreme attitudes of deficiency in respect to the physical aspects of love' (158–9).

> In virtuous lore to traine his tender youth
> And all that gentle noriture ensu'th:
> And that so soone as ryper yeares he raught,
> He might for memorie of that dayes ruth,
> Be called *Ruddymane*, and thereby taught,
> T'avenge his Parents death on them that had it wrought.
> (II.iii.2)

Medina's tutelage in maintaining a balance of extremes will help Ruddymane to undo the curses of his parents' concupiscence.

So Ruddymane is not an allegorical image of original sin, although Guyon momentarily may think so. I would like to suggest that, instead, the strikingly disturbing image of the infant Ruddymane's dabbling in his mother's blood is an illustration of Aristotle's statement in the *Nichomachaean Ethics* that self-indulgence is a childish refusal to control one's appetites through reason:

> The name self-indulgence is applied also to childish faults; for they bear a certain resemblance to what we have been considering .... that which desires what is base and which develops quickly ought to be kept in a chastened condition, and these characteristics belong above all to appetite and to the child, since children in fact live at the beck and call of appetite, and it is in them that the desire for what is pleasant is strongest. If, then, it is not going to be obedient and subject to the ruling principle, it will go to great lengths; for in an irrational being the desire for pleasure is insatiable even if it tries every source of gratification, and the exercise of appetite increases its innate force, and if appetites are strong and violent they even expel the power of calculation. Hence they should be moderate and few, and should in no way oppose the rational principle—and this is what we call an obedient and chastened state—and as the child should live according to the direction of his tutor, so the appetitive element should live according to rational principle.[25]

Ruddymane begins his story by self-indulgently playing in his dying mother's blood, but Guyon provides him with a tutor who will teach him to live 'according to the rational principle'.[26]

Spenser emphasizes Ruddymane's connection to self-indulgence when he says of Amavia's infant:

---

[25] *NE*, III. 12, 983–4. I quote from Aristotle, *Ethica Nichomachea*, in *The Basic Works of Aristotle*, trans. W. D. Ross, ed. Richard McKeon (New York: Random House, 1941), 927–1112. Also available at *The Constitution Society*, www.constitution.org/ari/ethic, accessed 3 March, 2005.

[26] William F. DeMoss saw this episode's connection to this passage in Aristotle, but associated the tutor Aristotle mentions with the Palmer and the pupil with Guyon (cit. *Variorum*, 420.)

> Als in her lap a louely babe did play
> His cruel sport, in stead of sorrow dew;
> For in her streaming blood he did embay
> His little hands, and tender ioynts embrew;
> Pitiful spectacle, as euer eye did view
> (II.i.40)

and later describes the baby as unperturbed by his parents' deaths:

> Thus when *Sir Guyon* with his faithfull guide
> Had with due rites and dolorous lament
> The end of their sad Tragedie vptyde,
> The little babe vp in his armes he hente;
> Who with sweet pleasance and bold blandishment
> Gan smyle on him that rather ought to weepe,
> As careless of his woe, or innocent
> Of that was doen, that ruth emperced deepe
> In that knight's heart, and wordes with bitter teeres did steepe.
> (II.ii.1).

Ruddymane thus seems to be an appropriate image of the childishness that lives only 'at the beck and call of appetite ... in opposition to the rational principle' (Aristotle) and which must remain under the control of its tutor (Medina) in order to keep it from indulging its insatiable desires. Unconstrained, the child exhibits cruelty as extreme as Furor's or Acrasia's. Spenser thus creates in Ruddymane an allegorical embodiment of the Aristotelian idea that the naturally self-indulgent child must be taught to control his (or her) desires with reason, and that without such tutoring, that childish self-indulgence in adults leads to human tragedy. Spenser's method here is almost entirely metaphorical, clothing a thin line of exemplary actions with the allegorical imagery that gives those actions their meaning.

Sidney's genius tends more towards the exemplary, as indicated by his own statement of theory in the 'Defence'. In the *Arcadia*s, the metaphorical technique is present only in the sporadic transportation of contemporary political and social figures into the work's characters. Several scholars have pointed to isolated passages in the *Arcadia*s which refer to Sidney's friends, or to contemporary political figures or events. Hanford and Watson, for example, associate the Lelius of *The New Arcadia* with Sir Henry Lee,[27] a friend with whom Sidney once jousted in a tournament, and Marcus Goldman points out many elements in the *Arcadia*s which seem to have been transported out of contemporary politics and social life.[28] Perhaps the most interesting such study is the

---

[27] James Holly Hanford and Sara Ruth Watson, 'Personal Allegory in the *Arcadia:* Philisides and Lelius', *Modern Philology*, 32 (1934), 1–10.

[28] *Sir Philip Sidney and The Arcadia*, University of Illinois Studies in Language and Literature, vol. 17 (1934).

essay by David McPherson. He suggests that Mopsa was transported into the *Arcadia* from a Brueghel engraving which ironically depicted a verse from Vergil's ecologues.[29]

Given the intimate circle of family and literary friends for whom Sidney wrote the *Arcadia*s, it is to be expected that he would carry into his works incidents and people whose recognition would amuse his audience. But such contemporary references do not play a major role in developing his foreconceit. The pleasure these sporadic metaphorical touches provide is incidental to the exemplary function of characters who stand alone and solid within their fictional world.

Travis Curtwright has recognized that Sidney's formation of character is based upon the concept of *ethos* as laid out in Aristotle's *Poetics*. He determines that 'by transforming Aristotelian mimesis and character, Sidney will create a doctrine of Ideas that delights audiences by showing them examples of good and evil'.[30] The rhetorical figure of the *paradigma* or example is, as Curtwright suggests, at the heart of Sidney's artistic formation of character. The 'Defence' says a great deal about the use of characters as examples; indeed, it is through the poetic example that Sidney reconciles Philosophy and History within poetry, saying,

> The philosopher therefore, and the historian are they which would win the goal, the one by precept, the other by example. But both, not having both, do halt ... . Now doth the peerless poet perform both: for whatsoever the philosopher saith should be done, he giveth a perfect picture of it in someone by whom he presupposeth it was done; so as he coupleth the general notion with the particular example. (221)

His summary of the poetic process also clearly demonstrates his conviction that examples and the admiration examples inspire are the key to a poet's success:

> for any understanding knoweth the skill of each artificer standeth in that *idea*, or fore-conceit of the work, and not in the work itself. And that the poet hath that *idea* is manifest, by delivering them forth in such excellency as he had imagined them. Which delivering forth also is not wholly imaginative, as we are wont to say by them that build castles in the air; but so far substantially it worketh, not only to make a Cyrus, which had been but a particular excellency as nature might have done, but to bestow a Cyrus upon the world to make many Cyruses, if they will learn aright why and how that maker made them. (216–17)

---

[29] 'A Possible Origin for Mopsa in Sidney's *Arcadia*', *Renaissance Quarterly*, 21 (1968), 420–8.

[30] 'Sidney's *Defense of Poetry:* Ethos and Ideas', *Ben Jonson Journal: Literary Contexts in the Age of Elizabeth, James and Charles*, 10 (2003), 101–15, here 103.

Sidney's concept of poetry moves from the foreconceit or universal truth, through the 'delivering forth' of imitation, down to the specific nature and action of the exemplary character, and culminates finally in the instruction of the reader by admiration of the fictional character and his virtues. To Sidney, poetry's effectiveness depends upon the quality of the poet's examples.

Shakespeare's characterization is not so easily defined. At first glance, he seems to create exemplary characters, but closer analysis shows that metaphorical characterization is firmly in his repertoire and that even his most 'realistic' exemplary characters contain significant metaphorical elements. The remainder of this essay attempts to unpack the fusion of exemplary and metaphorical characterization in *King Lear* that makes that play so uniquely and powerfully Shakespearean.

Like Spenser's *Book of Temperance, King Lear*, too, can be seen as a study of intemperance and, as such, a companion, analogue, or perhaps an overgoing of Spenser's *Book II*. Judith Anderson has identified many thematic parallels between the two works,[31] and the influence of Spenser's allegory upon *King Lear* has been noted not only in the use of the Lear story from *FQ* II.x, but also, albeit less convincingly, in structural echoes of the Malbecco episode in *The Faerie Queene* III.x.[32] However, *King Lear* follows Sidney's theory more closely than Spenser's metaphorical images, presenting to the theatre audience exemplary characters that embody the *mores* of intemperance in their actions. Lear, for example, acts out the hasty anger that in Spenser's work almost overcomes Guyon as he challenges Redcrosse (II.i.8–9). Although Helen Gardner argues that Lear is more patient than we are wont to give him credit for,[33] what we remember about him is his rag-

---

[31] 'Conspiracy of Realism', 16–23.

[32] Martin Coyle, '*King Lear* and *The Faerie Queene*', *Notes and Queries*, 31:229 (1984), 205–7; J. J. M. Tobin, 'Malbecco, Yet Again', *Notes and Queries*. 32:230 (1985), 478–9.

[33] '*King Lear:* The John Coffin Memorial Lecture delivered before the University of London on 2 March 1966' (London: The Athlone Press, 1968). She argues that 'Much has been said of Lear's impatience of temperament; but along with it there goes from the beginning a generous unwillingness to see offence before he must ... along with this impatience over trifles, there is a touching striving after fairness ... when, as he goes out into the storm, he cries "O fool, I shall go mad!" he shows he understands the dangers of a passionate temper that he has attempted and does attempt to master. It is not wholly true that "he hath ever but slenderly known himself". It might more truly be said that what he has to learn is less his own nature than the nature of the world, "how the world goes". And if his impatience at the beginning has been exaggerated and his efforts at self-control passed over, by those critics who would make the theme of the play Lear's moral redemption, the rage and cries for vengeance that alternate with his moments of gentleness and pity and self-reproach have been perhaps rather overlooked too ... with Lear we explore passionate experience: his discovery of what the world offers to a heart that loves and asks for love in return', 20–1.

ing anger, first at Cordelia, then at Regan and Goneril, and finally at the storm into which he plunges himself.

Moreover, just as Shakespeare analyzes ambition in more depth than does Marlowe, so, too, in *King Lear*, he explores in depth a particular aspect of intemperance that Spenser merely suggests with the image of Ruddymane, showing it indeed to be the root cause of intemperate behaviour. *King Lear* is about children and about adults who revert to childishness, and through these characters Shakespeare unfolds various ways in which childish self-indulgence motivates cruel intemperance to generate an extremity of human suffering even more horrifying than that of Amavia's death and Acrasia's power.

John P. Cutts analyzes the influence of Ruddymane upon the images of bloody hands and bloody babes in *Macbeth*, demonstrating the resonance that this Spenserian character had for Shakespeare during his writing of the great tragedies,[34] and as Gardner says of Goneril and Regan:

> No suggestion is ever hazarded [in the play] as to why they are as they are. It is enough that they simply are. They are embodiments of monstrous implacability, incarnations of the uncompassionate selfishness, the cruel egoism that is a dark streak in most human hearts. They are the next generation, ruthlessly claiming its right to shoulder the old out of its way.[35]

Like Ruddymane, they and Edmund think nothing of sating their appetites by playing in their fathers' heart blood.

When Regan shuts the eighty year old Lear out in the storm without shelter, we witness an active example of what Ruddymane represents by metaphor—the almost unthinkable physical cruelty of the self-centered, ill-governed, grown child. She plays in her father's misery as cruelly and selfishly as Ruddymane plays in his mother's blood, showing how Ruddymane's metaphorical behavior can manifest itself in adult human actions.

In contrast, Cordelia and Edgar exemplify the ways in which a child's passions are tempered by love and reason. Each denies his or her appetites: Cordelia gives up her inheritance for the sake of exercising a reasonable, temperate expression of love, and Edgar at first goes to ascetic extremes as Mad Tom, giving up more than his inheritance. Like Malbecco in his grief over the loss of Hellenore, or like Guyon after his self-denial in the House of Mammon, he gives up his humanity and almost his life. He recovers himself in aiding his father, and

---

[34] John P. Cutts, 'Spenser, Shakespeare, and the "Bloody Babe"', *Neuphilologische Mitteilungen: Bulletin de la Societe Neophilologique/Bulletin of the Modern Language Society*, 86:4 (1985), 506–14.

[35] *Lear*, 5.

ultimately exhibits a just and temperate anger in finally punishing his brother's faults. There is no self-indulgent rage in that fight—just clear, impassionate justice, as he says to the defeated Edmund:

> Let's exchange charity,
> I am no less in blood than thou art, Edmund.
> If more, the more ignobly thou has wronged me.
> *He takes off his helmet*
> My name is Edgar, and thy father's son
> The gods are just, and of our pleasant vies
> Make instruments to scourge us.
> The dark and vicious place where thee he got
> Cost him his eyes.[36]

Edgar and Cordelia provide foils of kind and self-effacing temperance that bring into sharp relief the cruel self-indulgence of their siblings.

Shakespeare deepens his portrayal of temperance even further, however, by making Lear not just a victim of his childrens' intemperate self-indulgence, but also an example himself of the same intemperance that his self-centered daughters demonstrate. His childish self-indulgence matches theirs, and so he becomes a victim of his own failings as well as of those of his children.

Not only does Lear furiously banish Cordelia for remaining silent, but when he strikes and then encourages Kent to, quite childishly, trip Oswald (scene 4, 69–75), it is difficult not to have some sympathy for Goneril's complaints about the disrespect and rowdiness of Lear and his attendants. That Lear's fool enters immediately upon Oswald's exit in this scene and offers Lear his coxcomb (4.82) seems visually (and metaphorically) to underscore the foolishness of Lear's self-indulgent irascibility.

His daughters' response to this behavior ultimately reduces him to a crying infant. He tells Goneril,

> Life and death! I am ashamed
> That thou hast power to shake my manhood thus,
> That these hot tears, that break from me perforce
> And should make thee—worst blasts and fogs upon thee!
> Untented woundings of a father's curse
> Pierce every sense about thee!
> (4.274–9)

Lear's intemperate wrath, deriving from the childish self-indulgence that leads him to abrogate his responsibilities without being willing to

---

[36] 24.167. I have chosen to use the Norton edition of *The History of King Lear* (Q1) as being theoretically, at least, closest to the play's original form (Greenblatt, ed. *Lear*, 2308). All references to the play come from this text.

give up the privileges of kingship, contributes significantly to the events that lead to his madness, to his drenching in the storm, and to the sickness that ultimately reduces him to a state of infancy.

Instead of rationally facing the reality of his situation, Lear rages, storms, cajoles, and generally throws a tantrum, running away into the storm in a fit of wrath. His actions exemplify what Aristotle warns against when he says, in the passage already quoted from the *Nichomachaean Ethics*:

> If, then, it [self-indulgence] is not going to be obedient and subject to the ruling principle [reason], it will go to great lengths; for in an irrational being the desire for pleasure is insatiable even if it tries every source of gratification, and the exercise of appetite increases its innate force, and if appetites are strong and violent they even expel the power of calculation. (III.12.984)

Lear has indulged his old age and irascibility, and once having chosen to ignore reason, his desire for self gratification tries every source (both daughters), grows in force, and becomes so 'strong and violent' that it expels any 'power of [rational] calculation' to cope with the situation realistically. The child is without, yes, but also within, and it is the childish intemperance within Lear that gives his intemperately ambitious children the wherewithal to vicitimize him. As Barbara L. Estrin points out,

> Goneril and Regan emerge as mothers to his self, definers of his being. Reduced to nothing, Lear becomes the controlled object of his daughters' imaginations ... when he understands his diminution, the first frame of the play ends and Lear—the proud parent—becomes the humbled child of the enclosed story.[37]

Lear is his own Ruddymane to his own Amavia. Abandoned by these bad mothers, Lear becomes lost and finally dependent upon his daughter Cordelia for mothering, just as Ruddymane ends up in the arms of Medina.

While Spenser identifies in the single, emblematic figure of Ruddymane, the quality of childish self-indulgence that characterizes the intemperate person, Shakespeare takes the same concept and exemplifies it. Both methods can be called 'allegorical', because ultimately both techniques develop an abstract, philosophical understanding of intemperance; and in a very true sense, Shakespeare is transporting a figure from Spenser's work into his play and giving it various forms, just as Spenser transports the image from Aristotle into his own work.

---

[37] *The Raven and the Lark: Lost Children in Literature of the English Renaissance* (Lewisburg, PA: Bucknell University Press, 1985), 172–3.

However, while *The Book of Temperance* consistently points us towards the ideas that inform and form its text, *King Lear* draws us through the behavior of the characters away from abstraction and into specific, concrete, human experience. In this process, it takes us beyond the judgmental rejection of Lear's self-indulgence, such as that expressed by Estrin, to a transcendent image that returns the allegorical to the text and through a fusion of exemplary and metaphorical characterization creates the 'explosion of emotion' that Anderson describes.

This movement away from exemplary allegory into human experience takes place, ironically, in the most metaphorical moment in the play—when Lear plunges into the storm. The storm represents the kind of rage exhibited by Spenser's Furor, and Lear himself emphasizes its metaphorical quality, suggesting that the external tempest reflects the rage at his daughters' filial ingratitude that has characterized his intemperance from the first scene in the play:

> This tempest in my mind
> Doth from my sense take all feeling else
> Save what beats there: filial ingratitude.
> (11.12–14)

However, this metaphorical moment points us not towards analysis of the nature or consequences of intemperance, but instead to the chaos and pain of human experience. We are soon caught up in the shivering of the Fool and the ramblings of Poor Tom, all thought reduced to irrational expressions of shock, confusion, and grief that defy allegorical interpretation. The lessons about temperance and intemperance to be gained by observing the characters' behavior, fade away into a tone poem of human tragedy and empathetic pity. The study of temperance becomes a study of human pain, and like Edgar at this moment (12.93–103), we leave the abstractions of the mind to concentrate upon the horrifying realities of someone else's suffering and a forlorn hope of reconciliation.

Before reconciliation, however, we find horror. Edmund's insatiable urge to satisfy his own desires results in one of the cruelest scenes in Shakespeare's canon. Nevertheless, Shakespeare seems deliberately to distance this scene from the allegory of childish self-indulgence by making Edmund pointedly absent from the location of his father's blinding, sent away by Cornwall because, 'The revenges we are bound to take upon your traitorous father are not fit for your beholding' (14.5–7). This small detail of the plot effectively separates the scene from the image of Ruddymane, preventing us from seeing Edmund bespattered with his father's blood. Instead of reinforcing the concept borrowed from Spenser, then, this scene directs our attention to the concrete action of Cornwall's grinding out Gloucester's eyes. We forget the dysfunctional parent-child relationships in our fascinated horror at the violence itself that we are viewing and at Gloucester's subsequent sufferings.

By the time Gloucester is wandering with bleeding eyes towards Dover, the idea of self-indulgent intemperance as exemplified in childish and insensitive behavior has been subsumed into nihilism: 'As flies to wanton boys are we to th' gods / They kill us for their sport' (15.35–6). Is this line an echo of Ruddymane's 'cruel sport'? Is the reference to 'wanton boys' meant to recall the image of Ruddymane that Cornwall's actions have temporarily misplaced? If so, then just as Archimago's meaning shifts in Spenser's work, so now Ruddymane is no longer the image of Aristotle's cruel and intemperately self indulgent human child but a representation of all the gods of the universe. Regan and Goneril's behavior is not a matter of refusing to listen to reason, but synecdoche for the very nature of life itself. The whole world has been rendered intemperately, self-indulgently cruel, denying rational sense to this excruciatingly raw moment in the play. Shakespeare has gone beyond Aristotle and intemperance, Ruddymane and rage, into experiential misery. Here is the moment of 'wonder' that Aristotle, Longinus, and the commentators find so important to tragedy; here is the moment when emotion explodes, overwhelming reason and the capacity to make knowledge out of allegory.

T. G. Bishop, Peter G. Platt, and J. V. Cunningham all point out that the view of 'wonder' in Renaissance poetics is of two kinds—that which leads to knowledge, inspiring us to ask why or how such horror has occurred, and sending us back to our reason to find the answer, and secondly a theory associated with Plato, Longinus, or Longinus through Patrizi, that sees wonder as affectively transporting the audience, involving them in the play in a way that diminishes reason.[38] So, Platt explains:

> In Aristotle's system, a mind stimulated by wonder sought a larger rational 'design', whether in the world at large or in a work of art, and this exercise was part of an even greater move in the mind from ignorance to knowledge. Wonder, Aristotle claimed, was the origin of our interest in anything. ... More specifically, the encounter with all mimetic art forms engaged human beings in the epistemological process: '... great pleasure is derived from exercising the understanding, not just for philosophers but in the same way for all men, though their capacity for it may be limited. It is for this reason that men enjoy looking at images, because what happens is that, as they contemplate them, they apply their understanding and reasoning to each element ... '. Wonder and the pursuit and acquisition of knowledge were fundamentally linked

---

[38] See Cunningham, *Woe or Wonder*, 67–84; Platt, *Reason Diminished*, 1–18, and Bishop, *Shakespeare*, 21–41.

in the Aristotelian scheme, and this dynamic was often triggered by an encounter with art.[39]

Spenser uses the image of Ruddymane to excite wonder in just the way Aristotle describes here—to lead us to what Cunningham calls 'inquiry',[40] to seeking knowledge about what Ruddymane represents and what we can learn from him about temperance.

However, other trends in the critical discussions of 'wonder' in Plato, Aristotle, and the rhetoricians also see it as leading beyond reason to, as Platt says, diminish reason. In discussing Patrizi's unusual commentary on Artistotle, Platt traces his ideas about wonder back to Longinus:

> For Longinus, like Patrizi, advocated a poetical form of fragmentary, scattered bursts that, on account of their wonderful and incredible nature, had the power to take the audience 'out of themselves'. ... Finally, Longinus's anti-Aristotelian preference of wondrous 'transport' to rational persuasion is of crucial importance to Patrizi's theory of poetry.[41]

Platt believes that Shakespeare's concept of 'wonder' as the transporting of the audience out of reason and into emotional involvement with the scenes and characters of the play, may have come from the critical tradition represented by Patrizi.[42] Certainly the wonder-full moments in *King Lear* are much more akin to the transportation out of oneself that Longinus describes than to the rational process of wonder's leading to inquiry that we see in Spenser's work. Spenser captured this effect of wonder through the horrific image of Ruddymane's playing in the gushing blood of his dying mother. But that image shocks only briefly and is very soon turned into a logical puzzle as Guyon tries to explain his inability to wash the baby's hands clean. By the time Guyon hands Ruddymane over to Medina, the wonder is long past and the question answered or forgotten. Ruddymane's influence is not enough to explain fully the emotional power of that tragic wonder we find in *King Lear*.

It is significant that the shift from analysis to emotion in the storm scene is reinforced by the Gloucester subplot, taken from Sir Philip Sidney's *New Arcadia*, for it is to Sidney's influence, I believe, that *King Lear* owes its success in achieving its explosively emotional 'wonder'.[43]

---

[39] *Reason Diminished*, 3. Platt is quoting here from Aristotle, *Poetics*, 4.

[40] *Woe or Wonder*, 81.

[41] *Reason Diminished*, 16.

[42] *Ibid.*, 17.

[43] For a valuable analysis of the relative influence of Sidney and Spenser upon *King Lear*, but in the context of the nature of influence and intertextuality in the Renaissance, see Andrew Weiner, 'Sidney/Spenser/Shakespeare: Influence/Intertextuality/Intention', in *Influence and Intertextuality in Literary History*, ed. Jay Clayton and Eric Rothstein (Madison: University of Wisconsin Press, 1991), 245-270.

David Richman follows Cunningham in stressing the rhetorical nature of the tradition of wonder, writing that,

> One of the strongest tenets in the long tradition of rhetorical and poetic theory, from Aristotle through Longinus down to Sidney, is that poetry at its most elevated can move wonder, or to use Sidney's phrase, can 'stir the effects of a well raised admiration'. Effects of astonishment can result from unusual diction and rhythm as well as from unusual events. Wonder can be a response to style as well as to subject.[44]

Sidney, indeed, as Richman suggests, tends more towards the rhetorical than to the inquiry-focused tradition of wonder or admiration. Whereas Spenser uses imagery to create a sense of wonder that in good Aristotelian fashion leads immediately to knowledge-seeking, Sidney uses rhetoric in the fashion of Longinus to establish and maintain a wonder of emotion.

In Sidney's *New Arcadia,* the Paphlagonian king's story, like those of Amavia and Lear, is a story of intemperance and its results, told in exemplary fashion. Plexirtus, Edmund's counterpart in the story, is as ambitious, self-indulgent, and unfilial as Edmund is. Like *King Lear,* it is a story that stresses the pain of familial conflict, and Leonatus's royal father drives home this focus through his polyptoton upon the word 'grief':

> nobody daring to show so much charity as to lend me a hand to do this kind office you see him perform towards me—to my unspeakable *grief,* not only because his kindness is a glass even to my blind eyes of my naughtiness, but that, above all *griefs,* it *grieves* me he should desperately adventure the loss of his so well-deserving life for mine. (182, italics mine)

Musidorus picks up the same rhetorical technique in his summary of the story: 'The matter in itself *lamentable, lamentably* expressed by the old prince which needed not to take to himself the gestures of pity, since his face could not put off the marks thereof, greatly moved the two princes to compassion' (183, italics mine). These uses of polyptoton point us to the privately emotional impact of intemperate ambition and self-indulgence and contribute to the emotional power of the passage and towards wonder at Plexirtus's filial cruelty.

In borrowing this story for *King Lear,* Shakespeare transports the grief that Sidney emphasizes rhetorically into a dramatic portrayal of Lear's and Gloucester's misery. Under Sidney's influence, the storm scene and the Gloucester subplot shift the play's focus from an exemplary allegory to a portrayal of human suffering. As Edgar leads

---

[44] *Laughter, Pain, and Wonder,* 93.

Gloucester towards the 'cliff', we think very little about self-indulgence and a great deal about what it must feel like to wander the fields with blind and bleeding eyes.

Shakespeare carries the shift from abstraction to experience forward into the main plot as well by transforming the character of Lear from an example of self-indulgence and intemperate governance into an image of human misery to which we can relate only emotionally, without hope of rational analysis to make sense of what we are seeing. When Lear joins Tom in his mad ramblings (13.10ff), when he wakes from his sleep in the care of Cordelia (21.42ff), and when he howls with pain at her death (24.252), we are taken beyond reason and rhetoric into sensation, the gut experience of human emotion. Although *King Lear* makes the transition into emotion more powerfully than does Sidney's *New Arcadia*, it seems that Sidney's work may have provided the inspiration for that move.

There is an additional element of the Paphlagonian king's story and its aftermath that has not yet been noticed but which is perhaps the most emotionally poignant borrowing that Shakespeare made. The ultimate effect of Plexirtus's self-indulgent, ambitious fraud is the death of his daughter, Zelmane, who pines away for love of Pyrocles and for shame at her father's betrayal of the princes (265). Echoes of Zelmane ring most loudly in Shakespeare's *Twelfth Night*, particularly in Viola's description of the pining of the sister who:

> never told her love,
> But let concealment, like a worm i'th' bud,
> Feed on her damask cheek. She pined in thought,
> And with a green and yellow melancholy
> She sat like patience on a monument,
> Smiling at grief. Was not this love indeed?
> (II.v.109–14)

However, Zelmane appears not only as an important image in *Twelfth Night*: Cordelia too 'never tells her love', at least until her father awakens from his sleep. Her refusal to express that love, like Zelmane's, leads ultimately to her death. And like Zelmane, although her father is a seriously flawed man, Cordelia's devotion to him is unshaken. One of Zelmane's dying wishes is that Pyrocles and Musidorus will 'pardon my father the displeasure you have justly conceived against him, and for this once succor him out of the danger wherein he is' (268.5–9); one can imagine Cordelia's making that same plea to her husband, the King of France, upon hearing about Lear's deteriorating situation.

Furthermore, in describing Zelmane's death, Pyrocles tells Philoclea that it is the experience of having been so tragically loved by Zelmane that opens Pyrocles's heart to love. Previously focused upon heroism alone, Pyrocles showed little interest in the private virtue of love. But now he tells Philoclea:

> And then kissing me, and often desiring me not to condemn her of lightness, in mine arms she delivered her pure soul to the purest place, leaving me as full of agony as kindness, pity, and sorrow could make an honest heart—for I must confess for true, that if my stars had not wholly reserved me for you, there else perhaps I might have loved, and, which had been most strange, begun my love after death ... something there was, which, when I saw a picture of yours, brought again her figure into my remembrance, and made my heart as apt to receive the wound, as the power of your beauty with unresistable force to pierce. (268.23–34)

Zelmane's love has a transformative effect upon the hitherto action-focused Pyrocles. It elevates his physical desire for Philoclea to something more transcendent and powerful than mere sexual attraction.

The same motif of transformative love that results from a death brought on by silence is well established in *King Lear*. Lear's statement that 'nothing will come of nothing' seems to come true as he first descends into madness, and then suffers first Cordelia's death, and finally his own. But the play's final scene promises redemption through the transcendence of death by a love purer than can be expressed in words. Cordelia, like Zelmane, functions as an example of the silent and transcendent love that is, as Greenblatt suggests,[45] the only answer to the pain that the play depicts and the only hope of redemption from human tragedy. Cordelia neither retreats into madness and rage, as do Edgar and Lear; nor does she remain passive. Like Zelmane, she brings her love to bear on the situation and sacrifices herself to it.

In concluding her lecture on *King Lear*, Gardner suggests that the image of Lear's holding Cordelia in his arms transports into the text a 'scene carved and painted all over Europe for three centuries before Shakespeare wrote *King Lear*'.[46] 'With this secular *Pieta*', she says, 'Shakespeare ends his greatest play' (28). She believes that because of the non-Christian environment of the play, 'No consolation is offered us, for there is none which this world, the world of the play, can offer' (28), but there is consolation in those last lines—consolation in the ending of a long and painful life, and consolation in the thought that there will be a less painful future for the young who 'Shall never see so much, nor live so long' (24.320). In the end, also, there is a triumph of the temperate integrity for which Cordelia has died: Albany says that they must 'Speak what we feel, not what we ought to say' (24.318). No longer will words be put to the service of cruel self-indulgence; honest emotions alone will be voiced. Cordelia has not died in vain, then,

---

[45] Ed., *Lear*, 2314.
[46] *Lear*, 27.

and that is some consolation. Ultimately, the play says, any philosophical and moral condemnation of intemperate, childish self-indulgence cannot rationalize away the pain that self-indulgence causes. Love, not philosophy—love as silent and powerful as that exemplified by Zelmane's love for Pyrocles, Mary's love for Jesus, Jesus's love for humankind, Cordelia's love for Lear and, finally, Lear's for Cordelia—is the only redemptive possibility for that pain.

Although Greenblatt believes that in *Lear*, 'An apocalyptic dream of last judgement and redemption hovers over the entire tragedy, but it is a dream forever deferred', he also asserts that 'Shakespeare's tragedy asks us not to turn away from evil, folly, and unbearable human pain but, seeing them face-to-face, to strengthen our capacity to endure and to love'.[47] The infusion of Sidney's Zelmane into the intemperate world of Spenser's Ruddymane suggests a solution to the horrors of intemperance that is both more poignantly sad and more emotionally powerful than the cold undoing of Acrasia's Bower with which Spenser's *Book of Temperance* ends. Guyon cleanses his world of the self-indulgent source of its pain. Shakespeare denies that such cleansing can take place, but provides examples of filial love that can make living in a self-indulgent world bearable, and, perhaps, even meaningful.

Tom McAlindon once argued against reducing *King Lear* to political ideology, suggesting that the play's greatness lies in tragedy's 'capacity to fill the audience with a sense of woe and wonder, and to leave them at the last mute, and pale, and very thoughtful'.[48] A. Kent Hieatt captured the difference between Shakespeare's genius and Spenser's when he said in his article on Shakespeare in *The Spenser Encyclopedia* that 'Spenser's magically resourceful thesaurus of symbolic transformations, through which a competent reader can imaginatively reconstitute a way of living in the world, contrasts with the intimate directness and dramatic finalities which Shakespeare offers for the same purpose' (63). In *King Lear*, it is Shakespeare's combination of techniques and borrowings that results in what Anderson calls the 'explosion' of human emotion in the play and in the sense that Lear's human character is breaking through the 'allegorical ground' that 'silhouettes his final moments'.[49] The allegorical method of *King Lear* fuses metaphorical and exemplary techniques and then abandons them to depict an extreme emotional experience that leaves abstractions behind, only to return to an allegorical image at the end that makes us appreciate more fully the human experience and pain for which the only balm is love. Is Shakespeare allegorical in the manner of Spenser? Yes, but with a difference inspired by his

---

[47] Ed., *Lear*, 2314.

[48] Tom McAlindon, '*King Lear* and the Politics of the Heart', *Shakespeare Survey*, 44 (1991), 85–90; here, 90.

[49] 'Conspiracy of Realism', 12.

command of poetic 'wonder' and by Sidney's models and rhetoric. In *King Lear*, Shakespeare overgoes both his great predecessors by fusing their exercise of Renaissance poetics into a unique mixture of his own.

What Means a Knight? Red Cross Knight and Edgar

Michael L. Hays

A word about this paper[1]—not only its subject and approach, but also its kind—to avoid false expectations. In considering Redcross Knight and Edgar as chivalric knights, I explore Spenser's and Shakespeare's respective uses of materials from the tradition of chivalric romance. So I rule out source or influence study. Shakespeare knew Spenser's version, among many versions, of the Lear story, but I neither trace the untraceable—exact and exclusive similarities between the two versions—nor appraise the authors' use of this story. Likewise, I rule out critical judgments about their better or worse use of the materials from the tradition. My purpose, which respects the integrity of each work, is to discover Spenser's and Shakespeare's attitudes toward knights and chivalry as possible indications of contemporary perspectives as the medieval world made the transition to the modern. So much for subject.

My approach is to view both works as I assume most contemporaries read or attended them—how they did so in light of what they knew of the tradition. Both authors would have expected contemporaries to read a book or attend a play as a one-time, front-to-back experience; they would not have imagined our scholarly ways of examining their texts. Thus, I do not view the first book of *The Faerie Queene* in light of later books, or earlier scenes in *King Lear* in light of later scenes. Spenser's audience would have read from the first to the third, then the fourth to the sixth, book. They might recall an earlier book when they read a later one, but not the converse, and I doubt that many looked back or read him twice. Shakespeare's audience would have attended scenes in sequence, from first to last, and, until his plays appeared in print, they could not go back to an earlier scene, short of attending another performance. This linearity of experience means two things. One, contemporaries either immediately apprehended materials akin to those in a literary tradition or not. Two, both authors had a pretty good sense of what their contemporaries would apprehend as conventional or general, or, if atypical or specific, from a work well known to them.

My approach is also to view both works as I assume most contemporaries would, in part through their intimate familiarity with chivalric romances and their conventional materials. Spenser was well-read in the tradition; his range of reference within that tradition, though mainly Arthurian, extends far more widely. First and obviously is the very first

---

[1] I wrote this paper at the invitation of Thomas Herron for the Spenser and Shakespeare seminar at the 2006 Shakespeare Association of America conference. I thank J. B. Lethbridge for his help in my modest revisions of this paper for publication.

line of Book I of *The Faerie Queene*, with its echo of Chaucer's 'Tale of Sir Thopas', a parody of chivalric romances. Shakespeare read chivalric romances but, with the exception of *Troilus and Cressida* and *The Two Noble Kinsmen*, made little direct use of them, especially in his tragedies. Thus, it is surprising that no one but me makes anything of lines quoted from *Bevis of Hampton*, in the center of *King Lear*.

One problem is that what Spenser's and Shakespeare's contemporaries knew almost intuitively—namely, the tradition, conventions, and materials of chivalric romance, and their signification—we know far less well. So we may have some difficulty identifying and interpreting them or, as the case may be, departures from them. Since we are not instinct with this literature, we may not know what is or is not conventional. Instance: some may regard the marriage of Redcross Knight and Una as contrary to romance convention. However, marriages not only occur in some chivalric romances, but also happen early or midway or late in them. In *Guy of Warwick*, Guy marries Felice early; in *Bevis of Hampton*, Bevis marries Josian medially; and in *The Wedding of Sir Gawain and Dame Ragnell*, the hero marries the lady late. *Guy* and *Bevis* represent the most popular chivalric romances at the time, with the possible exception of the Arthurian romances.

Increasing our difficulty is instructed ignorance; what we think we know about this tradition is often slanted by the works taken and taught as representative. One look at the titles above tell us that none occurs in the English curriculum, which, dominated by aesthetically superior works, misrepresents the literary experience of contemporaries. Most college survey courses teach (or taught) *Sir Gawain and the Green Knight*, a superb romance, but one unknown for over four centuries beyond the baronial West Midlands court in which it was written and read. So far as we know, it has existed in only one manuscript and was not printed until 1839.[2] But *Guy* and *Bevis*, both of which existed in many manuscripts and many printings (some of both surely unknown to us)—a sure sign of widespread reading—few, including specialists, read now. (A late ms. indicates a play on *Guy* circa 1593.[3]) Which is to say that most of the tradition, if cursorily acknowledged, is largely underappreciated for its influence, or, more precisely, its import, as a cultural basis for communication between these authors and their audiences.

In sum, my approach skirts two pitfalls common in criticism. First, it skips cross-book or cross-scene comparisons of similar materials because they rely on an inappropriate and anachronistic way to apprehend these works. Our scholarly way too often indulges such a mode of ap-

---

[2] J. Burke Severs and Albert E. Hartung, ed., *A Manual of the Writings in Middle English 1050–1500*, 9 vols. (New Haven: Connecticut Academy of Arts and Sciences, 1967–1993); Vol. I: Romances (1967), 238–9.

[3] Sylvia Stoler Wagonheim, ed., *Annals of the English Drama 975–1700*, 3rd ed. (London: Routledge, 1989), 60–1.

prehension. The tradition of chivalric romances contains multitudes, and its materials have many meanings, and specific meanings in different contexts.[4] So far as I can tell, Spenser is of mixed minds in different ways about many things. I am not sure that his meanings in one context more likely clarify than complicate, if not confuse or obscure, meanings in another, for a similarity of materials does not imply a similarity of meaning. Shakespeare may or may not be of many minds, but this problem is less acute and less common in criticism because most of his plays, his two tetralogies of history plays aside, stand alone. Second, my approach here spares me the pointless trouble, if not the impossible task, of tracing commonplace items derived from the tradition of chivalric romance to a particular source. I rely on chivalric romance materials intuitively understood by contemporaries from their prior literary experience and, for my purpose, interpret Spenser's and Shakespeare's texts on the basis of cultural meanings rarely indebted to a particular work.

Although I do, I hope, know the demands of a scholarly paper, I believe that its usual appurtenances and paraphernalia need not burden every one. What I have attempted is something else: what is known in the public policy world as a 'white paper', that is, a concept piece which sets forth an idea with only a sketch of argument and evidence. No doubt, given such broad-brush treatment, objections must arise and blemishes abound. I beg your indulgence because I think there is something to be said for starting up a hare and letting others run it down. So what I wrote as a labor of love I have revised for this venue only modestly in order to retain something of its exuberance and, if I may say so, the enthusiasm with which my fellow seminarians seemed to receive it.

This essay discusses the Redcross Knight in *The Faerie Queene*, Book I, and Edgar in *King Lear* as chivalric knights.[5] The Redcross Knight is obviously a chivalric knight. But the thick overlay of signification associated with him and his experiences likely distracts critics from considering his delineation as a knight in much detail. By contrast, Edgar is not obviously a chivalric knight, at least not until he engages Edmund in single combat. Perhaps critics assume that his appearance as a knight so late in the play occurs too late for them to consider his delineation as such earlier in the play.

In an allegory merging and investing features of both epic and romance, Spenser shapes his readers' perceptions by an introductory subtitle which denotes the Redcross Knight as a figure of holiness, known

---

[4] A recent and excellent account of meanings is Helen Cooper's *The English Romance in Time: Transforming Motifs from Geoffrey of Monmouth to the Death of Shakespeare* (Oxford: Oxford University Press, 2004).

[5] For Spenser, my text is Thomas P. Roche, Jr., ed. *Edmund Spenser: The Faerie Queene* (New Haven, CT: Yale University Press, 1978). For Shakespeare, my text is G. Blakemore Evans, ed. *The Riverside Shakespeare* (Boston: Houghton Mifflin, 1974).

at once and later named as St. George, the slayer of the Devil as dragon and the patron saint of England.[6] Thus, Spenser focuses his readers' attention on the allegorical tenor, not the chivalric vehicle, of Book I.

Although Redcross Knight is present in most of Book I, he is separated from Una, with whom he begins and ends his quest, for over half of it. In separating the two from each other, Spenser adopts the structural separation-and-reunion motif more common in Greek than chivalric romance. His point, plainly allegorical as it plays out in Redcross Knight's multiple failures, is to show that Holiness is not sufficient to stand without Truth-of-Faith to sustain it. Conversely, the same point is made when, in the presence of Una, he defeats the dragons in the Den of Error and in the final battle.

Shakespeare takes an opposite approach in *King Lear*, a drama regarded by others as tragedy but by me as romance.[7] From the beginning, he creates a feudal world of knights, with Kent and Edgar shown faithful in their allegiance to Lear. For all his moralizing, Edgar is no foil to Lear—Edgar, no naïve representative of a comforting, conventional morality, to Lear, a seer confronting dark truths about a nihilistic universe. Instead, making Edgar Lear's rightful successor, Shakespeare uses a chivalric vehicle to carry a romantic tenor.

Edgar's career proceeds from expulsion to recovery as he acts as a knight in difficult circumstances. Although one detail, a reference to Edgar's background, in a play otherwise devoid of explicit Christian reference implies Christian doctrine and ritual in his upbringing, Edgar succeeds on his initiative and self-reliance. In this respect, Shakespeare eschews allegory; at most, he assumes a Christianity comporting with chivalry but not controlling it.

So I affirm the fact of allegory in *The Faerie Queene*, Book I, and allow the possibility of allegory in *King Lear*.[8] However, I take a literal approach by considering Redcross Knight and Edgar as chivalric knights in light of contemporary understanding and expectations of such a figure as defined by the tradition of English chivalric romance. Typically, the figure implies high-born status, military training, and religious instruction. This background implies well-known commitments: loyalty to one's lord (later, one's nation), loyalty to one's lady, defense of the

---

[6] Holiness befits a saint, but, by Spenser's time, St. George had evolved into a figure more secular than religious, more English knight than Christian saint. Such is the case in Richard Johnson's *The Seven Champions of Christendom*, I (1596) and II (1597). Earlier, though the story remains much the same, the saint's life of St. Eustace evolved into the romance of Sir Placidas.

[7] Michael L. Hays, *Shakespearean Tragedy as Chivalric Romance: Rethinking 'Macbeth', 'Hamlet', 'Othello', and 'King Lear'* (London: Boydell & Brewer, 2003), specifically the concluding chapter, on *King Lear*, 191–210.

[8] For an extended discussion of my caveats and concerns about allegorical readings, see the extended note at the end of this paper.

faith, justice, and succor to the weak and poor, especially widows and orphans. Conflict between these commitments is the stuff of all but naïve romances celebrating exemplars. Various motifs carry these commitments, with the quest, courtly love, and single combat prominent among them.[9] Other motifs, like exile and return, and fair unknown more specifically address political succession or personal identity, respectively. Underlying the entire chivalric enterprise, especially in seeking justice, is the moral principle that right makes might.[10]

Spenser repeatedly represents or renders chivalric materials, and Redcross Knight's emotional and religious condition, in ways which make them ambiguous, doubtful, or problematic. Of these, the essential mo-

---

[9] A main difference between continental and English chivalric romances is their respective attitudes toward courtly love. Continental chivalric romances take a more indulgent, if not a more approving, attitude toward courtly love than English chivalric romances do. These different attitudes reflect ambiguities in Christianity and chivalry. Christianity can see the lady's ability to inspire virtue as a secular type of the Blessed Virgin Mary's inspiration, or her allure as an inducement to fornication or adultery. Military chivalry can regard the lady as either an inspiration to martial exertion or (often) marital enervation, with dalliance regarded as a cause of debility. Thus, Chaucer's palinode at the end of *Troilus and Criseyde* and Malory's denouement to *Le Morte D'Arthur*, and, to come close to home, both Spenser's showing Redcross Knight weakened when he is wooing Duessa as Fidessa, and Shakespeare's having Othello protest that the presence of Desdemona in Cyprus will not distract him from his mission. Spenser is in hearty accord with this attitude toward courtly love.

[10] I discuss these and other features in detail in the third chapter of *Shakesperean Tragedy*, 66–97.

The principle manifests itself, usually without remark, in the victory of one knight over many knights, large champions, or huge dragons by right prevailing over the apparently greater might of larger numbers or size, any reference to God or Christ notwithstanding. An unusual, because explicit, explanation occurs in *Bevis of Hampton*. Although an army far larger than his besieges his castle, Bevis plans to leave it in order to attack the enemy. His uncle Sabere advises that the six thousand defenders within the castle should not leave it to attack a Saracen foe nearly three times as large. Of course—and it is a matter of course—Bevis refuses this advice; he and his followers attack this huge force and rout it. We have to believe that the writer as well as his audience knew that a much smaller force could not ordinarily defeat a much larger one; Sabere voices this common sense. But the writer does not regard Bevis as a fool for refusing this advice because he troubles to have Bevis explain his refusal, which expresses one of the shaping themes of romance: 'For if they were as many mo, / Agaynst vs shulde they haue no myght: / They have the wronge, and we the ryght' (3028–3030). The same principle operates implicitly in romance after romance. The good knight defeats the larger and apparently stronger dragon or giant, the wronged knight prevails in single or judicial combat, the dispossessed knight reclaims his place in society. In all such cases, right is on the good knight's side, and victory rewards his virtue (of course, God's in the quarrel as the source of right).

What appears naïve to us might have been accounted wise in Shakespeare's time. Many Elizabethans would have offered arguments based on the facts of history. Thus, they would have cited the victories of smaller English forces over larger French armies at Crecy (1346), Poitiers (1356), and Agincourt (1415); over larger Scottish forces at Solway Moss (1542); and, more recently, over the larger Spanish Armada (1588). In this historical context, the principle may be wrong, but it is not obviously foolish or false, and its defenders might not necessarily have validated our modern views.

tif is Redcross Knight's quest. In chivalric quests, sundry adventures test the knight's mettle, show him worthy before the final encounter with the designated foe, and conclude with any number of conventional but triumphant endings: restoration of the kingdom to the rightful ruler, designation of the knight as his heir, and marriage to his daughter. Redcross Knight's quest accords with this overarching motif in large part. But many of his actions depart, some radically, from other conventions of chivalric romance.

The start of the quest and choice of knight are unusual. Una requests, and Gloriana assigns, Redcross Knight his first adventure, one to relieve Una's parents of a four-year siege by a dragon. Yet he has never wielded arms or worn armor, which shows 'old dints of deepe wounds' (I.i.1). We later learn that both come from Una, whose previous champions have failed her. It is unusual that a lady provides a knight with arms and armor, especially in damaged condition; that, given a record of choices failed, she selects a knight untested; and that, nevertheless, he is a warrior feared. Allegory can provide answers, but the tradition of chivalry and chivalric romance cannot.[11] Nevertheless, this first stanza concludes that a 'Full iolly knight he seemd'.

So far, so good, however odd. Except for the possible hint in 'seemd', the contrast with the first stanza in the turn to the second stanza is surprising: 'But on his brest a bloudie Crosse he bore' (i.2). Although he is 'Right faithful true... in deede and word,/... his cheere did seem too solemne sad'. The contrast with his appearance in the previous stanza suggests that the Redcross Knight is conflicted, more sad than glad. These first two stanzas present an ambivalent knight whose faith seems less than secure and strong, and thus at odds with the conventional hero-knight of chivalric romance. This ambivalence at the very outset suggests that he is something less than the nearly perfect or unblemished knight of many chivalric romances.

Even his first victory as a knight, over the dragon 'Errour', has its oddities as well. He extricates himself from the dragon's coil on Una's advice to 'Strangle' (i.19) it—not the usual recourse in battle—and finally delivers the deadly blow 'with more then manly force' (i.24). Allegorically, the episode shows his reliance on Una and divine strength to prevail. But the romance tradition shows knights sufficient to perform

---

[11] Allegory is not alone. In classical narratives, warriors sometimes borrow armor from others, and women sometimes provide such armor as a reminder of ancestral heroism and as a prompt to emulation. But I can think of no instance in chivalric romances of women providing used armor to knights.
    The association of Una's gift of 'pagan' armament with her Protestant affiliations is one of innumerable instances of Spenser's complicating artistry. It comports with a latter-day, Gothic-like Renaissance style which amalgamated classical, chivalric, Christian, and other elements not assimilated until the mid-seventeenth century. The Nine Worthies of pagan, Jewish, and Christian heroes are a good example of such mixtures.

deeds meriting and winning their ladies' love, usually without their advice or divine aid.

No less atypical are his vanity-driven fight for honor at, and his craven departure from, the House of Pride. In this central, two-canto episode, Redcross Knight fights with Sansjoy for the shield of Sansfoy, which Redcross Knight has won in his first battle. In fighting for the honor of retaining a trophy reflecting honor in battle, he fights for an honor derivative and debased. Spenser underlines the false moral conflict by likening both knights to monsters—one a 'Gryfon' (v.8), the other a 'Dragon' (presumably, importantly, and thus ironically, Redcross Knight)—and repeating the same ironic first line of this and the next stanza: 'So th' one for wrong, the other striues for right'. The moral ambiguity of this fight contrasts with conventional chivalric battles for honor in the service of a worthy cause (or in tourneys).[12]

Redcross Knight's craven departure from the House of Pride reflects no credit on him. Alerted by the Dwarf to a dungeon filled with prisoners of noble rank, Redcross Knight, though still recovering from his wounds, sneaks away out of fear that his pride will be similarly punished. His violation of the convention that hero-knights rescue or release captives of noble rank or chivalric standing is, I think, unique. The moral nature of the prisoners, imprisoned for sins represented by the counselors riding the beasts drawing Lucifera's coach, also violates convention and thus extenuates his conduct. The allegory is clear enough: pride consumes the proud, and the proud punish the proud. Clearer still, I suspect, are the disparities between allegory and convention, which Spenser's readers probably sensed, the more so since they exist elsewhere as well.

Strangely, from start almost to finish, Redcross Knight forgets his quest or discounts its purpose. Challenged by Despair about the worthlessness of it all, he fails to raise the value of his quest to defeat evil. Una must save him from suicide and chide him for thus fighting against himself instead of the dragon. Learning little in the House of Holiness, he acts on a narcissism contrary to Charissa's teaching when he elects the contemplative rather than the active life. Contemplation must remind him of his duty to serve Una and continue his quest. Typically, knights retire from action only when their work is done.[13]

---

[12] Additional overlaying of meaning appears in the dichotomous moral implications of the image of the dragon, suggesting either the emblem of Arthur or the enemy of the true faith.

Learned readings of this passage differ. As I see it, Redcross Knight wins Sansfoy's shield in battle; then Sansjoy seeks it; when they fight, presumably Redcross Knight puts it down, and it is held in escrow during combat, so neither possesses it. Thus, neither gryfon nor dragon holds it, and the extended simile does not strictly apply and leaves it up in the air which possesses it. A gryfon may be a symbol of Christ, but not always and, so far as I can tell, not here. The ambiguity abides.

[13] Spenser's ambivalence about chivalry from a Christian perspective reflects age-old

Finally, Redcross Knight defeats the dragon, betroths Una, and becomes her father's heir. These three story-ending conventions stand apart from reminders of his failures or departures from other conventions. First, he initially defers marriage 'to returne to that great Faerie Queene, / And her to serve six yeares in warlike wize' (xii.18), not the conventional seven-year period of service. Second, after Duessa's messenger delivers charges against him, he marries Una before he departs—a sign that he yet requires her as moral compass and prop. At the end, Redcross Knight is still not sufficient to stand alone; he appears neither to have acquired and absorbed truth, but requires Una's aid, nor to have demonstrated that he has become holy in the 'circumcision of his heart'.

Throughout Book I, Redcross Knight is peculiar in his passivity. Almost everything happens to him; he makes little happen, almost nothing without assistance or on his initiative, except when he is in Una's company or presence. For, whatever else it is, chivalry is nothing if not action, and knights are nobodies if not doers of deeds. But if a knight does not act and does not do what he is supposed to do on his own, what is he doing at all? As Spenser's readers assumed that a knight must be sound in faith in order to be strong in deed, they must have asked afterwards why Redcross Knight is 'pricking on the plaine' in the first place, before, as his belated religious education in the House of Holiness makes explicit, he is ready from a doctrinal point of view. And why the Faerie Queen sends a knight not only untested, but also religiously unready, on such a quest. And why Una wants such a knight, and with hands then clean of bloodshed since the quest will bloody them. His chivalry and his undertaking are odd indeed.[14]

---

questions about the relationship between chivalry and Christianity. For over four hundred years, the Church attacked chivalry for its 'open manslaughter' as well as its 'bold bawdry', as Roger Ascham put it two decades before Spenser wrote *The Faerie Queene*. Contemplation states exactly this objection when he informs Redcross Knight that, after he has won fame, he must cleanse himself. The turn which he urges is common to chivalric romances, notably traditional English ones like *King Horn* or *Guy of Warwick*. At the height of his prowess, Guy renounces chivalric honor for a pilgrimage to the Holy Land. Nevertheless, he finds himself engaging, as an unknown not seeking honor, in combat to right wrongs. A short stay in a hermitage ends his life and the romance. Nodding to the higher calling of a Christian but postponing a Christian life of penitence and prayer to its end, these chivalric romances keep their focus always on chivalry and the deeds of chivalry. Lancelot's retirement to a hermitage is hardly religiously motivated, for it occurs only after Guinevere, herself already in retirement at a nunnery, has refused his last advances.

[14] Redcross Knight's trajectory perhaps suggests, but is significantly different from, Edgar's progress as a Fair Unknown, discussed below. All knights on quests necessarily undertake to prove themselves. But the difference between their quests is great. Under Una's guidance, Redcross Knight grows and, as he grows, manifests his emerging character, martial and religious, though his identity—name, rank, and serial number, so to speak—is no secret. He is less unknown, except metaphorically, than undeveloped. By contrast, on his own initiative, Edgar manages his course of conduct from proscribed

And the relationship of Redcross Knight as a knight and Una as his lady is no less peculiar. Spenser contravenes the conventions of such a relationship in two distinctive ways. First, he makes his knight hardly inspired by and almost entirely reliant on his lady for success. Second, he has her love him for who he is, not for what he does or has done, indeed, despite his many failures: 'She did loue the knight of the *Redcrosse*; / For whose deare sake so many troubles her did tosse' (vii.27).[15] However, the nexus of chivalry and love in romance is a knight whose deeds, without help, prove his worth to a lady whose beauty, proxy for moral superiority, inspires him to those deeds which thereby deserve her love. The last thing which a knight is to his lady is a bother.

These departures and others (some noted, some to be noted) from the conventional, especially this unusual relationship between knight and lady, have a cumulative effect in questioning, if not undermining, Redcross Knight, the worth of chivalry, and chivalric undertakings. We can better see Spenser's dubiety in light of other authors' attitudes, as we look at their departures from the conventional. One result may be disparagement of chivalry, or at least false chivalry, as in the case of Shakespeare's *Troilus and Cressida*. Or it may be burlesque or spoof, as in the case of *The Tournament at Tottenham* (early fifteenth century) or Beaumont's *The Knight of the Burning Pestle* (1607), both of which use departures from the conventional for amusement or social satire. But Spenser's every departure from the conventional discredits knight or chivalry. Given both Christian reservations about, or objections to, chivalry, and Spenser's allegiance to the Protestant faith and his interest in holiness, which presumably shapes Redcross Knight's progress, I see his discrediting departures from conventions as signifying his view that chivalry is ultimately inadequate. In this sense, Redcross Knight is rather like a Lancelot forever incapable of becoming a Galahad.

Spenser could challenge but not expunge traditional expectations about knights with which his readers came to *The Faerie Queene*. His many departures from conventions of chivalric romance raise questions about his intended enterprise, an epic of twelve books, the hero-knight in each exemplifying a chivalric virtue, with Arthur as the figure of magnificence recapitulating and crowning them all. Spenser may have meant his work as a poetic courtesy book, but if so, he made trouble

---

felon to victorious knight, in part by controlling his identity, concealing it from all until he aptly reveals it to seal his success.

[15] Richard A. Levin, 'The Legende of the Redcrosse Knight and Una: Or, Of the Love of a Good Woman', *Studies in English Literature*, 31:1 (1991), 1–24, argues that Redcross Knight and Una are in, or falling in, love from the outset; thus, the silence between them. Two reasons suggest that his view may be tongue-in-cheek. First, it is hard to take seriously an argument, especially a long one, quite literally about and from silence. Second, so far as I know and, I assume, so far as Levin knows, chivalric romances do not indicate amorous feelings by nuance or silence.

for himself. Discussing arguably chivalric virtues independent of one another is one thing; presenting a knight associated with a set of chivalric virtues as a figure representing one virtue only is quite another. So what he made of the Redcross Knight as a figure of holiness—what he is or is not, does or does not—likely colored what his audience made of hero-knights in later books.

So, inevitably, Spenser's enterprise is beset by a dilemma. Either holiness in a knight like Redcross Knight (perhaps aided by a lady like Una) is necessary and sufficient to the success of his efforts or it is not. If it is, the importance of other virtues is much diminished and made contingent, not necessary though desirable, to true chivalry. The success or failure of each other knight would thus depend on holiness, not the virtue stressed in the book devoted to it. If not, then the reverse: holiness is contingent, not necessary though desirable. Later books do not raise the issue of their hero-knights' possession of true faith (or assistance by one providing it) or question their success in its absence. The argument might run that a virtue tested in one book is assumed in others. But Book I rebuts it: as a prelude to his many difficulties, Duessa repeatedly misleads or seduces Redcross Knight, and his lasciviousness, to whatever degree he carries it in canto vii, is far from the sexual restraint commended in Book III. Even so, his failures have nothing to do with departures from doctrine in the true faith, the essence of holiness. Inside *The Faerie Queene*, I, and, assuming Spenser's Protestant sympathies outside it, we can infer that only knights sufficient in true faith (and blessed with God's grace) can succeed in their efforts— which is to say that chivalry has almost nothing to do with achievement. Yet all, with Arthur's aiding interventions, succeed. I do not claim that Spenser's readers felt my puzzlement, but I would be surprised if many did not.

Book I is a work in progress, both literally and figuratively, toward holiness. I do not see that Redcross Knight actually becomes holy (or, given that he is but an earthly wight, holi*er*). Indeed, it discloses a disconnect between Spenser's allegorical tenor and his chivalric vehicle. Redcross Knight as saint, his religious nature signified by his name and insignia, leaves much to be acquired; St. George as knight, his chivalry more implied than implemented, leaves much to be desired.[16] Spenser

---

[16] Although Redcross Knight appears to some to undergo a kind of baptism and christening in the final battle, I do not see that he becomes holy. Holiness is an inward state; baptism and christening are all very good, but they do not make one holy, only clean of Original Sin. Book I ends before Redcross Knight shows himself holy in his conduct on the basis of his choices, even in resisting temptations of the kind which had earlier overcome him. We see no evidence of his 'circumcision of the heart'. By comparison, Lancelot tries to achieve the Grail and to be holy in success, but he fails and thereby shows himself to be less than holy. By contrast, Galahad, who is already holy, succeeds in the quest. Spenser seems to regard holiness as a state of soul, not an achievement of arms. In leaving Redcross Knight as less than a figure of perfect holiness, Spenser shows again the radical

makes this knight an exercise in errantry in a sequence of tableaux which do not much affect him. So we may wonder what moral or religious difference his allegory can have made to readers who saw the ineffectuality of episodic experiences to teach Redcross Knight much of anything or lead him to do much of anything unaided. Or whether Spenser thought knights and chivalry worthless both. Or whether we can do no better than treat *The Faerie Queene* as a work artistically rich and intricate but ethically incoherent, not susceptible of systematic allegory, but capable of only incidental allegorizing. Perhaps, in a larger sense, Spenser adumbrates the disparity between any allegorical schema or ethical system and human performance. Perhaps he asks whether we can be what we should be by doing what we should do; or whether, by doing what we should do, we can be what we should be. Either way, the questions are existentialist, and with us still.

By contrast, Shakespeare's delineation of Edgar and his career as a knight are no way problematic. His use of the conventions of chivalric romance not only does not question them, but also actually celebrates the virtues which they assume and enable, especially justice. The overarching structure of the narrative which traces Edgar's career in *King Lear* is the exile-and-return motif common in English chivalric romances. The first English romance, *King Horn*, begins with the father's death and Horn's forced expulsion at the hands of the champion of an invading army and ends with his recovery of his country. But the motif requires nothing more than the dispossession of the legitimate successor to an estate and his eventual repossession of it, as in *Bevis of Hampton*. The Gloucester-Edgar-Edmund parallel plot begins with Edmund's deception of his father and brother to dispossess his elder and legitimate sibling. Both men seem easily gulled; Edmund describes them as 'a credulous father and a brother noble, / Whose nature is so far from doing harms / That he suspects none; on whose foolish honesty / My practices ride easy' (I.ii.179–82). Edmund says so, but the play shows that neither has reason to suspect Edmund. Edgar's expulsion as a felon starts the exile-and-return motif.

His progress thereafter traces the motif of the fair unknown. Perhaps the best-known instance of this motif occurs in Malory's 'The Tale of Gareth'. In it, Gareth arrives at court without an identity, appears uncouth, receives the ironic name 'Beaumains' (i.e., beautiful hands, ironic since his hands are large and become rough with kitchen work), progressively displays his prowess to a scornful lady whom he serves, proves himself in battle by overcoming an oppressive knight, and defeats his brother Gawain, to whom he thereupon identifies himself. Like the banished Kent, the proscribed Edgar refuses exile, adopts a

---

rift, often glossed over by other writers, between chivalric works and Protestant faith.

disguise, and follows Lear.[17] As he goes into internal exile and settles on a disguise, he denies his identity: 'Edgar I nothing am' (II.iii.21). But in his disguise as Poor Tom, he reminds us of his status as a knight. First, Edgar speaks two lines from *Bevis of Hampton* which are appropriate to his condition: 'But mice and rats, and such small deer, / Have been Tom's food for seven long year' (III.iv.138–9).[18] Then, he refers to a story about 'Child [i.e., knight or noble youth before knighthood] Rowland [who] to the dark tower came, / His word was still, 'Fie, foh, and fum, / I smell the blood of a British man' (182–4), a reference which indicates his future action. When that moment arrives and the Herald readies the opponents for the fight, he asks Edgar his identity and rank—to which questions Edgar replies, 'Know, my name is lost' (V.ii.121) but claims a birth as noble as his adversary's. Only after he defeats his brother and his brother asks his identity does he reveal himself: 'My name is Edgar, and thy father's son' (170).

What brings an end to both motifs is the single combat between Edgar and Edmund as armed knights. Edgar's motives to fight are his desires not only to recover his identity and birthright, but also to defeat Edmund's political treachery. Acting on 'The privilege of mine honors, / My oath, and my profession', he aims to overthrow one 'False to thy gods, thy brother, and thy father, / Conspirant 'gainst this high illustrious prince' (129–31, 135–6). So, as in chivalric romances, the hero-knight engages in single combat to resolve issues of moment requiring the justice of righteous resistance to, and armed triumph over, wrong. By means of such motifs, Shakespeare establishes Edgar as a knight victorious in recovering what is his and restoring what is the kingdom's.

The question remains about his right to succession. The answer looks to his links to Lear. The play makes nothing of the relative status of its dukes, Cornwall and Albany, or its earls, Kent and Gloucester. But it makes everything of the closeness of Lear and Gloucester. The connection occurs when Regan, seeking to cast blame on Edgar, asks, 'Was he not companion with the riotous knights / That tended upon my father?' (II.i.94–5). This strong link is not so strong as the one a few lines earlier which critics overlook and in which Regan indicates incredulity at Edmund's report: 'What, did my father's godson seek your life?' (91). Edgar is Lear's 'godson'—a fact of which I make much, and not only because the term is unique in Shakespeare. It means that Lear assumed responsibility for Edgar's moral and religious instruction. Im-

---

[17] The parallel between Kent and Edgar, in their loyalty and service to Lear, is apparent and important. Like the Fool who appears in the first half of the play to be replaced by Cordelia in the second half, Kent plays a more significant role early and Edgar a more significant role later in the play. At the end, it is the older knight who gives way to the younger in a gesture which reflects both retirement and assured political succession.

[18] This two-line quotation is the longer of two in Shakespeare from a chivalric romance. A third line often set off with these two does not occur in this romance.

plications radiate, two mainly. First, it ratifies Edgar's moralizing sententiae. Shakespeare's audience not only accepted such aphorisms, but also probably noted Lear's affinity for Edgar-as-Poor-Tom and his repeated references to him as a 'philosopher'. Second, it permits succession based not on birth and noble rank, but on merit and moral authority.

If we view Edgar in light of Lear, we see that Edgar's moral authority is a matter not only of church rite and catechistic rearing, but also of right conduct learned from Lear. Lear experiences the intensifying ingratitude, insult, and abuse of his elder daughters; suffers the consequent discomforts of body and disorders of mind on the heath; and, in his madness, conducts a trial indicting social injustice of all kinds, in the course of which, he refers to Edgar-as-Poor-Tom as a 'robed man of justice' (III.vi.36). He regains his wits, repents his sins, and reunites with, and recovers his love for, his youngest and dearest daughter. Then, suddenly, he witnesses her slain savagely before his eyes, when he has little life beyond a moment left to him. So, when Lear enters with the dead Cordelia in his arms, he seems a man bereft of everything of value, and his death in agony at her death or in self-delusion that she lives seemingly instances this nihilism.

We must not know seems. Recovered from madness, with its sweeping indictment of all justice, Lear accepts not only the possibility, not only the promise, but also the fact, of chivalric justice. At the last, in reminiscence of his earlier life, he relishes his final deed as a chivalric knight. When, with the dead Cordelia in his arms, he addresses her, 'I kill'd the slave that was a-hanging thee' (V.iii.275), he offers them both the comfort, cold and small as it may be, that although he could not avert her murder, he could avenge it—his final act of chivalric justice which suggests a youth of many acts of justice. Indeed, when a gentleman attests to the truth of his claim, Lear rejoices in an old man's boast, 'Did I not, fellow? / I have seen the day, with my good biting falchion / I would have made [him] skip'. Speaking with pride in his chivalric prowess and recalling the deeds of his youthful days, he sanctions what Edgar has spoken and acted in the play, the life of a chivalric knight doing justice. Indeed, the question of justice, which looms large in the play, accords with, if it does not arise from, the chivalric background of both men. Lear is Edgar's godfather not only in church and catechism, but also in word and deed. So the power to rule England transfers by moral succession. What Lear has forgotten, Edgar has learned. What Lear has been, Edgar has become, and wiser for bearing witness to Lear. Lear dies, a tragic figure; Edgar, the knight redeeming England, lives on, a chivalric hero. The king is dead, long live the king. So Edgar renews the hope implicit in chivalric romance for justice done on earth as it is in heaven.

Spenser and Shakespeare plainly regarded knights, with their implicit code of chivalry, very differently. Where the former was ambivalent, the latter was decided. But paradox rules. Spenser wrote as the military and religious threat from Spain was at its greatest and as England refreshed its regard for knights and chivalry. The sudden outpouring of chivalric romances, old and new, beginning in 1588 and ending in 1603, attended the acme of the neo-chivalric revival, now turned to foreign as well as domestic uses in rallying as well as rousing the nation. Yet, at this very moment, Spenser picks as his hero the knight best known as the defender of the faith and of the country, and undermines him. In his treatment of his hero-knight, Spenser may have been prescient. After Elizabeth's death, favorable attitudes toward knights and chivalry declined. For all his ersatz archaism, Spenser seems to have sensed the future.

Shakespeare began writing plays while Spenser was writing *The Faerie Queene*, in the hey-day of the neo-chivalric revival. Fifteen years later, Shakespeare informed his best-known tragedies with the figures, motifs and other materials, and the shape and spirit of chivalric romances, despite the reaction to them which had already set in. Although we think of him as forward-looking, even, perhaps especially, in *King Lear*, he looked back to knights and chivalry with respect and with regret at a time long gone. In this regard, I think that Edgar speaks for him: 'The oldest hath borne most; we that are young / Shall never see so much, nor live so long' (V.iii.326–7).

Additional Note

The most notable recent effort to read *King Lear* in the way of allegory is Judith H. Anderson, 'The Conspiracy of Realism: Impasse and Vision in King Lear', *Studies in Philology*, 84:1 (1987), 1–23. Following her distinction, I use the term 'allegory' to imply as well, as context requires, allegorizing.

My response to such efforts is, however, a cautious one. I recognize both an inevitable tendency in reading fiction to move from the literal to the figurative and inescapable difficulties in distinguishing what is allegorical from what is not, and in determining specific allegorical meanings. Such recognitions prepare me to guard against an impulse to indicate allegory and to identify allegorical meaning, both of which can be premature and may be mistaken.

I offer as an extended example the episode in which Lear poses a question to his three daughters and receives their answers. Critics view this part of the scene in various terms—historical, fairytale, or allegorical. I have seen its similarity to a court of love. Whatever—and any, some, or all of these possibilities may apply—we all have culturally based expectations that, in fiction, where three children are involved, the elder two will be bad and the youngest good. Whether and how these expectations are fulfilled is the question.

As I see it, critics exalt Cordelia, wittingly or not, under the influence of the motif of two elder sisters and a 'Cinderella'. Ergo, Goneril and Regan are wrong, and Cordelia is right (not to mention that Lear is wrong). Almost all interpretations of *King Lear* accept without question the conclusion at the very least compatible with this cultural expectation. Their views vary in detail, but critics concur that Goneril and Regan speak falsely to gain material advantage; they further concur that Cordelia does the only thing suitable in such circumstances, namely, not answer her father's question in a forum in which her dishonest and dishonorable sisters have corrupted protestations of love (and in which they should never have to make them). However insightful these analyses are and smart in praise of her conduct, they celebrate Cinderella and preemptively clear her of responsibility for any of the consequences of her actions here.

Edgar thinks no better of such views than I do. He closes the play with an injunction hearkening back to this episode, that we must 'Speak what we feel, not what we ought to say' (V.iii.325). His sharp distinction between speech expressing feelings and speech discharging obligations indicts, perhaps too strongly, Cordelia's misconduct; something may be said for 'nothing' but not much. For her 'nothing' is a misleading, if not a false, response. So it makes some sense to see Cordelia at fault though less so than her sisters.

'Nothing' is the third response by the third daughter to Lear's question, 'Which of you shall we say doth love us most?' (I.i.51). His question is ugly in many ways, including its incestuous overtones (echoing the story of Antiochus). Thus, it—that is, its 'most'—almost stipulates materialistic answers like those rendered obediently by daughters first and second. His question is absurd as well; when Lear asks it, answers do not matter, for he has divided the kingdom beforehand and left the best part to last (who shall be first and inherit the earth, so goes a certain text).

The cultural imperative of the three-children motif inclines us to look to the speakers who answer the question, not to the speaker who asks it. But we should, and what we see may affect what we deem appropriate as answers. We see an old man who is both king of a country and father of three mature daughters. We see him more as a father than as a king because he and others refer to Goneril, Regan, and Cordelia as his daughters, not as his subjects. We see an aging parent who needs, and bribes to get, expressions of love from his children, and who willingly and happily pays for them. We should ask whether such conduct, however unpleasant, in such a parent is unnatural or implausible. We should ask why such a parent would ask such a question—what is the need? should we reason the need?—and, depending on the answer, we should ask what answer a child should give to it. Shakespeare's audience was not lacking in expectations on this point. For in European literature and life as far back as their respective records go, parents often expect or seek some late-life reassurance of their children's affection and, in most cases, their children feel obliged to give it. (All else being equal, it probably still seems best in most cases to err on the side of words of comfort, even if they conflict with truth.)

So Goneril and Regan make their answers. After each one, Cordelia comments in asides: after Goneril, 'What shall Cordelia speak? Love, and be silent' (I.i.62); after Regan, 'Then poor Cordelia! / And yet not so, since I am sure my love's / More ponderous than my tongue' (75–7). Cordelia's words about her sisters' language indicate that she reacts to the rhetoric of their responses and regards their rhetoric as so corrupt as to make any response of hers appear similarly corrupt. Indeed, 'ponderous' suggests a love which is palpable on the verge of materialistic. By contrast, 'Nothing, my lord' (87) is striking in its terse and apparent honesty.

Yet I think that we have one inadequate rhetoric after another. Although Cordelia recognizes and rejects the materialistic strains in her sisters' evidently insincere words, she does not articulate an alternative set of values in a sincere expression of her love. She need not give 'nothing' as an answer to avoid giving a materialistic answer. Indeed, her answer is false; she knows and everyone knows—Kent knows, and I think that Lear knows—that she loves her father exceedingly. Worse, her asides reveal what can be regarded only as narcissism; she thinks of herself and how her answer will or will not represent her. She does not think of her father or his needs in asking his question; she reasons, not his needs, but hers. Far from giving him comfort, she is insistently and insultingly impudent; her response provokes a second chance, to which her repetition provokes anger. So seeing Cordelia as right, even righteous, in light of the convention of the three children, not wrong in her way, though less so than her sisters, moves us away from a sufficient, literal reading of this episode. Indeed, in the end, Cordelia must and does reconcile with Lear as much as he with her, in both conduct and conversation. Her 'No cause, no cause' (IV.vii.74) tacitly admits her infuriating fault, for she accepts that she has no complaint to make of him; that is, he was not wrong to be wroth with her.

In this opening scene, Shakespeare exploits his audience's cultural expectations only to qualify them and, in just yesterday's critical parlance, unsettle its expectations. His stratagem wants a closer look, a second opinion, so to say; he does not want his audience to see the opening as an introduction to a Cinderella story, or only such a story, and, in the end, he does not give it one or anything so simple. He gives it something else, something more complex, and thereby challenges his audience's tendency to abstract, to move from the basic facts of human existence—one of the issues in the play. Likewise, a close look at any text requires a diligent effort to stay as close as we can to seeing what the meanings of the lines construct, with a first (but not only) check against the life represented by the figures as people conceived in contemporary terms. This approach seems important to avoid pre-emptive readings, especially since they can lead to allegorizing far removed from the experience represented in literature and its meaning at the level of life as it invites us to imagine it lived.

The Seven Deadly Sins and Shakespeare's Jacobean Tragedies

Ronald Horton

This essay will consider the ubiquitous concept of the seven deadly sins as a track for Shakespeare's featured motivating vices in the tragedies following *Hamlet*. It will refer to Spenser's account of them in the *Faerie Queene,* Book I, canto 4, as a natural source for Shakespeare. The evidence is abundant that Shakespeare was well acquainted with the 1590 edition of *The Faerie Queene*,[1] and it seems beyond question that Spenser's memorable tableau of the seven sins would have remained etched in his mind.

We recall that in canto 4 the Redcross Knight is brought by Duessa to the palace of a proud, cruel princess to find rest for the night. Her court is a trap for the unwary, those who come prepared to lose their humanity and their spiritual good in order to gain material wealth and status. Since pride is the Ur sin from which the other sins came and the root of subsequent sinning, Lucifera, queen of pride, is associated by name with the grand perpetrator of all sin and pictorially with the other six of the deadly sins. These sins appear in established iconographic attributes as figures riding beasts harnessed to her coach. The set of seven came to Spenser from centuries of popular admonitory writing and preaching as well as doctrinal comment going back to and beyond Gregory the Great in the sixth century, whose *Moralia* gave the classic formulation.[2] Their arrangement by Spenser draws from two millennia of moral philosophy.

---

[1] A. Kent Hieatt has summarized the evidence that Shakespeare knew intimately the 1590 edition of *The Faerie Queene* in 'Shakespeare', *Spenser Encyclopedia*, ed. A. C. Hamilton (Toronto: University of Toronto Press, 1990), 641–3. For evidence of Shakespeare's knowledge and use also of the 1596 edition, see Judith H. Anderson, 'The Conspiracy of Realism: Impasse and Vision in *King Lear'*, *Studies in Philology*, 84:1 (1987), 1–23, and her paper in the present collection. For the Arthur and Gloriana story as a mocked subtext of *A Midsummer Night's Dream*, see Robert L. Reid's paper in the present collection, and sources there listed.

[2] For the medieval history and prevalence of this topos, see Morton W. Bloomfield, *The Seven Deadly Sins* (East Lansing, MI: Michigan State University Press, 1952); for its widespread medieval and Tudor pictorial representations, see Samuel C. Chew, *The Pilgrimage of Life* (New Haven, CT: Yale University Press, 1962). A review of knowledge of the sins up to 1968 with suggestions for further investigation, including a valuable account of their history and influence, is Siegfried Wenzel's 'The Seven Deadly Sins: Some Problems of Research', *Speculum*, 43:1 (1968), 1–22. See also Joan Heiges Blythe, 'Spenser and the Seven Deadly Sins: Book I Cantos iv and v', *ELH*, 39 (1972), 342–52, and 'Seven Deadly Sins' in *The Spenser Encyclopedia*; and Ronald B. Bond, 'Sins, Seven Deadly', in *The Dictionary of Biblical Tradition in English Literature*, ed. David Lyle Jeffrey (Grand Rapids, MI: Eerdmans, 1992). The structural function of the sins in Book II of

There is precision in the order and coupling of the six vices. Yoked in the lead are Idleness and Gluttony, followed by Lechery and Avarice, and these four by Envy and Wrath, lashed on by Satan, who sits on the wagon beam. Following in the coach is Lucifera, queen of the Palace of Pride, completing the seven. The sequence of the six pulling vices was discussed in an article twenty years ago by John M. Crossett and Donald V. Stump, whose analysis I will follow and amend.[3]

         Envy (5)   Avarice (4)   Idleness (1)
Pride <Satan>
         Wrath (6)   Lechery (3)   Gluttony (2)

Plato's threefold division of the soul, displayed in the *Phaedrus* as a chariot with driver and team, distinguishes the intellectual, spirited, and appetitive parts, located respectively in the mind, the heart, and the liver. Aristotle in *Nicomachean Ethics* and *De Anima* analyzes the soul into three ascending powers: the nutritive, the sensitive, and the rational. The sensitive power divides into the irascible and concupiscible passions and, together with the rational, yields a tripartite scheme broadly similar to Plato's.

So it is that in Spenser's display of the vices the first team, yoking Idleness and Gluttony, and second team, yoking Lechery and Avarice, present sinful tendencies associated with the appetitive nature or concupiscible passions. Gluttony, Lechery, and Avarice are Spenser's 'forward' acquisitive desires responsive to attraction. Idleness, though not itself a sin of sensual desire, is the fertile condition for sins of the concupiscent nature. Guyon must cross Idle Lake to reach Mammon's delve and Acrasia's Bower. Cupid's Masque in the House of Busirane is introduced by a character named Ease (III.vii.3–4). The association of Idleness with lechery in particular was a medieval commonplace.[4]

The Faerie Queene is argued in J. Holloway, 'The Seven Deadly Sins in *The Faerie Queene*, Book II', *RES*, ns 3:9 (1952), 13–18, and in Robert C. Fox, 'The Seven Deadly Sins in *The Faerie Queene*, Book II', *RES*, ns 12:45 (1961), 1–6. *The Seven Deadly Sins: From Communities to Individuals*, ed. Richard Neuhauser (Leiden: Brill, 2007), treats the sins as cultural constructions of medieval society.

[3] 'Spenser's Inferno: The Order of the Seven Deadly Sins at the Palace of Pride', *Journal of Medieval and Renaissance Studies*, 14 (1984), 203–18. The authors see each vice and its companion across the wagon tree as a contrasting pair: Idleness is lean, Gluttony fat; Avarice is miserly, Lechery prodigal; Envy cowardly, Wrath bold. As contrasting sets, the one is associated with inwardness, coldness, deficiency; the other with extroversion, heat, and excess according to the Aristotelian Golden Mean. The application of Spenser's 'froward' and 'forward' to the virtues on either side of the beam is less convincing.

[4] Crossett and Stump, 'Spenser's Inferno', cite Bloomfield, *Seven Deadly Sins*, on this commonplace, noting that it is Ease who announces the Masque of Cupid and the maiden Sloth who opens the garden gate to the lover in Guillaume de Lorris's part of the *Romance of the Rose* (212n24). Lechery 'is closely allied to Idleness', observes Chew (*Pilgrimage*, 104),

Idleness is associated with sensuality not only as its inducing condition but also as its aftermath. Redcrosse's 'manly forces gan to fayle' (I.vii.6)[5] after his sexual dalliance with Duessa, figured in his drinking from the enfeebling fountain. In Acrasia's Bower Verdant lies immobilized, asleep, his head in the lap of the fair enchantress, a noble life in waste. 'The young man sleeping by her, seemd to be / Some goodly swayne of honorable place. . . . His warlike Armes, the ydle instruments / Of sleeping praise, were hong vpon a tree'. Disregardful of honor, 'in lewd loues, and wastfull luxuree, / His dayes, his goods, his bodie he did spend' (II.xii.79–80). Accordingly the description of Idleness in Lucifera's procession suggests sensual exhaustion, not abstention: 'His life he led in lawlesse riotise', the cause of his disease and enervation (I.iv.20).

The third team, yoking Envy and Wrath, presents sins of the spirited nature or irascible passions, Spenser's 'froward' emotions of repulsion and negation. They appear yoked in the conventional Gregorian order next to Satan, forming with pride his primary moral attributes.[6] Satan, the chariot driver, energizes, drives, the six harnessed sins. He himself is energized and directed by Pride, an intellectual sin, located appropriately behind him and the others. Pride was responsible for Satan's fall and the subsequent fall of the human race. It begot and begets the other sins. But Idleness, as noted, pulls first of the yoked sins, and properly so. It is the incipient vice, the 'nourse of sin' (I.vi.18), which draws after it its fellows. Its yokemate, leading the vices on the right side of the wagon beam, is Gluttony, responsible for the first human sin, Eve's eating the forbidden fruit.[7] In Spenser's pageant Idleness precedes psychologically, gluttony historically, and pride primordially. In loose Aristotelian terms, pride is the *final cause* of vicious character and behavior, their ultimate cosmic explanation; gluttony the *efficient cause,* their particular originating agency; and sloth the *material cause,* their practical occasioning condition.

In Plato's allegory of the charioteer, the charioteer, reason, drives a yoke of ill-matched horses, of which the noble ireful steed tries to lead and keep to the path the recalcitrant, libidinous nag. Spenser's al-

---

recalling that idleness preceded David's adultery with Bathsheba and that Idleness leads Lechery in William Dunbar's *Dance of the Sevin Deidly Synis.* Sloth is a sin of commission in Wyclif's *Trialogus* (Bloomfield, 188).

[5] Citations of *The Faerie Queene* will refer to *Spenser: The Faerie Queene*, ed. A. C. Hamilton, 2nd ed. (London: Longman, 2001).

[6] In his *Tractatus,* Wyclif treats envy and wrath as offspring of pride and connects all three with the devil (Bloomfield, *Seven Deadly Sins,* 188).

[7] John Cassian, whose account of the deadly vices (eight rather than seven) in his *Institutes of Cenobites* preceded Gregory's by a century and a half, treats gluttony as the first sin (Bond,'Seven Deadly Sins', 698); Susan E. Hill, ' "The Ooze of Gluttony": Attitudes towards Food, Eating, and Excess in the Middle Ages', in Newhauser, 59–60.

legory not only adds Satan to the conveyance but also shows both the concupiscible and irascible powers in decay. The powers associated with Plato's black nag are leading those associated with his spirited steed, giving a picture of total psychic disintegration in which sinful tendencies have taken over the soul.

The figure of Lucifera projects pride in its internal and external aspects as personal vanity and worldly ambition. She is described as a vain queen, obsessed with her fair countenance, narcissistically gazing at her image in a hand mirror. She is also the medieval Dame Fortune, dealing out worldly favors to fawning suitors on the stairs beneath her throne. In her dungeon lie famed conquerors brought low by their service to the goddess. Both aspects of pride are implied in Gregory's vainglory, the first in his list of the seven sins.[8] In canto 7 the allegory will center on pride as personal vanity in the description of the giant Orgoglio, a puffed-up wind-filled bladder, reduced by Arthur's sword to utter emptiness. It is this species of pride that pertains most to the internal concerns of the Book of Holiness.

Spenser's movable tableau of the seven vices thus fuses classical and medieval doctrine and display. It is precisely in accord with inherited moral theory. And its subject had more than antiquarian interest during his time. Tudor zealots thought it important enough to plaster over its depiction on church walls.[9]

The continuing vitality of the seven deadly sins in the writing of this era has been well documented by Samuel Chew and others. Examples include Thomas Lodge's moral treatise *Wits Miserie and the Worldes Madness* (1596), which expounds the seven deadly sins in seven chapters, following the Gregorian scheme, associating them with seven devils. In Thomas Nashe's pamphlet *Pierce Pennilesse* (1592) the sins provide a framework for social satire directed especially at avarice and sloth. Anthony Munday's *The Mirrour of Mutabilitie, or Principall part of the Mirrour for Magistrates* (1579) presents 'tragedies' of biblical characters and, notably for our purpose, one for each of the seven deadly sins.[10] In Thomas Dekker's popular *Seven Deadly Sins of London,* which appeared in 1606, the sins are less a theological heptad than a vehicle of social commentary.[11]

---

[8] Gerald Morgan in ' "Add faith unto your force": The Perfecting of Spenser's Knight of Holiness in Faith and Humility', *Renaissance Studies*, 18:3 (2004), 449–74, cites Aquinas (*ST* 2a 2ae 132.2,4) on Gregory (*Moralia,* 31.45), for whom pride had a special status as queen of all the vices, producing vainglory, the first of the seven deadly sins (463).

[9] A few mural paintings of the sins remain in England ('About twenty, often in poor condition'); in sculpture they are 'very rare' (Bloomfield, *Seven Deadly Sins*, 103).

[10] Willard Farnham, *The Medieval Heritage of Elizabethan Tragedy* (New York: Barnes & Noble, 1950), 306–9.

[11] Bond, 'Seven Deadly Sins', 700.

In drama, besides scattered appearances including the farcical pageant of the seven sins in *Dr. Faustus,* outlines of two seven-deadly-sins plays from this period are extant: one by Richard Tarleton from the repertoire of the Queen's Men in the late 1580s; the other, anonymous, from the repertoire of the Admiral's or Lord Strange's Men about 1590.[12] We are concerned with, of course, a commonplace of commonplaces, and it should not surprise us to find reflections of it in the work of its leading dramatist.

Within a year or so of James's accession to the throne, Shakespeare composed a tragedy whose antagonist was thought by Coleridge to be without adequate motivation. A 'motiveless malignity' drives his behavior. This impression has persisted despite opening speeches that make it clear Iago hates his general for passing over him in promoting Cassio. 'I do hate him as I do hell-pains', Iago tells Roderigo (1.1.154).[13] The hatred, directed mainly toward Othello rather than as jealousy might suggest against Cassio, has seemed disproportional to the cause. Iago is driven by radical ill will arising from an angered sense of inferior status. It rankles Iago that the vacant lieutenancy has been filled by presumed merit rather than by seniority. Iago later seems aware that Cassio is indeed his natural better in personal qualities when he admits to himself, 'He hath a daily beauty in his life / That makes me ugly' (5.1.19–20). Iago is Spenser's 'most enuious man, that grieues at neighbours good' (*FQ* I.ix.39). He recalls Spenser's Envy in Book V, who 'scratched her cursed head, although it itched naught' (5.12.29.3–4). Grief at others' good and joy at their mishap are the essence of envy, a vice characterized by hatred beyond occasion.

Envy contrasts with its close cousin, jealousy, by this very feature of lacking a plausible cause. Iago, the man of envy, has been deprived of what he never possessed or knows he deserved. He toys with thoughts of justifiable cause—vague notions of Othello's involvement with Emilia—but they prove only a momentary rationalization for the visceral malice ('I hate the Moor' [1.3.366]) that possesses him. Iago's full motivation must remain a mystery, for there is no explicable cause of hellish envy. Othello before he dies asks Iago's motive and gets only a curt refusal: 'Will you, I pray, demand that demi-devil, / Why he hath thus ensnar'd my soul and body?' Iago replies, 'Demand me nothing; what you know, you know: / From this time forth I never will speak word' (5.2.301–4).

Othello, on the other hand, has lost what he believes to be a rightful possession. As a jealous man he has been deprived of what he possessed

---

[12] E[dmund] K. Chambers, *William Shakespeare: A Study of Facts and Problems,* vol. I (Oxford: Clarendon Press, 1930), 33, 44.

[13] Citations of the plays will refer to *The Riverside Shakespeare,* 2nd ed. (Boston: Houghton Mifflin, 1997).

and thinks he deserves. At the beginning of the last scene Othello reassures himself he is justifiably motivated: 'It is the cause, it is the cause', he tells himself as he prepares to execute his justice on Desdemona.[14]

And yet, Othello himself is tempted toward envy by Iago's suggestions that he never truly possessed the heart of Desdemona, that she was never really his. Iago is not content to see his general suffering as a dispossessed jealous man. He would plant envy in his mind as well. As Othello speaks of Desdemona as the enemy of all good and contemplates with Iago a suitably painful death for her, his jealousy seems about to be overtaken by Iago's vice of envy. He feels himself brought low by her and wishes to bring her down. Iago would have Othello as well as Roderigo infected with his own irrational ill will, the rankling resentment of the have-nots.

Iago not only is presented in such a way as to establish a groundless hatred as his motive, the vice of envy. He appears also from the start a master of calumny, arousing Brabantio against Othello and later Othello against Cassio. Critics have remarked on Iago's skill and gleefulness in stirring disorder through vociferous slander. Calumny was closely associated with envy as its natural expression.[15] In Book IV Sclaunder's defamation of Amoret and Aemylia ('Her nature is all goodness to abuse, / And causelesse crimes continually to frame, / With which she guiltlesse persons may accuse, / And steal away the crowne of their good name', IV.viii.25) reminds of Iago's device concerning Desdemona 'to turn her virtue into pitch' (2.3.360). Iago's words, like Sclaunder's, 'were not, as common words are ment, / T'expresse the meaning of the inward mind, / But noysome breath, and poysnous spirit sent / From inward parts, with cancred malice lind' (IV.viii.26).

Spenser's knight of Justice at the end of Book V restrains Talus from punishing the railing hags Envy and Detraction just as Arthur had refrained from punishing Sclaunder. The defeat of Envy and its calumnious expression, Detraction, must await the efforts of the knight of Courtesy in Book VI. There they will be embodied in the doglike backbiting Blatant Beast.[16] The dog was part of the iconography of Envy, who rides upon a wolf in Spenser's procession. (Lear speaks of Goneril's 'wolvish visage' [1.4.308]; Kent, of Lear's 'dog-hearted daughters' [4.3.45].) Thus the dying Roderigo cries, 'O damn'd Iago! O inhuman dog!' (5.1.62). Lodovico in the play's closing speech addresses Iago as 'Spartan dog' (5.2.352)—a quietly persistent envy-driven killer. Envy is the generative and presiding motive of the play.

---

[14] He will be no comic cuckold, like Spenser's Malbecco, who metamorphizes from an example of jealousy into jealousy itself (III.x.60).

[15] Chew, *Pilgrimage*, 88.

[16] Cf. the barking, backbiting Sclaunder, who 'Like as a curre doth felly bite and teare / The stone, which passing straunger at him threw' (IV.iii.36).

Envy's location immediately before Lucifera's coach and Satan is in keeping with the Gregorian sequence of the vices and traditional moral thought. Expressions associating the 'demi-devil' Iago with Satan and reprobation keep before us the link between envy and Satanic pride. 'Hell and night / Must bring this monstrous birth to the world's light' (1.3.403–4). 'Divinity of hell! / When devils will the blackest sins put on, / They do suggest at first with heavenly shows, / As I do now' (2.3.350–3). The location also seems right psychologically, for envy can stem from wounded pride, the motive of Milton's Satan. Whereas a successful person may be driven by pride, it is the unsuccessful who are driven by envy. Whereas pride is the most odious of sins against God, envy, exulting in other's loss and grieving at other's gain, is the most contemptible of sins against another human being. Both show elemental disregard of due right. That such should be so is no wonder, for the one gives birth to the other.

Appropriately *King Lear* and *Macbeth*, appearing in successive years after *Othello*, present tragic action originating in pride. Pride is featured as personal vanity in Lear and as worldly ambition in Macbeth. Lear's troubles come on him because of his desire to be publicly adored in keeping with his sense of central importance. The desire is no less serious for being attributable to senility. It derives also from a fixed habit of mind, if we may allow weight to Regan's words to Goneril: ' "Tis the infirmity of his age, yet he hath ever but slenderly known himself' (1.1.293–4).

Pride as inordinate ambition overtakes the Thane of Glamis. Macbeth, says his Lady, is 'not without ambition, but without / The illness should attend it', the willingness to use unholy means (1.5.19–20). Macbeth complains, 'I have no spur / To prick the sides of my intent, but only / Vaulting ambition, which o'erleaps itself' (1.7.25–7), after which, Enter Spur, Lady Macbeth, who will supply what in her husband is lacking. Pride here has its conventional connections. Its association with Satan's ambition is reflected in the demonic backdrop of Macbeth's rise and fall. It is pride that awakens the envy of Malcolm in Macbeth and wrath in both Lear and Macbeth, for it is of the nature of a vice to engage its near fellows and pull with them in the harnessed set.[17]

---

[17] Wenzel, in his survey of the scholastic models of the vices, quotes Gregory on the concatenation of the vices: 'Each of these vices is linked to the others by such kinship that one is brought forth (*proferatur*) from the other'. Pride generates envy of rivals, and envy, chafing inwardly, produces anger, and so forth. Gregory's linking of the sins, says Wenzel, 'became commonplace among medieval theologians' (4). Bloomfield cites Wyclif on the concatenation of the sins, whose *Tractatus de civili dominio* in the latter part 'develops the theme that just as all virtues are linked, so are all sins inextricably connected, *superbia* with *invidia*, *invidia* with *ira*', etc. (*Seven Deadly Sins*, 190–1).

Within a year after *Macbeth* by most reckonings, Shakespeare returned to Plutarch to compose a tragedy of a great man who fell in political life from inclinations deadly to the performance of military duty. In the opening lines, two Roman soldiers, one Caesar's and one his own, chorus-like decry the shameful spectacle of the 'triple pillar of the world' mired in lechery and sloth (1.1.12). Antony says in scene 2, 'I must from this enchanting queen break off; / Ten thousand harms, more than the ills I know, / My idleness doth hatch' (1.2.128–30). Pompey expresses surprise that so small a conflict by Antony's reckoning could have drawn Antony from his slack life in the East. 'I did not think / This amorous surfeiter would have donn'd his helm / For such a petty war. His soldiership / Is twice the other twain; but let us rear / The higher our opinion, that our stirring / Can from the lap of Egypt's widow pluck / The [ne'er-] lust-wearied Antony' (2.1.32–8). 'The beds i' th' East are soft', Antony tells Pompey five scenes later (2.6.50).

Whether the Roman view of Antony is to be taken as normative for interpretation is not at issue here or necessary to my point. Critical sentiment generally finds inadequate Plutarch's explanation of Antony's behavior, in which 'the horse of the minde as Plato termeth it, that is so hard of rayne (I mean the unreyned lust of concupiscence) did put out of Antonius heade, all honest and commendable thoughts',[18] finding Shakespeare inclining instead, in the Egyptian case, to Claudio's view concerning lechery that 'Sure it is no sin, / Or of the deadly seven it is the least' (*Measure for Measure,* 3.1.109–10). Yet the play does attend to moral consequences. The vices of lechery and sloth, like envy in *Othello* and pride in *Lear,* are placed in high relief at the outset and kept before us as inimical to Antony's judgment and self-mastery and as causes of his defeat. Verdant can become absolute Mortdant in Cleopatra's bower.[19] In Egypt lechery enervates, sloth brings sleep, and sleep forbodes of death.

With idleness and lechery is associated concomitantly the vice of gluttony, to make up a trio of concupiscent failings—the first three sins in Spenser's order of mention. Pompey, himself a victim of gluttony, desires that it will join with lechery and sloth to weaken Antony.

> But all the charms of love,
> Salt Cleopatra, soften thy wan'd lip!
> Let witchcraft join with beauty, lust with both,
> Tie up the libertine in a field of feasts,
> Keep his brain fuming; epicurean cooks

---

[18] 'The Life of Marcus Antonius', *Plutarch's Lives of the Noble Grecians and Romans,* trans. Sir Thomas North (1579), in *Narrative and Dramatic Sources of Shakespeare,* ed. Geoffrey Bullough, vol. 5 (London: Routledge, 1964), 283.

[19] Anderson in 'Beyond Binarism' in the present volume sees Adonis and Verdant (and pietà figures) in the recumbent, wounded Antony, dying in the lap of an attentive maternal-like possessor.

> Sharpen with cloyless sauce his appetite,
> That sleep and feeding may prorogue his honor,
> Even till a Lethe'd dullness.
>   (2.1.20–7)

In *Plutarch* Shakespeare found two other stories eked out by a third to fill out his work in tragedy. The first provided a play in which the main challenge to the tragic hero is the management of anger. As in *Antony and Cleopatra*, the hero's moral defect is signaled at the outset, but unlike in the earlier play, it is for a time inadequately defined. The true nature of Coriolanus's flaw is identified only gradually. It is clarified in response to a false hypothesis, voiced by the citizens and tribunes. In the opening dialogue, the First Citizen charges that Coriolanus (then known as Caius Martius) has performed his exploits not for the good of the commonwealth but for his mother and from pride; for proud he is 'even to the altitude of his virtue' (1.1.40). This view is seconded by the tribunes, appointed to represent the commons in its plea for food. 'Was ever man so proud as is this Martius?' asks Sicinius. 'He has no equal', replies Brutus (1.1.252–3). Their assessment seems warranted from Coriolanus's vituperation toward the assembled mob and his ferocity in responding to his summons to war against the Volscians. But it does not prove out as the play continues.

In Act 2, scene 1, Menenius, alone with Sicinius and Brutus, rejects their interpretation of Coriolanus's character and turns the charge of pride back on them and their fellows. If the two tribunes would examine themselves, they would 'discover a brace of unmeriting, proud, violent, testy magistrates (alias fools) as any in Rome' (2.1.43–5). Their judgment, says Menenius, is worthless.

> When you speak best unto the purpose, it is not worth the wagging of your beards, and your beards deserve not so honorable a grave as to stuff a botcher's cushion, or to be entombed in an ass's pack-saddle. Yet you must be saying Martius is proud; who, in a cheap estimation, is worth all your predecessors since Deucalion, though peradventure some of the best of 'em were hereditary hangmen. (2.1.86–93)

In the next scene Coriolanus 'rises and offers to go away' to escape hearing his praises. 'I had rather have my wounds to heal again', he says, 'Than hear say how I got them' (2.2.69–70). He shows no personal vanity.

That Coriolanus also lacks personal ambition is confirmed by his rival general, Cominius, in the same scene:

> Our spoils he kick'd at,
> And look'd upon things precious as they were
> The common muck of the world. He covets less

> Than misery itself would give, rewards
> His deeds with doing them, and is content
> To spend the time to end it.

To which Menenius replies, 'He is right noble. / Let him be call'd for' (2.2.124–30), and presents Coriolanus to the applauding Senate. Later Menenius again defends Coriolanus's character against charges of ambition from the tribunes: 'His nature is too noble for the world: / He would not flatter Neptune for his trident, / Or Jove for's power to thunder' (3.1.254–6). He cares only for success in what he is given to do.

This is not false modesty. The tribunes Brutus and Sicinius are deep-dyed cynics, viscerally hostile to Coriolanus, determined subverters of his name. They can see only pride as responsible for Coriolanus's unwillingness to conciliate the populace and accept its approval and praise. The possibility that he would act in a people's best interest neglectful of their good will and disregardful of his own gain is beyond their comprehension. From their limited moral categories they can see his behavior only as ill-tempered pride. Even after the banishment of Coriolanus, their public view of him remains unchanged: 'Caius Martius was / A worthy officer i' th' war, but insolent, / O'ercome with pride, ambitious past all thinking, self-loving—'And affecting one sole throne / Without assistance'. To which Menenius replies, 'I think not so' (4.6.29–33). Subsequent action will prove Menenius right and the tribunes wrong.[20]

In private conversation, however, the tribunes show an understanding of Coriolanus's real weakness and in fact plan to act on this knowledge. Having publicly accused Coriolanus of prideful disregard of the people, they privately plan to attack him at his truly vulnerable point. 'If, as his nature is, he fall in rage / With their refusal, both observe and answer / The vantage of his anger' (2.3.258–60). Later at the Forum, Brutus reminds Sicinius of their agreed strategy.

> Put him to choler straight, he hath been us'd
> Ever to conquer, and to have his worth
> Of contradiction. Being once chaf'd, he cannot
> Be rein'd again to temperance; then he speaks
> What's in his heart, and that is there which looks
> With us to break his neck.
>
> (3.3.25–30)

---

[20] I find credible Francis Ferguson's 'wise old Menenius, ... the only character in the play with a disinterested love of Rome and a balanced view of what the community should be' (*Shakespeare: The Pattern in His Carpet* [New York: Dell, 1958], 265) rather than Harold Goddard's 'muddle-headed' descendant of Polonius, of whom 'the best that can be said ... is that he loves Coriolanus—in his doting fashion—and Coriolanus loves him', whose 'graciousness is largely veneer' and 'underneath [which] is a hypocrite, a fool, and a snob' (*The Meaning of Shakespeare*, vol. II [1951; Chicago, IL: University of Chicago Press, 1964], 224–5).

The plot of the tribunes is dependent upon Coriolanus's propensity to wrath, a quality less serviceable against political cunning than against open opposition in battle. Of the Volsces Coriolanus says, 'They do disdain us much beyond our thoughts, / Which makes me sweat with wrath' (1.4.26–7). That Coriolanus is capable of more than wrath in battle is clear when he asks Cominius to release to freedom a poor prisoner who had once befriended him, whose plea Coriolanus had forgotten in battle when 'wrath o'erwhelmed my pity' (1.9.86). But the propensity to this behavior is ever present. Coriolanus is being tempted to wrath by villains just as Othello is tempted to jealousy by Iago—simple protagonists inapt to coping with complexities and frustration and vulnerable to clever provocations.

It is given to his friend Menenius to reconcile Coriolanus's flaw with his genuine nobility of character, a surly virtue (as Boswell says of Johnson's) that eschews falseness, laxity, cowardice, and empty ceremony with the same angry contempt that energizes him in battle.

> His nature is too noble for the world;
> He would not flatter Neptune for his trident,
> Or Jove for's power to thunder. His heart's his mouth;
> What his breast forges, that his tongue must vent,
> And, being angry, does forget that ever
> He heard the name of death.
> (3.1.254–9)

This fault, says Menenius, echoing Plutarch, derives from a defective education, which, directed toward the making of a warrior, omitted the control of anger. 'Consider this: he has been bred i' the wars / Since 'a could draw a sword, and is ill school'd / In bolted language; meal and bran together / He throws without distinction' (3.1.318–21). To judge him solely on this flaw and link it to arrogant ambition is, Menenius says, a misreading of his character. He was home-schooled in anger by his mother, who formed him after her own example. Volumnia, grieving over the banishment of her son, refuses Menenius's invitation to supper, explaining 'Anger's my meat' and declaring she will lament 'In anger Juno-like' (4.2.50, 53). In the last scene the Volscian general Aufidius knows how to unravel his rival's composure with a single word, that of 'traitor', echoing the taunt of the tribunes (5.6.84), and Coriolanus comes apart in soaring rage. The play features wrath.[21]

Having completed *Coriolanus*, or while doing so, Shakespeare had yet to raise to special prominence as motivating vices the remaining

---

[21] Coriolanus obviously has no monopoly on wrath among the protagonists of Shakespeare's Jacobean tragedies. Othello, Lear, Macbeth, Antony, and Timon rage no less fiercely than Coriolanus. Their wrath however is a consequence, rather than the instigating vice, of their falls.

two sins of the deadly seven: avarice and gluttony.[22] Of the seven vices these would seem the least promising for raising tragic interest, though elsewhere they had served him well enough. In Plutarch's *Life of Antony* and *Life of Alcibiades*, which he had used for the two plays just discussed, Shakespeare found references to an Athenian nobleman driven to misanthropy and malice toward his city by the ingratitude of friends. From these fragments and others in the Timon tradition, including a dialogue of Lucian and perhaps an earlier Timon play, Shakespeare put together a story of a foolishly generous nobleman who in willful ignorance incited a stream of flattering parasites to devour his wealth.[23]

A commonplace of *Timon* criticism, echoing Lucian, is the association of avarice and eating, notable in the two banquet settings and in the persistent imagery in which Timon's guests are both eating his food and eating him. Timon asks, 'Wilt dine with me, Apemantus?' The dour seer replies, 'No; I eat not lords' (1.1.203–4). At the banquet Apemantus exclaims, 'O you gods! What a number of men eats Timon, and he sees 'em not. It grieves me to see so many dip their meat in one man's blood' (1.2.39–41). For Apemantus, remarks R. C. Fulton, 'dining *with* Timon is equivalent to dining *on* Timon'. Apemantus sees the banquet as 'a cannibal's feast'.[24] Timon's disheartened steward, Flavius, tells his master of his anguish, 'When all our offices have been oppress'd / With

---

[22] Gluttony, though a consort of lechery and sloth in Pompey's speech, is not featured in Antony's fall as are the other two. Besides being less prominent, it is not distinctive of Egyptian Antony. The Romans are overfeasting drunkards as well.

[23] John C. Briggs notes that Shakespeare added generosity to Timon's character from Plutarch's Alcibiades in his *Life* of the Athenian general. Alcibiades in the play is reduced to a soldier-hero, not altogether admirable, whereas in Plutarch he is not only a noble warrior but also a man of wealth and munificence who charms the Athenians, those who dislike him. Shakespeare's Timon 'splits Plutarch's hero [Alcibiades] between Timon and Alcibiades'. The other part of Timon, his crazed anger, is 'an exaggerated version of Coriolanus', ' "Within Athens' Shadow": The Ghost of Plutarch in Shakespeare's *Timon of Athens*', *Poetica*, 48 (1997), 128–30. Bart Westerweel suggests that Shakespeare intended *Coriolanus* and *Timon of Athens* to parallel each other in the manner of Plutarch's *Lives* of Coriolanus and Alcibiades, 'Plutarch's *Lives* and *Coriolanus*: Shakespeare's View of Roman History', *Recreating Ancient History: Episodes from the Greek and Roman Past in the Arts and Literature of the Early Modern Period* (Leiden: Brill, 2001), 187–211. It is interesting in this regard that in the Book of Justice we meet the contempt for the rabble and severe measures of Coriolanus and in the Book of Courtesy the generosity and decorum of Timon and the cannibalism figuratively attributed to his greedy guests. In Coriolanus is shown just due without generosity; in Timon generosity without just due—the positives appearing in complementary relation in emergent virtues and their heroes of Books V and VI. It is plausible that the two plays were conceived as a pair with Spenser at least distantly in mind. Timon's foolish beneficence is indeed a culpable error in judgment. Chaucer's Parson warns against overcorrecting avarice by 'fool-largesse' in 'Relevacio contra peccatum Avaricie', *The Parson's Tale* (F. N. Robinson, ed., *The Works of Geoffrey Chaucer*, 2nd ed. [Boston: Houghton Mifflin, 1957], 254). Prodigality and avarice as opposite sins are punished on the fifth terrace of Dante's *Purgatorio*.

[24] '*Timon*, Cupid, and the Amazons', *Shakespeare Studies*, 9 (1976), 283–93, cit. Karl Klein, ed., *Timon of Athens* (Cambridge: Cambridge University Press, 2001), 26.

riotous feeders, when our vaults have wept / With drunken spilth of wine' (2.2.158–60). He laments, 'How many prodigal bits have slaves and peasants / This night englutted' (2.2.165–6). At the end of Act 3, when Timon's appeals for a generous return from his beneficiaries have proved fruitless, Timon draws the carnivores once again to their feeding site for a mock banquet of warm water and drives them with cursing from his hall. Three scenes later, the hermit Timon discovers gold—while digging for something to eat.

Shakespeare's generous host beset with avaricious gormandizing flatterers occurs in an overlooked passage in Horace's *Ars Poetica*, one that may have seeded his mind with some particulars. Horace's host however is a poet, inverting the Timon story.

> Just like the herald at an auction who collects a crowd in order to sell his merchandise, the poet who is rich in lands, rich in money lent out for interest, bids flatterers with an eye on profit to assemble. If in fact he is someone who can properly serve up a lavish banquet and go bail for a fickle, poverty-stricken client and can extricate someone from distressing lawsuits, I will be surprised if the blessed fellow can tell a liar from a true friend. You, then, if you have given, or plan to give, a gift to someone, must refuse to invite him, full of joyful gratitude, to a reading of poems you have written. For he will shout, 'Beautiful!' 'Great!' 'Right on!' He will turn pale over them, he will even let dew drip from his friendly eyes, he will dance and pound the pavement with his foot.[25]

What we know of Shakespeare the man indicates he was too practically shrewd to fall into the trap Horace warns about. What we can infer of him from the plays indicates a contempt for slothful, avaricious flatterers. It is not surprising Shakespeare would attempt a tragedy featuring as generating vices gluttony and avarice to finish out his account of the seven deadly sins, whatever misgivings he may have had about its likely success.

In positing a scheme for the tragedies that follow *Hamlet*, a play in a different mold, I am not proposing a view of the plays that distributes them reductively in a moral grid. Nor am I insisting that the moral qualities raised to prominence as motivating vices take us necessarily to the centers of the plays in which they appear. Nor need I claim that Shakespeare had in mind from the beginning the deadly sins as a track

---

[25] *Horace for Students of Literature: The 'Ars Poetica' and Its Tradition*, O. B. Hardison, Jr. (ed. and commentator) and Leon Golden (trans.) (Gainesville: University Press of Florida, 1995), 20–1, lines 419–37. Tom Adair finds, in addition to the unmistakable allusion to Horace's *Epistles* in Timon's 'They say, my lords, "*Ira furor brevis est*"' (I.ii.28), a less conspicuous one in the Poet's comparison of his medium to 'a gum, which oozes / From whence 'tis nourished' (I.i.21–5): 'Shakespeare's Horatian Poet', *Notes and Queries*, ns 45:3 (1998), 353–5. The *Ars Poetica* begins like *Timon* with a poet and a painter.

for his tragedies. I am suggesting that at some point after the accession of James I, perhaps as late as the appearance of Dekker's tract, the year of *Macbeth,* Shakespeare, not caring to repeat himself, may have become aware that his work in tragedy was proceeding along the lines of the traditional set of deadly vices and decided to complete the account—an account of the attack of vice not on the city of London, as in Dekker, but on the soul.

This hypothesis has interesting implications for the unfinished state of *Timon of Athens*. With *Timon,* as noted, Shakespeare faced a special challenge, centering a tragedy upon two vices better suited to comedy. He devised, I think, an elegant structure in support of incisive moral critique and laced it with splendid invective but realized he could not overcome the inherent weakness in tragic interest, due to the limitations of the motivating vices and their location in peripheral characters. Giving up his attempt to make it work, he abandoned his notion to complete the vices and proceeded to the Late Romances. Surviving as a space filler in the First Folio, *Timon* evidently had not been staged by 1623 and may not have been performed until Shadwell's adaptation in 1678. My hypothesis addresses not only the question of why the play is unfinished but also and perhaps more basically the question (not intended disparagingly) of why the play was ever begun. The allure of an idea may have proved too strong.

It seems then that Spenser's display of the vices may have amounted in Shakespeare to more than a shadowy recollection. Having waded this far in speculation, we may wade farther. If Shakespeare were to have read Spenser's series of the vices in an alternating manner, in which each successive pair begins at the left, rather than in the serpentine order intended (in which 'next to him' means directly behind), the correspondence of Spenser's incontinent set with Shakespeare's commonly supposed order of composition would be especially striking. After Pride (as in Lear and Macbeth) and Envy (as in Othello) would be, on the left side facing forward, Lechery and Idleness (as in Antony), and then, on the right facing forward from the chariot, Wrath (as in Coriolanus) and Avarice and Gluttony (as in Timon). Misread in this way, Spenser's order of the pulling beasts and their riders after Pride and Envy would parallel the usual dating of the plays.

	Serpentine				Alternating	
	5	4	1	5	3	1
	Envy	Avarice	Idleness	Envy	Lechery	Idleness
Pride				Pride		
	Wrath	Lechery	Gluttony	Wrath	Avarice	Gluttony
	6	3	2	6	4	2

The serpentine order has obvious symbolic value for a sinister unfolding of the sins in Spenser's pageant and can hardly be accidental, and yet the order could easily go undiscerned by a busy practicing dramatist.

In any case, it seems beyond conjecture to this reader that the seven vices are given prominence in the Jacobean tragedies through overt moralism and reiteration well beyond dramatic necessity and more than plausible that at some point Shakespeare recognized their value as a paradigm for his remaining work in tragedy and decided to carry it through. If so, it follows naturally that Shakespeare would have turned to a familiar source, the poetry of Spenser, for a concentrated treatment of the seven sins—a brilliant pictorial account that had already served paradigmatic purposes for the grandest attempt in epic in sixteenth-century Europe and that might also for him. I will not contend for the *inherent* appeal of these materials for this subtle master while allowing that the expression *poet-moralist* might not for a dramatist of his era have seemed oxymoronic.

Of Shakespeare's general medieval affinities there should be less doubt. Years ago Hardin Craig in 'Morality Plays and Elizabethan Drama' described the importance of the morality play in Tudor drama.[26] Morality plays 'continued to be written throughout the whole Tudor period' and 'form a very extensive element in Tudor drama' (68). Having surveyed the early Tudor and Elizabethan examples of the genre, Craig made his case concerning Shakespeare's indebtedness, remarking that 'it is part of his greatness that practically all of his characters have general as well as individual significance'. Furthermore, '[i]n many of his major characters there is a definite pattern of aberration like that of the full-scope morality' (71). Similar consequences follow. Macbeth, like Everyman, 'goes down fighting' but 'does go down, and at the end he stands, as mankind must stand, face to face with divine retribution'. The ending, notes Craig, is not required by the story. It 'is Shakespeare's own, and ... embodies a definition of evil which Shakespeare everywhere endorses and which does not differ one iota from the conception of evil which pervades the morality plays' (72).

The moral-allegorical nature of Shakespeare's plays remains a delicate question. There is broad recognition among critics that allegory plays a part in at least some of them and, if we stretch the concept, in many of them, but how much of a part it is and what that part may be is far from settled. The answer is no doubt determined as much by one's notion of allegory as by one's idea of the plays. Anderson ('Conspiracy') contends that, while *King Lear* is not an allegory, to experience it fully, especially on the macro level, requires appreciating its allegorical features, those it shares with Spenser's *Faerie Queene*. In her article in the

---

[26] 'Morality Plays and Elizabethan Drama', *Shakespeare Quarterly* 1:2 (1950), 64–72.

present collection she claims the same for *Antony and Cleopatra*. Susan Oldrieve in an article also in the present collection, finds *Lear* moving from Spenserian metaphorical abstraction through Sidnean concrete example to a fusion of the two in transcendent allegorical tableaux.

The sticking point is the function of allegory as moral-didactic vehicle. In 'We Came Crying Hither,' Maynard Mack observes of *Lear* that 'most of the characters are unabashed *exempla* of evil and good' and that there is 'a somewhat schematic variety in the play's characterization of Lear and Gloucester' (177). Moral energies drive the play. In the first scene are coiled consequences waiting to be sprung. In the course of the play all the major characters have to take a stand and deal with the effects of it. Indeed in *Lear* 'there is much of the morality play'. But the morality content 'is not used toward a morality thesis' (177).[27] For Lyle Glazier, writing a half century ago, there was no need to finesse the moral-allegorical question. *King Lear*, like the story of Redcross, presents us minimally with 'the graph of virtue and vice'.[28]

Concerning allegorical spectacle, there is little disagreement. D. D. Carnicelli in the introduction to his edition of Lord Morley's translation of the *Triumphs* of Petrarch finds Shakespeare along with Spenser responding imaginatively to the allegorical triumphal pageantry for notable occasions and likely to the *Triumphs* themselves, most notably and directly in *Love's Labour's Lost* but frequently elsewhere.[29] The importance of medieval romance materials in Shakespeare is evident from Michael L. Hays's discussion of *King Lear* as chivalric romance in the present collection and developed powerfully in Helen Cooper's *The English Romance in Time: Transforming Motifs from Geoffrey of Monmouth to the Death of Shakespeare*.[30] Recently Cooper, in her inaugural lecture on succeeding to the Cambridge chair of Medieval and Renaissance English Literature, urges greater attention to medieval elements in Shakespeare. She sees Shakespeare in the 1590's 'opening himself increasingly to the Middle Ages' and 'at the end of his career' turning 'more and more back to total theatre, to dramaturgy of the home-grown medieval variety', in mentality as well as mode.[31]

The evidence is before us in *Timon of Athens*. A medieval-allegorical, let us say Spenserian, moment occurs in the first scene in the Poet's

---

[27] '"We Came Crying Hither:" An Essay on Some Characteristics of *King Lear*', *Yale Review*, 44:2 (1964), 61–86.

[28] 'The Struggle Between Good and Evil in the First Book of *The Faerie Queene*', *College English*, 11 (1950), 384.

[29] *Lord Morley's 'Tryumphes of Fraunces Petrarcke'*, ed. D. D. Carnicelli (Cambridge, MA: Harvard University Press, 1971), 57–65.

[30] Oxford: Oxford University Press, 2004. For Shakespeare's use of the romance model in the comedies and in *Romeo and Juliet*, see 260–68. For the romance model recast as tragedy in *King Lear*, see 405.

[31] *Shakespeare and the Middle Ages* (Cambridge: Cambridge University Press, 2006), 29.

conversation with the Painter. The Poet has written a poem for Timon that places him among the suitors of Dame Fortune. The 'sovereign lady' is enthroned like Lucifera 'upon a high and pleasant hill'. Among the suitors is one 'of Lord Timon's frame, / Whom Fortune with her ivory hand wafts to her' (1.1.63–70). As he ascends, his former rivals 'Follow his strides' to rise with him. They will not fall with him.

> When Fortune in her shift and change of mood
> Spurns down her late beloved, all his dependants
> Which labor'd after him to the mountain's top
> Even on their knees and [hands], let him [slip] down,
> Not one accompanying his declining foot.
> (1.1.84–88).

The conversation is a chorus providing moral pointing like that which opens *Antony and Cleopatra*. Here it evokes a medieval rather than Roman world.

Stephen Spender once ventured the observation that 'the fundamental aim of modernism was the confrontation of the past with the present'.[32] Spender's observation might extend to postmodernism as well except that for postmodernism the past is not fixed but malleable, ultimately a fiction. An equally useful standpoint is the confrontation of the present with the past, one which I believe appears in the two authors treated here. The exact nature of the confronting past in Shakespeare is perhaps endlessly arguable. One may be convinced as I am of the responsiveness of Shakespeare to the medieval content within his mixed culture, and of his kinship with Spenser in this regard, and yet be persuaded that his writing like Spenser's instantiates the premises of an Elizabethan Protestant England. Still, these premises, as both poets show, were not altogether discontinuous with those of the preceding age.

---

[32] 'The Modern as Vision of a Whole Situation', *Partisan Review*, 29 (1962), 351.

Works Cited

Addison, Catherine. 'Little Boxes: The Effects of Stanza on Poetic Narrative.' *Style* 37 (2003): 124–43.
Addison, Catherine. 'Rhyming Against the Grain: A New Look at the Spenserian Stanza.' *Edmund Spenser: New and Renewed Directions*. Ed. J. B. Lethbridge. Madison: Fairleigh Dickinson University Press, 2006. 337–51.
Adelman, Janet. *Suffocating Mothers: Fantasies of Maternal Origin in Shakespeare's Plays, 'Hamlet' to 'The Tempest'*. New York: Routledge, 1992.
Adelman, Janet. *The Common Liar: An Essay on 'Antony and Cleopatra'*. New Haven: Yale University Press, 1973.
Adelman, Janet. 'Hugh Maclean Memorial Lecture: "Revaluing the Body in *The Faerie Queene*."' *The Spenser Review* 36 (2005): 15–25.
Akrigg, G. P. V. *Shakespeare and the Earl of Southampton*. London: Hamish Hamilton, 1968.
Albright, Evelyn May. 'The Folio Version of *Henry V* in Relation to Shakespeare's Times.' *PMLA* 43 (1928): 722–56.
Allen, D. C. *Mysteriously Meant: The Rediscovery of Pagan Symbolism and Allegorical Interpretation in the Renaissance*. Baltimore: Johns Hopkins University Press, 1970.
Alpers, Paul. *What is Pastoral?* Chicago: University of Chicago Press, 1996.
Alpers, Paul. 'How to Read *The Faerie Queene*.' *Essays in Criticism* 18 (1968): 426–43.
Alpers, Paul. 'Narration in The Faerie Queene.' *ELH* 44 (1977): 19–39, and *The Poetry of 'The Faerie Queene'*. Princeton: Princeton University Press, 1967.
Alvis, John. *Shakespeare's Understanding of Honor*. Durham: Carolina Academic Press, 1990.
Anderson, Judith H. *Biographical Truth: The Representation of Historical Persons in Tudor-Stuart Writing*. New Haven: Yale University Press, 1984.
Anderson, Judith H. *Growth of a Personal Voice: 'Piers Plowman' and 'The Faerie Queene'*. New Haven: Yale University Press, 1976.
Anderson, Judith H. *Translating Investments: Metaphor and the Dynamic of Cultural Change in Tudor-Stuart England*. New York: Fordham University Press, 2005.

Anderson, Judith H. '*Venus and Adonis*: Spenser, Shakespeare, and the Forms of Desire.' *Grief and Gender, 700–1700*. Ed. Jennifer C. Vaught and Lynne Dickson Bruckner. New York: Palgrave, 2003. 149–60.

Anderson, Judith H. *Words That Matter: Linguistic Perception in Renaissance English*. Stanford: Stanford University Press, 1996.

Anderson, Judith H. 'Flowers and Boars: Surmounting Sexual Binarism in Spenser's Garden of Adonis.' Forthcoming, *Spenser Studies* 23 (2008).

Anderson, Judith H. 'Prudence and Her Silence: Spenser's Use of Chaucer's Melibee.' *ELH* 62 (1995): 29–46.

Anderson, Judith H. 'The Conspiracy of Realism: Impasse and Vision in *King Lear*.' *Studies in Philology* 84.1 (1987): 1–23.

André, Bernard. *Historia Regis Henrici Septimi* [c. 1502]. Ed. James Gairdner. London: Longman et al., 1858.

Apuleius. *The Golden Ass*. Trans. William Adlington. London, 1566.

Aquinas, Thomas. *Saint Thomas Aquinas: Philosophical Texts*. Selected and trans. Thomas Gilby. New York: Oxford University Press, 1960.

Aquinas, Thomas. *The Summa Theologica of Saint Thomas Aquinas*. Trans. Fathers of the Dominican Province. Chicago: Encyclopedia Britannica, 1952.

Aristotle. *Ethica Nichomachea. The Basic Works of Aristotle*. Trans. W. D. Ross, ed. Richard McKeon. New York: Random House, 1941. 927–1112.

Aristotle. *The Complete Works of Aristotle*, The Revised Oxford Translation, 2 vols. Ed. Jonathan Barnes. Princeton: Princeton UP, 1995.

Armstrong, Edward A. *Shakespeare's Imagination: A Study of the Psychology of Association and Inspiration*. 1946: Lincoln: University of Nebraska Press, 1963.

Arnold, Matthew. *On Translating Homer*. London: Longman, Green, Longman, and Roberts, 1861.

Atchity, Kenneth J., ed. *'Eterne in Mutabilitie': The Unity of 'The Faerie Queene'*. Hamden: Archon Books, 1972.

Attridge, Derek. *The Rhythms of English Poetry*. London: Longman, 1982.

'Augsburg Confession', The *Creeds of the Churches: A Reader in Christian Doctrine from the Bible to the Present*. 3rd ed. Ed. John H. Leith. Louisville: John Knox Press, 1982. 84–5.

Augustine. *The City of God*. Trans. John Healey. London: J.M. Dent, 1950.

Baker, Herschel. *The Image of Man*. New York: Barnes and Noble, 1952. (Orig. *The Dignity of Man*. Harvard: Harvard University Press, 1947.)

Baldwin, William, et al. *The Mirror for Magistrates*. Ed. Lily B. Campbell. 1938. New York: Barnes and Noble, 1960.

Barber, Charles Laurence. *The Idea of Honour in the English Drama 1591–1700*. Göteborg: Blom, 1957.

Barclay, Alexander. *The Eclogues of Alexander Barclay from the Original Edition by John Cawood.* Ed. Barbara White. 1928. London: Oxford University Press for Early English Text Society, 1960.
Barkan, Leonard. *The Gods Made Flesh: Metamorphosis and the Pursuit of Paganism.* New Haven: Yale University Press, 1986.
Bate, Jonathan. *Shakespeare and Ovid.* Oxford: Clarendon Press, 1993.
Battenhouse, Roy W. 'Henry V in the Light of Erasmus.' *Shakespeare Studies* 17 (1985): 77–88.
Battenhouse, Roy W. *Shakespearean Tragedy: Its Art and Christian Premises.* Bloomington: Indiana University Press, 1969.
Battenhouse, Roy W. *Shakespeare's Christian Dimension: An Anthology of Commentary.* Bloomington: Indiana University Press, 1994.
Battenhouse, Roy W. 'The Doctrine of Man in Calvin and in Renaissance Platonism.' *Journal of the History of Ideas* 9.4 (1948): 447–71.
Battenhouse, Roy W. 'The Relation of *Henry V* to *Tamburlaine*.' *Shakespeare Studies* 27 (1974): 71–9.
Beal, Peter. *Index of English Literary Manuscripts.* 4 vols. London: Mansell, 1980.
Beckwith, Sarah. 'Shakespeare's Resurrections.' Unpublished paper.
Bednarz, James P. *Shakespeare and the Poets' War.* New York: Columbia University Press, 2001.
Bednarz, James P. 'Imitations of Spenser in *A Midsummer Night's Dream*.' *Renaissance Drama* 14 (1983): 79–102.
Beecher, Donald. 'Introduction.' *Rosalind: Euphues' Golden Legacy Found After His Death in his Cell in Silexedra.* (1590.) Thomas Lodge. Ed. Donald Beecher. Ottawa: Dovehouse Editions, 1997.
Bellamy, Elizabeth J. 'Colin and Orphic Interpretation: Reading Neoplatonically on Spenser's Acidale.' *Comparative Literature Studies* 27 (1990): 172–92.
Bellamy, Elizabeth J. *Translations of Power: Narcissism and the Unconscious in Epic History.* Ithaca: Cornell University Press, 1992.
Bellamy, Elizabeth J. 'The Vocative and the Vocational: The Unreadability of Elizabeth in *The Faerie Queene*.' *ELH* 54 (1987): 1–30.
Belsey, Catherine. 'Love as Trompe-L'Oeil: Taxonomies of Desire in *Venus and Adonis*.' *Shakespeare Quarterly* 46 (1995): 257–76.
Benbow, R. M. 'The Providential Theory of Historical Causation in Holinshed's Chronicles 1577 and 1587.' *Texas Studies in Literature and Language* 1 (1959): 264–76.
Berger, Harry, Jr. 'Actaeon at the Hinder Gate: The Stag Party in Spenser's Gardens of Adonis.' *Desire in the Renaissance: Psychoanalysis and Literature.* Ed. Valeria Finucci and Regina Schwartz. Princeton: Princeton University Press, 1994. 91–119.
Berger, Harry, Jr. 'Archimago: Between Text and Countertext.' *Studies in English Literature* 43.1 (2003): 19–64.

Berger, Harry, Jr. 'A Secret Discipline: *The Faerie Queene* Book VI.' *Revisionary Play*. 215–42.
Berger, Harry, Jr. 'Bodies and Texts.' *Situated Utterances*. 99–128.
Berger, Harry, Jr. *Imaginary Audition: Shakespeare on Stage and Page*. 1989. Berkeley: University of California Press, 1991.
Berger, Harry, Jr. *Revisionary Play: Studies in the Spenserian Dynamics*. 1961. Berkeley: University of California Press, 1988.
Berger, Harry, Jr. *Situated Utterances: Texts, Bodies, and Cultural Representations*. New York: Fordham University Press, 2005.
Berger, Harry, Jr. *The Allegorical Temper: Vision and Reality in Book II of Spenser's 'Faerie Queene'*. New Haven: Yale University Press, 1957.
Berger, Harry, Jr. 'Narrative as Rhetoric in *The Faerie Queene*.' *English Literary Renaissance* 21 (1991): 3–48.
Berger, Harry, Jr. 'The Origins of Bucolic Representation: Disenchantment and Revision in Theocritus's Seventh Idyll.' *Situated Utterances*. 131–72.
Berger, Karol. 'Prospero's Art.' *Shakespeare Studies* 10 (1977): 211–39.
Bernheimer, Richard. *Wild Men in the Middle Ages*. Cambridge: Harvard University Press, 1952.
Berry, Philippa. *Shakespeare's Feminine Endings: Disfiguring Death in the Tragedies*. London: Routledge, 1999.
Bieman, Elizabeth. *Plato Baptized: Towards the Interpretation of Spenser's Mimetic Fictions*. University of Toronto Press, 1988.
Bion. 'Great Lament for Adonis.' *The Greek Bucolic Poets*. Trans. A. S. Gow. Cambridge: Cambridge University Press, 1953. 147.
Bishop, T. G. *Shakespeare and the Theatre of* Wonder. Cambridge: Cambridge University Press, 1996.
Blanc, Pauline. '"All Joy of the Worm": Tragi-Comic Tempering in Shakespeare's *Antony and Cleopatra*.' *Q/W/E/R/T/Y* 10 (2000): 5–18.
Bloomfield, Morton W. *The Seven Deadly Sins*. East Lansing: University of Michigan Press, 1952.
Bloom, Harold. *Shakespeare: The Invention of the Human*. New York: Riverhead, 1998.
Bloom, Harold. *The Anxiety of Influence*. New York: Oxford University Press, 1973.
Blythe, Joan Heiges. 'Spenser and the Seven Deadly Sins: Book 1, Cantos 4 and 5.' *ELH* 39 (1972): 342–52.
Boccaccio, Giovanni. *Genealogiae Joannis Boccatii*. (Venice 1494). Facsimile edition. Ed. Stephen Orgel. New York: Garland, 1976.
Bogel, Fredric V. *The Difference Satire Makes: Rhetoric and Reading from Jonson to Byron*. Ithaca: Cornell University Press, 2001.
Bolzani, G. P. Valeriano. *Hieroglyphica* (1556). Trans. (French) Jean de Montlyart. Lyon, 1615. Facsimile edition. Ed. Stephen Orgel. New York: Garland, 1976.

Bonciani, Francesco. 'Lezione Della Prosopopea' (1578). *Trattati del Poetica e Retorica del Cinquecento*. Vol. 3. Ed. Bernard Weinberg. Bari: Scrittori D'Italia, 1972.
Bongiorno, Andrew. *Castelvetro on the Art of Poetry: An Abridged Translation of Lodovico Castelvetro's* Poetica d'Aristotele Vulgarrizzata et Sposta. Binghamton: Center for Medieval and Renaissance Texts and Studies, 1984.
Bonjour, Adrian. 'From Shakespeare's Venus to Cleopatra's Cupids.' *Shakespeare Survey* 15 (1962): 73–80.
Bono, Barbara J. *Literary Transvaluation: From Vergilian Epic to Shakespearean Tragicomedy*. Berkeley: University of California Press, 1984.
Borris, Kenneth. '"Diuelish Ceremonies": Allegorical Satire of Protestant Extremism in *The Faerie Queene* VI.viii.31–51.' *Spenser Studies* 8 (1987): 175–209.
Borris, Kenneth. *Allegory and Epic in English Renaissance Literature: Heroic Form in Sidney, Spenser, and Milton*. Cambridge: Cambridge University Press, 2000.
Bradby, G. F. *Short Studies in Shakespeare*. London: J. Murray, 1929.
Brietz Monta, Susannah. *Martyrdom and Literature in Early Modern England*. Cambridge: Cambridge University Press, 2005.
Broaddus, James W. *Spenser's Allegory of Love*. Newark: University of Delaware Press, 1999.
Brooks-Davies, Douglas. *Spenser's 'Faerie Queene': A Critical Commentary on Books I and II*. Manchester: Manchester University Press, 1977.
Brooks-Davies, Douglas. 'Una.' *SpEncy*. Ed. A. C. Hamilton et al.
Brower, Reuben A. *Hero and Saint: Shakespeare and the Graeco-Roman Tradition*. Oxford: Oxford University Press, 1971.
Bruns, Gerald. *Modern Poetry and the Idea of Language: A Critical and Historical Study*. New Haven: Yale University Press, 1974.
Bruster, Douglas. *Quoting Shakespeare: Form and Culture in Early Modern Drama*. Lincoln: University of Nebraska Press, 2000.
Buchanan, George. *Ane Detectioun of the Duinges of Marie Quene of Scottes*. London, 1571.
Bullough, Geoffrey, ed. *Narrative and Dramatic Sources of Shakespeare*. 1960. London: Routledge and Kegan Paul, 1964.
Burchmore, David. 'Triamond, Agape, and the Fates: Neoplatonic Cosmology in Spenser's Legend of Friendship.' *Spenser Studies* 5 (1984): 45–64, 273–87.
Burrow, Colin. *Epic Romance: Homer to Milton*. Oxford: Clarendon, 1993.
Burrow, Colin. 'Original Fictions: Metamorphoses in *The Faerie Queene*.' *Ovid Renewed: Ovidian Influences on Literature and Art from the Middle Ages to the Twentieth Century*. Ed. Charles Martindale. Cambridge: Cambridge University Press, 1988. 99–119.

Burton, J. Anthony. 'Hamlet, Osric, and the Duel.' *Shakespeare Bulletin* 2.10 (1984): 5–7, 22–5.
Bush, Douglas. *Mythology and the Renaissance Tradition in English Poetry.* Rev. ed. Minneapolis: University of Minnesota Press, 1964.
Butler, Christopher and Alastair Fowler. 'Time-Beguiling Sport: Number Symbolism in Shakespeare's *Venus and Adonis*.' *Shakespeare 1564–1964*. Ed. Edward A. Bloom. Providence: Brown University Press, 1964. 124–33.
Butler, Todd. 'That "Saluage Nation": Contextualizing the Multitudes in Edmund Spenser's *The Faerie Queene*.' *Spenser Studies* 19 (2004): 93–124.
Cain, Thomas H. 'Elizabeth, Images of.' *SpEncy*. Ed. A. C. Hamilton et al.
Calepinus, Ambrosius. 'Adonis.' *Dictionarium . . . Additamenta Pauli Manutii*. Venice, 1571.
Campbell, Oscar James. *Shakespeare's Satire.* 1943. New York: Gordian Press, 1971.
Carlson, David. 'The Princes' Embrace in *Richard III*.' *Shakespeare Quarterly* 41 (1990): 344–7.
Carriero, Alessandro. *Breve e Ingenioso Discorso Contra L'Opera di Dante* (1582). *Trattati di Poetica e Retorica del Cinquecento.* Vol. 3. Ed. Bernard Weinberg. Bari: Laterza, 1972.
Carroll, William. *The Metamorphoses of Shakespeare's Comedy.* Princeton: Princeton University Press, 1985.
Carscallen, J. 'Temperance.' *SpEncy*. Ed. A. C. Hamilton et al.
Cartari, Vincenzo. *Les Images des Dieux des Anciens*. Lyon, 1581.
Cartelli, Thomas. *Marlowe, Shakespeare, and the Economy of Theatrical Experience.* Philadelphia: University of Pennsylvania Press, 1991.
Castelvetro, Ludovico. *Poetica D'Aristotele Vulgarizzata et Sposta per Lodovico Castelvetro.* Basle, 1576.
Celovsky, Lisa. 'Early Modern Masculinities and *The Faerie Queene*.' *English Literary Renaissance* 35 (2005): 210–47.
Charney, Maurice. *Style in Hamlet.* Princeton: Princeton University Press, 1969.
Chaudhuri, Sukanta. *Renaissance Pastoral and Its English Developments.* Oxford: Oxford University Press, 1989.
Chaudhuri, Supriya 'Metamorphosis.' *SpEncy*. Ed. A. C. Hamilton et al.
Cheney, Donald. *Spenser's Image of Nature.* New Haven: Yale University Press, 1966.
Cheney, Patrick. *Marlowe's Counterfeit Profession: Ovid, Spenser, Counter-Nationhood.* Toronto: University of Toronto Press, 1997.
Cheney, Patrick. *Shakespeare, National Poet-Playwright.* Cambridge: Cambridge University Press, 2004.

Cheney, Patrick. *Shakespeare's Literary Authorship*. Cambridge: Cambridge University Press, 2007.
Cheney, Patrick. *Spenser's Famous Flight: A Renaissance Idea of a Literary Career*. Toronto: University of Toronto Press, 1993.
Cheney, Patrick. 'Shakespeare's Sonnet 106, Spenser's National Epic, and Counter-Petrarchism.' *English Literary Renaissance* 31 (2001): 331–64.
Cheney, Patrick. 'Spenser's Pastorals: *The Shepheardes Calender* and *Colin Clouts Come Home Againe*.' *The Cambridge Companion to Spenser*. Ed. Andrew Hadfield. Cambridge: Cambridge University Press, 2001. 79–105.
Cheney, Patrick. 'The Old Poet Presents Himself: *Prothalamion* as a Defense of Spenser's Career.' *Spenser Studies* 8 (1990): 211–38.
Coddon, Karin S. '"Suche Strange Desygns": Madness, Subjectivity, and Treason in *Hamlet* and Elizabethan Culture.' *Renaissance Drama* 20 (1989): 51–75.
Comalada, Miguel de. *Desiderius, a Most Godly, Religious, and Delectable Dialogue, Teaching the True and Ready Way, by which we may Attayne to the Perfect Loue of God* .(1604). Ed. D. M. Rogers. Menston: Scolar Press, 1971.
Cook, Carol. 'The Fatal Cleopatra.' *Shakespearean Tragedy and Gender*. Ed. Shirley Nelson Garner and Madelon Sprengnether. Bloomington: Indiana University Press, 1996. 241–67.
Cooper, Helen. *The English Romance in Time: Transforming Motifs from Geoffrey of Monmouth to the Death of Shakespeare*. Oxford: Oxford University Press, 2004.
Cooper, Helen. 'Pastoral.' *SpEncy*. Ed. A. C. Hamilton et al.
Council, Norman. *When Honour's at the Stake: Ideas of Honour in Shakespeare's Plays*. London: George Allen and Unwin, 1973.
Covington, Sarah. *The Trail of Martyrdom: Persecution and Resistance in Sixteenth-Century England*. Notre Dame: University of Notre Dame Press, 2003.
Craft, William. *Labyrinth of Desire: Invention and Culture in the Work of Sir Philip Sidney*. Newark: University of Delaware Press, 1994.
Craft, William. 'Remaking the Heroic Self in the *New Arcadia*.' *Studies in English Literature* 25 (1985): 45–67.
Crewe, Jonathan. *Trials of Authorship: Anterior Forms and Poetic Reconstruction from Wyatt to Shakespeare*. Berkeley: University of California Press, 1990.
Crollius, Osvaldus. *Traité des signatures*. Lyon, 1624. In: Michel Foucault. *Order of Things: An Archaeology of the Human Sciences*. New York: Random House, 1973.
Crossett, John M. and Donald V. Stump, 'Spenser's Inferno: The Order of the Seven Deadly Sins at the Palace of Pride.' *Journal of Medieval and Renaissance Studies* 14 (1984): 203–18.

Cummings, Robert. 'Spenser's "Twelve Private Morall Virtues."' *Spenser Studies* 8 (1990): 35–59.
Cunningham, J. V. *Woe or Wonder: The Emotional Effect of Shakespearean Tragedy*. Denver: University of Denver Press, 1951.
Curtwright, Travis. 'Sidney's Defense of Poetry: Ethos and Ideas.' *Ben Jonson Journal* 10 (2003): 101–15.
Cutts, John P. 'Spenser, Shakespeare, and the "Bloody Babe."' *Neuphilologische Mitteilungen* 86.4 (1985): 506–14.
Cyr, Gordon C. 'Polonius as Lord Burleigh: Oxford's Revenge on His Father-in-Law?' *The Shakespeare Newsletter* 30.6 (1980): 48.
Deats, Sara Munson, ed. *'Antony and Cleopatra': New Critical Essays*. London: Routledge, 2005.
Deats, Sara Munson. 'Shakespeare's Anamorphic Drama: A Survey of *Antony and Cleopatra* in Criticism.' *'Antony and Cleopatra'*. Ed. Sara Munson Deats. 1–93.
De Grazia, Margreta. *Shakespeare Verbatim: The Reproduction of Authenticity and the 1790 Apparatus*. Oxford: Clarendon, 1991.
De Man, Paul. 'The Rhetoric of Temporality.' *Interpretation: Theory and Practice*. Ed. Charles S. Singleton. Baltimore: Johns Hopkins University Press, 1969. 173–209.
DeMoss, William F. *The Influence of Aristotle's 'Politics' and 'Ethics' on Spenser*. Chicago: University of Chicago Press, 1920.
DeMoss, William F. 'Spenser's Twelve Moral Virtues "According to Aristotle."' *Modern Philology* 16.5 (1918): 245–70.
De Nores, Giason. *Discorso Intorno a Que' Principii, Cause et Accrescimenti che la Comedia, La Tragedia, et il Poema Eroico Ricevono dalla Filosofia Morale e Civile e Da' Governatori delle Repubbliche* (1587). *Trattati di Poetica e Retorica del Cinquecento*. Vol. 3. Ed. Bernard Weinberg. Bari: Laterza, 1972.
Devereux, E. J. 'Sacramental Imagery in *The Tempest*.' *Bulletin de l'Association Canadienne des Humanités* 19 (1968): 50–62.
D'Ewes, Simonds, ed. *The Journals of all the Parliaments, during the Reign of Queen Elizabeth, Both of the House of Lords and House of Commons*. London, 1682.
Dixon, Michael F. N. *The Polliticke Courtier: Spenser's 'The Faerie Queene' as a Rhetoric of Justice*. Montreal and Kingston: McGill-Queen's University Press, 1996.
Dobson, Michael. *The Making of the National Poet: Shakespeare, Adaptation, and Authorship, 1660–1769*. Oxford: Clarendon, 1992.
Doerksen, Daniel W., and Christopher Hodgkins. *Centered on the Word: Literature, Scripture, and the Tudor-Stuart Middle Way*. Newark: University of Delaware Press, 2004.
Donaldson, E. Talbot. *The Swan at the Well: Shakespeare Reading Chaucer*. New Haven: Yale University Press, 1985.

Donnelly, M. L. 'The Life of Vergil and the Aspirations of the "New Poet."' *Spenser Studies* 17 (2003): 1–35.
Donno, E. S. 'Some Aspects of Shakespeare's Holinshed.' *Huntington Library Quarterly* 50 (1987): 229–48.
Du Bartas, Sieur. *The Divine Weeks and Works of Guillaume de Saluste.*. Ed. Susan Snyder. Trans. Josuah Sylvester. Oxford: Clarendon Press, 1979. I: 141–2.
Dughi, Thomas A. 'Redcrosse's "Springing Well" of Scriptural Faith.' *Studies in English Literature* 37 (1997): 21–38.
Duncan-Jones, Katherine. *Sir Philip Sidney: Courtier Poet*. New Haven: Yale University Press, 1991.
Duncan-Jones, Katherine. *Ungentle Shakespeare: Scenes from His Life*. Arden Shakespeare, 3rd Series. London: Thomson Learning, 2001.
Duncan-Jones, Katherine. 'Much Ado with Red and White: The Earliest Readers of Shakespeare's *Venus and Adonis* (1593).' *Review of English Studies* 44 (1993): 479–501.
Duncan-Jones, Katherine. 'Was the 1609 Shake-Speares Sonnets Really Unauthorized?' *RES* 34 (1983): 151–71.
Dunlop, Alexander. 'Number Symbolism, Modern Studies in.' *SpEncy*. Ed. A. C. Hamilton et al.
Dunlop, Alexander. 'The Drama of *Amoretti*.' *Spenser Studies* 1 (1980): 107–20.
Dunlop, Alexander. 'The Unity of Spenser's *Amoretti*.' *Silent Poetry*. Ed. Alastair Fowler. London: Routledge, 1970. 153–69.
Durling, Robert M., ed. and trans. *Petrarch's Lyric Poems: The "Rime sparse" and Other Lyrics*. Cambridge, MA: Harvard University Press, 1976.
Dutton, Richard, Alison Findlay, and Richard Wilson, ed. *Region, Religion, and Patronage: Lancastrian Shakespeare*. Manchester: Manchester University Press, 2003.
Dutton, Richard. '*Volpone* and Beast Fable: Early Modern Analogic Reading.' *Huntington Library Quarterly* 67 (2004): 347–70.
Dutton, Richard. Review of *Shakespeare, National Poet-Playwright* by Patrick Cheney. *Shakespeare Quarterly* 56 (2005): 371–4.
Eccles, Mark. 'Burghley, William Cecil, Lord.' *SpEncy*. Ed. A. C. Hamilton et al.
Eggert, Katherine. *Showing like a Queen: Female Authority and Literary Experiment in Spenser, Shakespeare, and Milton*. Philadelphia: University of Pennsylvania Press, 2000.
Eliot, T. S. 'Christopher Marlowe.' *Selected Essays*. New ed. New York: Harcourt, Brace & Co., 1950. 100–6.
Elliott, W. E. Y. 'A Touchstone for the Bard.' *Computers and the Humanities*, 25 (1991): 199–209.

Ellison, James. 'The Winter's Tale and the Religious Politics of Europe'. *Shakespeare's Romances*. Ed. Alison Thorne. New Casebooks. Basingstoke: Palgrave Macmillan, 2003. 171–204.

To the Seminarye Priests lately come ouer some like Gentlemen, some like Marchants, some like Seruing-men, and some like Maymed Soldiours: who in Wordes Speake like Angelles of Light, but are Angelles of Darkenes, and so Proued in this Small Pamphlet. London, 1592.

Enos, Carol. 'Catholic Exiles in Flanders and *As You Like It*; or, What If You Don't Like It At All?' *Theatre and Religion: Lancastrian Shakespeare*. Ed. Richard Dutton, Alison Findlay, and Richard Wilson. Manchester: Manchester University Press, 2003. 130–42.

Enterline, Lynn. *The Rhetoric of the Body: From Ovid to Shakespeare*. Cambridge: Cambridge University Press, 2000.

Erasmus, Desiderius. 'Adonidis horti.' *The Adages of Erasmus*. Ed. William Barker. Toronto: Toronto Univ. Press, 2001. 31–2.

Erasmus, Desiderius. *Enchiridion Militis Christiani, An English Version*. Ed. Anne M. O'Donnell. S.N.D. for Early English Text Society. Oxford: Oxford University Press, 1981.

Erickson, Peter. *Rewriting Shakespeare, Rewriting Ourselves*. Berkeley: University of California Press, 1991.

Erne, Lukas. *Shakespeare as Literary Dramatist*. Cambridge: Cambridge University Press, 2003.

Esler, Anthony. *The Aspiring Mind of the Elizabethan Younger Generation*. Durham: Duke University Press, 1966.

Esolen, Anthony. '"The Isles Shall Wait for His Law": Isaiah and *The Tempest*.' *Studies in Philology* 94 (1997): 221–48.

Estienne, Charles. 'Adonis.' *Dictionarium Historicum, Geographicum, Poeticum* [1553; Paris, 1596]. Facsimile edition. Ed. Stephen Orgel. New York: Garland: 1976.

Estrin, Barbara L. *The Raven and the Lark: Lost Children in Literature of the English Renaissance*. Lewisburg: Bucknell University Press, 1985.

Estrin, Barbara. 'The Foundling Plot: Stories in *The Winter's Tale*.' *Modern Language Studies* 7 (1977): 27–38.

Fichter, Andrew. *Poets Historical: Dynastic Epic in the Renaissance*. New Haven: Yale University Press, 1982.

Fletcher, Angus. *Allegory: The Theory of a Symbolic Mode*. Ithaca: Cornell University Press, 1964.

Forker, Charles R. 'Perdita's Distribution of Flowers and the Function of Lyricism in *The Winter's Tale*.' *Fancy's Images: Contexts, Settings, and Perspectives in Shakespeare and His Contemporaries*. Carbondale: Southern Illinois University Press, 1990. 113–26.

Fowler, Alastair. 'Emanations of Glory: Neoplatonic Order in Spenser's *Faerie Queene*.' *A Theatre for Spenserians*. Ed. Judith M. Kennedy and James M. Reither. Toronto: University of Toronto Press, 1973. 53–82.

Fowler, Alastair. *Conceitful Thought: The Interpretation of English Renaissance Poems*. Edinburgh: University of Edinburgh Press, 1975.
Fowler, Alastair. *Spenser and the Numbers of Time*. London: Routledge and Kegan Paul, 1964.
Fowler, Alastair. 'Spenser's *Prothalamion*.' *Conceitful Thought: The Interpretation of English Renaissance Poems*. Edinburgh: University of Edinburgh Press, 1975. 79–85.
Fracastoro, Girolamo. *Naugerius, Sive De Poetica Dialogus*. Trans. Ruth Kelso. Chicago: University of Illinois Press, 1924.
Freinkel, Lisa. *Reading Shakespeare's Will: The Theology of Figure from Augustine to the Sonnets*. New York: Columbia University Press, 2002.
Freinkel, Lisa. 'The Name of the Rose: Christian Figurality and Shakespeare's Sonnets.' *Shakespeare's Sonnets: Critical Essays*. Ed. James Schiffer. New York: Garland, 1999. 241–61.
Fruen, Jeffrey P. 'The Faerie Queene Unveiled? Five Glimpses of Gloriana.' *Spenser Studies* 11 (1994): 53–88.
Fruen, Jeffrey P. '"True Glorious Type": The Place of Gloriana in *The Faerie Queene*.' *Spenser Studies* 7 (1987): 147–73.
Frye, Northrop. 'Recognition in *The Winter's Tale*.' *Fables of Identity: Studies in Poetic Mythology*. New York: Harcourt-Harbinger, 1963. 107–18.
Fulke, William. *A Treatise Against the Defense of the Censure* [...]. Cambridge, 1586.
Garber, Marjorie. *Shakespeare After All*. New York: Pantheon, 2004.
Garber, Marjorie. *Shakespeare's Ghost Writers: Literature as Uncanny Causality*. New York: Routledge, 1987.
Gardner, Helen. *'King Lear': The John Coffin Memorial Lecture delivered before the University of London on 2 March 1966*. London: The Athlone Press, 1968.
Gilbert, Allan H., ed. *Literary Criticism: Plato to Dryden*. 1940. Detroit: Wayne State University Press, 1962.
Gless, Darryl J. *Interpretation and Theology in Spenser*. Cambridge: Cambridge University Press, 1994.
Gless, Darryl J. 'Nature and Grace.' *SpEncy*. Ed. A. C. Hamilton et al.
Goddard, Harold C. *The Meaning of Shakespeare*. 1951. 2 vols. Chicago: University of Chicago Press, 1960.
Goldberg, Jonathan. *Endlesse Worke: Spenser and the Structures of Discourse*. Baltimore: Johns Hopkins University Press, 1981.
Goldman, Marcus. *Sir Philip Sidney and 'The Arcadia'*. Urbana: University of Illinois, 1934.
Goldman, Michael. '*Antony and Cleopatra*: Action as Imaginative Command.' *Shakespeare's Late Tragedies: A Collection of Critical Essays*. Ed. Susanne L. Wofford. Upper Saddle River: Prentice Hall, 1996. 249–67.

Googe, Barnabe. *Eclogues, Epitaphs, and Sonnets*. Ed. Judith M. Kennedy. Toronto: University of Toronto Press, 1989.
Gottfried, Rudolph B. 'Spenser's *View* and Essex.' *PMLA* 52 (1937): 645–51.
Greenblatt, Stephen. *Renaissance Self-Fashioning*. Chicago: University of Chicago Press, 1980.
Greenblatt, Stephen. *Will in the World: How Shakespeare Became Shakespeare*. New York: Norton, 2004.
Greenblatt, Stephen. *King Lear. The Norton Shakespeare*. Ed. Stephen Greenblatt. New York: Norton, 1997. 2307–2316.
Greenblatt, Stephen J. *Shakespearean Negotiations: The Circulation of Social Energy in Renaissance England*. Oxford: Clarendon Press, 1990.
Greenfield, Sayre. 'Allegorical Impulses and Critical Ends: Shakespeare's and Spenser's Venus and Adonis.' *Criticism* 36 (1994): 475–98.
Green, Martin. *Wriothesley's Roses in Shakespearean Sonnets, Poems and Plays*. Baltimore: Clevedon Books, 1993.
Gregerson, Linda. *The Reformation of the Subject: Spenser, Milton, and the English Protestant Epic*. Cambridge: Cambridge University Press, 1995.
Gregory, Brad S. *Salvation at Stake: Christian Martyrdom in Early Modern Europe*. Cambridge, MA: Harvard University Press, 1999.
Grell, Ole Peter, and Bob Scribner, ed. *Tolerance and Intolerance in the European Reformation*. Cambridge: Cambridge University Press, 1996.
Grell, Ole Peter. 'Exile and Tolerance.' *Tolerance and Intolerance in the European Reformation*. Ed. Ole Peter Grell and Bob Scribner. 182–98.
Gross, Kenneth. *Spenserian Poetics: Idolatry, Iconoclasm, and Magic*. Ithaca: Cornell University Press, 1985.
Grossman, Marshall. *The Story of All Things: Writing the Self in English Renaissance Narrative Poetry*. Durham, NC and London: Duke University Press, 1998.
Guillory, John. 'Milton, Narcissism, Gender: On the Genealogy of Male Self-Esteem.' *Critical Essays on John Milton*. Ed. Christopher Kendrick. New York: G.K. Hale, 1995. 194–233.
Guy-Bray, Stephen. '*The Winter's Tale.*' *Homoerotic Space: The Poetics of Loss in Renaissance Literature*. Toronto: University of Toronto Press, 2002. 198–215.
Hadfield, Andrew. *Edmund Spenser's Irish Experience: Wilde Fruit and Salvage Soyl*. Oxford: Clarendon Press, 1997.
Hadfield, Andrew. *Shakespeare, Spenser, and the Matter of Britain*. New York: Palgrave Macmillan, 2004.
Hadfield, Andrew. 'The "Sacred Hunger of Ambitious Minds": Spenser's Savage Religion.' *Edmund Spenser*. Ed. Andrew Hadfield. London: Longman, 1996. 177–95.

Hadfield, Andrew. '"Who knowes not Colin Clout?" The Permanent Exile of Edmund Spenser.' *Politics and National Identity: Reformation to Renaissance.* Ed. Cambridge: Cambridge University Press, 1994. 170–201.

Haebreo, Jacob Mantino Hispano. *Aristotelis De Rhetorica, Et Poetica Libri cum Averrois in Eosdem Paraphrasibus, Venetiis apud Junctas.* 1562. Vol. 2. Facsimile edition. Frankfurt am Main: Minerva Press, 1962.

Hall, Edward. *The Union of the Two Noble and Illustre Famelies of Lancastre and Yorke.* London, 1548.

Hamilton, A. C. 'A Theological Reading of *The Faerie Queene,* Book II.' *ELH* 25.3 (1958): 155–62.

Hamilton, A. C. *The Structure of Allegory in* The Faerie Queene. Oxford: Clarendon Press, 1961.

Hamilton, A. C., gen. ed. *Spenser Encyclopedia.* Toronto: University of Toronto Press, 1990.

Hamilton, A. C. 'The *Architectonike* of the Poem.' *The Structure of Allegory.* 89–123.

Hamilton, A. C. 'Venus and Adonis.' *Studies in English Literature* 1 (1961): 1–15.

Hamilton, Donna. *Anthony Munday and the Catholics.* Aldershot: Ashgate, 2005.

Hamilton, Donna. *Virgil and 'The Tempest': The Politics of Imitation.* Columbus: Ohio State University Press, 1990.

Hammer, Paul E. J. 'Devereux, Robert, Second Earl of Essex.' *Oxford Dictionary of National Biography.* Vol. 15. Oxford: Oxford University Press, 2004.

Hammer, Paul E. J. *The Polarization of Elizabethan Politics: The Political Career of Robert Devereux, 2nd Earl of Essex, 1585–1597.* Vol. 1. Cambridge: Cambridge University Press, 1999.

Hanford, James Holly and Sara Ruth Watson. 'Personal Allegory in the *Arcadia*: Philisides and Lelius.' *Modern Philology* 32 (1934): 1–10.

Hanham, Alison. *Richard the Third and his Early Historians.* Oxford: Clarendon Press, 1975.

Hankins, John Erskine. *Source and Meaning in Spenser's Allegory: A Study of 'The Faerie Queene'.* Oxford: Clarendon, 1971.

Harris, Brice. 'The Ape in *Mother Hubberds Tale.*' *Huntington Library Quarterly* 4 (1941): 191–203.

Harrison, G. B. *The Life and Death of Robert Devereux, Earl of Essex.* New York: Henry Holt, 1937.

Harrison, Thomas P. *They Tell of Birds: Chaucer, Spenser, Milton, Drayton.* Austin: University of Texas Press, 1956.

Hart, Alfred. 'The Growth of Shakespeare's Vocabulary.' *Renaissance English Studies* 75 (1943): 242–54.

Hart, Alfred. 'Vocabularies of Shakespeare's Plays.' *Renaissance English Studies* 74 (1943): 128–40.

Harvey, Gabriel. *Foure Letters and Certaine Sonnets*. 1592. *Spenser: The Critical Heritage*. Ed. R. M. Cummings. London: Routledge and Kegan Paul, 1971.
Harwood, Ellen A. 'Venus and Adonis: Shakespeare's Critique of Spenser.' *Journal of the Rutgers University Libraries* 39 (1977): 44–60.
Hatto, A. T. 'Venus and Adonis – and the Boar.' *Modern Language Review* 41 (1946): 353–61.
Haynes, Alan. *Robert Cecil, Earl of Salisbury, 1563–1612: Servant of Two Sovereigns*. London: Peter Owen, 1989.
Hays, Michael L. *Shakespearean Tragedy as Chivalric Romance: Rethinking 'Macbeth', 'Hamlet', 'Othello', and 'King Lear'*. London: Boydell and Brewer, 2003.
Hedrick, Donald K. '"It Is No Novelty for a Prince to Be a Prince": An Enantiomorphous Hamlet.' *Shakespeare Quarterly* 35 (1984): 72–6.
Heffner, Ray. 'Essex and Book Five of *The Faerie Queene*.' *ELH* 3 (1936): 67–82.
Heffner, Ray. 'Essex, the Ideal Courtier.' *ELH* 1 (1934): 7–36.
Heinemann, Margot. '"Let Rome in Tiber Melt": Order and Disorder in *Antony and Cleopatra*.' *New Casebooks: 'Antony and Cleopatra'*. Ed. John Drakakis. London: Macmillan, 1994. 166–81.
Helgerson, Richard. *Self-Crowned Laureates: Spenser, Jonson, Milton, and the Literary System*. Berkeley: University of California Press, 1983.
Heninger, S. K., Jr. *Touches of Sweet Harmony: Pythagorean Cosmology and Renaissance Poetics*. San Marino: Huntington Library, 1974.
Herendeen, W. H. 'Gloriana.' *SpEncy*. Ed. A. C. Hamilton et al.
Herron, Thomas. 'Exotic Beasts: The Earl of Ormond and Nicholas Dawtry in "Mother Hubberds Tale."' *Spenser Studies* 19 (2004): 245–51.
Hibbard Loomis, Laura A. *Medieval Romance in England*. 1924. New York: Burt Franklin, 1960.
Hieatt, A. Kent. *Short Time's Endless Monument: The Symbolism of the Numbers in Edmund Spenser's "Epithalamion."* New York: Columbia Univerity Press, 1960.
Hieatt, A. Kent. 'Shakespeare, William.' *SpEncy*. Ed. A. C. Hamilton et al.
Hieatt, A. Kent. 'The Genesis of Shakespeare's Sonnets: Spenser's *Ruines of Rome: By Bellay*.' *PMLA* 98 (1983): 800–14.
Highley, Christopher. *Shakespeare, Spenser, and Ireland*. Cambridge: Cambridge University Press, 1997.
Highley, Christopher. '"Lost British Lamb": English Catholic Exiles and the Problem of Britain.' *British Identities and English Renaissance Literature*. Ed. David J. Baker and Willy Maley. Cambridge: Cambridge University Press, 2002.
Hinds, Stephen. *The Metamorphosis of Persephone: Ovid and the Self-Conscious Muse*. Cambridge: Cambridge University Press, 1997.

Hirsch, James. 'Rome and Egypt in *Antony and Cleopatra* and in Criticism of the Play.' *'Antony and Cleopatra'*. Ed. Sara Munson Deats. 175–91.
Holahan, Michael. '*Iamque Opus Exegi*: Ovid's Changes and Spenser's Brief Epic of Mutability.' *English Literary Renaissance* 6 (1976): 244–70:
Holahan, Michael. 'Ovid.' *SpEncy*. Ed. A. C. Hamilton et al.
Hopkins, Lisa. 'Cleopatra and the Myth of Scota.' *'Antony and Cleopatra'*. Ed. Sara Munson Deats. 231–42.
Horton, Ronald A. 'Aristotle and his Commentators.' *SpEncy*. Ed. A. C. Hamilton et al.
Horton, Ronald A. *The Unity of 'The Faerie Queene'*. Athens: University of Georgia Press, 1978.
Horton, Ronald A. 'Virtues.' *SpEncy*. Ed. A. C. Hamilton et al.
Hotson, Leslie. *The First Night of 'Twelfth Night'*. London: Hart-Davis, 1954.
Howell, Roger. *Sir Philip Sidney: The Shepherd Knight*. Toronto: Little, Brown and Company, 1968.
Hughes, Merrit Y. *Virgil and Spenser*. Berkeley: University of California Press, 1929.
Hulse, Clark. 'Shakespeare's Myth of Venus and Adonis.' *PMLA* 93 (1978): 95–105.
Hume, Anthea. 'Love's Martyr, "The Phoenix and the Turtle," and the Aftermath of the Essex Rebellion.' *Review of English Studies* 40 (1989): 48–71.
Humfrey, Belinda. 'Dragons.' *SpEncy*. Ed. A. C. Hamilton et al.
Hunter, Edwin R. *Shakespeare and the Common Sense*. Boston: Christopher Publishing, 1954.
Hunter, Robert G. *Shakespeare and the Comedy of Forgiveness*. New York: Columbia University Press, 1965.
Hunt, Maurice. 'A Speculative Political Allegory in *A Midsummer Night's Dream*.' *Comparative Drama* 34 (2000–1): 423–53.
Hunt, Maurice. '"Standing in Rich Place": The Importance of Context in *The Winter's Tale*.' *Rocky Mountain Review of Language and Literature* 38 (1984): 13–33.
Ide, Richard S. *Possessed with Greatness: The Heroic Tragedies of Chapman and Shakespeare*. Chapel Hill: University of North Carolina Press, 1980.
Iser, Wolfgang. *The Fictive and the Imaginary: Charting Literary Anthropology*. Baltimore: Johns Hopkins University Press, 1993.
James, Heather. *Shakespeare's Troy: Drama, Politics, and the Translation of Empire*. Cambridge: Cambridge University Press, 1997.
James, Heather. 'Ovid and the Question of Politics in Early Modern England.' *Images of Matter: Essays on British Literature of the Middle Ages*

and *Renaissance*. Ed. Yvonne Bruce. Newark: University of Delaware Press, 2005. 92–122.

James, Heather. 'The Politics of Display and the Anamorphic Subjects of *Antony and Cleopatra*.' *Shakespeare's Late Tragedies: A Collection of Critical Essays*. Ed. Susanne L. Wofford. Upper Saddle River: Prentice Hall, 1996. 208–34.

James, Mervyn. *Society, Politics and Culture: Studies in Early Modern England*. Cambridge: Cambridge University Press, 1986.

Javitch, Daniel: 'Rescuing Ovid from the Allegorizers.' *Comparative Literature* 30 (1978): 97–107.

Jerome, Saint. *Certain Selected Epistles of S. Hierome as also the Liues of Saint Paul the First Hermite, of Saint Hilarian the First Monke of Syria* [...]. Trans. Henry Hawkins. Saint Omer, 1630.

Jerome, Saint. *Vitas Patrum*. (Wesmynstre, 1495). Amsterdam: Theatrum Orbis Terrarum, 1977.

Johnson, W. R. 'The Problem of the Counter-Classical Sensibility and Its Critics.' *California Studies in Classical Antiquity* 3 (1970): 123–51.

Jordan, Constance. *Shakespeare's Monarchies: Ruler and Subject in the Romances*. Ithaca: Cornell University Press, 1997.

Judson, A. C. 'Mother Hubberd's Ape.' *Modern Language Notes* 63 (1948): 145–9.

Kahan, Jeffrey. 'Shakespeare's *Julius Caesar* and the Anticipation of 1603.' *Cithara* 44 (2004): 3–21.

Kahn, Coppélia. *Roman Shakespeare: Warriors, Wounds, and Women*. London: Routledge, 1997.

Kane, Sean. *Spenser's Moral Allegory*. Toronto: University of Toronto Press, 1989.

Kaplan, M. Lindsay, and Katherine Eggert. '"Good Queen, my Lord, Good Queen": Sexual Slander and the Trials of Female Authority in *The Winter's Tale*.' *Renaissance Drama* 25 (1994): 89–118.

Kaske, Carol V. 'Amavia, Mortdant, Ruddymane.' *SpEncy*. Ed. A. C. Hamilton et al.

Kaske, Carol V. 'Spenser's *Amoretti* and *Epithalamion* of 1595: Structure, Genre, and Numerology.' *English Literary Renaissance* 8 (1978): 271–95.

Kaske, Carol V. 'The Dragon's Spark and Sting and the Structure of Red Cross's Dragon-Fight: *The Faerie Queene*, I xi-xii.' *Studies in Philology* 66 (1969): 609–38.

Kastan, David Scott. *Shakespeare and the Book*. Cambridge: Cambridge University Press, 2001.

Kelley, Henry A. *Divine Providence in the England of Shakespeare's Histories*. Cambridge, MA: Harvard University Press.

Kelsey, Harry. *Sir Francis Drake: The Queen's Pirate*. 1998. New Haven: Yale University Press, 2000.

Kennedy, William J. 'Diana.' *SpEncy*. Ed. A. C. Hamilton et al.

Kennedy, William J. 'Paynims.' *SpEncy*. Ed. A. C. Hamilton et al.
Kennedy, William J. 'Shakespeare and the Development of English Poetry.' *The Cambridge Companion to Shakespeare's Poetry*. Ed. Patrick Cheney. Cambridge: Cambridge University Press, 2007. 14–32.
Kennedy, William J. 'Virgil.' *SpEncy*. Ed. A. C. Hamilton et al.
Kermode, Frank. *Shakespeare's Language*. London: Allen Lane, 2000.
Kernan, Alvin. *The Cankered Muse: Satire of the English Renaissance*. New Haven: Yale University Press, 1959.
Kiernan, Pauline. *Shakespeare's Theory of Drama*. Cambridge: Cambridge University Press, 1996.
King, Andrew. *The Faerie Queene and Middle English Romance: The Matter of Just Memory*. Oxford: Oxford University Press, 2000.
King, John N. *Spenser's Poetry and the Reformation Tradition*. Princeton: Princeton University Press, 1990.
Kinney, Clare R. 'Feigning Female Faining: Spenser, Lodge, Shakespeare, and Rosalind.' *Modern Philology* 95.3 (1998): 291–315.
Klein, Joan Larsen. 'Bacchus.' *SpEncy*. Ed. A. C. Hamilton et al.
Kliman, Bernice W. 'Three Notes on Polonius: Position, Residence, and Name.' *Shakespeare Bulletin* 20 (2002): 5–7.
Kolin, Philip C. *'Venus and Adonis': Critical Essays*. New York: Garland, 1997.
Kott, Jan. 'The *Aeneid* and *The Tempest*.' *Arion* 3.4 (1976): 424–51.
Kott, Jan. '*The Tempest*, or Repetition.' *Mosaic* 10 (1977): 9–36.
Kouwenhoven, Jan Karel. *Apparent Narrative as Thematic Metaphor: The Organization of The Faerie Queene*. Oxford: Clarendon Press, 1983.
Krier, Theresa M. 'Mother's Sorrow, Mother's Joy: Mourning Birth in Edmund Spenser's Garden of Adonis.' *Grief and Gender, 700–1700*. Ed. Jennifer C. Vaught and Lynne Dickson Bruckner. New York: Palgrave, 2003. 133–47.
Lacey, Robert. *Robert, Earl of Essex: An Elizabethan Icarus*. London: Weidenfeld and Nicolson, 1971.
Lakowski, Romuald Ian. 'From History to Myth: the Misogyny of Richard III in More's History and Shakespeare's Play.' *Q/W/E/R/T/Y* 9 (1999): 15–23.
Lall, Rama Rani. *Satiric Fable in English: A Critical Study of the Animal Tales of Chaucer, Spenser, Dryden, and Orwell*. New Delhi: New Statesman Publishing, 1979.
Langston, Beach. 'Essex and the Art of Dying.' *Huntington Library Quarterly* 2 (1950): 109–29.
Laqueur, Thomas. *Making Sex: Body and Gender from the Greeks to Freud*. Cambridge, MA: Harvard University Press, 1990.
Latham, Agnes. 'Introduction.' *The Arden Edition of the Works of William Shakespeare: As You Like It*. Ed. Agnes Latham. London: Methuen, 1975. i–xcv.

Latz, Dorothy. 'Introduction.' *Neglected English Literature: Recusant Writings of the 16th–17th Centuries*. Salzburg: Institut für Anglistik und Amerikanistik Universität Salzburg, 1997.
Le Comte, Edward S. 'The Ending of *Hamlet* as a Farewell to Essex.' *ELH: Journal of English Literary History* 17 (1950): 87–114.
Lee, John. *Shakespeare's 'Hamlet' and the Controversies of Self*. Oxford: Oxford University Press, 2000.
Legge, Thomas. *The Complete Plays. Volume 1: Richardus Tertius*. Ed. and trans. Dana F. Sutton. New York: Peter Lang, 1993.
Lepage, John Louis. 'Mutability.' *SpEncy*. Ed. A. C. Hamilton et al.
Leslie, Michael. *Spenser's 'Fierce Warres and Faithfull Loves': Martial and Chivalric Symbolism in 'The Faerie Queene'*. Cambridge: Cambridge University Press, 1983. 68–84.
Lethbridge, J. B. 'Introduction.' *Edmund Spenser: New and Renewed Directions*. Ed. J. B. Lethbridge. Madison: Fairleigh Dickinson University Press, 2006. 15–57.
Lethbridge, J. B. 'Spenser's Last Days: Ireland, Career, Mutability, Allegory.' *Edmund Spenser: New and Renewed Directions*. Madison: Fairleigh Dickinson University Press, 2006. 302–36.
Lever, J. W. 'Venus and the Second Chance.' *Shakespeare Survey* 15 (1962): 81–8.
Levin, Richard A. 'The Legende of the Redcrosse Knight and Una: Or, Of the Love of a Good Woman.' *Studies in English Literature* 31.1 (1991): 1–24.
Leyburn, Ellen Douglas. *Satiric Allegory: Mirror of Man*. New Haven: Yale University Press, 1969.
Lindheim, Nancy. 'The Shakespearean *Venus and Adonis*.' *Shakespeare Quarterly* 37 (1986): 190–203.
Littlehales, Margaret Mary. *Mary Ward: Pilgrim and Mystic 1585–1645*. 1998. London: Burns and Oates, 2001.
Lloyd, Lodowick. *First Part of the Diall of Daies*. London, 1590.
Logan, Robert A. '"High Events as These": Sources, Influences, and the Artistry of *Antony and Cleopatra*.' *'Antony and Cleopatra'*. Ed. Sara Munson Deats. 153–74.
Loomba, Ania. 'Theatre and the Space of the Other in *Antony and Cleopatra*.' *Shakespeare's Late Tragedies: A Collection of Critical Essays*. Ed. Susanne L. Wofford. Upper Saddle River: Prentice Hall, 1996. 235–48.
Loomba, Ania. '"Travelling Thoughts": Theatre and the Space of the Other.' *New Casebooks: 'Antony and Cleopatra'*. Ed. John Drakakis. London: Macmillan, 1994. 279–307.
Lyotard, Jean-François. 'The Dream-Work Does Not Think.' Trans. Mary Lydon. *The Lyotard Reader*. Ed. Andrew Benjamin. Oxford: Blackwell, 1989. 19–55.

MacLachlan, Hugh, and Philip B. Rollinson. 'Magnanimity, Magnificence.' *SpEncy*. Ed. A. C. Hamilton et al.
MacLure, Millar. 'Nature and Art in *The Faerie Queene*.' *Critical Essays on Spenser from 'ELH'*. Baltimore: Johns Hopkins University Press, 1970. 138–57.
Macrobius. *The Saturnalia*. Trans. and ed. Percival Vaughan Davies. New York: Columbia University Press, 1969. 141–2.
Magnusson, Lynne. 'Finding Place for a Faultless Lyric: Verbal Virtuosity in *The Winter's Tale*.' *Upstart Crow* 9 (1989): 96–106.
Mallette, Richard. 'Book Five of *The Faerie Queene*: An Elizabethan Apocalypse.' *Spenser Studies* 11 (1994): 129–59.
Mallette, Richard. *Spenser and the Discourses of Reformation England*. Lincoln: University of Nebraska Press, 1997.
Mallette, Richard. 'Rosalind.' *SpEncy*. Ed. A. C. Hamilton et al.
Mallin, Eric S. *Inscribing the Time: Shakespeare and the End of Elizabethan England*. Berkeley: University of California Press, 1995.
Mallin, Eric S. 'Emulous Factions and the Collapse of Chivalry: *Troilus and Cressida*.' *Representations* 29 (1990): 145–79.
Mantuanus, Baptista (Spagnoli). *Adulescentia: The Eclogues of Mantuan*. Ed. and trans. Lee Piepho. New York: Garland, 1989.
Marcus, Leah S. *Puzzling Shakespeare: Local Reading and Its Discontents*. Berkeley: University of California Press, 1988.
Marotti, Arthur F. 'Alienating Catholics in Early Modern England: Recusant Women, Jesuits and Ideological Fantasies.' *Catholicism and Anti-Catholicism in Early Modern English Texts*. Ed. Arthur F. Marotti. New York: Macmillan, 1999. 1–34.
Marotti, Arthur F. *Religious Ideology and Cultural Fantasy: Catholic and anti-Catholic Discourses in Early Modern England*. Notre Dame: University of Notre Dame Press, 2005.
Marotti, Arthur F. '"Love Is Not Love": Elizabethan Sonnet Sequences and the Social Order.' *ELH* 49 (1982): 396–428.
Marotti, Arthur F. 'Manuscript Transmission and the Catholic Martyrdom Account in Early Modern England.' *Print, Manuscript, and Performance: The Changing Relations of the Media in Early Modern England*. Ed. Arthur F. Marotti and Michael D. Bristol. Columbus: Ohio State University Press, 2000. 172–99.
Marquis, Paul A. 'Problems of Closure in *The Faerie Queene*.' *English Studies in Canada* 16 (1990): 149–63.
Martindale, Charles, and Colin Burrow. 'Clapham's *Narcissus*: A Pretext for Shakespeare's *Venus and Adonis*? (text, translation, commentary)' *English Literary Renaissance* 22 (1992): 147–76.
Maslen, R.W. '*Venus and Adonis* and the Death of Orpheus.' *The Glasgow Review* 1 (1993): 67–78. 1 December 2007. http://www.arts.gla.ac.uk/sesll/stella/comet/glasrev/issue1.

Mayor, Joseph B. *Chapters on English Metre*. 2nd ed. Cambridge: Cambridge University Press, 1901.
McAlindon, Tom. '*King Lear* and the Politics of the Heart.' *Shakespeare Survey* 44 (1991): 85–90.
McCabe, Richard A. *Spenser's Monstrous Regiment: Elizabethan Ireland and the Poetics of Difference*. Oxford: Oxford University Press, 2002.
McCabe, Richard A. *The Pillars of Eternity: Time and Providence in 'The Faerie Queene'*. Dublin: Irish Academic Press, 1989.
McCoy, Richard C. '"A Dangerous Image": The Earl of Essex and Elizabethan Chivalry.' *Journal of Medieval and Renaissance Studies* 13 (1983): 313–29.
McDonald, Russ. *Shakespeare and Jonson / Jonson and Shakespeare*. Lincoln: University of Nebraska Press, 1988.
McDonald, Russ. 'Marlowe and Style.' *The Cambridge Companion to Christopher Marlowe*. Ed. Patrick Cheney. Cambridge: Cambridge University Press, 2004. 55–69.
McLane, Paul E. *Spenser's 'Shepheardes Calender': A Study in Elizabethan Allegory*. Notre Dame: University of Notre Dame Press, 1961.
McNamee, Maurice B. *Honor and the Epic Hero: A Study of the Shifting Concept of Magnanimity in Philosophy and Epic Poetry*. New York: Holt, Rinehart and Winston, 1960.
McPherson, David C. 'A Possible Origin for Mopsa in Sidney's *Arcadia*.' *Renaissance Quarterly* 21 (1968): 420–8.
McRae, Andrew. *Literature, Satire, and the Early Stuart State*. Cambridge: Cambridge University Press, 2004.
Mebane, John S. *Renaissance Magic and the Return of the Golden Age: The Occult Tradition and Marlowe, Jonson, and Shakespeare*. Lincoln: University of Nebraska Press, 1989.
Menon, Madhavi. 'Spurning Teleology in *Venus and Adonis*.' *GLQ: A Journal of Lesbian and Gay Studies* 11 (2005): 491–519.
Meres, Francis. *Palladis Tamia* (London, 1598). *Shakespeare Allusions and Parallels*. 2 vols. Ed. A. Bruce Black and Robert Metcalf Smith. Bethlehem: Lehigh University Press, 1931.
Merrix, Robert P. '"Lo, in This Hollow Cradle Take Thy Rest: Sexual Conflicht in *Venus and Adonis*.' *'Venus and Adonis'*. Ed. Philip C. Kolin. 341–58.
Miller, David Lee. 'Abandoning the Quest.' *ELH* 46 (1979): 173–92.
Miller, Lewis H., Jr. 'A Secular Reading of *The Faerie Queene*, Book II.' *ELH* 33.2 (1966): 154–69.
Miller, Robert P. 'The Myth of Mars's Hot Minion in *Venus and Adonis*.' *ELH* 26 (1959): 470–81.
Milton, John. 'Paradise Lost.' *John Milton: Complete Poems and Major Prose*. Ed. Merritt Y. Hughes. New York: Odyssey, 1957.
Milward, Peter. *Religious Controversies of the Elizabethan Age: A Survey of Printed Sources*. London: Scolar Press, 1977.

Miola, Robert. 'Vergil in Shakespeare: From Allusion to Imitation.' *Vergil at 2000.* Ed. John D. Bernard. New York: AMS Press, 1986. 254–6.
Montrose, Louis A. '"Eliza, Queene of the Shepherdes," and the Pastoral of Power.' *English Literary Renaissance* 10 (1980):153–82.
Montrose, Louis A. 'New Historicisms.' *Redrawing the Boundaries: The Transformation of English and American Literary Studies.* Ed. Stephen J. Greenblatt and Giles Gunn. New York: Modern Language Association of America, 1992. 392–418.
Montrose, Louis A. 'Of Gentlemen and Shepherds: The Politics of Elizabethan Pastoral Form.' *ELH* 50 (1983): 415–59.
Montrose, Louis A. 'The Elizabethan Subject and the Spenserian Text.' *Literary Theory / Renaissance Texts.* Ed. Patricia Parker and David Quint. Baltimore: Johns Hopkins University Press, 1986. 303–40.
More, Thomas. *The History of King Richard III.* Ed. Richard Sylvester. New Haven, 1963.
Morgan, Gerald. '"Add faith vnto your force": The Perfecting of Spenser's Knight of Holiness in Faith and Humility.' *Renaissance Studies* 18 (2004): 449–74.
Morgan, Gerald. 'Aquinas.' *SpEncy.* Ed. A. C. Hamilton et al.
Morgan, Gerald. 'Holiness as the First of Spenser's Aristotelian Moral Virtues.' *Modern Language Review* 81 (1986): 817–37.
Morgan, Gerald. 'Spenser's Conception of Courtesy and the Design of the *Faerie Queene*.' *Review of English Studies* 32 (1981): 17–36.
Morgan, Gerald. 'The Idea of Temperance in the Second Book of *The Faerie Queene*.' *Review of English Studies* 37 (1986): 11–39.
Morris, Helen. 'Queen Elizabeth I "Shadowed" in Cleopatra.' *Huntington Library Quarterly* 32 (1969): 271–8.
Mortimer, Anthony. *Variable Passions: A Reading of Shakespeare's 'Venus and Adonis'.* New York: AMS Press, 2000.
Moulton, Ian Frederick. '"A Monster Great Deformed": The Unruly Masculinity of Richard III.' *Shakespeare Quarterly* 47 (1996): 251–68.
Mounts, Charles E. 'Spenser and the Earl of Essex.' *Renaissance Papers* (1958–1960): 12–19.
Murrin, Michael. *The Allegorical Epic: Essays in Its Rise and Decline.* Chicago: University of Chicago Press, 1980.
Nancy, Jean-Luc. *The Ground of the Image.* Trans. Jeff Fort. New York: Fordham, University Press, 2005.
Neely, Carol Thomas. *Broken Nuptials in Shakespeare's Plays.* 1985. Urbana: University of Illinois Press, 1993.
Nelson, William. *The Poetry of Edmund Spenser: A Study.* 1963. New York: Columbia University Press, 1965.
Neuse, Richard. 'Adonis, Gardens of.' *SpEncy.* Ed. A. C. Hamilton et al.
Neuse, Richard. 'Book Six as Conclusion of *The Faerie Queene*.' *ELH* 35 (1968): 329–53.

Neuse, Richard. "Pastorella'. *SpEncy*. Ed. A. C. Hamilton et al.
Niccols, Richard. *The Beggers Ape* [London, 1627]. Eugene: Renascence Editions, 2000. 7 December 2006. http://www.uoregon.edu/~rbear/ape.html.
Nicoll, Allardyce. *Stuart Masques and the Renaissance Stage*. London: George G. Harrap, 1937.
Nohrnberg, James. *The Analogy of 'The Faerie Queene'*. Princeton: Princeton University Press, 1976.
Northrop, Douglas A. 'The Uncertainty of Courtesy in Book VI of *The Faerie Queene*.' *Spenser Studies* 14 (2000): 215–32.
Nosworthy, Jim. 'The Narrative Sources of *The Tempest*.' *Review of English Studies* 24 (1948): 281–94.
Nuttall, A. D. 'Ovid's Narcissus and Shakespeare's Richard II: The Reflected Self.' *Ovid Renewed: Ovidian Influences on Literature and Art from the Middle Ages to the Twentieth Century*. Ed. Charles Martindale. Cambridge: Cambridge University Press, 1988. 137–50.
O'Callaghan, Michelle. *The 'Shepheards Nation': Jacobean Spenserians and Early Stuart Political Culture, 1612–1625*. Oxford: Clarendon Press, 2000.
O'Callaghan, Michelle. '"Talking Politics": Tyranny, Politics, and Christopher Brooke's *The Ghost of Richard the Third* (1614).' *The Historical Journal* 41 (1998): 97–120.
O'Connell, Michael. *Mirror and Veil: The Historical Dimension of Spenser's 'Faerie Queene'*. Chapel Hill: University of North Carolina Press, 1977.
O'Connell, Michael. 'The Experiment of Romance.' *The Cambridge Companion to Shakespearean Comedy*. Ed. Alexander Leggatt. Cambridge: Cambridge University Press, 2002. 215–29.
O'Donovan, Oliver. *The Problem of Self-Love in St. Augustine*. New Haven: Yale University Press, 1980.
Oestreich-Hart, Donna J. '"Therefore, Since I Cannot Prove a Lover."' *Studies in English Literature* 40.2 (2000): 241–60:
Olson, Greta. 'Richard III's Animalistic Criminal Body.' *Philological Quarterly* 82 (2003): 301–24.
Olson, Paul F. '*A Midsummer Night's Dream* and the Meaning of Court Marriage.' *ELH* 24 (1957): 95–119.
Oram, William A. 'Spenserian Paralysis.' *SEL: Studies in English Literature* 41 (2001): 49–70.
Oras, Ants. *Pause Patterns in Elizabethan and Jacobean Drama; an Experiment in Prosody*. Gainsville: University of Florida Press, 1960.
Orgel, Stephen. *The Jonsonian Masque*. New York: Columbia University Press, 1967.
Ornstein, Robert. *A Kingdom for a Stage*. Cambridge, MA.: Harvard University Press, 1972.
Orr, Mary. *Intertextuality: Debates and Contexts*. Cambridge: Polity, 2003.

Padhi, Shanti. 'Hamlet's Satirical Rogue.' *Hamlet Studies* 6 (1984): 68–71.
Paglia, Camille. *Sexual Personae: Art and Decadence from Nefertiti to Emily Dickinson*. 1990. New York: Random House, 1991.
Paglia, Camille. 'The Apollonian Androgyne and *The Faerie Queene*.' *English Language Review* 9 (1979): 42–63.
Palfrey, Simon. *Late Shakespeare: A New World of Words*. Oxford: Clarendon Press, 1997.
Panofsky, Erwin, *Studies in Iconology: Humanistic Themes in the Art of the Renaissance*. London and New York: Harper and Row, 1972.
Parker, Patricia A. *Inescapable Romance: Studies in the Poetics of a Mode*. Princeton: Princeton University Press, 1979.
Patterson, Annabel. *Pastoral Ideology: Virgil to Valery*. Berkeley: University of California Press, 1987.
Patterson, Annabel. *Shakespeare and the Popular Voice*. Cambridge, MA: Basil Blackwell, 1989.
Payne, Michael. 'Erotic Irony and Polarity in *Antony and Cleopatra*.' *Shakespeare Quarterly* 24 (1973): 265–79.
Peacham, Henry. *The Garden of Eloquence*. (London, 1577). Scolar Press Facsimile. Ed. R.C. Alson. Menston: Scolar Press, 1971.
Pearlman, E. 'The Invention of Richard of Gloucester.' *Shakespeare Quarterly* 43 (1992): 410–29.
Perkins, William. *A Golden Chaine: Or, The Description of Theologie*. London, 1600.
Peters, Julie Stone. *The Theatre of the Book, 1480–1880: Print, Text, and Performance in Europe*. Oxford: Oxford University Press, 2000.
Peterson, Richard S. 'Laurel Crown and Ape's Tail: New Light on Spenser's Career from Sir Thomas Tresham.' *Spenser Studies* 12 (1998): 1–35.
Petrarca, Francesco. *Bucolicum Carmen*. Trans. Thomas G. Bergin. New Haven: Yale University Press, 1974.
Petrarca, Francesco. *The Life of Solitude*. 1924. Trans. Jacob Zeitlin. Westport: Hyperion Press, 1978.
Petti, Anthony G. 'Beasts and Politics in Elizabethan Literature.' *Essays and Studies* 16 (1963): 68–90.
Philmus, Maria R. Rohr. '*The Faerie Queene* and Renaissance Poetics: Another Look at Book VI as "Conclusion" to the Poem.' *English Studies* 76 (1995): 497–519.
Piepho, Lee. 'Mantuan's Eclogues in the English Reformation.' *Sixteenth Century Journal* 25.3 (1994): 623–32.
Pincombe, Michael. 'The Ovidian Hermaphrodite: Moralizations by Peend and Spenser.' *Ovid and the Renaissance Body*. Ed. Goran V. Stanivukovic. Toronto: University of Toronto Press, 2001. 155–70.
Pitcher, John. 'A Theatre of the Future: *The Aeneid* and *The Tempest*.' *Essays in Criticism* 34 (1984): 193–215.

Pitcher, John. 'Essex, Robert Devereux, Second Earl of.' *SpEncy*. Ed. A. C. Hamilton et al.
Pitcher, John. 'Some Call Him Autolycus.' *In Arden: Editing Shakespeare: Essays in Honour of Richard Proudfoot*. Ed. Ann Thompson and Gordon McMullan. London: Arden Shakespeare, 2003. 252–68.
Platt, Peter G. *Reason Diminished: Shakespeare and the Marvellous*. Lincoln: University of Nebraska Press, 1997.
Plutarch. *Moralia*. Trans. Frank Cole Babbitt. 1936. Cambridge, MA: Harvard University Press, 2003.
Plutarch. *The Lives of the Noble Grecians and Romanes*. Trans. Thomas North from the French of J. Amyot. London, 1579.
Plutarch. 'Gryllus.' *Moralia*. Trans. Harold Cherniss. Cambridge, MA: Harvard University Press, 1984. XII: 493–533.
Plutarch. 'The Life of Marcus Antonius.' *Plutarch's Lives of the Noble Grecians and Romanes*. Trans. Sir Thomas North. In: *Narrative and Dramatic Sources of Shakespeare*. Ed. Geoffrey Bullough. London: Routledge and Kegan Paul, 1964. V: 254–321.
Podro, Michael. 'Depiction and the Golden Calf.' *Philosophy and the Visual Arts: Seeing and Abstracting*. Ed. Andrew Harrison. Dordrecht and Boston: Royal Institute of Philosophy Conferences, 1987. 3–28.
Pomponazzi, Pietro. 'On the Immortality of the Soul.' *The Renaissance Philosophy of Man*. Ed. Ernst Cassirer, Paul Oskar Kristeller and John Herman Randall, Jr. 1948. Chicago: University of Chicago Press, 1956. 257–381.
Potts, Abbie Findlay. *Shakespeare and 'The Faerie Queene'*. Ithaca: Cornell University Press, 1958.
Prescott, Anne Lake. 'Complicating the Allegory: Spenser and Religion in Recent Scholarship.' *Renaissance and Reformation* 24.4 (2001): 9–23.
Prescott, Anne Lake. 'Refusing Translation: The Gregorian Calendar and Early Modern English Writers.' *Year in English Studies* 36 (2006): 1–11.
Primaudaye, Pierre de la. *The Second Part of The French Academie* (Paris, 1586). London, 1618.
Pugh, Syrithe. *Spenser and Ovid*. Aldershot: Ashgate, 2005.
Puttenham, George. *The Arte of English Poesie*. 1589. Ed. Edward Arber. London: 1869.
Questier, Michael C. *Catholicism and Community in Early Modern England: Politics, Aristocratic Patronage and Religion, c. 1550–1640*. Cambridge: Cambridge University Press, 2006.
Quilligan, Maureen. *The Language of Allegory: Defining the Genre*. Ithaca: Cornell University Press, 1979.
Quitslund, Jon. *Spenser's Supreme Fiction: Platonic Natural Philosophy and 'The Faerie Queene'*. Toronto: University of Toronto Press, 2001.
Rajan, Balachandra. 'Closure.' *SpEncy*. Ed. A. C. Hamilton et al.

Rajan, Balachandra. *The Form of the Unfinished: English Poetics from Spenser to Pound*. Princeton: Princeton University Press, 1985.
Raleigh, Sir Walter. *Milton*. London: Edward Arnold, 1922.
Reames, Sherry L. 'Prince Arthur and Spenser's Changing Design.' *Eterne in Mutabilitie*. Ed. Kenneth J. Atchity. 180–206.
Rebhorn, Wayne A. 'The Crisis of the Aristocracy in *Julius Caesar*.' *Renaissance Quarterly* 43 (1990): 75–111.
Reid, Robert L. 'Alma's Castle and the Symbolization of Reason in *The Faerie Queene*.' *Journal of English and Germanic Philology* 80 (1981): 512–27.
Reid, Robert L. *Shakespeare's Tragic Form*. Newark: University of Delaware Press, 2000.
Reid, Robert L. 'Holiness, House of.' *SpEncy*. Ed. A. C. Hamilton et al.
Reid, Robert L. 'Humoral Psychology in Shakespeare's *Henriad*.' *Comparative Drama* 30 (1996–7): 471–502.
Reid, Robert L. 'Man, Woman, Child or Servant: Family Hierarchy as a Figure of Tripartite Psychology in *The Faerie Queene*.' *Studies in Philology* 78 (1981): 370–90.
Reid, Robert L. 'Psychology, Platonic.' *SpEncy*. Ed. A. C. Hamilton et al.
Reid, Robert L. 'Spenserian Psychology and the Structure of Allegory in Books 1 and 2 of *The Faerie Queene*.' *Modern Philology* 79 (1982): 359–75.
Reid, Robert L. 'The Fairy Queen: Gloriana or Titania?' *The Upstart Crow* 13 (1993): 16–32.
Reid, Robert L. 'The Problem of Self-Love in Shakespeare's Tragedies and in Renaissance and Reformation Theology.' *Shakespeare's Christianity: The Protestant and Catholic Poetics of 'Julius Caesar', 'Macbeth', and 'Hamlet'*. Waco: Baylor University Press, 2006.
Richman, David. *Laughter, Pain, and Wonder: Shakespeare's Comedies and the Audience in the Theater*. Newark: University of Delaware Press, 1990.
Ricoeur, Paul. *Time and Narrative*. Trans. Kathleen McLaughlin and David Pellauer. Vol. 1. Chicago: University of Chicago Press, 1984.
Rinehart, Keith. 'Shakespeare's Cleopatra and England's Elizabeth.' *Shakespeare Quarterly* 23 (1972): 81–6.
Roberts, Julian, and A. G. Watson. *John Dee's Library Catalogue*. London: Bibliographical Society, 1990.
Robertson, David. *'My Self / Before Me': Self-Love in the Works of John Milton*. Tampere: University of Tampere, 1992.
Rogers, William Elford. 'Proserpina in *Prothalamion*.' *American Notes and Queries* 15 (1977): 131–5.
Ronan, Clifford J. 'Sallust, Beasts That "Sleep and Feed," and *Hamlet*, 5.2.' *Hamlet Studies* 7 (1985): 72–80.

Ronsard, Pierre de. 'Elegie XXIV.' *Oeuvres Complètes*. Ed. Jean Céard et al. Paris: Gallimard, 1994. II: 409.
Rosenberg, Marvin. *The Masks of Hamlet*. Newark: University of Delaware Press, 1992.
Rosenheim, Judith. 'Allegorical Commentary in *The Merchant of Venice*.' *Shakespeare Studies* 24 (1996): 156–210.
Røstvig, Maren-Sofie. *Configurations: A Topomorphical Approach to Renaissance Poetry*. Oslo: Scandinavian University Press, 1990.
Røstvig, Maren-Sophie. 'Number Symbolism, Tradition of.' *SpEncy*. Ed. A. C. Hamilton et al.
Rowland, Beryl. *Birds with Human Souls: A Guide to Bird Symbolism*. Knoxville: University of Tennessee Press, 1978.
Saintsbury, George. *A History of English Prosody from the Twelfth Century to the Present Day*. 3 vols. 2nd ed. 1908; London: Macmillan, 1923.
Sale, Roger. *Reading Spenser: An Introduction to 'The Faerie Queene'*. New York: Random House, 1968.
Sarrazin, G. 'Wortechos bei Shakespeare I.' *Jahrbuch der deutschen Shakespeare-Gesellschaft* (1897): 121–65.
Sarrazin, G. 'Wortechos bei Shakespeare II.' *Jahrbuch der deutschen Shakespeare-Gesellschaft* (1898): 119–69;
Saunders, J.W. 'The Stigma of Print: A Note on the Social Bases of Tudor Poetry.' *Essays in Criticism* (1951): 139–64.
Schanzer, Ernest. 'The Tragedy of Shakespeare's Brutus.' *ELH* 22 (1955): 1–15.
Schmidgall, Gary. *Shakespeare and the Courtly Aesthetic*. Berkeley: University of California Press, 1981.
Schmidgall, Gary. *Shakespeare and the Poet's Life*. Lexington: University Press of Kentucky, 1990.
Schmidt, Alexander. *Shakespeare Lexicon and Quotation Dictionary: A Complete Dictionary of all the English Words, Phrases and Constructions in the Works of the Poet*. 3rd ed. revised and enlarged by George Sarrazin. 2 vols. Berlin, 1902; New York: Dover Publications, 1971.
Schoenbaum, Samuel. *Shakespeare's Lives*. 1970. Oxford: Clarendon Press, 1991.
Schoenfeldt, Michael. 'The Construction of Inwardness in *The Faerie Queene*, Book 2.' *Worldmaking Spenser*. Ed. Patrick Cheney and Lauren Silberman. Lexington: University of Kentucky Press, 2000. 234–43.
Scipio Gentili. *La Gerusalemme Liberata di Torquato Tasso con le annotationi di Scipion Gentili, e di Giulio Gustavini, e li argomenti I Orazio Ariosto*. Geneva, 1617.
Scott-Giles, C.W. *Shakespeare's Heraldry*. London, 1950.
Severs, J. Burke, and Albert E. Hartung, gen. ed. *A Manual of the Writings in Middle English 1050–1500*. 9 vols. New Haven: Connecticut Academy of Arts and Sciences, 1967–1993. Vol. 1: *Romances* (1967).

Shackford, Martha Hale. '*Rose* in Shakespeare's Sonnets.' *Modern Language Notes* 33 (1918): 122.
Shapiro, James. *A Year in the Life of William Shakespeare 1599*. New York: HarperCollins, 2005.
Shapiro, James. *Rival Playwrights: Marlowe, Jonson, Shakespeare*. New York: Columbia University Press, 1991.
Shapiro, James. 'The Invisible Armada.' *A Year in the Life of William Shakespeare*. New York: Harper Collins, 2005. 173–87.
Sharrock, Alison. 'Ovid and the Discourses of Love: The Amatory Works.' *The Cambridge Companion to Ovid*. Ed. Philip Hardie. Cambridge: Cambridge University Press, 2002. 150–62.
Shaver, Anne. 'Rereading Mirabella.' *Spenser Studies* 9 (1991): 211–26.
Sheidley, William E. '"Unless it be a Boar": Love and Wisdom in Shakespeare's *Venus and Adonis*,' *Modern Language Quarterly* 35 (1974): 3–15.
Sherman, William. 'The Place of Reading in the Renaissance: John Dee Revisited.' *The Practice and Representation of Reading in England*. Ed. James Raven, Helen Small, and Naomi Tadmor. Cambridge: Cambridge University Press, 1996. 62–75.
Shorney, David. *Protestant Nonconformity and Roman Catholicism: A Guide to the Sources in the Public Record Office*. London: PRO Publications, 1996.
Sidney, Philip. *The Defence of Poesie*. (London, 1595). Eugene: Renascence Editions, 1992. 12 December 2006. http://darkwing.uoregon.edu/~rbear/defence.html.
Sidney, Sir Philip. *An Apology for Poetry*. Ed. Geoffrey Shepherd. 1965. Manchester: Manchester University Press, 1973.
Sidney, Sir Philip. *The Countess of Pembroke's Arcadia (The New Arcadia)*. Ed. Victor Skretkowicz. Oxford: Clarendon Press, 1987.
Sidney, Sir Philip. 'The Defence of Poesy.' *The Oxford Authors: Sir Philip Sidney*. Ed. Katherine Duncan-Jones. New York: Oxford University Press, 1989. 212–50.
Silberman, Lauren. '*The Faerie Queene*, Book V, and the Politics of Text.' *Spenser Studies* 19 (2004): 1–16.
Sims, James H. 'Perdita's "Flowers o' th' spring" and "vernal flowers" in *Lycidas*.' *Shakespeare Quarterly* 22 (1971): 87–90.
Singh, Jyotsna G. 'The Politics of Empathy in *Antony and Cleopatra*: A View from Below.' *A Companion to Shakespeare's Works. Vol. I: The Tragedies*. Ed. Richard Dutton and Jean E. Howard. Oxford: Blackwell, 2003. 411–29.
Sirluck, Ernest '*The Faerie Queene*, Book II, and the *Nicomachean Ethics*.' *Modern Philology* 49 (1951): 73–100.
Slater, Ann P. 'Variations within a Source: From Isaiah XXIX to *The Tempest*.' *Shakespeare Studies* 25 (1972): 125–35.

Slover, George. 'Magic, Mystery, and Make-Believe: An Analogical Reading of *The Tempest*.' *Shakespeare Studies* 11 (1978): 180–205.

Sokol, B. J. 'Perdita's Tale: Dubious Piedness.' *Art and Illusion in The Winter's Tale.* Manchester: Manchester University Press, 1994. 116–41.

Spagnuoli, Baptista. *The Eclogues of Mantuan.* Trans. George Tuberville (1567). Ed. Douglas Bush. New York: Scholars' Facsimiles and Reprints, 1937.

Spurgeon, Caroline. *Shakespeare's Imagery and What It Tells Us.* 1935. Cambridge: Cambridge University Press, 1999.

Stapleton, M. L. *Harmful Eloquence: Ovid's 'Amores' from Antiquity to Shakespeare.* Ann Arbor: University of Michigan Press, 1996.

Starks, Lisa S. '"Immortal Longings": The Erotics of Death in *Antony and Cleopatra*.' *'Antony and Cleopatra'*. Ed. Sara Munson Deats. 243–58.

Steadman, John M. 'Una and the Clergy: The Ass Symbol in *The Faerie Queene*.' *Journal of the Warburg and Courtauld Institutes* 21 (1958): 134–7.

Stewart, Stanley. 'Sir Calidore and "Closure."' *Studies in English Literature* 24 (1984): 69–86.

Stillman, Robert E. 'The Perils of Fancy: Poetry and Self-Love in *The Old Arcadia*.' *Texas Studies in Literature and Language* 26 (1984): 1–17.

Stillman, Robert E. 'The Truths of a Slippery World: Poetry and Tyranny in Sidney's "Defense."' *Renaissance Quarterly* 55 (2002): 1287–1319.

Stoler Wagonheim, Sylvia, ed. *Annals of the English Drama 975–1700.* 3rd ed. London: Routledge, 1989.

Strier, Richard. *Resistant Structures: Particularity, Radicalism, and Renaissance Texts.* Berkeley: University of California Press, 1995.

Stump, Donald V., and John M. Crossett. 'Spenser's Inferno: The Order of the Seven Deadly Sins at the Palace of Pride.' *Journal of Medieval and Renaissance Studies* 14 (1984): 203–18.

Stump, Donald V. 'Pride.' *SpEncy*. Ed. A. C. Hamilton et al.

Tassi. Marguerite A. 'O'erpicturing Appelles: Shakespeare's *Paragone* with Painting in *Antony and Cleopatra*.' *'Antony and Cleopatra'*. Ed. Sara Munson Deats. 291–307.

Tasso, Torquato. *Scritti Sull'Arte Poetica.* Vol. 2. Ed. Ettore Mazzali. Milano: Ricciardi, 1959.

Taylor, A. B. *Shakespeare's Ovid: The Metamorphoses in the Plays.* Cambridge: Cambridge University Press, 2000.

Taylor, Gary. 'Forms of Opposition: Shakespeare and Middleton.' *English Literary Renaissance* 24 (1994): 283–314.

Taylor, James. '*Hamlet*'s Debt to Sixteenth-Century Satire.' *Modern Language Studies* 22 (1986): 374–84.

Terry, Reta A. '"Vows to the Blackest Devil": *Hamlet* and the Evolving Code of Honor in Early Modern England.' *Renaissance Quarterly* 52 (1999): 1070–86.
Teskey, Gordon. 'Arthur in *The Faerie Queene*.' *SpEncy*. Ed. A. C. Hamilton et al.
Teskey, Gordon. ' "And therefore as a stranger give it welcome:" Courtesy and Thinking.' *Spenser Studies* 18 (2003): 343–59.
Thompson, Ann. *Shakespeare's Chaucer: A Study in Literary Origins*. Liverpool: Liverpool University Press, 1978.
Thompson, Ann. 'Philomel in *Titus Andronicus* and *Cymbeline*.' *Shakespeare Survey* 31 (1978): 23–32.
Tiffany, Grace. 'Shakespeare's Dionysian Prince: Drama, Politics, and the "Athenian" History Play.' *Renaissance Quarterly* 52 (1999): 366–83.
Tilley, Morris Palmer. *A Dictionary of the Proverbs in England in the Sixteenth and Seventeenth Centuries*. Ann Arbor: University of Michigan Press, 1950.
Tipton, Alzada. 'The Transformation of the Earl of Essex: Post-Execution Ballads and "The Phoenix and the Turtle."' *Studies in Philology* 99 (2002): 57–80.
Tobin, J. J. M. 'Apuleius.' *SpEncy*. Ed. A. C. Hamilton et al.
Tobin, J. J. M. *Shakespeare's Favorite Novel: A Study of* The Golden Asse *as Prime Source*. Lanham: University Press of America, 1984.
Tonkin, Humphrey. *Spenser's Courteous Pastoral: Book Six of 'The Faerie Queene'*. Oxford: Clarendon Press, 1972.
Tonkin, Humphrey. '*The Faerie Queene*, Book VI.' *SpEncy*. Ed. A. C. Hamilton et al.
Tonkin, Humphrey. 'Spenser's Garden of Adonis and Britomart's Quest,' *PMLA: Publications of the Modern Language Society* 88 (1973): 408–17.
Traister, Barbara. *Heavenly Necromancers: The Magician in English Renaissance Drama*. Columbia: University of Missouri Press, 1984.
Traub, Valerie. *Desire and Anxiety: Circulation of Sexuality in Shakespearean Drama*. London: Routledge, 1992.
Treip, Mindele Anne. *Allegorical Poetics and the Epic: The Renaissance Tradition to Paradise Lost'*. Lexington: University Press of Kentucky, 1994.
Trevor, Douglas. 'Sadness in *The Faerie Queene*.' *Reading the Early Modern Passions*. Ed. Gail Kern Paster, Katherine Rowe, and Mary Floyd-Wilson. Philadelphia: University of Pennsylvania Press, 2004. 240–52.
Trissino, Giovanni Georgio. *La Quinta e la Sesta Divisione della Poetica* (1562). *Trattati di Poetica e Retorica del Cinquecento*. Vol. III. Ed. Bernard Weinberg. Bari: Laterza, 1972.
Truax, Elizabeth. *Metamorphosis in Shakespeare's Plays: A Pageant of Heroes, Gods, Maids and Monsters*. Lewiston: Edwin Mellen, 1992.

Tudeau-Clayton, Margaret. *Jonson, Shakespeare, and Early Modern Virgil.* Cambridge: Cambridge University Press, 1998.
Tuve, Rosemund. *Allegorical Imagery: Some Medieval Books and Their Posterity.* Princeton: Princeton UP, 1966.
Uhlig, Claus. '"The sobbing Deer": *As You Like it* and the Historical Context.' *Renaissance Drama* 3 (1970): 79–109.
Van Dyke, Carolynn. *The Fiction of Truth: Structures of Meaning in Narrative and Dramatic Allegory.* Ithaca: Cornell University Press, 1985.
Vanhoutte, Jacqueline. 'Antony's "secret house of death": Suicide and Sovereignty in *Antony and Cleopatra.*' *Philological Quarterly* 79 (2000): 153–75.
Vergil, Polydore. *Historie of England.* Ed. Sir Henry Ellis. London: Camden Society, 1844.
Versteegan, Richard. *Thétre des Cruatés des Hérétiques de Notre Temps.* Ed. Frank Lestringant. Paris: Editions Chandeigne, 1995.
Vickers, Brian. *Shakespeare, 'A Lover's Complaint', and John Davies of Hereford.* Cambridge: Cambridge University Press, 2007.
Virgil. *The Eclogues.* Trans. Guy Lee. 1980. London: Penguin Books, 1984.
Walker, Claire. *Gender and Politics in Early Modern Europe: English Convents in France and the Low Countries.* Basingstoke: Palgrave Macmillan, 2003.
Walker, Julia M. *Medusa's Mirrors: Spenser, Shakespeare, Milton, and the Metamorphosis of the Female Self.* Newark: University of Delaware Press, 1998.
Wall, John N. *Transformations of the Word: Spenser, Herbert, Vaughan.* Athens: University of Georgia Press, 1988.
Wall, Wendy. *The Imprint of Gender: Authorship and Publication in the English Renaissance.* Ithaca: Cornell University Press, 1993.
Wall, William G. 'The Importance of Being Osric: Death, Fate, and Foppery in Shakespeare's *Hamlet.*' *Shakespeare Newsletter* 42 (1992): 62.
Walsham, Alexandra. *Church Papists.* Suffolk: Boydel Press, 1993.
Walsingham, Thomas. *De Archana Deorum.* Ed. Robert A. van Kluyve. Durham: Duke University Press, 1968.
Watkins, W. B. C. *Shakespeare and Spenser.* 1950. Cambridge, MA: Walker-de-Berry, 1961.
Watson, Curtis Brown. *Shakespeare and the Renaissance Concept of Honor.* Princeton: Princeton University Press, 1960.
Watson, Thomas. *An Eglogue Upon the Death of the Right Honorable Sir Francis Walsingham.* London, 1590.
Weatherby, Harold. *Mirrors of Celestial Grace.* Toronto: University of Toronto Press, 1994.
Webbe, William. 'A Discourse of English Poetrie.' *Elizabethan Critical Essays.* Ed. Gregory Smith. Oxford: Oxford University Press, 1971.

Webb, W.S. 'Vergil in Spenser's Epic Theory.' *ELH* 4 (1937): 62–84.
Weimann, Robert. *Shakespeare and the Popular Tradition in the Theater: Studies in the Social Dimension of Dramatic Form and Function.* Ed. Robert Schwarz. Baltimore: Johns Hopkins University Press, 1978.
Weimann, Robert. 'Mimesis in *Hamlet*.' *Shakespeare and the Question of Theory.* Ed. Patricia Parker and Geoffrey Hartman. New York: Methuen, 1985. 275–91.
Weimann, Robert. 'Towards a Literary Theory of Ideology: Mimesis, Representation, Authority.' *Shakespeare Reproduced: The Text in History and Ideology.* 1987. Ed. Jean E. Howard and Marion F. O'Connor. New York: Routledge, 1993. 265–72.
Weiss, Paul. *Modes of Being.* Carbondale: Southern Illinois University Press, 1958.
Wells, Robin Headlam. 'Blessing Europe: Virgil, Ovid, and Seneca in *The Tempest*.' *Shakespeare and Intertextuality: The Transition of Cultures Between Italy and England in the Early Modern Period.* Ed. Michele Marrapodi. Rome: Bulzoni, 2000. 69–84.
Wells, William, ed. *Spenser Allusions in the Sixteenth and Seventeenth Centuries.* Chapel Hill: University of North Carolina Press, 1972.
Welsford, Enid. *The Court Masque.* Cambridge: Cambridge University Press, 1927.
Wentersdorf, Karl P. 'Animal Symbolism in Shakespeare's *Hamlet*.' *Comparative Drama* 17 (1983): 348–82.
Wilkinson, L. P. *Ovid Recalled.* Cambridge: Cambridge University Press, 1955.
Williams, Gordon. 'The Coming of Age in Shakespeare's Adonis.' *Modern Language Review* 78 (1983): 769–76.
Williams, Juanita Sullivan. *Towards a Definition of Menippean Satire.* Ann Arbor: University Microfilms, 1969.
Wilson, Harold S. '"Nature and Art" in *The Winter's Tale*.' *Shakespeare Association Bulletin* 18 (1943): 114–20.
Wilson, J. Dover. *The Essential Shakespeare.* Cambridge: Cambridge University Press, 1932.
Wilson, Richard. *Secret Shakespeare: Studies in Theatre, Religion, and Resistance.* Manchester: Manchester University Press, 2004.
Wiltenberg, Robert. 'The *Aeneid* in *The Tempest*.' *Shakespeare Studies* 39 (1987): 159–68.
Wiltenburg, Robert. *Ben Jonson and Self-Love.* Columbia: University of Missouri Press, 1990.
Wind, Edgar. *Pagan Mysteries in the Renaissance.* Rev. ed. Harmondsworth: Penguin, 1967.
Wolf, Janet S. '"Like an Old Tale Still": Paulina, "Triple Hecate," and the Persephone Myth in *The Winter's Tale*.' *Images of Persephone: Feminist Readings in Western Literature.* Ed. Elizabeth T. Hayes. Gainesville: University of Florida Press, 1994. 32–44.

Womersley, David. 'Why Is Falstaff Fat?' *Review of English Studies* 47 (1996): 1–22.
Woodcock, Matthew. *Fairy in The Faerie Queene: Renaissance Elf-Fashioning and Elizabethan Myth-Making.* Aldershot: Ashgate, 2004.
Woodhouse, A. S. P. 'Nature and Grace in *The Faerie Queene*.' *ELH* 16 (1949): 194–228.
Woodman, David. *White Magic and English Renaissance Drama.* Rutherford: Fairleigh Dickinson University Press, 1973.
Wood, Rufus. *Metaphor and Belief in 'The Faerie Queene'.* Basingstoke: Macmillan, 1997.
Woods, Susanne. 'Closure in *The Faerie Queene*.' *Journal of English and Germanic Philology* 76 (1977): 195–216.
Worthen, W. B. 'The Weight of Antony: Staging "Character" in *Antony and Cleopatra*.' *Studies in English Literature* 26 (1986): 295–308.
Yeats, W. B. *Essays and Introductions.* New York: Collier Books, 1968.
Yoder, Audrey. *Animal Analogy in Shakespeare's Character Portrayal.* New York: King's Crown Press, 1947.
Young, George. *An English Prosody on Inductive Lines.* Cambridge: Cambridge University Press, 1928; New York: Greenwood Press, 1969.

Bibliography of Books and Papers on Spenser and Shakespeare

Adelman, Janet. *The Common Liar: An Essay on 'Antony and Cleopatra'.* New Haven: Yale University Press, 1973.

Alpers, Paul. *What is Pastoral?* Chicago: University of Chicago Press, 1996.

Anderson, Judith H. 'The Conspiracy of Realism: Impasse and Vision in *King Lear*.' *Studies in Philology* 84.1 (1987): 1–23.

Anderson, Judith H. *Words that Matter: Linguistic Perception in Renaissance English.* Stanford: Stanford University Press, 1996.

Anderson, Judith H. '*Venus and Adonis*: Spenser, Shakespeare, and the Forms of Desire.' *Grief and Gender, 700–1700.* Ed. Jennifer C. Vaught and Lynne Dickson Bruckner. New York: Palgrave, 2003. 149–60.

Andrews, Michael Cameron. ' "Music's Sound": A Note on *Romeo and Juliet*.' *Notes and Queries* 36 (1989): 32–3.

Ardolino, Frank. 'The Influence of Spenser's *Faerie Queene* on Kyd's *Spanish Tragedy*. *EMLS* 7.3 (2002).

Bakeless, John. *The Tragical History of Christopher Marlowe.* 2 vols. Cambridge, MA: Harvard University Press, 1942

Baldwin, T. W. 'The Genesis of Some Passages Which Spenser Borrowed from Marlowe.' *ELH* 3 (1942): 157–87.

Baldwin, T.W. 'The Genesis of Some Passages Which Spenser Borrowed from Marlowe.' *ELH* 12 (1945): 165.

Barthel, Carol. 'Prince Arthur and Bottom the Weaver: The Renaissance Dream of the Fairy Queen.' *Spenser: Classical, Medieval, Renaissance, and Modern.* Ed. David A. Richardson. Cleveland: Cleveland State University Press, 1977. 72–83.

Bednarz, James P. 'Imitations of Spenser in *A Midsummer Night's Dream*.' *Renaissance Drama* 14 (1983): 79–102.

Blake, N. F. *A Grammar of Shakespeare's Language.* Houndmills, Basingstoke: Palgrave, 2001.

Blythe, David-Everett. 'Ox-eyed Phebe.' *Shakespeare Quarterly* 33.1 (1982): 101–2.

Boss, Judith E. 'The Golden Age, Cockaigne, and Utopia in *The Faerie Queene* and *The Tempest*.' *Georgia Review* 26 (1972): 145–55.

Brooks, Harold, ed. *A Midsummer Night's Dream.* Arden 2. (1979). London: Thomas Learning, 2002. xxxiv–xxxix, lviii–lvii.

Brooks, Harold F. 'Richard III: Antecedents of Clarence's Dream.' *Shakespeare Survey: An Annual Survey of Shakespeare Studies and Production* 32 (1979): 145–50.

Brown, James Neil. ' "A Calendar, a Calendar! Look in the Almanac".' *Notes and Queries* 27 (1980): 162–5.
Bruce, Donald. 'Spenser's Poetic Pictures: a Vision Of Beauty.' *Contemporary Review* 288.1680 (2006) 73–86.
Burrow, Colin. *William Shakespeare: The Complete Sonnets and Poems.* Oxford: Oxford University Press, 2002.
Bush, Douglas. '*Hero and Leander* and *Romeo and Juliet*.' *Philological Quarterly* 9 (1930): 396–9.
Bush, Douglas. 'Marlowe and Spenser.' *Times Literary Supplement* (Jan 1, 1938): 12.
Bush, Douglas. 'Notes on Shakespeare's Classical Mythology.' *Philological Quarterly* 6 (1927): 301.
Campana, Joseph. 'On Not Defending Poetry: Spenser, Suffering, and the Energy of Affect.' *PMLA* 120.1 (2005): 33–48.
Celovsky, Lisa. 'Early Modern Masculinities and *The Faerie Queene*.' *English Literary Renaissance* (2005): 210–47.
Cheney, Patrick. *Shakespeare, National Poet-Playwright.* Cambridge: Cambridge University Press, 2004.
Cheney, Patrick. ' "O, Let My Books Be ... Dumb Presagers": Poetry and Theater in Shakespeare's Sonnets.' *Shakespeare Quarterly* 52.2 (2001): 222–54.
Cheney, Patrick. 'Shakespeare's *Sonnet 106*, Spenser's *National Epic*, and Counter-Petrarchism.' *English Literary Renaissance* 31 (2001): 331–64.
Coatalen, Guillaume. '*The Faerie Queene*, VI.viii.32.1, *A Midsummer Night's Dream*, II.i.2, and *Paradise Lost*, IV.538.' *Notes and Queries* 51 (2004): 360–1.
Coyle, Martin. '*King Lear* and *The Faerie Queene*.' *Notes and Queries* 31 (1984): 205–7.
Crawford, Charles. 'Edmund Spenser, "Locrine", and "Selimus".' *Notes and Queries* 9th ser. 7 (1901): 61–3, 101–3, 142–4, 203–5, 261–3, 324–5, 384–6.
Cutts, John P. 'Spenser, Shakespeare, and the "Bloody Babe".' *Neuphilologische Mitteilungen* (1985): 506–14.
Daniell, David. 'Explorers of the Revelation: Spenser and Shakespeare.' *Shakespeare's Christianity: Catholic-Protestant Presence in 'Julius Caesar', 'Hamlet', and 'MacBeth'.* Ed Beatrice Bartson. Waco: Baylor University Press, 2006. 19–34.
Dauber, Antionette B. 'Allegory and Irony in *Othello*.' *Shakespeare Survey* 40 (1988): 123–44.
Doloff, Steven. 'Francisco, Hamlet, and God's Faithful Sentries.' *Notes and Queries* 44 (1997): 498.
Donow, Herbert S. *A Concordance to the Sonnet Sequences of Daniel, Drayton, Shakespeare, Sidney, and Spenser.* Carbondale: Southern Illinois University Press, 1969.

Dzelzainis, Martin. 'Antony and Cleopatra, I.iii.102–5 and Spenser's Ruines of Rome.' Notes and Queries 45 (1998): 345–6.
Edwards, Philip. 'The Rapture of the Sea.' Shakespearean Continuities. Ed. John Batchelor, Tom Cain, and Claire Lamont. New York: St. Martin's, 1997. 175–89.
Esolen, Anthony. 'Not a Hair Shall Perish.' Touchstone: A Journal of Mere Christianity 20.1 (2007): 34–5.
Fitzpatrick, Joan. 'Shakespeare's Titus Andronicus and Bandello's Novelle as Sources for the Munera Episode in Spenser's Faerie Queene, Book 5, Canto 2.' Notes and Queries 52 (2005): 196–8.
Gibbons, Brian. 'Fabled Cymbeline.' Deutsche Shakespeare-Gesellschaft. West: Jahrbuch, 1987. 78–99. Bochum: Kamp, 1987.
Gough, Melinda J. ' "Her filthy feature open showne" in Ariosto, Spenser, and Much Ado about Nothing.' Studies in English Literature 1500–1900 39 (1999): 41–67.
Gray, Henry D. 'Shakespeare's Rival Poet.' Journal of English and Germanic Philology 47 (1948): 365–73.
Greenfield, Sayre N. 'Allegorical Impulses and Critical Ends: Shakespeare's and Spenser's Venus and Adonis.' Criticism 36 (1994): 475–98.
Guenther, Genevieve. 'Spenser's Magic, or Instrumental Aesthetics in the 1590 Faerie Queene.' English Literary Renaissance 36.2 (2006): 194–226.
Hadfield, Andrew. 'Tamburlaine as the "Scourge of God" and The First English Life of King Henry the Fifth.' Notes and Queries 50 (2003): 399–400.
Haley, David. 'Gothic Armaments and King Hamlet's Poleaxe.' Shakespeare Quarterly 29.3 (1978): 407–13.
Hamlin, William M. 'Making Religion of Wonder: The Divine Attribution in Renaissance Ethnography and Romance.' Renaissance and Reformation 18.4 (1994): 39–51.
Harrison, Thomas P., Jr. 'Aspects of Primitivism in Shakespeare and Spenser.' Studies in English (1941): 39–71.
Harrison, Thomas P. Jr. 'Flower Lore in Spenser and Shakespeare: Two Notes.' Modern Language Quarterly 7 (1946): 175–8.
Hart, Alfred. 'The Growth of Shakespeare's Vocabulary.' Renaissance English Studies 19 (No. 75) (1943): 242–54.
Hart, Alfred. 'Vocabularies of Shakespeare's Plays.' Renaissance English Studies 19 (No. 74) (1943): 128–40.
Hecht, Paul J. 'Spenser Out of His Stanza.' Style 39.3 (2005): 316–35.
Hieatt, A. Kent, and Charles W. Hieatt. 'Shakespeare's Early "Fair".' Notes and Queries 45 (1998): 315–18.
Hieatt, A. Kent, Charles W. Hieatt, and Anne Lake Prescott. 'When Did Shakespeare Write Sonnets 1609?.' Studies in Philology 88.1 (1991): 69–109.

Hieatt, A. Kent. '*Cymbeline* and the Intrusion of Lyric into Romance Narrative: *Sonnets*, "A Lover's Complaint", Spenser's *Ruines of Rome*.' *Unfolded Tales: Essays on Renaissance Romance*. Ed. George M. Logan and Gordon Teskey. Ithaca: Cornell University Press, 1989. 98–118.

Hieatt, A. Kent 'Shakespeare, William.' *The Spenser Encyclopedia*. Gen. Ed. A. C. Hamilton. Toronto: University of Toronto Press, 1990. 641–3.

Hieatt, A. Kent, T. G. Bishop and E. A. Nicholson. 'Shakespeare's Rare Words: "Lover's Complaint", *Cymbeline*, and *Sonnets*.' *Notes and Queries* 34 (June 1987): 219–24.

Hieatt, A. Kent. 'The Genesis of Shakespeare's *Sonnets*: Spenser's *Ruines of Rome: by Bellay*.' *PMLA* 98 (1983): 800–14.

Hieatt, Charles. 'Dating *King John*: The Implications of the Influence of Edmund Spenser's *Ruins of Rome* on Shakespeare's Text.' *Notes and Queries* 35 (1988): 458–63.

Hieatt, Constance B. 'Stooping at a Simile: Some Literary Uses of Falconry.' *Papers on Language and Literature* 19.4 (1983): 339–60.

Holderness, Graham. ' "The Scripture Moveth Us in Sundry Places...": Strategies of Persuasion in Sixteenth Century Anglican Liturgy.' *Reformation & Renaissance Review: Journal of the Society for Reformation Studies* 2 (1999): 20–38.

Hunt, Maurice. 'Wrestling for Temperance: *As You Like It* and *The Faerie Queene*, Book II.' *Allegorica: A Journal of Medieval and Renaissance Literature* 16 (1995): 31–46.

Hutchinson, D.S. *Shakespeare and the Poets' War*. New York: Columbia University Press, 2001.

Hutchinson, D.S. 'The Cynicism of Jaques: A New Source in Spenser's *Axiochus*.' *Notes and Queries* 39 (1992): 328–30.

Iyengar, Sujata. ' "Handling Soft the Hurts": Female Healers and Manual Contact in Spenser, Ariosto and Shakespeare.' *In Sensible Flesh: On Touch in Early Modern Culture*. Ed. Elizabeth D. Harvey. Philadelphia: University of Pennsylvania Press, 2003. 39–61.

Jackson, MacDonald P. 'Indefinite Articles in *Titus Andronicus*, Peele, and Shakespeare.' *Notes and Queries* 45 (1998): 308–11.

Jackson, MacDonald P. 'Shakespeare's *Sonnet CXI* and John Davies of Hereford's *Microcosmos* (1603).' *Modern Language Review* 102.1 (2007): 1–10.

Jackson, M.P. 'Echoes of Spenser's *Prothalamion* as Evidence against an Early Date for Shakespeare's *A Lover's Complaint*.' *Notes and Queries* 37 (1990): 180–2.

Jump, John D. 'Spenser and Marlowe.' *Notes and Queries* 11 (1964): 261–2.

Kay, D.C. 'A Spenserian Source for Shakespeare's *Claribel*?' *Notes and Queries* 31 (1984): 217.

Kinney, Clare R. 'Feigning Female Faining: Spenser, Lodge, Shakespeare, and Rosalind.' *Modern Philology* 95 (1998): 291–315.
Kuhl, E. P. 'Hercules in Spenser and Shakespeare.' *Times Literary Supplement* (1954): 860.
Kuin, Roger. 'Two-Part Invention: "Love Ruins" Shakespeares Sonnets.' *Chamber Music: Elizabethan Sonnet Sequences and the Pleasure of Criticism*. Toronto: University of Toronto Press, 1998. 77–100.
Lancashire, Anne. 'Timon of Athnes: Shakespeare's Dr Faustus.' *Shakespeare Quarterly* 21.1 (1970): 35–44.
Lever, J. W. 'Venus and the Second Chance.' *Shakespeare Survey* 15 (1962): 81–8.
Logan, Robert A. *Shakespeare's Marlowe: The Influence of Christopher Marlowe on Shakespeare's Artistry*. Aldershot: Ashgate, 2007.
Luckyj, Christina. 'Rachel Speght and the "Criticall Reader".' *English Literary Renaissance* 36.2 (2006): 227–49.
Mack, Peter. *Elizabethan Rhetoric: Theory and Practice*. Cambridge: Cambridge University Press, 2002.
Maley, Willy. ' "This ripping of auncestors": the ethnographic present in Spenser's *A View of the State of Ireland*.' *Textures of Renaissance Knowledge*. Ed. Philipa Berry and Margaret Tudeau-Clayton. Manchester: Manchester University Press, 2003. 117–34.
Marder, Louis. 'New Source for Sonnets Discovered in Spenser's *Ruines of Rome*.' *Shakespeare Newsletter* 32 (1982): 17–18.
Marx, Steven. ' "Fortunate Senex": The Pastoral of Old Age.' *SEL: Studies in English Literature, 1500-1900* 25.1 (1985): 21–44.
Mayhall, Jane. 'Shakespeare and Spenser: A Commentary on Differences.' *Modern Language Quarterly* 10 (1949): 356–63.
McCown, Gary M. ' "Runnawayes Eyes" and Juliet's Epithalamium.' *Shakespeare Quarterly* 27.2 (1976): 150–70.
McEvoy, Jaqueline. 'Prophetic Authority and Error: An Biblical *View of the Present State of Ireland*.' *Renaissance Papers* (1998): 1–18.
McPeek, James A. S. 'The Genesis of Caliban.' *Philological Quarterly* 25 (1946): 378–81.
Merriam, Thomas. 'Linguistic Computing in the Shadow of Postmodernism.' *Linguistic and Literary Computing* 17.2 (2002): 181–92.
Merriam, Thomas. 'Low Frequency Words, Genre, Date, and Authorship.' *Notes and Queries* 53 (2006): 495–8.
Merriam, Thomas. 'The Tenor of Marlowe in *Henry V*.' *Notes and Queries* 45 (1998): 318–25.
Nearing, Homer, Jr. 'Caesar's Sword (*Faerie Queene* II. x. 49; *Love's Labour's Lost* v.ii.615).' *Modern Language Notes* 63.6 (1948): 403–5.
Neill, Kirby. 'More Ado About Claudio: An Acquittal for the Slandered Groom.' *Shakespeare Quarterly* 3.2 (1952): 91–107.

Nohrnberg, James, C. 'Alençon's Dream / Dido's Tomb: Some Shakespearean Music and a Spenserian Muse.' *Spenser Studies* XXII (2007): 73–102.

Norton-Smith, John. 'Marlowe's *Faustus* (I. iii, 1–4).' *Notes and Queries* 25 (1978): 436–7.

Nuttall, A. D. 'Spenser and Elizabethan Alienation.' *Essays in Criticism* 55.3 (2005): 209–25.

Paglia, Camille. *Sexual Personae: Art and Decadence from Nefertiti to Emily Dickinson*. New Haven: Yale University Press, 1990.

Peck, D. C. 'Raleigh, Sidney, Oxford, and the Catholics, 1579.' *Notes and Queries* 25 (1978): 427–31.

Pincombe, Michael. 'Classical and Contemporary Sources of the "Gloomy Woods" of *Titus Andronicus*: Ovid, Seneca, Spenser.' *Shakespearean Continuities: Essays in Honor of E.A.J. Honigmann*. Ed. John Batchelor, Tom Cain, and Claire Lamont. Basingstoke: Macmillan, 1997. 40–55.

Pirnajmuddin, Hossein. 'Spenser's *The Faerie Queene*.' *The Explicator* 64.3 (2006): 132–3.

Potts, Abbie Findlay. *Shakespeare and 'The Faerie Queene'*. Ithaca: Cornell University Press, 1958.

Potts, Abbie Findlay. 'Hamlet and Gloriana's Knights.' *Shakespeare Quarterly* 6 (1955): 31–43.

Potts, Abbie F. 'Spenserian "Courtesy" and "Temperance" in *Much Ado about Nothing*.' *Shakespeare Association Bulletin* 17 (1942): 103.

Prescott, Anne Lake, and A. Kent Hieatt. 'Shakespeare and Spenser.' *PMLA* 100.5 (1985): 820–2.

Prescott, Anne Lake. 'Complicating the Allegory: Spenser and Religion in Recent Scholarship.' *Renaissance and Reformation* 25.4 (2001): 9–23.

Quint, David. 'Bragging Rights: Honor and Courtesy in Shakespeare and Spenser.' *Creative Imitation: New Essays on Renaissance Literature in honor of Thomas M. Greene*. Ed. David Quint, Margaret W. Ferguson, G.W. Pigman III, and Wayne A. Rebhorn. Binghamton: Medieval and Renaissance Texts and Studies, 1992. 391–430.

Rabl, Kathleen. 'Taming the "Wild Irish" in English Renaissance Drama.' *Literary Interrelations: Ireland, England, and the World*. Ed. Wolfgang Zach and Heinz Kosok. Tübingen: G. Narr Verlag, 1987. 47–59.

Reid, Robert L. 'The Fairy Queen: Gloriana or Titania?' *The Upstart Crow* 13 (1993): 16–32.

Rhu, Lawrence. 'Agons of Interpretation: Ariostan source and Elizabethan Meaning in Spenser, Harington, and Shakespeare.' *Renaissance Drama* 24 (1993): 171–88.

Ringler, William A., Jr. 'Spenser, Shakespeare, Honor, and Worship.' *Renaissance News* 14.3 (1961): 159–61.

Roberts, Gareth, 'Three Notes on Uses of Circe by Spenser, Marlowe and Milton.' *Notes and Queries* 25 (1978): 433–5.
Roe, John, ed. *The Poems*. By William Shakespeare. New Cambridge Shakespeare. Cambridge: Cambridge University Press, 1992.
Rosaye, Jean-Paul. 'Tradition and Meaning: One Interpretation of Renaissance Theology in the Twentieth Century.' *Reformation & Renaissance Review: Journal of the Society for Reformation Studies* 2 (1999): 9–20.
Sagaser, Elizabeth Harris. 'Shakespeare's Sweet Leaves: Mourning, Pleasure, and the Triumph of Thought in the Renaissance Love Lyric.' *English Literary History* 61 (1994): 1–26.
Sarrazin, G. 'Wortechos bei Shakespeare I.' *Jahrbuch der deutschen Shakespeare-Gesellschaft*. 1897. 121–65
Sarrazin, G. 'Wortechos bei Shakespeare II.' *Jahrbuch der deutschen Shakespeare-Gesellschaft*. 1897. 119–69.
Schmidgall, Gary, and A. Kent Hieatt. 'Shakespeare's Sonnets.' *PMLA* 99.2 (1984): 244–5.
Schoeneich, Georg. *Der litterarische Einfluss Spensers auf Marlowe*. Halle: Diss., 1907.
Scott, William O. 'Proteus in Spenser and Shakespeare: The Lover's Identity.' *Shakespeare Studies* (1965): 283–93.
Sims, James H. 'Perdita's "Flowers O' Th' Spring" and "Vernal Flowers" in Lycidas.' *Shakespeare Quarterly* 22.1 (1971): 87–90.
Slater, Eliot. 'Shakespeare: Word Links Between Poems and Plays.' *Notes and Queries* 22 (April 1975): 157–63.
Sokol, B.J. 'A Spenserian Idea in *The Taming of the Shrew*.' *English Studies* 66 (1985): 310–15.
Stapleton, M.L. 'Spenser, the *Antiquitez de Rome*, and the Development of the English Sonnet Form.' *Comparative Literature Studies* 27.4 (1990): 259–74.
Taylor, A. B. 'Britomart and the Mermaids: A Note on Marlowe and Spenser.' *Notes and Queries* 18 (1971): 224–5.
Taylor, Anthony Brian. 'The Elizabethan Seneca and Two Notes on Shakespeare and Spenser.' *Notes and Queries* 34 (1987): 193–5.
Thaler, Alwin. 'Mercutio and Spenser's *Phantastes*.' *Philological Quarterly* 16 (1937): 405–7.
Thaler, Alwin. 'Shakespeare and Spenser.' *Shakespeare Association Bulletin* 10 (1935): 192–211.
Thaler, Alwin. 'Shakespeare and Spenser.' *Shakespeare Association Bulletin* 11 (1936): 34–40.
Thaler, Alwin. 'Spenser and *Much Ado about Nothing*.' *Studies in Philology* 37 (1940): 225–35.
Thomas, Sidney. 'On the Dating of Shakespeare's Early Plays.' *Shakespeare Quarterly* 39.2 (1988): 187–94.

Tilley, Morris P. 'The Organic Unity of *Twelfth Night.*' *PMLA* 29.4 (1914): 550–66.
Tobin, J.J.M. '"A Calandar, A Calandar! Look in the Almanac."' *Notes and Queries* 27 (1980): 162–5.
Tobin, J.J.M. 'Malbecco, Yet Again.' *Notes and Queries* 32 (1985): 478–9.
Tobin, John. 'Spenserian Parallels.' *Essays in Criticism: A Quarterly Journal of Literary Criticism* 29 (1979): 264–9.
Tosello, Matthew. 'Spenser's Silence about Dante.' *Studies in English Literature* 17:1 (1977): 59–66.
van Kranendonk, A.G. 'Spenserian Echoes in *A Midsummer Night's Dream.*' *English Studies* 14 (1932): 209–11.
Walley, Harold R. 'Shakespeare's Debt to Marlowe in *Romeo and Juliet.*' *Philological Quarterly* 21.3 (1942): 257–67.
Watkins, W. B. C. *Shakespeare and Spenser*. Princeton: Princeton University Press, 1950.
Watkins, W. B. C. 'The Plagiarist: Spenser or Marlowe?' *English Literary History* 11.4 (1944): 249–65.
Weatherby, H. L. 'Spenser and Shakespeare at Sonnets.' *Sewanee Review* 108:1 (2000): 124–31.
Weiner, Andrew D. 'Sidney/Spenser/Shakespeare: Influence/Intertextuality/Intention.' *Influence and Intertextuality in Literary History*. Madison: University of Wisconsin Press, 1991. 245–70.
White, R.S. 'Metamorphosis by Love in Elizabethan Romance, Romantic Comedy and Shakespeare's Early Comedies.' *Review of English Studies* n.s. 35 (1984): 14–64.
White, R.S. 'Shakespearian Source-Material in Spenser.' *Notes and Queries* 38 (1991): 60.
Williams, Christopher. 'Hume on the Tedium of Reading Spenser.' *British Journal of Aesthetics* 46.1 (2006): 1–16.
Woodbridge, Linda. ' "Fire in Your Heart and Brimstone in Your Liver:" Towards an Unsaturnalian Twelfth Night.' *Southern Review: Literary and Interdisciplinary Essays* 17.3 (1984): 270–91.
Worthen, W. B. 'The Weight of Anthony: Staging Character in Anthony and Cleopatra.' *Studies in English Literature* 26:2 (1986): 295–308.
Yuasa, Nobuyuki. 'The Art of Naming: A Study of Fictional Names as an Element of Style in Chaucer, Spenser and Shakespeare.' *Poetica: An International Journal of Linguistic-Literary Studies* 41 (1994): 59–83.

Index

Addison, Catherine, 8n, 29n
Adelman, Janet, 57, 58, 58n, 60, 61n, 62, 62n, 65
Akrigg, G.P.V., 113n
Albright, Evelyn May, 117n
Allen, D.C., 82n, 84n, 115n
Allen, William, 158n
Alpers, Paul, 7n, 12n, 16n, 24n, 125n, 131n
Alvis, John, 101n
Anderson, Judith H., 7n, 25n, 80, 81n, 86n, 88n, 95, 95n, 97, 97n, 160n, 168, 168n, 173n, 176, 177n, 201, 201n, 202, 214, 218, 224, 239, 242n, 249n, 256
André, Bernard, 178, 178n, 179, 179n
Apuleius, 91, 91n
Aquinas, Thomas, 79n, 87n, 100, 101n, 102, 104, 105, 106n, 109, 109n, 110, 118, 245n
Aristotle, 62, 63n, 79, 80n, 82, 85, 87, 101, 104, 109, 109n, 202, 206, 207, 211, 211n, 212, 213, 217, 219, 220, 220n, 221, 243
Arnold, Matthew, 14n, 43
Atchity, Kenneth J, 81n, 85n
Attridge, Derek, 16n
Augustine, 102, 104, 104n, 109n, 110, 110n, 124n, 145n

Baker, Herschel, 79n, 144n
Baldwin, William, 2n, 15n, 179n
Barber, Charles Laurence, 101n
Barclay, Alexander, 146, 146n
Barkan, Leonard, 81, 82n, 170n

Bate, Jonathan, 81n, 123n, 133n
Battenhouse, Roy W., 72n, 86n, 94n, 97n, 117, 118
Beal, Peter, 189n
Beckwith, Sarah, 139n
Bednarz, James P., 90n, 92n, 99, 99n, 124, 125n, 128n
Beecher, Donald, 153n
Bellamy, Elizabeth J., 87n, 102n, 127n
Belsey, Catherine, 184n
Benbow, R.M., 93n
Berger, Harry, Jr., 12n, 60n, 62n, 70n, 81n, 85n, 103n, 122n, 132n, 143n, 171n, 210n
Berger, Karol, 97n
Bernheimer, Richard, 91n
Berry, Philippa, 61n, 78n
Bieman, Elizabeth, 86n
Bion, 175, 176n
Bishop, T.G., 202n, 219, 219n
Blanc, Pauline, 54n
Blisset, William, 8n
Bloom, Harold, 96, 96n, 129n, 135n
Bloomfield, Morton W., 99n, 242–245n, 248n
Blythe, Joan Heiges, 99n, 242n
Boccaccio, Giovanni, 146n, 172
Bogel, Fredric V., 191, 192n
Bolzani, G.P. Valeriano, 172n
Bonciani, Francesco, 203n, 206n
Bongiorno, Andrew, 207n
Bonjour, Adrian, 57
Bono, Barbara J, 57n, 65n, 75n, 77n, 97n, 123n
Borris, Kenneth, 86n, 91n
Bradby, G.F., 155n

Brietz Monta, Susannah, 151n
Broaddus, James W., 80n, 102, 102n
Brooks-Davies, Douglas, 91n
Brower, Reuben A., 123n
Bruns, Gerald, 65, 65n
Bruster, Douglas, 124n
Buchanan, George, 173, 173n
Bullough, Geoffrey, 75n, 180n, 249n
Burchmore, David, 86n
Burrow, Colin, 82n, 112n, 126n
Burton, J. Anthony, 80, 198, 199n
Bush, Douglas, 81n, 146n
Butler, Christopher, 170n
Butler, Martin, 125, 126, 126n
Butler, Todd, 143n
Byron, George Gordon, Lord, 18n, 23n, 136n, 192n

Cain, Thomas H., 84n
Calepinus, Ambrosius, 172n
Calvin, John, 86n, 106, 106n, 109n, 155, 155n
Campbell, Oscar James, 179n, 193n
Carlson, David, 179n
Carroll, William, 81n, 160n
Carscallen, J., 209n
Cartari, Vincenzo, 172, 174n
Cartelli, Thomas, 124n
Castelvetro, Ludovico, 62n, 203n, 207, 207n
Celovsky, Lisa, 70n
Charney, Maurice, 187n
Chaudhuri, Sukanta, 146n
Chaudhuri, Supriya, 82n
Cheney, Donald, 81n, 160n
Cheney, Patrick, 2, 3n, 4, 4n, 39n, 35–44, 47, 47n, 48–51, 60n, 80n, 104n, 116n, 122n, 123, 123–125n, 127, 128n, 131n, 133, 134n, 137, 138n, 141, 142n, 160n
Coddon, Karin S., 199n
Collingwood, Robin George, 1n
Comalada, Miguel de, 147n
Cook, Carol, 61n, 67n, 71n, 76n
Cooper, Helen, 39n, 129n, 228n, 257
Council, Norman, 101n
Covington, Sarah, 151n
Coyle, Martin, 214n
Craft, William, 98, 99n
Crawford, Charles, 28n
Crewe, Jonathan, 124n
Crollius, Osvaldus, 175n
Crossett, John M., 243
Crossett, John M., 99n, 243n
Cummings, Robert, 85, 86n, 189n
Cunningham, J.V., 202n, 219, 219n, 220, 221
Curtwright, Travis, 213
Cutts, John P., 215, 215n
Cyr, Gordon C., 196n

D'Ewes, Simonds, 158n
Davis, Walter R., 154n
De Grazia, Margreta, 122n
De Man, Paul, 57n
De Nores, Giason, 203n
Deats, Sara Munson, 54n, 57n, 61n, 65, 66n, 72n, 75, 76n
DeMoss, William F., 79n, 211n
Devereux, E.J., 92, 93n, 97n, 115, 115, 116n, 188
Dixon, Michael F.N., 85n
Dobson, Michael, 122n
Doerksen, Daniel W., 143n
Donaldson, E. Talbot, 123n
Donnelly, M.L., 80n
Donno, E.S., 93n
Du Bartas, Sieur, 176, 176n
Dughi, Thomas A., 107, 108n

Duncan-Jones, Katherine, 42n, 124n, 169n, 202n, 205n
Dunlop, Alexander, 84n, 103, 103n, 106n
Durling, Robert M., 131n
Dutton, Richard, 54n, 122n, 143, 144n, 188n, 190, 190n

Eccles, Mark, 100n
Eggert, Katherine, 58n, 79n, 87n, 96n, 131n
Eliot, T.S., 5n, 16n, 43, 117
Ellison, James, 125n, 136n
Enos, Carol, 144n
Enterline, Lynn, 81n, 124n
Erasmus, Desiderius, 91, 91n, 94n, 109, 109n, 175, 175n
Erickson, Peter, 117n
Erne, Lukas, 122, 122n, 123
Esler, Anthony, 117n
Esolen, Anthony, 97n
Estienne, Charles, 172, 172n
Estrin, Barbara L., 125n, 217, 218

Fichter, Andrew, 80n
Findlay, Alison, 143, 144n
Fitzpatrick, Joan, 2n
Fletcher, Angus, 66, 66n
Forker, Charles R., 137n
Fowler, Alastair, 84n, 85, 85, 86n, 115, 116n, 170n
Fracastoro, Girolamo, 203n
Fraunce, Abraham, 170
Freinkel, Lisa, 113n, 124n, 145n
Fruen, Jeffrey P., 89n
Frye, Northrop, 138, 138n
Fulke, William, 173n

Garber, Marjorie, 122, 123n, 137n, 139, 140n
Gardner, Helen, 214, 215, 223
Gilbert, Allan H., 62n

Gless, Darryl J., 81, 82n, 86n, 91n, 107n
Goddard, Harold C., 60n, 94n, 134, 135n, 251n
Goldberg, Jonathan, 54, 85n
Goldman, Marcus, 75n, 212
Googe, Barnabe, 146, 146n
Gottfried, Rudolph B., 115n
Green, Martin, 94n, 113n
Greenblatt, Stephen, 1n, 98, 98n, 121n, 122, 123n, 197n, 201, 201n, 216n, 223, 224
Greenfield, Sayre, 169, 169n
Greenlaw, Edwin, 188n, 210n
Gregerson, Linda, 80n, 102, 116, 117n
Gregory, Brad S., 100n, 109n, 151, 151, 152n, 174, 204n, 242, 244n, 245, 245n, 248n
Grell, Ole Peter, 144n
Grice, H. Paul, 1n
Gross, Kenneth, 69n, 70, 72n
Grossman, Marshall, 87n
Guillory, John, 99n
Guy-Bray, Stephen, 125n, 132n

Hadfield, Andrew, 82n, 85n, 91n, 106n, 127n, 143n, 150n
Haebreo, Jacob Mantino Hispano, 203n
Hall, Edward, 93, 93n, 178, 178n
Hamilton, A.C., 54n, 69n, 72n, 79n, 81, 82n, 84, 84n, 121n, 139, 170, 170n, 209, 210n, 242n, 244
Hamilton, Donna, 97n, 123n, 143n
Hammer, Paul E.J., 93, 93, 94n, 116n
Hanford, James Holly, 212, 212n
Hanham, Alison, 178n
Hankins, John Erskine, 69n, 73n

Harris, Brice, 188, 189n
Harrison, G.B., 116n
Harrison, Thomas P., 197, 197n
Hartung, Albert E., 227n
Harvey, Gabriel, 126n, 189, 189n, 207
Harwood, Ellen A., 168n
Hatto, A.T., 177n
Haynes, Alan, 200n
Hays, Michael L., 39n, 229n, 257
Hecht, Paul J., 8n
Hedrick, Donald K., 199n
Heffner, Ray, 115, 115n
Heinemann, Margot, 54, 54n
Helgerson, Richard, 80n, 106n, 123n, 125n, 128n, 140, 159, 159n
Heninger, S.K., Jr., 84n, 86n
Herendeen, W.H., 89n
Herron, Thomas, 160n, 197n, 226n
Hibbard Loomis, Laura A., 155n
Hieatt, A. Kent, 3–5n, 8, 25, 28n, 31n, 33n, 35, 40n, 42n, 44–48, 84n, 125n, 191, 191n, 224, 242n
Highley, Christopher, 144n, 150n
Hinds, Stephen, 138n
Hirsch, James, 65n, 71n
Hodgkins, Christopher, 143n
Holahan, Michael, 82n
Homer, 5n, 8n, 9, 9n, 12, 14n, 15, 17, 80n, 101, 123, 123n, 127, 204, 260n
Hopkins, Lisa, 72n
Horton, Ronald A., 79, 80n, 82n, 85, 85n
Hotson, Leslie, 96n
Howell, Roger, 202n
Hughes, Merrit Y., 72n, 80n
Hulse, Clark, 170n

Hume, Anthea, 117n
Humfrey, Belinda, 107n
Hunt, Maurice, 3n, 43n, 92, 92n, 135n
Hunter, Edwin R., 140n
Hunter, Robert G., 97n

Ide, Richard S., 117n, 123n
Iser, Wolfgang, 65, 65n

James, Heather, 68n, 73n, 81, 82n, 97n, 123n
James, Mervyn, 101n
Javitch, Daniel, 82n
Jerome, Saint, 147, 147n, 172n
Johnson, Richard, 180, 229n
Johnson, W.R., 125n
Jordan, Constance, 132
Judson, A.C., 188n

Kahan, Jeffrey, 117n
Kahn, Coppélia, 71n
Kane, Sean, 82n
Kaplan, M. Lindsay, 131n
Kaske, Carol V., 84n, 107n, 210n
Kastan, David Scott, 121, 122n
Kelley, Henry A., 179n
Kellogg, Robert, 100n
Kelsey, Harry, 158n
Kennedy, William J., 80n, 84, 84n, 86n, 141n, 146n
Kermode, Frank, 124n, 142n
Kernan, Alvin, 194n
Kiernan, Pauline, 55, 56n, 60, 60n, 61, 61n, 62, 62n, 63–65, 65n, 78n
King, Andrew, 39n
King, John N., 106n, 108n
Kinney, Clare R., 145n
Klein, Joan Larsen, 82n
Kliman, Bernice W., 192n, 196, 196n
Kolin, Philip C., 168n, 170n
Kott, Jan, 97n

Index

Kouwenhoven, Jan Karel, 85n
Krier, Theresa M., 176, 176n

Lacey, Robert, 116n
Lakowski, Romuald Ian, 177n
Lall, Rama Rani, 194n
Lamont, Claire, 5n
Langston, Beach, 118n
Laqueur, Thomas, 68n
Latham, Agnes, 152n, 154n
Latz, Dorothy, 144n
Le Comte, Edward S., 117, 118n, 199n
Lee, John, 136, 136n
Legge, Thomas, 180, 180n
Leith, John H., 147, 148n
Lepage, John Louis , 82n
Leslie, Michael, 103n
Lethbridge, J.B., 1n, 8n, 79n, 85n, 179, 187n, 226n
Lever, J.W., 57
Levin, Richard A., 234n
Leyburn, Ellen Douglas, 194n
Lindheim, Nancy, 170n
Littlehales, Margaret Mary, 144n
Lloyd, Lodowick, 174n
Logan, Robert A., 75n
Lombardi, Bartolomeo, 203n
Loomba, Ania, 54, 54n, 66n
Lyotard, Jean-François, 59n

MacLachlan, Hugh, 87n
MacLure, Millar, 139n
Macrobius, 171, 171n, 172, 172n
Magnusson, Lynne, 135n
Mallette, Richard, 89n, 96n, 108n, 150, 150n
Mallin, Eric S., 94, 94n, 117n
Mantuanus, Baptista Spagnoli, 146n
Marcus, Leah S., 96n
Marlowe, Christopher, 2, 2, 3n, 6, 10, 11, 13–15, 15, 16n, 17, 18, 18n, 19, 20, 20n, 21, 21n, 22, 23, 24n, 28n, 25–35, 37, 41, 43, 51, 97n, 99, 110, 111, 123, 124n, 141n, 205, 215
Marotti, Arthur F., 103n, 143n, 151n, 158n
Marquis, Paul A., 85n
Martindale, Charles, 81n, 112n
Maslen, R.W., 168, 168n
Mayhall, Jane, 3n
Mayor, Joseph B., 16n
McAlindon, Tom, 224, 224n
McCabe, Richard A., 85n, 128n, 138n
McCoy, Richard C., 116n
McDonald, Russ, 16n, 124n
McLane, Paul E., 159n
McNamee, Maurice B., 101, 101n, 102
McPherson, David C., 213
McRae, Andrew, 189n
Mebane, John S., 97n
Menon, Madhavi, 171n
Meres, Francis, 80, 81, 81n
Merrix, Robert P., 170n
Miller, David Lee, 80n, 85n, 103n, 115n
Miller, Lewis H., Jr., 210, 210n
Miller, Robert P., 170n
Milton, John, 9, 18n, 58n, 72, 72n, 75n, 86, 87n, 99, 99n, 102, 102n, 122, 123, 123n, 126n, 150n, 159n, 197n, 248
Milward, Peter, 147n, 152n, 158n, 162, 162n
Minturno, Antonio Sebastiano, 203, 203n
Miola, Robert, 97n
Montrose, Louis A., 8n, 129, 130, 130n, 131, 131n, 135, 146n, 160n
More, Thomas, 177n, 178, 178n
Morgan, Gerald, 79n, 82n, 143n, 245n

Morris, Helen, 96n
Mortimer, Anthony, 168, 168n, 169
Moulton, Ian Frederick, 171n, 177n
Mounts, Charles E., 115, 115n
Murrin, Michael, 80n

Nancy, Jean-Luc, 76, 77n
Neely, Carol Thomas, 76n
Nelson, William, 105, 105n, 209n
Neuse, Richard, 72n, 84n, 121, 125n, 129n, 137, 138n
Nicoll, Allardyce, 84n
Nohrnberg, James, 69, 70n, 73n, 80n, 82n, 85, 85, 86n, 88, 89n, 91n, 107n, 210n
Northrop, Douglas A., 89n
Nosworthy, Jim, 97n
Nuttall, A.D., 7n, 81n

O'Callaghan, Michelle, 184n, 189n
O'Connell, Michael, 80n, 125n, 159n
O'Donovan, Oliver, 110n
Oestreich-Hart, Donna J., 182n
Olson, Greta, 178n
Olson, Paul F., 84n
Oram, William A., 73n, 80n, 89n, 103n, 138n, 189n
Oras, Ants, 17n
Orgel, Stephen, 84n, 125–127n, 129n, 132n, 138, 139n, 172, 173n
Ornstein, Robert, 184, 184n
Orr, Mary, 61n, 64n
Osgood, Charles Grosvenor, 210n

Padelford, Frederick Morgan, 210n
Padhi, Shanti, 194n

Paglia, Camille, 58, 59, 80, 80n, 82, 136, 136n, 142n
Palfrey, Simon, 125n
Panofsky, Erwin, 6n
Parker, Patricia A., 63n, 88n, 130n
Parsons, Robert, 157n
Patterson, Annabel, 93n, 117n, 144n
Payne, Michael, 68n
Peacham, Henry, 80, 173, 204, 204n
Pearlman, E., 182n
Perkins, William, 106n
Perrot, Francois, 146n
Peters, Julie Stone, 122n
Peterson, Richard S., 188, 189n
Petrarca, Francesco, 80n, 92, 103, 123, 131, 131n, 145n, 146, 146n, 147, 149, 160n, 183, 257, 257n
Petti, Anthony G., 188n, 195n, 199, 199n
Philmus, Maria R. Rohr, 85n
Piepho, Lee, 146n
Pincombe, Michael, 5n, 82n
Pitcher, John, 97n, 115n, 125n, 127, 128, 128n
Platt, Peter G., 202n, 219, 219n, 220, 220n
Plutarch, 71n, 75n, 77, 77n, 173, 173n, 174, 174n, 249, 249n, 250, 252, 253, 253n
Podro, Michael, 6n
Pomponazzi, Pietro, 62n
Potts, Abbie Findlay, 3n, 191, 191n, 197, 197n, 199n
Prescott, Anne Lake, 25n, 44, 45n, 50, 70, 71n, 116n, 143n
Primaudaye, Pierre de la, 109, 110, 110n
Pugh, Syrithe, 72n, 81n
Puttenham, George, 62n, 206, 206n

Index

Questier, Michael C., 156, 157, 157n
Quilligan, Maureen, 201, 201n
Quitslund, Jon, 70n, 73n, 82n, 85, 85n

Rajan, Balachandra, 85n
Reames, Sherry L., 85n
Rebhorn, Wayne A., 94, 94n, 117n
Reid, Robert L., 3n, 12n, 15n, 26n, 49, 50, 79, 79, 80n, 83n, 88n, 90n, 92n, 95n, 102n, 109n, 199n, 242n
Richman, David, 202n, 221
Ricoeur, Paul, 63
Rinehart, Keith, 96n
Roberts, Julian R., 202n
Robertson, David, 99n
Rogers, D.M., 147n
Rogers, William Elford, 138n
Rollinson, Philip B., 87n
Ronan, Clifford J., 192n
Ronsard, Pierre de, 175, 176, 176n
Rosenberg, Marvin, 198n
Rosenheim, Judith, 96n
Rossaeo, G. Guilielmo [William Rainolds], 157n
Rowland, Beryl, 197, 198n
Røstvig, Maren-Sofie, 84n

Saintsbury, George, 16n
Sale, Roger, 7n, 23, 24n
Sanders, Arnold A., 210n
Saunders, J.W., 134n
Schanzer, Ernest, 118
Schmidgall, Gary, 44, 45n, 47, 97n, 142n
Schoenbaum, Samuel, 143n
Schoenfeldt, Michael, 104, 105
Scipio Gentili, 203n
Scott-Giles, C.W., 178n
Severs, J. Burke, 227n
Shackford, Martha Hale, 113n

Shapiro, James, 117n, 124n, 152n
Sharrock, Alison, 131n
Shaver, Anne, 89n
Sheidley, William E., 171n
Sherman, William, 202n
Shorney, David, 144n
Sidney, Sir Philip, 60, 61n, 62, 64, 64n, 65, 65n, 86n, 98, 98, 99n, 106n, 108, 110, 111, 114, 115, 123, 125n, 139, 154n, 159, 160, 175, 194, 194n, 202, 202n, 204, 205, 205n, 206, 212, 212n, 213, 213n, 214, 220–222, 224, 225
Silberman, Lauren, 104n, 143n
Sims, James H., 125n
Singh, Jyotsna G., 54n
Sirluck, Ernest, 79n
Slater, Ann P., 97n
Slover, George, 97n
Sokol, B.J., 125n
Spagnuoli, Baptista, 146n
Spurgeon, Caroline, 187n
Stapleton, M.L., 81n, 187n
Starks, Lisa S., 76n
Steadman, John M., 91n
Steele, Oliver, 100n
Stewart, Stanley, 85n
Stillman, Robert E., 98n
Strier, Richard, 145, 145n
Stump, Donald V., 99n, 103n, 243, 243n

Tassi, Marguerite A., 61n
Tasso, Torquato, 62n, 169, 203n
Taylor, A.B., 81n
Taylor, Gary, 121n, 125n
Taylor, James, 194n
Terry, Reta A., 101n
Teskey, Gordon, 1n, 86n
Thaler, Alwin, 3n
Thompson, Ann, 123n, 125n, 134n
Tiffany, Grace, 80n

Tilley, Morris Palmer, 193n
Tipton, Alzada, 117n
Tobin, J.J.M., 25n, 91n, 214n
Tonkin, Humphrey, 84n, 89n, 91n, 125n, 139n, 183, 183n
Traister, Barbara, 97n
Traub, Valerie, 68n
Treip, Mindele Anne, 62n
Trevor, Douglas, 105n
Trissino, Giovanni Georgio, 203n
Truax, Elizabeth, 81n
Tudeau-Clayton, Margaret, 97n, 123n
Tuve, Rosemund, 85, 85, 86n, 99n, 100, 201, 201n

Uhlig, Claus, 155n

Van Dyke, Carolynn, 58n
Vanhoutte, Jacqueline, 75n
Vergil, Polydore, 178, 178n
Versteegan, Richard, 150, 150n
Vickers, Sir Brian, 45, 46n
Virgil, 9, 14, 50, 57n, 72, 73, 73n, 80, 80–82n, 85, 89, 97, 97n, 101, 123, 123n, 125n, 126, 126n, 130, 131, 131n, 132, 137, 144n, 145, 146n, 197, 213

Wagonheim, Sylvia Stoler, 227n
Walker, Claire, 144n
Walker, Julia M., 75n
Wall, John N., 108n
Wall, Wendy, 134n
Wall, William G., 198, 199n
Walsham, Alexandra, 147n
Walsingham, Thomas, 172, 172n
Watkins, W.B.C., 2n, 7n, 15n, 56, 56n, 66, 72, 191n
Watson, A.G., 202n

Watson, Curtis Brown, 101n, 102, 102n
Watson, Sara Ruth, 212, 212n
Watson, Thomas, 80, 80n, 173n
Weatherby, Harold, 107n
Webb, W.S., 80n
Webbe, William, 204, 204n
Weimann, Robert, 63n
Weiss, Paul, 82, 82n
Wells, Robin Headlam, 97n
Wells, William, 80n, 189, 190n
Welsford, Enid, 84n
Wentersdorf, Karl P., 187n, 195, 196n
Wilkinson, L.P., 81n
Williams, Gordon, 70n
Williams, Juanita Sullivan, 194n
Wilson, Harold S., 138, 138n
Wilson, J. Dover, 117n, 125n
Wilson, Richard, 143, 144n
Wilson-Okamura, David Scott, 8n
Wiltenberg, Robert, 97n
Wind, Edgar, 71n
Wolf, Janet S., 138, 138n
Womersley, David, 93n
Wood, Rufus, 66
Woodcock, Matthew, 90n
Woodhouse, A.S.P., 81n
Woodman, David, 97n
Woods, Susanne, 8n, 85n
Worthen, W.B., 61n

Yeats, William Butler, 5n, 18n, 24n
Yoder, Audrey, 187n
Young, Sir George, 16n

EU authorised representative for GPSR:
Easy Access System Europe, Mustamäe tee 50,
10621 Tallinn, Estonia
gpsr.requests@easproject.com

www.ingramcontent.com/pod-product-compliance
Lightning Source LLC
Chambersburg PA
CBHW051049230426
43666CB00012B/2617